IRELAND'S
LITERARY
RENAISSANCE

IRELAND'S LITERARY RENAISSANCE

by ERNEST *Augustus* BOYD

BARNES & NOBLE, Inc.
NEW YORK
PUBLISHERS & BOOKSELLERS SINCE 1873

First published, 1916
By Alfred A. Knopf, Inc.

New revised edition, 1922
This edition published, 1968
By Barnes & Noble, Inc.

L. C. Catalog Card Number: 68-20700

Printed in the United States of America

TO
M. E. B.

PREFACE TO NEW EDITION

*Since the Easter rising of 1916 there has been re-
newed in Ireland that sense of national identity which
never fails to assert itself in the Irish people when the
spirit of nationality seems near the point of extinction.
On every such occasion this resurgent nationalism has
become articulate and has seriously affected the literature of the time, but it has not been until the inevitable
lull, following the storm of politics, that this feeling has
flowered in prose and poetry. The so-called literary
renaissance followed the political aftermath of 1848,
and the Fenian movement, when the patriotic literature
of the Thomas Davis school made way for a literature
whose patriotism had its roots in the rich soil of the
Gaelic tradition, and was only incidentally concerned
with the political passions of nationalism. Rescued
from neglect by the pioneer editors and translators of
the old literature, Irish culture began once more to live
in the songs and stories of the poets, instead of dying
slowly in the folk-tales of the peasantry. The creation
of the Gaelic League and the heightening of the national
consciousness, which were the cultural achievements of
Sinn Féin, brought about a renaissance of which Anglo-Irish literature was but one aspect. That new spirit
has culminated in the rising of 1916, and the subsequent exacerbation of the national temper, so that the
circle of experience is completed, and Ireland finds herself in literature and politics back in the era of Davis
and Mangan.*

5

The most obvious result of this change has been the recrudescence of pamphleteering and the predominantly political character of the current writing. As in the eighteenth century, Dublin teems with pamphlets and jail journals: economic histories, and various types of historical and political essay absorb the energies of the writers involved in the Sinn Féin mêlée. The majority of these are without any literary value whatsoever, and it is even doubtful if many will be of more than passing interest to the future historian as records of the time. It is only necessary to look at John Mitchel's "Jail Journal" (1854) in order to see that, whereas he added a masterpiece to Anglo-Irish literature, his imitators of recent years are simply journalists of varying skill. The finest piece of political writing which these years of stress have produced is "The National Being," by A. E., whose ideas are as far beyond the average politician in Ireland as elsewhere. But it has become a convenient fiction that the policy of Sinn Féin can be identified with the best thought of certain individuals, simply because these individuals are not in opposition to the ideals of Sinn Féin.

It is one of the peculiarities of the relationship between Sinn Féin and the contemporary Irish writers that, whereas the doctrinaire exponents of the former have never lost an opportunity of belittling and ridiculing the work of the Anglo-Irish writers, the latter have ignored this abuse and have not been deterred from giving expression to their sense of national solidarity. Many of the leaders of Sinn Féin dismiss the Anglo-Irish writers as unnational because they have used English as their medium. The rank and file of the Sinn Féin movement has made a virtue of its ignorance of and contempt for the literature which has done more than anything else to draw the attention of the outside world to the separate national existence of Ireland. Synge was denounced as an un-Irish decadent by the leading Sinn Féiners of his time, and to this day the Irish Theatre is regarded askance by the ultra-patriotic. Hence the error, into which outside observers commonly fall, of associating with Sinn Féin all the movements of modern Ireland which are a creditable manifestation of the awakening of the national spirit. These are attributable to Sinn Féin to the extent that they are a part of the general revival of nationalism, but the politicians of republicanism, like their predecessors, the politicians of parliamentary home rule, cannot claim any share in these intellectual and artistic developments.

Now that political preoccupations are supreme, literature in Ireland has been relegated to the second plane. The energies of a new generation are once more absorbed in the material struggle for national existence. There is no sign of the influence of James Joyce in his own country, although his daring technique has manifestly arrested the attention of some of his English contemporaries. Irish criticism is too largely the monopoly of the patriotic, whose unimpeachable sentiments concerning Ireland are regarded as entitling them to pass judgment upon questions of æsthetics.

In times like the present these tendencies have grown more pronounced, and it seems as if a great deal of the ground were lost which had been gained by the generation of W. B. Yeats, when they revolted against the purely political nationalism of their predecessors. When John Eglinton wrote of the necessity for the "de-Davisisation" of Irish literature, the shaking off of the tradition of Thomas Davis, when W. B. Yeats fought for Synge against the exigencies of mob patriotism, they were clearing the ground for the development of a free criticism and a literature whose nationalism was not to be tested by the crude standards of the political market-place. Much was accomplished under that impulse, and the group of writers whose work forms the substance of what is called the Irish literary renaissance stand as a justification of the ideals at stake. But the last few years have not left Ireland untouched by the universal malady, in which all forms of disinterested intellectual activity have suffered an eclipse. Everywhere literature is being harnessed to the preaching of theses and the exposition of theories. Material problems, domestic and international, are imposed upon the attention of every individual, and until we recover something of that freedom from care, that leisure of mind, without which the creative impulse is arrested, we cannot expect the arts to flourish. Ireland is going yet again through a period of national travail, out of which another era will be born. Then a new singer will rise who will find perhaps in some scrap of to-day's history the inspiration of a new song.

E. B.

New York, June, 1922.

PREFACE TO THE FIRST EDITION

The purpose of this book is to give an account of the literature produced in Ireland during the last thirty years, under the impulse of the Celtic Renaissance. The generation which succeeded the Anglicised Irish writers of the eighteenth century was the first conscious expression of national feeling since the passing of Gaelic as a literary medium. But, in spite of such fine personalities as William Carleton and Thomas Davis, the early nineteenth century was associated chiefly with "the stage Irishism" of Charles Lever, and the fierce political nationalism of the patriot poets of "The Nation." It was not until the Eighties that nationalism made way for nationality, and a literature came into existence which bore the imprint of the latter. The rise of the Language Movement, and the return to Celtic sources, gave a colour and tradition to the new literature unknown to the older exponents of Anglicisation or nationalism, and rendered it more akin to the Gaelic than the English genius. Consequently, it was no more related to the political than to the Anglicised literature which had preceded it, for which reason no reference has been made in this work to the later writers who have followed either school. Such names as Oscar Wilde and Bernard Shaw belong as certainly to the history of English literature as Goldsmith and Sheridan, whereas the term Irish (or Anglo-Irish) can be most properly reserved for that literature which, although not written in Gaelic, is none the less informed by the spirit of the race.

Given this limitation of the subject, it will be evident that the estimates and judgments expressed in the course of this history are relative, and must always be referred to the fundamental condition upon which Anglo-Irish literature exists. As a rule, studies of Irish writers, whether articles or monographs, are written from an essentially English point of view. The subject is conceived, in other words, as part of English literature, and every effort is made to challenge attention by claiming for some Irish work a place amongst the masterpieces of the English genius. Sometimes these claims are allowed to pass, but more often they are resented by susceptible champions of England's literary supremacy. While we may understand the patriotic indignation of the latter, we cannot admit the theory that every word of praise bestowed upon Irish poetry is a tribute filched from Keats or Shelley. It is true that certain critics demand recognition for the subject of their enthusiasm upon terms which seem overgenerous to those most predisposed to sympathy, and thereby they render a great disservice to the literature of contemporary Ireland. The fact is, the same misconception exists on both sides of the controversy. Irish criticism is not interested in such comparisons, being primarily concerned in establishing a ratio of national literary values for Irish literature. If comparisons between English and Irish poets are called for, they must be made upon some reasonable basis. It will not do to dismiss Yeats or A. E. by contrasting their achievement with that of the greatest writers in the English language. To us, in Ireland, Yeats may well be the national counterpart of England's Shelley, and as such he claims our attention. In comparative literature his rank may be different. We are satisfied that the poetry of the Revival is, to say the least, equal to that written in England during the same period. But needless to say such speculations, however interesting to the English historian, have no place in the present volume. The writers have been studied as part of our national literature, and have been estimated accordingly. Their work has been considered solely in so far as it reveals those artistic and racial qualities which constitute the raison d'être of the Celtic Renaissance, and the terms of appreciation are strictly relative to the scope of Anglo-Irish literature.

With few exceptions, the subjects of the following chapters have all placed me under obligations by the kind manner in which they responded to my inquiries concerning matters which absence from Ireland prevented me from verifying at first hand. For the same reason, I owe many thanks to my friend, Miss J. Taylour, of Dublin, who so patiently elucidated doubtful points of bibliographical interest, and to Mr. John Quinn, of New York, who generously gave me access to his rare collection of Irish books, at a time when no other sources of reference were at my disposal.

E. B.

Baltimore, September, 1916.

CONTENTS

CONTENTS

IRELAND'S LITERARY RENAISSANCE

CHAPTER I

PRECURSORS

JAMES CLARENCE MANGAN.   SIR SAMUEL FERGUSON

THE nineteenth century saw the definite eclipse of the Irish language, and, consequently, the beginnings of a genuine Anglo-Irish literature.   At first England predominated, as in the work of Thomas Moore, whose songs familiarised the English people with Irish conditions, and constituted him our literary ambassador in England.   These Irish melodies, which he clothed in the music of his country, are the first flutterings of the Irish spirit in English literature.   Moore was followed by Jeremiah Joseph Callanan, who opened up the path along which Mangan was to follow and to out-distance him.   Most of Callanan's work is of little value, being an imitation in form and manner of Byron, Scott and Moore.   Fortunately, his knowledge of Irish gave him access to sources which saved him from the Anglicisation that renders so many of his predecessors and contemporaries negligible. The essentially Irish metre of the *Outlaw of Loch Lene*, and the passionate *Dirge of O'Sullivan Bear*, are fine illustrations of Callanan's powers as translator.

The best of his original poems is probably *Gogaune Barra*, with its characteristically Gaelic rhymes, and its proud consciousness of Irish tradition.

Three years after Callanan's death, in 1842, Sir Charles Gavan Duffy founded *The Nation*, a newspaper of great importance in the evolution of Anglo-Irish poetry. Primarily the organ of the Young Ireland Party, *The Nation* was born to awaken the spirit of Irish nationality. The essays of Thomas Davis and others were appeals for national unity, an attempt to revive a sense of history, of pride in the traditions of Ireland, in a people ignorant and enslaved, and lost to all consciousness of the past achievement of their race. This propaganda of nationalism was greatly strengthened by Gavan Duffy's proposal to enlist the aid of the poets. Davis's *Lament for the Death of Owen Roe O'Neill*, probably his finest verse, was the first of the series of national songs and ballads which afterwards became famous as *The Spirit of the Nation*. A volume of poetry was poured into this channel from all quarters, obscure peasant girls, men well-known in the struggle for political freedom, succeeded one another in the pages of *The Nation*. All were inspired by a like fervour of patriotism, while the sincerity of their emotion, and the vigour of its expression, earned for them the appreciation of such unlikely admirers as Lord Jeffrey and Macaulay. There can be little doubt of the influence of these poets upon their contemporaries. The idea of Irish nationality had become revitalised, and became a living thing to many distinguished Irishmen of the period, whose training and circumstances would ordinarily have directed their minds in another direction. Of these Sir Samuel Ferguson may be mentioned, as he was later to appear as the most remarkable poet of this century, and to share with Mangan the claim to be the immediate forerunner of the Literary Revival.

The poets of *The Nation*, for all their intensity of patriotic feeling, followed the English rather than the Celtic tradition, their work has a political rather than a literary value, and bears little upon the development of modern Irish verse. The literature of the Revival is no longer concerned with the political revolt against England. It has lost the passionate cry of aggressive patriotism, the wail of despair, and has entered into possession of the vast field of Irish legend. Here, in the interpretation of the Celtic spirit, it has found a truer and more steadfast expression of Irish nationality. The circumstances propitious to such outbursts as characterised the patriot poets of the mid-nineteenth century have altered. Patriotic revolt is not a sufficient guarantee of good poetry, and the Irish Muse has found a quieter and more lasting inspiration. With the exception of Mangan, none of *The Nation* poets has left work whose appeal is likely to endure. Mangan was something more than a patriot, he was a poet of genius, and his work has a value transcending that of the writers with whom he was accidentally associated. In him one can detect the presence of influences which were absent from the work of his contemporaries, and which make him the true father of the modern poets. Contact with the pure stream of Irish culture, Gaelic literature, so moulded the mind of the poet as to constitute his work the first utterance of Celtic Ireland in the English tongue. Patriot though he was, like Davis, McGee and the others, he required the stimulus of some ancient Gaelic song or legend to bring out the great power that was in him. Even the essentially patriotic and familiar *Dark Rosaleen* owes its existence to Mangan's reading of *Roisin Dubh*, the work of an obscure Elizabethan bard. It was not, moreover, until he had produced two less felicitous versions that he attained the perfection of form in which it is now best known.

The existence of these three versions, written at considerable intervals, indicates to what extent Mangan's imagination was haunted by this song. As he brooded over its passionate theme, becoming more deeply stirred by its beauty, his soul vibrated to the music of the Gaelic minstrel, until, carried away by his awakened inspiration, he gave his noble and almost perfect rendering. A comparison of these versions, verse by verse, reveals everywhere the same differences; the contrast between translation and inspiration is in every line. As the poem departs more and more from the text, it comes nearer and nearer to the conception of the Gaelic poet, and becomes at the same time an original creation. In exchange for verbal fidelity Mangan offers such personal contribution as "your holy delicate white hands," nowhere to be discovered in the text. In short he treats his subject as the moderns have treated theirs. The latter, absorbing the legends and stories of their country, have identified themselves with the spirit of Ireland's past, and renewed the tradition of Irish literature. Mangan, however, was not always so happily inspired by Gaelic themes, and in many instances his successor, Samuel Ferguson, has surpassed him, without possessing more than a tithe of his poetic genius. Ferguson's profound knowledge of Irish often enables him to succeed, in a measure, where Mangan has failed. Owing to the absence of inspiration to compensate for the lack of scholarship, Mangan's *The Fair Hills of Ireland* is inferior to Ferguson's *The Fair Hills of Éire, O.*   Mangan has notes which Ferguson could never hope to reach, but his fire is spasmodic, and flickers in a manner utterly incompatible with the steady, if somewhat dead, level of Ferguson's work. His finest achievement is *Dark Rosaleen.* Noisy and sincere patriotism were then, and have since been, the frequent inspiration of Irish poetry, but that wonderful paraphrase has a beauty and a poignant intensity which have never been equalled.

The squalid shiftlessness of Mangan's own life made him the responsive interpreter of Ireland's sorrowful history of former splendour contrasted with an ever-present misery.   Here he could lose himself in the hopes, laments and memories of the Gael, and satisfy the vague longings of his idealism. Weak and purposeless himself, he had not that joy of living which alone can create eternal beauty.   It was only when he caught the fervour of some old Irish poet that he became truly inspired.   Even then, he could not say yea to life.   As in his original work, so in his poems of Gaelic origin, his themes are of sorrow, despair and death.   His verse is filled with tears, and seems, as it were, the *caoine* of an entire race.   Apart from Gaelic sources Mangan is as commonplace as Moore.   His work is often shallow and arid, filled with rhetoric which not even his unusual command of rhyme and rhythm, his skilful versification, can conceal.   He was devoid of the self-control which enables the great artist to select and fashion his material at will.   His genuine culture and love of literature constituted him a somewhat unique figure in his time.   In him the authentic voice of Celtic Ireland was heard for the first time in Anglo-Irish poetry, and he indicated the way of escape from the dominance of England, which his successors have followed.

Unlike Mangan, Ferguson was a distinguished Gaelic scholar. His studies in archæological research gave him direct access to the treasures of Ireland's ancient history and literature, which were only imperfectly revealed to Mangan in the literal translations from the Gaelic, furnished by his learned friends O'Daly and O'Curry. With the intuition of genius, Mangan was able to sense the spirit that lay behind these transcriptions. Ferguson infused his verse with that spirit as the reward of years of antiquarian labours. His work was not confined to literature, but covered the whole field of Irish culture, history, architecture, law, music and antiquities. The public recognition of his services to Irish scholarship was his appointment as Deputy Keeper of the Records, and subsequently his election as President of the Royal Irish Academy. He set himself to lay the foundations of a national literature worthy of Ireland, realising that something more substantial than the aggressive patriotism of *The Nation* must provide the subject matter of Irish art.

While a young man Ferguson attracted attention as a poet in the pages of *Blackwood's Magazine*, and between the ages of twenty and thirty he contributed to the *Dublin University Review* the series of historic tales afterwards published as *The Hibernian Nights' Entertainments*. These were his first attempts to put the old legends and stories into circulation. In 1867 he published his first volume of verse, *Lays of the Western Gael*, which was followed in 1872 by the more ambitious epic, *Congal*. A volume of collected *Poems* appeared in 1880, and attached directly to the first book of *Lays*, by its treatment of further incidents in the Red Branch legendary cycle. These two works gave a strong impulse to the return to Irish legend which is so distinctive a feature of the Revival. This rendering in English verse of the Conorian cycle of the Red Branch history is the foundation of a new literature. Here, for the first time in Anglo-Irish poetry, is outlined the tragic history of the House of Usnach, of the loves of Naisi and Deirdre, the Helen and Paris of Ireland's antiquity, and the mighty deeds of Cuchulain, who dominates Irish bardic history, as Achilles dominated the Greek epic.

The older,—Conorian,—legend has always found more favour than the later Ossianic. The love story of Deirdre, for example, has never ceased, since Ferguson, to engage the attention of the poets. As early as 1876 the *Deirdre* of R. D. Joyce awakened popular response, and since 1880, the date of Ferguson's version, the subject has been treated by Douglas Hyde, John Todhunter, T. W. Rolleston, A.E., J. M. Synge, W. B. Yeats, and others of lesser importance. On the other hand, the corresponding tale of Diarmuid and Grania from the later legend has attracted comparatively few, none of whom has been quite successful. Ferguson, in his *Lays*, has treated the pathetic incident of the death of Diarmuid and his last meeting with Finn. Katharine Tynan, in her second volume of verse, *Shamrocks*, gave a sympathetic rendering of the story, but it still awaits a worthy interpretation. The dramatists have similarly failed in their treatment. Neither the *Diarmuid and Grania* due to the strange collaboration of George Moore and W. B. Yeats, nor the recent *Grania* of Lady Gregory, can be compared with the dramas which have had Deirdre for their subject. The latter, it is true, offers material of a naturally more dramatic quality. The story falls of its own accord into the five acts of classical tragedy, and, involving as it does the destiny of the entire House of Usnach, it is not surprising that it should transcend the more circumscribed interest of the Diarmuid and Grania episode. The Fate of the Sons of Usnach seems from the earliest times to have been sung by the bards, for whom the tragedy had the same fascination it has exercised upon the modern poets. Indeed, as Dr. Sigerson has pointed out, there is reason to suppose that Deirdre was the first tragedy, outside of the classic languages, in the literature of Europe.

It was natural that Ferguson, with his ambition to found a national literature, should think of writing an Irish epic. In *Lays of the Western Gael* he had already adapted to English verse portions of the great Gaelic epic, the *Tain-Bo-Cuaigne*, but these episodes were never welded together, and made no pretence of fufilling the need of Anglo-Irish literature for a work of epical dimensions. For this purpose something more was demanded of the poet than that he should be a translator or adapter. It was necessary to take the material supplied by the transcripts of the ancient tales of the bards, to divest it of many of the extravagancies which conceal the true grandeur and poetry of the bardic songs, and to remould it into one of those beautiful, homogeneous narratives with which we associate the great epic poems of literature. In the bardic romance known as *The Battle of Moyra*, Ferguson believed he had found a subject susceptible of such treatment, and for some years he strove to embody it in a poem of epic quality. The result of his labours was the publication in 1872 of *Congal*. This, however, was but the partial fulfilment of his original purpose. As he confessed in his preface, the "inherent repugnancies"

of the subject proved "too obstinate for reconcile-
ment." Instead of following the plan of the original
story, he was obliged to recast the material, and to
concentrate his attention upon Congal, the principal
personage in the Gaelic text, while retaining the
Battle of Moyra as the culminating incident.

The theme seems, indeed, peculiarly adapted to
epic treatment, possessing, as it does, breadth of significance and unity and continuity of action. The
struggle between the forces of Congal and Domnal
transcend the interest of simple warfare, and the
battle at Moyra marks the last stand of bardic and
pagan Ireland against the forces of Christianity and
clericalism. In spite of having abandoned his first
project, Ferguson succeeded in imparting to *Congal*
some of the qualities which his original conception
would naturally have possessed. He peoples his
narrative of the expedition of Prince Congal against
Domnal, king of Erin, with the terrible, gigantic
figures of Celtic mythology. Mananan mac Lir,
the great sea-god of Irish antiquity, strides through
these pages with giant steps, while the ghastly
Washer of the Ford, most horrible of banshees, is
evoked with the vividness of reality.

Ferguson's work is valuable as representing a definite stage in the development of Anglo-Irish literature. It must be judged by its relative rather than
by its absolute merits. As we have seen, he was
more than a poet, he was an antiquarian whose man-
ifold activities, though all directed towards the
reconstruction of the Gaelic past, could not but interfere with his efforts in the field of pure literature.
He did not bring to poetry that concentration of
purpose and jealous care for perfection of finish,
which are necessary to the creation of great verse.
The most effective passages in *Congal* are marred by

metrical weaknesses, the clashing of consonants and awkward cæsuræ, all indicating a certain roughness of composition also visible in the shorter poems. Frequently, on the other hand, there is a vigour and freshness which enable Ferguson to achieve his effects, in spite of poor craftmanship. It is necessary to remember the difficulties with which he had to contend.

We are now so familiar with the material that we forget how strange it was in Ferguson's time. To the natural difficulties of all pioneer work must be added the problem of finding euphonious equivalents for the old Gaelic names and of grappling in English with the redundant fluency of the old language. In his notes to *Congal* Ferguson refers to these "word-cataracts," where such orgies of descriptive epithet abound as the following:

The deep-clear-watered, foamy crested, terribly-resounding,
Lofty leaping, prone-descending, ocean-calf-abounding,
Fishy fruitful, salmon-teeming, many-coloured, sunny beaming,
Heady-eddied, horrid thund'ring, ocean-prodigy-engend'ring,
Billow-raging, battle waging, merman-haunted, poet-vaunted,
Royal, patrimonial, old torrent of Eas-Roe.

That he should have risen so successfully to the exigencies of his task must weigh with us in estimating the defects and qualities of Ferguson's verse. If we miss the more delicate verbal effects to which many of his successors have attained, we find in him a grasp of subject, a simple grandeur, with frequent passages of genuine inspiration, which compensate the absence of a more perfect technique. At times, especially in his longer works, we are more sensible of the hand of the scholar than of the poet. It was fortunate that, sometimes, at least, scholarship and poetry were combined. The disappearance of Gaelic from the mainstream of Irish life was so complete that it seemed condemned to exist obscurely in the libraries of the learned societies. Once having lapsed into the domain of scholarship, the annals and achievement of Gaelic Ireland could only be restored through the intervention of a scholar, but a scholar who would reach the ear of the unlearned.

The work of restoration demanded the co-operation of learning and imagination, and in Ferguson a man was found who combined the necessary qualifications. He was able to see the past with the eyes of a scholar and to interpret it with the mind of a poet. It was thus his privilege to possess the key that unlocked the gates through which the stream of modern Irish literature was to pass. He set free the Celtic spirit, imprisoned in the shell of an almost extinct language, and obscured by the dust of political turmoil. It is significant that Ferguson obtained immediate recognition from Aubrey de Vere, William Allingham, and such of his contemporaries as were to prepare the way of the new poetic revival. The year of his death, 1886, saw the publication of *Mosada*, the first book of W. B. Yeats, who has since been so completely identified with the Celtic spirit in Irish literature. As indicating the relation of Ferguson to the young generation, and, consequently, his influence upon the Literary Revival, Yeats's criticism of that date may be quoted: "The author of these poems is the greatest poet Ireland has produced, because the most central and the most Celtic. Whatever the future may bring forth in the way of a truly great and national literature . . . will find its morning in these three volumes of one who was made by the purifying flame of national sentiment, the one man of his time who wrote heroic poetry."

CHAPTER II

SOURCES

I

MANGAN and Ferguson may be rightly regarded as the precursors of the Literary Revival, for their work contains more in common with that of their successors than with that of the poets who preceded them, under the leadership of Thomas Davis. Patriotic as was *The Nation* group, it cannot in the proper sense of the word be described as national. Davis and his followers expressed too narrow a phase of Irish life to merit so comprehensive a term. Mangan and Ferguson, on the other hand, were the interpreters of a wider and purer nationalism, existing independent of political sentiment. They lifted national poetry out of the noisy clamour of politics, and thereby effected that dissociation of ideas which was most essential to the existence of national literature, and which remains the characteristic of all the best work of the modern Irish poets. The substitution of a sense of nationality for aggressive nationalism is the factor in the poetry of Mangan and Ferguson which distinguishes them from all their predecessors, and brings them nearer to our own time than to theirs.

While thus introducing a new element into Irish

26

literature, they lacked, nevertheless, the qualification which we shall find in those who were the true initiators of the Revival. Something more powerful than intermittent flashes of Mangan's wayward genius, something more ardent than the conscious scholarship of Ferguson, was needed to produce the extraordinary awakening known as the Irish Literary Revival. The occasion demanded a writer who, combining the imaginative intensity of the former, with the scholarly attainments of the latter, would illumine the entire field of Ireland's antiquity with the vivifying flame of romance and poetry. It so happened that, about the year 1872, a young student of Dublin University was obliged to spend a wet day indoors at a country house where he was visiting. While exploring the bookshelves he came upon the three volumes of O'Halloran's *History of Ireland*, where he made the discovery that his country had a great past—an interesting, but awkward fact, which had been well hidden from him, in accordance with the current precepts of Irish Protestant education. His interest and excitement kindled, this youth returned to Dublin and plunged into the records of his newly discovered country, preserved in the Royal Irish Academy. A few years later he introduced himself to the public as Standish O'Grady, a name which has ever since been familiar by its constant association with every form of literary, political and economic activity, that called for noble enthusiasm and lofty idealism. To this accidental contact with O'Halloran we owe a most remarkable renascence of Irish literature. The publication in 1878 of O'Grady's *History of Ireland: Heroic Period*, marked the advent of a new spirit, and this work, with its concluding volume in 1880, must be regarded as the starting-point of the Literary Revival.

That a great stream of poetry should have its fountain-head in a work of prose, and a prose history, moreover, may be sufficiently unusual to explain the prevailing ignorance of the authentic origin of the poetic renascence in Ireland. It is a commonplace of literary evolution that prose should issue from poetry, and that the latter should be concerned in its beginnings with historical themes. The reversal of the process in the present instance was all the more calculated to escape the notice of criticism, inasmuch as the existence of the preceding generations of Irish poets indicated them as the obvious source from which to trace their successors. To do so, however, is to assume that the Literary Revival is merely a continuation of the Anglicised Irish literature of the eighteenth and early nineteenth centuries, whereas it is, in reality, the creation of a national literature in the English language. But the growth of this literature has necessarily been a departure from the normal process of evolution. Ireland already possessed the literary forms perfected and handed down both by English and Gaelic writers, so that it was not a question of evolving the framework of literature, but of renewing the substance which was to be poured into the existing moulds. In the circumstances, therefore, we need no longer be surprised that two volumes of historical prose should prove the starting point of a rich vein of poetry. It was not the form but the matter and spirit of literature that were changed, in order that Ireland might be adequately expressed in the language which had supplanted her own tongue. We have seen that neither Mangan nor Ferguson was sufficiently equipped for such a task, still less their predecessors. What the older poets were unable to achieve in verse was accomplished by the prose of Standish O'Grady. This

poet, disguised in the mantle of an historian, infused the new spirit which was to revitalise Irish
literature.

Nothing further from the ordinary conception of
historical writing can be imagined than these two
volumes relating the history of Ireland's heroic age.
That they should differ from the manner of Keatinge,
O'Curry, and other orthodox historians, was necessary and inevitable, if we view them in the light of
their ultimate destiny, for how otherwise could a
young and comparatively unknown barrister achieve
such extraordinary results in a field already laboured
by recognised authorities? But it did not require
the confirmation of subsequent events to emphasise
the fact that with Standish O'Grady a new method
of treating Irish history was inaugurated. In his
Preface the author himself clearly indicated his own
attitude towards history, and the faults of his predecessors which he proposed to remedy. Nowhere
more than in Ireland had the historian of antiquity
been content to accumulate names and dates, and
to tabulate events, solely with a view to presenting
as exhaustive a mass of antiquarian research as
possible. The ignorance of Irish laws, customs and
traditions, resulting from the desuetude into which
the language had fallen, explains to some extent the
character of Irish history. So many facts had
become obscured, so much literature was threatened
with oblivion by the spread of Anglicisation, that the
work of translation and excavation seemed at once
the most imperative and the most important. But,
as Standish O'Grady pointed out, a generation of
workers had laboured patiently at this task, the
bardic writings had been largely translated, the
remains of ancient Ireland had been investigated,
and a large quantity of material now lay within easy

reach of the true historian. At the same time, a
precedent had unfortunately been created, with the
result, as he says, that "the province of archæology
has so extended its frontiers as to have swallowed
up the dominion of pure history altogether." The
antiquarians have unearthed "mounds of ore," to
be smelted and converted into current coin of the
realm, but they stand "in their gaunt uselessness,"
awaiting literary exploitation.

It was O'Grady who came with the fire of imagination which transmuted this ore into gold. Leaving
aside all the preoccupations of archæology, the inquiries and investigations, the balancing of statements and probabilities, he undertakes "the reconstruction by imaginative processes of the life led
by our ancestors in this country." Taking the
material furnished by the antiquarians, he remoulds
and absorbs it, reducing to its artistic elements the
entire history of the heroic period as revealed in
bardic literature. To Standish O'Grady these great
figures of an age of heroes are something more than
the vague and remote shadows that strive to live
in the pages of the Publications of the Gaelic and
Ossianic Societies. He so immerses himself in the
past that he identifies himself with his heroes and
heroines, they cease to be legendary and become
for him living men like himself, moving about the
same country, treading the same earth—his ancestors, as they are the ancestors of every Irishman.
As he ponders over the bardic tales he catches their
note of epic grandeur, and the spaciousness of diction which characterised the bards of old is reflected
in his own style. Thus he describes heroic Ireland
as he sees it in the dazzling light of the bardic
imagination:

"But all around, in surging, tumultuous motion, come and go the gorgeous, unearthly beings that long ago emanated from bardic minds, a most weird and mocking world. Faces rush out of the darkness, and as swiftly retreat again. Heroes expand into giants and dwindle into goblins, or fling aside the heroic form and gambol as buffoons; gorgeous palaces are blown asunder like smoke wreaths; kings with wands of silver and ard-roth of gold, move with all their state from century to century; puissant heroes, whose fame reverberates through battles, are shifted from place to place . . . buried monarchs reappear. . . . The explorer visits an enchanted land where he is mocked and deluded. Everything is blown loose from its fastenings. All that should be most stable is whirled round and borne away like foam or dead leaves in a storm."

As befits a work destined to be the source of a literature, O'Grady's History has a certain primitive energy, a naïve amplitude such as we expect in epic narrative. Not content with the vast uncharted territory before him, in which the annals of the bards are but stepping stones "set at long distances in some quaking Cimmerian waste," he must begin with the Pleistocene epoch, and briefly trace the transformations which preceded the inhabitation of Ireland by the human species! One feels that he is attracted to these periods by the immensity of the events which they cover and by the gigantic creatures to which they gave birth. We see him linger with the delight of Homeric simplicity over mastodon and megatherium, pleiseosauros and trogatherium, the size of these monsters fills him with the same satisfaction as he experiences when describing Ireland, sinking beneath the slowly descending glaciers that covered Europe, or submerged by the waters of the ocean, "as with a vast millennial suspiration, the earth's bosom fell." But these chapters are merely the preliminary exercises of a mind enamoured of greatness, whether material or spiritual. They hardly bear more relation to scientific accuracy, than the geology and geography of the Iliad. The historian soon reaches the borders of the vast dominion, where the legendary and the historical mingle in a shadowy confusion, which he has undertaken to survey. Here he pauses for a moment, arrested by the thought of separating the facts of history from the visions of the bards, but his scruples vanish as he recollects the beauties of the legend and their significance in the life of a people. "They are that kind of history a nation desires to possess. They betray the ambition and ideals of the people, and, in that respect, have a value beyond the tale of actual events and duly recorded deeds." In his eyes "Achilles and Troy appear somehow more real than Histiœus and Miletus; Cuculain and Emain Macha than Brian Boromh and Kincorah."

Standish O'Grady sees the gods and demigods, the heroes and kings of Irish history, with the eyes of an epic imagination. He is not concerned with deciding the exact point at which the legends merge into history, but embraces the whole epoch, assimilating all that is best and most lordly in the bardic compositions with the knowledge gleaned from all manner of sources, contemporary documents and recent commentaries. The result is an astonishingly vigorous narrative, which rolls along with a mighty sweep, carrying the reader into the very midst of the great life of the heroic period. The past lives again in these pages, lit up by the brilliance of a mind stored with a wealth of romantic vision.

The first volume of the History begins, properly speaking, with the foundation of Emain Macha, and relates mainly to the incidents of the Cattle Spoil of Coolney, or *Tain Bo-Cuailgne*. Incidentally the story of Deirdre is told, and the whole work is inter-

woven with numerous myths and charming snatches
of Celtic folk-lore. Valuable as they are in creating
atmosphere and in renewing tradition, they do not
constitute the greatest merit of the book. Its real
distinction lies in the wonderful series of graphic
pictures which the author has drawn of the great
spoil. This, the chief of the epic romances of Irish
literature, is conceived in truly epical spirit. The
protagonists, Maeve, Fergus, Ferdia, on the one side,
Conchobar, Laeg and, above all Cuculain, on the
other—these stand out in fine relief. We move
between the camps of the contending hosts, we
attend their councils of war, we hear their cries of
joy and grief, we sit amid their feasts. As he nar-
rates the events of this struggle between Maeve and
the Red Branch, Standish O'Grady attains to something of the style of the Greek historians. His
manner of rendering the speeches of the chieftains
and warriors reminds us, sometimes of the simplicity—so penetrating and effective—of Herodotus,
sometimes of the terse word-painting of Thucydides.
When he leaves the main course of events to evoke
some picture of contemporary manners, the feasting
of the heroes, the domestic employments of the
women, the games of the children, the contests of the
youths, he achieves, at his best, the *naïveté* and
simple grandeur of Homer. He has the truly Celtic
love of the sonorous phrase, but his style bears
traces of his classical scholarship.

The finest qualities of the historian are revealed
by his treatment of the story of Cuculain. Step
by step this heroic and lordly nature is unfolded
before us with the skill and sympathy which come
of deep understanding coupled with a power of
vision and expression. We feel that there is a harmony between the author and his subject to which

we owe this great and spirited re-creation. We see the child, his eager mind filled with the stories of his country's heroes, meditate his escape to the martial life of Emain Macha. A charming picture he presents, this child of ten years old, as he eludes his mother's anxious vigilance and sets out for Emain, armed with his wooden shield and little sword of lath. In his first trial of strength with his contemporaries we are made to feel the promise of his future exploits, the incident is all the more real, too, because of the natural way in which it is described as arising out of a quarrel between a group of Ultonian boys, playing at hurling, and the intruding stranger. Similarly, the legend of the naming of Cuculain, so remote and colourless in Ferguson's poem, is impressed upon the reader by an equal freshness and vivacity of narrative. In the glow of his enthusiasm and imagination, Cuculain lives as he could never have lived in the cold precision of Ferguson's *Lays*. With what skill he evokes Cuculain's life at Emain, his military training under Fergus, his ever-increasing prowess at arms, and finally his knighthood, preparatory to his entry upon the great stage which he was to dominate—the battlefields of heroic Ireland. Cuculain submits all the proofs of strength and military science exacted by his judges, and at last receives the chariot which is to be his aid and witness in the mighty deeds which he subsequently performed on behalf of Ultonia.

"Like a hawk swooping along the face of a cliff when the wind is high, or like the rush of the March wind over the smooth plain, or like the fleetness of the stag roused from his lair by the hounds, and covering his first field, was the rush of those steeds when they had broken through the restraint of the charioteer as though they galloped over fiery flags, so that the earth shook and trembled with the velocity of their motion, and all the time the great car

brayed and shrieked as the wheels of solid and glittering bronze
went round, for there were demons that had their abode in that
car.''

We enter now upon the most significant and illus-
trious phase of Cuculain's career. With the breath-
less interest of romance the History carries us along
from one scene to another in the dramatic struggle
of Maeve against the Ultonians. The long series of
single combats in which the champions of Maeve,
in their turn, stand against Cuculain, the sole
guardian of his clan, alternate with the plots and
schemes of the Queen to remove by some trick this
youth who bars the path of her march northward.
Admiration is divided between the vigorous intensity
with which these great duels are described and the
telling effect of the descriptions of Maeve's relations
with her soldiers and advisers. In the former, with
all the attendant circumstances of supernatural
phenomena, demons and gods who participate only
to heighten the fierceness and terror of the struggle,
the gigantic figures of the combatants are as near
to us and as real as though they were men of to-day.
In the latter, we learn to know Maeve, not merely
as the warrior-queen and rival of Conchobar, but as
a woman, spiteful, unscrupulous and headstrong,
and of a temper so quick that when her counsellor
Fergus remonstrated at her imprudence, she hurled
a spear at him. "But ere she could seize another,"
we are told, "he ran to her, and seized her with his
strong hands and forced her back into her throne,
and held her still, and she spat at him." In their
strength and weakness these semi-legendary figures
are wonderfully near to common humanity as they
move across the pages of Standish O'Grady's history.

The finest chapters are those of the latter portion
of the book in which we find Cuculain forsaken, but

unconquerable, as he holds the ford against his adversaries. Day after day he struggles with a new champion, and emerges a victor from the encounter, but in his lonely mountain hiding-place his mind is torn with grief and wonder at the continued absence of his kinsmen. The arrival of his father serves to settle his doubts, for now he learns of the spell that has been cast upon the Red Branch, so that they are unconscious of the peril of Cuculain and of his valour on their behalf. The pathos of this scene, the old man powerless to assist his son, the latter's tender care for his father in spite of exhaustion and danger, these are the traits which help us to realise the nobility of Cuculain. With consummate insight Standish O'Grady contrives to give the necessary light and shade to the portrayal of this heroic being. While bringing into prominence the terrible strength, the extraordinary skill and endurance of Cuculain, he never fails to illustrate his contrasting qualities of gentleness and kindness which excite the love and admiration of his enemies. Thus we see Cuculain conquer Maeve herself, in a moment of truce, by the loveliness of his disposition, we hear his touching conversation with Fergus who, forgetting his office of Councillor and General to Maeve, steals off at night to the mountains to comfort his former pupil, whom he is debarred from assisting by the rules of warfare. Especially beautiful is the account of the final encounter which closes the first volume. Using the most unscrupulous means Maeve persuades Ferdia to engage with Cuculain, his old friend and comrade at arms. When Cuculain sees this new adversary, he is overcome by emotion, the fierce warrior that is in him is subdued for a moment by the voice of memory and friendship. The combatants appeal to

one another in the name of their affection, each
entreating the other to surrender, that he may be
spared the pain of inflicting death to one beloved.
Skilfully the dialogue passes from affectionate en-
treaty to sterner remonstrance, then to reproaches
and upbraidings, taunt follows taunt, until the
irreparable words are spoken and the two mighty
champions are engaged.

"Then drew Fardia his mighty sword that made a flaming crescent as it flashed most bright and terrible, and rushed headlong
upon Cuculain, and they met in the midst of the ford. But
straightway there arose a spray and a mist from the trampling of
the heroes, and through the mist their forms moved hugely, like
two giants of the Fomoroh contending in a storm. But the war-
demons too, contended around them fighting, the Bocanah and
Bananahs, the wild people of the glens and the demon of the air,
and the fiercer and more blood-thirsty of the Tuatha de Danan.
. . . But the warriors of Maeve turned pale, and the war-steeds
brake loose and flew through the plain with the war-cars, and the
women and camp-followers brake forth and fled, and the upper
water of the divine stream gathered together for fear, and reared
itself aloft like a steed that has seen a spectre, with jags of torn
water and tossing foam."

Fierce and bloody the horrible struggle continues,
accompanied by the dreadful shouts of the people of
Ferdia, only restrained from aiding their chief by
the forcible intervention of Fergus. At last Cuculain is victorious, his friend lies torn and mutilated
at his feet, dead like all the other champions who
tried to force the gates of the north. But soon the
war-demons pass out of him, and he joins the enemy
in lamenting the dead. The narrative concludes:

"He took off the cath-barr from the head of Fardia, and un-
wound his yellow hair, tress after bright tress, most beautiful,
shedding many tears, and he opened the battle-dress and took out
the queen's brooch—that for which his friend had come to slay
him—and he cursed the lifeless metal, and cast it from him into
the air, southwards over the host, and men saw it no more."

Then Cuculain strides to his resting-place in the mountains where Laeg comes to his assistance. The book closes upon the scene of the hero resting under the care of his faithful friend who in a vision had seen his plight, and roused the spellbound men of the Red Branch from their unnatural inertia. In a magnificent closing chapter we see Cuculain visited by the gods throughout Erin, the Sidh from the bright land of Tir-na-noge, the Tuatha de Danaan, all come to pay homage to, and comfort, the brave warrior who was able to converse with them, "being noble of heart like themselves."

II

The second part of the *History of Ireland* did not appear until 1880. Meanwhile, in 1879, appeared the interesting essay on Early Bardic Literature, which provided an instructive exegesis on the entire History, and was subsequently reprinted as an Introduction to the concluding volume. Here Standish O'Grady makes an eloquent plea on behalf of the bardic remains of Ireland, pointing out their value as historical documents, and vindicating them against the neglect of the English-speaking literary world. Ancient Irish literature "with its hundred epics" is relegated to the care of pure scholarship, whereas its great antiquity should give it a peculiar interest to all Aryan nations. The Nibelungenlied, a modern production beside some of the bardic tales, secures attention, even MacPherson's Ossian is familar to the literary classes, as O'Grady indignantly observes, but the wonderful epic cycles of Ireland are unknown or ignored. In thus asserting the claims of bardic literature, he is obviously proclaiming the intention of his own work and, as we know, his appeal was not in vain, so far as his own countrymen are concerned. Circumstances have since rendered most of his arguments inapplicable to present conditions, but without under-estimating labours of recent writers in the same field, we cannot but recognise in Standish O'Grady the pioneer. By an unusual combination of scholarly precept with literary practice he succeeded in dispersing the clouds of prejudice and ignorance that obscured a glittering source of inspiration from the eyes of the poets.

Valuable as this essay is as the preliminary manifesto of the Literary Revival, and as a succinct statement of the main facts relating to the ancient literature of Ireland, it derives an incidental interest as a sort of apologia for the author's conception of history as revealed in his first book. This latter, it goes without saying, possessed none of the charms of the usual, and the critics, with one or two exceptions, accorded it the traditional reception extended to innovators. In the course of a remarkably appreciative criticism, *The Spectator*, it is true, displayed unique foresight and sympathy by enquiring why the Irish poets have left unwrought "this rich mine of the virgin poetry of their country." "Why does not some one arise among them," the reviewer asks, "aspiring to do for these legends what Tennyson has done for the legends of King Arthur and the Knights of the Round Table?"

This solitary instance of a genuine insight into the author's purpose was nevertheless not sufficient to allay the fears awakened in him by the hostile references to his naïve geology, his fantastic geography and the general incoherence of his want of historical method. It is evidently with such faultfinders in his mind that he emphasises the difficulties of the historian who has to deal with the bardic material; the impossibility of distinguishing between truth and fiction as evidenced by the presence or absence of the marvellous, the enormous mass of literature to be considered, and the necessity for considering every document. Thus he is led to declare that the only effective method of treating this heroic literature in connection with the history of Ireland would be to print it exactly as it is without excision or condensation, adopting the order determined by the bards themselves. Such a task, however, is beyond the power of any single individual, and must be performed under the supervision of the Royal Irish Academy. Having thus suggested the ideal history, he rapidly dismisses as out of the question the familiar method of tabulating names and dates, and falls back upon his own plan, on the ground of its being justified by the circumstances explained. Admitting that his mode of writing history is open to "many obvious objections," he once again formulates his intention, this time in words curiously prophetic of his ultimate success:

"I desire to make this heroic period once again a portion of the imagination of the country, and its chief characters as familiar in the minds of our people as they once were. . . . If I can awake an interest in the career of even a single ancient Irish king, I shall establish a train of thoughts, which will advance easily from thence to the state of society in which he lived, and the kings and heroes who surrounded, preceded or followed him. Attention and interest once fully aroused, concerning even one feature of this landscape of ancient history, could be easily widened and extended in its scope."

In spite of this confession of faith, when the concluding volume of the History appeared in 1880, it was prefaced by a chronological sketch of the entire period covered by the two volumes. This was clearly a concession to the demand for definite outlines and precise facts. Without it, the author feared his History might be referred "to a different order of romantic composition than that to which it really belongs." While admitting that this sketch is not without its utility, most readers will wish that it had been an appendix, rather than that it should interrupt the narrative which is here continued to the death of Cuculain. The insertion of both the introductory essay on bardic literature and this preface, between the points at which the story breaks off in the first volume and begins in the second, constitutes a blunder in form which might easily have been avoided.

Nevertheless these defects do not seriously detract from the merits of this final portion of the History, in which the Cuculain epic reaches its apogee, losing none of its sublime grandeur and weird terror in the process of reconstruction. When the narrative is resumed the hero is still lying weak and in the care of Laeg after the last great duel with Ferdia. While he thus remains in the background the history is concerned with Maeve and her followers. A succession of striking pictures explains the course of events in the camp of the Queen, who has invaded and plundered Ultonia during the temporary cessation of Cuculain's activities, while incidentally enabling the reader to obtain a vivid insight into the life and customs of the heroic age. The great feast at which Maeve and her courtiers celebrate their invasion of Ultonia, the songs of the bard, as he entertains the warriors with the incidents of the Tain from earliest days of the Red Branch down to the events in which his hearers had just participated, the visions and portents that strike fear into the hearts of the revellers, the prophecies of the Druid Cailitin, and finally, the hurried preparations to meet the host of Concobar approaching to intercept the retreat of the invaders— these are the preliminary graphic touches filling in the foreground of the canvas upon which the artist is to evoke the apotheosis of heroic Ireland.

The ensuing battle of Gaura is related with that spirit and extraordinary power of visualisation which have endowed the work of Standish O'Grady with such a special significance in the revival of Irish literature. We see the great plain filled with mighty hosts of the Four Provinces of Erin and the men of the Red Branch; the shouts of the warriors, the rattle of the chariots, are the roar of this sea of giant humanity. The chieftains move before us with their men, and each is made to stand out by some deft touch which heightens the relief, so that, immense as the picture is, it is not blurred or confused, but is a clear visualisation. In contrast to the swaying, struggling masses on the plain, we are shown Cuculain asleep in his tent, his strength visibly returning as he slumbers and dreams, unconscious of the peril of the Red Branch. In his sleep comes a vision, the god Lu appears summoning him to the battle, and promising him divine aid to overcome the supernatural forces he will have to encounter. Cuculain arises, goes into the field and surpasses in strength, valour, magnanimity all that men had imagined. Surrounded by tutelary gods and demons of slaughter, he sweeps the armies of Maeve before him; his form is now seen in the mist of panic and terror, gigantic, invulnerable, invincible. Cuculain here enters upon the greatest and last phase of his career where, without ceasing to be human, he has taken on the attributes of divinity.

"Out of his countenance there went as it were lightnings, showers of deadly stars rained forth from the dark western clouds above his head, and there was a sound as of thunder round him, and cries not of his own coming from unseen mouths, and dreadful faces came and went upon the wind, and visages not seen in Erin for a thousand years were present around the hero that day."

Thus he is shown to us as he goes forth to battle against the Four Provinces, and so he appears throughout many fine pages of the History.

In the end, however, the forces of his divine protectors are unable to withstand the powers of evil, he loses his magic attributes and is vanquished in the final downfall of the Ultonians. In describing the last hosting of the Four Provinces against Cuculain O'Grady loses none of his effective power. The concluding chapters relating the distress of Cuculain as he fights against the demons and invisible hosts of darkness, the hero's farewell to his wife Emer, his desperate struggles when, shorn of his glory, he goes to war "like one who has devoted himself to death," and finally his death from the spear which passed first through his body before piercing that of Laeg—these chapters sustain the lofty note which characterises the whole History. There is the same evidence of imagination and sympathy in the picture of Cuculain as he leaves his wife, with his little son clinging to him and asking when he will return, as in this tragic scene when the hero falls mortally wounded:

"Thereat the sun darkened, and the earth trembled, and a wail of agony from immortal mouths shrilled across the land and a pale panic smote the host of Maeve when, with a crash, fell that pillar of heroism, and that flame of the warlike valour of Erin was extinguished."

The book closes upon the mighty figure as he stands on an eminence, sword in hand and with the rays of the setting sun upon his helmet, for he has bound himself to a pillar that he may die neither sitting or lying, as was prophesied. From a distance it seems to the host of Maeve that he is immortal, so that even in the agony of death he strikes terror into the hearts of his enemies.

III

As we have seen, Standish O'Grady's method of writing history drew upon him the adverse criticism of those who held to the orthodox conception of historiography, so much so, in fact, that in his second volume he felt called upon to make certain concessions to such critics and to enter a defence of his own style. Not content with this, he published in 1881 the first volume of a *Critical and Philosophical History*, which was by way of redeeming his former errors, and offering to the public a more conventional study of the same period traversed by his earlier work. This History, however, was never completed, and now serves only to bear witness to the soundness of the instinct which prompted the author to abandon himself in the first instance to the visualisation of a naturally epic imagination. Perhaps it may be profitably regarded as a commentary or appendix to the *Bardic History*. O'Grady strives earnestly to conform to the traditional manner, quoting dates, citing authorities, and explaining legends, but beneath the array of facts is felt the throb of romance and of poetry. At times this restraint is relaxed and the bardic note is heard again. Sometimes he interpolates passages from the earlier history, and even elaborates them, as in the famous dialogue between Ossian and St. Patrick, sometimes he simply follows the bent of his mind, forgetting the critics he would placate, and once more the material of heroic Ireland glows with the life breathed into it by the epic spirit. The following description of Cuculain on the field of battle might well be mistaken for a passage from the *Bardic History:*

"Fear and Panic go out before him; from his eyes glare vivid lightnings; the lips shrink away from his mouth, and between his crashing teeth a voice like near thunder bellows. . . . Black clouds gather round him pouring forth showers of deadly stars, the blood starts from his hair which lashes the wind with gory whips, and all the demons that exult in carnage and in blood roar around him, while like the sound of a mighty drum his heart beats."

The imaginative element is too strong to be long held in check, and in the pages of this volume it frequently preponderates at the expense of the critical and philosophical intentions of the author. Unfortunately such passages derive an inevitable incongruity from their juxtaposition with matter of a purely prosaic and historic nature, and seem curiously out of place in a work of this kind. It is easy, therefore, to understand why the second volume was never published. The first remains, odd and inconclusive, to emphasise the essentially epical and poetic quality of Standish O'Grady's genius and to illustrate his inability to break the mould of his mind.

Unable or unwilling to adopt the conventional historical methods, O'Grady was forced to find some other medium by which to give expression to his peculiar talent for historic reconstruction. Given the preponderance of the romantic and imaginative in his work, it was clear that the most obvious path must lead him to the novel. Henceforward we shall find him employing his activities, almost exclusively in the field of romance. It is true that he did not altogether forsake pure history, but his editorship of *Pacata Hibernia* in 1897 does not call for consideration in a study of the Literary Revival in Ireland.

Similarly, his political writings, *The Crisis in Ireland* (1882), *Toryism and the Tory Democracy* (1889) and *All Ireland* (1898) need only be mentioned in passing. They all possess unusual qualities and have more claim to be considered as literature than might be anticipated from their original scope and purpose. *Toryism and the Tory Democracy*, in particular, is an interesting instance of the application of O'Grady's method to history somewhat less remote than that of heroic Ireland, to the period preceding and covering the first years of the union of the English and Irish Parliaments. Most remarkable is the section *Ireland and the Hour*, in which, continuing *The Crisis in Ireland*, the author addresses the Irish landowners. This eloquent indictment of a worthless aristocracy, lost to all sense of its duties, clinging fearfully to the protection of England, and devoid of those intellectual and spiritual qualities which alone could justify its privileges or excuse its insolence—this indictment is one of the finest pieces of political writing in Irish literature. The pen that wrote the *Bardic History* is easily recognisable, whether it be in the passages that so remorselessly sum up the continued years of incompetence and neglect, or those in which the glories of the great Irish aristocracies of the past are evoked in forcible contrast. It is surely the mark of genius that a work written for the moment should endure by its intrinsic worth. Like the pamphlets of Swift, O'Grady's *Tory Democracy* possesses those qualities of style and emotion which enable such writings to retain their interest when their object has long since been accomplished, or has ceased to engage public attention. The landed aristocracy is no longer a factor in Irish life, other economic problems have taken the place of that which exercised the scorn, the eloquence and the intelligence of Standish O'Grady. As indicating how his influence has transcended the occasion of its immediate exercise, it is significant that, in indicating the class which has replaced the landowners in the economic struggle, the poet, A. E., has been inspired to renew the eloquent tradition of *Ireland and the Hour*.

The series of historical romances which followed the publication of the histories fall into two groups, the one dealing with heroic age, the other with the Elizabethan Ireland. Contrary to what might be expected, it was not from the bardic material that O'Grady's first novel was fashioned, fresh as this material must have been in his mind. Perhaps, indeed, the comprehensive studies he had already given of heroic Ireland, induced him to break new ground by turning to the Elizabethan period, and to come forward as a novelist in 1889 with *Red Hugh's Captivity*. In describing this work as a novel, advantage has been taken of the proverbial amorphousness of the *genre*. *Red Hugh's Captivity* hesitates between the history and the novel, and might almost indifferently be attributed to either, particularly in view of the author's conception of history. From the Introduction it is evident that O'Grady intends to do for Irish history in the sixteenth century what he had previously done for the heroic period. Now, however, instead of the bardic literature, contemporary State papers and subsequent histories provide him with a vast field in which his restless imagination and inventive genius are given free play.

In selecting the Elizabethan era Standish O'Grady found himself in the presence of conditions somewhat analogous to those that gave birth to his *Bardic History*. The work of the various historians, excellent as it was from the technical standpoint, could never hope to bring the period vividly home to the minds of the vast general public. *The Annals of the Four Masters*, O'Clery's *Bardic Life of Hugh Roe*, or the more recent works of Froude and others, were no more likely to reach the uninitiated than the writings of the ancient bards or the studies of Keatinge and O'Curry. If the fruit of their researches and labours was to become part of the national inheritance, it was essential that some one should appear with sufficient energy, enthusiasm and literary ability to remould this material and throw it into common circulation. As O'Grady had lighted up the obscure region of Irish legend and mythology with the flashes of a brilliant imagination, so he undertook to illumine the gloomy waste of sixteenth-century Irish history.

This century is one of vital interest to Irishmen, for it witnessed the struggle of Gaelic Ireland against her assimilation by England, resulting in the incorporation of the Irish with the English-speaking race. The age was crowded with remarkable personalities, the Irish chiefs and petty kings whose resistance to England constituted the last stand of the old Gaelic and feudal order against English civilisation. Naturally, however, the more general histories of the time could not do justice to these figures, and the events in which they were concerned, so, as a rule, they were hastily sketched in as very minor detail in a large picture. While recognising this as inevitable in the circumstances, Standish O'Grady determined to devote a series of smaller pictures to filling in precisely this detail, so important to Irishmen, and so neglected in the comprehensive studies of the professional historians. Shane O'Neill, Feagh mac-Hugh O'Byrne, Red Hugh O'Donnell—all the great

chieftains are rescued from what he describes so
aptly as "the sombre immortality of the bookshelf."
They and their followers are presented in the setting
of their own stirring times, a background filled with
patiently elaborated sketches of feudal life and
customs.

In *Red Hugh's Captivity*, as has been suggested,
O'Grady does not seem quite sure of his style, which
oscillates between pure history and romance. The
narrative is too frequently obscured or interrupted
by the clumsy interposition of historical data, as
though the author were overburdened with the results of his researches in the archives. Conscious,
apparently, of the ineffectiveness of his attempt, he
returned in 1897 to the same story of Red Hugh's
escape from Dublin Castle, and in *The Flight of the
Eagle* gave to Irish literature one of its most spirited
and beautifully written romances. Here the skele-
ton of history is concealed by a vesture of fine prose,
the spoils of the Record Office no longer obtrude
themselves, but are discreetly added for reference
in an appendix, and the whole episode is welded into
a harmonious narrative. The episode of Red Hugh's
capture and flight is the most famous and significant
of the dramas enacted in Elizabethan Ireland, marking, as it did, the beginning of the Nine Years' War
which proved to be the greatest obstacle to the establishment of English rule, and might have changed
the destiny of the Irish people. *The Flight of the
Eagle* is a fascinating picture of the social and political life of the time, and is probably the only work
at all worthy of the picturesque and daring young
rebel whose story is related. Its many beautiful
passages entitle it to rank with the *Bardic History*.
The magnified apostrophe of Lough Liath towards
the end, when the young hero's successful flight has

brought him safe to his mountain home, is justly celebrated. This lonely lake, high upon the mountain-top of Slieve Gullion, is identified with the greatest periods of Gaelic history, with the druidic mysteries of earliest antiquity, with Finn, Cuculain and all the heroic mythological figures of Irish legend. In an eloquent rhapsody O'Grady evokes the great deeds and personages grouped around this cradle and keystone of Celtic Ireland, and closes his narrative with the picture of Red Hugh O'Donnell at the foot of this historic mountain, the last champion of the old ideals with which Lough Liath is inseparably and so intimately connected.

If *The Flight of the Eagle* represents such an advance upon *Red Hugh's Captivity*, and is the finest work O'Grady has done outside of the heroic period, it is doubtless because the years intervening between the two had seen the publication of almost all his work in the field of historic romance. The charming volume of Elizabethan stories, *The Bog of Stars*, in 1893 enabled him to add to his saga of Red Hugh by the addition of incidents in the life of the hero and his associates, not directly part of the events with which the two main narratives are concerned. At the same time he extended the scope of his historic reconstructions by the elaboration of various important phases of the struggle against the Tudor dynasty. The appearance of *Ulrick the Ready* in 1896 marked the last stage of his advance in the art of narration. The manner in which he handles his historical material has lost all the clumsiness of his first effort at long narrative, the odour of the archives no longer hangs about his pages, and the ease and fluency of the story indicates a complete mastery of detail. Indeed he is now threatened with the dangers of this facility and succumbs to

the extent of writing *In the Wake of King James.*
Here he reveals all the faults of a certain type of
popular pseudo-historical novel, in which an historical setting is exploited as a pretext for the telling
of some banal tale of love and adventure. Fortunately, instead of continuing in this direction
O'Grady bethought himself of his first work, and
returned to the half-accomplished task of *Red
Hugh's Captivity* with the fortunate results already
described.

In considering the group of stories based upon
bardic literature little can be added to what has been
said of the history of the heroic period. With the
exception of *Finn and His Companions* (1892), a simple retelling of some of the principal incidents of
the Ossianic cycle addressed to children, the remaining works are adaptations from the histories. *The
Coming of Cuculain* was published in 1894, and consisted almost entirely of a literal transcription of the
earlier chapter relating to the childhood and youth
of Cuculain, in the first volume of the *History of
Ireland.* At that date, as we have seen, O'Grady
was practising his skill as a novelist, and this book
may be regarded as an exercise, for he has taken his
earlier material and elaborated and rearranged it
to form a continuous narrative. Some years later,
in 1901, he remodelled similarly the concluding
chapters of the same volume, and *In the Gates of the
North* presented the story of Cuculain's manhood,
concluding with the hero's splendid defence of
Ulster, single-handed, against the champions of
Maeve. These accounts of Cuculain thus presented in the form of historic romance lose nothing
in the process, and are, therefore, significant as indicating the essentially imaginative, romantic quality
of O'Grady's mind. In this form, moreover, they

must have reached a public not likely to be attracted
to a work ostensibly of pure history, and consequently they have helped materially to attain the
chief end their author had in view: to rehabilitate
the bardic literature of Ireland and to place the
Irish people in possession of their lost national
heritage.

It is, however, as an historian that Standish
O'Grady exercised the greatest influence upon the
Literary Revival. With a fine sense of what was
needed to give nerve and backbone to Irish literature
he turned in succession to the two epochs in the history of Ireland when the national spirit was most
strongly and truly defined; the heroic age, when the
Celtic soul had reached its plenitude, the Elizabethan age, when the last sunset glow of the old
ideals flared up to show the final rally and dispersion
of Gaelic civilisation. His *History of Ireland* offends
against most of the accepted canons of historical
writing, his novels are marred by faults of construction at which the most commonplace "circulationist"
would smile, but all these faults are redeemed by the
inner quality which they derive from burning idealism and epic grandeur of the mind that conceived
these works. The *Bardic History*, in particular,
was a veritable revelation. Here at last was heard
the authentic voice of pagan and heroic Ireland; in
the story of Cuculain, modern Irish literature had
at length found its epic. How pale is Ferguson's
Congal beside this glowing prose, where poetry
springs from the very power and beauty of the
imagination as it conceives the life and struggles of
the divine being. With his proud affirmations of
belief in the ancient deities, and his wonderful evocation of the past, Standish O'Grady revealed to his
countrymen the splendour of their own idealism,

and restored to them their truly national tradition.
All eyes were now turned towards the shining land
of heroic story and legend, the footsteps of all were
directed upon the path which led back to the sources
of Irish nationality.

There is not an important writer of the Revival
but has acknowledged his debt to Standish O'Grady,
more particularly the generation just springing up
when his best work appeared. A. E., whose mind
and work are perhaps most akin to his, shows con-
tinual traces of O'Grady's influence, and has repeatedly testified to the importance of the *Bardic
History;* Todhunter's *Three Bardic Tales* are the
direct result of the contact thus afforded with Irish
legend, while W. B. Yeats has directly and indirectly
admitted his obligation to the same source. It was
further given to O'Grady to foster the growth of
Irish literature both as a publisher and an editor.
He founded in 1900, and conducted for some six
years, *The All Ireland Review,* which was, at the time,
the only journal in Ireland devoted to letters. This
periodical became in due course a real centre of
culture and ideas, and was the soil from which some
of the best fruits of the Literary Revival sprang.

It was not the least of his achievements that, as a
publisher, O'Grady was responsible for the appearance of a volume of essays unique in the history of
the Revival, *Pebbles from a Brook,* the best work of
John Eglinton, that subtle essayist who alone up-
holds the traditions of this *genre* in contemporary
Irish literature. Historian, dramatist, novelist, editor, publisher, poet and even economist, Standish
O'Grady was, above all, and always, an idealist,
and in every phase of his activities he has never
failed to champion the great ideals which first attracted him to the noblest period in the story of his

race. As a personality he has exerted a profound influence upon the literary generation whose ardour he had already kindled by his re-creation of heroic Ireland. As he was the first to reveal a truly noble tradition, it was fitting that he should create, and for a time watch over, the medium through which so much was expressed that was the direct outcome of his own teaching and example, and that he should finally become sponsor for some of the children of his own literary offspring. It is with a peculiar sense of appropriateness, therefore, that we may salute in Standish James O'Grady the father of the Literary Revival in Ireland.

CHAPTER III

SOURCES

WHILE Standish O'Grady revealed the wonders of Irish bardic literature, and sent the poets to the heroic age for the themes of a new song more truly expressive of the national spirit, it was left to others to explore fields hardly less rich in unexploited treasures of the Celtic imagination. The Literary Revival has been characterised, not only by the resuscitation of the great historical figures and events of Irish antiquity, but also by the restoration to letters of the beautiful songs and stories of folk-lore, which were being rapidly obliterated by the increasing Anglicisation of the countryside. The work of the translators and folklorists who collected, transcribed and translated these folk tales and songs, in which the old Celtic traditions still lived, was an important element in the forces that went to the formation of modern Anglo-Irish literature. It is true, however, that this work did not give so direct an impulse to the literary renascence as that of Standish James O'Grady, and belongs more properly to the history of the Gaelic movement, which has done so much to preserve the Irish language, literature and customs. Nevertheless, certain of these writers have exercised a greater influence upon Anglo-Irish letters than

others, an influence beyond that which might be
expected from mere translation, and cannot, therefore, be omitted from a consideration of the Literary
Revival. Moreover, as the language movement was
coincident with the Revival, and has undoubtedly
strengthened it, the interaction of the two may best
be studied in those writers who belonged to both,
while primarily concerned with the restoration of
Gaelic.

In the field of translation George Sigerson may be
said to occupy a position somewhat similar to that of
Standish O'Grady in the history of Anglo-Irish literature proper, and to share the honours with him
as *doyen* of the Revival. Born in 1839, he is not only
O'Grady's senior in years, but as a poet he had
become known some twenty years before the *Bardic
History* was published. As far back as 1855 he was
a contributor to *The Harp*, and much of his early
verse appeared in Davis' paper, *The Nation*, during
the last phase of its existence. Under the pseudonym "Erionnach," Sigerson was familiar to readers of Irish periodicals, but excellent as is much of
his original verse, it has never been collected, and is
only accessible in the various anthologies, of which
there is rather an unfortunate profusion in Ireland.
Apart from his activities on behalf of the National
Literary Society, which we shall notice later, his
influence has been strongest as a translator of the
old Gaelic poets, and it is upon his achievement in
this direction that his claim to distinction must rest.

Sigerson's first permanent contribution to literature was the publication, in 1860, of the second part
of the *Poets and Poetry of Munster*, the first series of
which had been contributed by Mangan, and was
published posthumously in 1850. Thus, by an interesting coincidence, George Sigerson serves as a living

link between the precursors of the Revival and its
initiators, joining up the age of Mangan and Ferguson with that of the new literature whose seed
was germinating in their work. The *Poets and
Poetry of Munster*, which contained the text of about
fifty very beautiful Irish poems, with those metrical
translations which were to become the special study
of the author, was the first effective contribution to
the Gaelic movement. It marks the beginning of
the Celtic Revival which subsequently made such
headway under the leadership of Douglas Hyde.
Indeed, the later vigour to which the language
movement attained would certainly have been re-
tarded, if not rendered absolutely impossible, had
it not been for the work of Sigerson and of John
O'Daly, the editor of both series of Munster Poets.
For many years these two fought alone against the
indifference of the public towards Gaelic literature,
the repository of Irish nationality.

The justification of their faith, and the measure
of their success, were demonstrated by the very different conditions in which Sigerson presented his
second work dealing with the poets and poetry of
ancient Ireland. When *Bards of the Gael and Gall*
appeared, in 1897, it was not the offering of an
enthusiastic young student to an apathetic public,
but the contribution of a ripe scholar to a subject
for which an appreciative audience had in the mean-
time developed. The National Literary Society in
Dublin and the Irish Literary Society in London
had come into being, and it was as President of the
former that Sigerson was able to dedicate the volume
to Gavan Duffy, the President of the sister society,
and to Douglas Hyde, the President of the Gaelic
League. This dedication is, so to speak, a synthesis
of the various activities of literary Ireland since the

publication of the second series of *Poets and Poetry of Munster*. It is a sign-post whereon are inscribed the names which point out the two directions taken by the national current in literature. On the one hand are evoked the struggles of those who strove to restore the language and letters of the Gael, and on the other, the crystallisation of the efforts to create a national literature in English by the absorption and remoulding of the Gaelic material.

Bards of the Gael and Gall was addressed to both the Gaelic and the Anglo-Irish sections by the dual nature of its appeal. To the one it offered the interest of its extraordinarily faithful, and metrically skilful, renderings of the original texts; to the other it presented an imposing anthology of Irish poetic literature, enhanced by a scholarly history of Gaelic verse and a vindication of the greatness of Celtic culture. Dispensing with the original texts, which had become more accessible since the days when he translated the Munster poets, Sigerson was able to bring together eight times as many poems as in his first collection. These range from earliest lays of the Milesian invaders to folk-songs of the eighteenth century, and extend over a period of some two thousand years. All the great epochs of Irish history are represented, the age of Cuculain, the age of Finn, the age of Ossian, the dawn of Christianity and the Gaelic-Norse period, the whole constituting an almost unparalleled poetic lineage, which could not but strengthen the growing sense of Irish nationality in literature. With such an ancestry, the poets were emboldened to proclaim themselves as voicing something more than a mere province of England. The material of Gaelic literature and history had been released by the magic touch of O'Grady; Sigerson, Hyde and others were kindling the torch of Gaelic civilisation, and had drawn to the service of the Irish language many of the younger writers. A literature was in the process of formation, which attached itself directly to the original stem of national culture. This new branch, though its outer covering was of a different texture from the parent tree, derived its sap from the same roots. The spirit was Celtic, if the form was English. Even the form, however, has inevitably taken on something of the colour of its environment. Thus, while in Ireland some critics have questioned the possibility of an Irish literature in the English language, in England the contrary criticism has been raised. So successfully have Irish writers adapted English to the expression of national characteristics, so deeply have they marked it with the Gaelic imprint, that they have been accused of deforming the English language.

Such critics will find nothing to reassure them in *Bards of the Gael and Gall*. At a first glance they might, perhaps, be misled into believing that the book contained nothing dangerous to the integrity of English. They will not find any words, phrases or turns of speech of an emphatically Gaelic complexion, none of these flamboyant, exotic passages with which Synge, particularly, startled the unaccustomed ear. Nevertheless Sigerson is, in their sense, a more serious source of danger than most of his successors. His metrical translations are, in fact, a unique instance of the adaptation of a foreign language to the needs of the user. It is not very difficult for an Irish poet to catch the spirit of a Gaelic text; so far we have seen that it was done to a varying extent both by Ferguson and Mangan. Sigerson, however, succeeds in achieving the far more difficult feat of rendering the music of the original, in addition to its spirit. The popular heptasyllabic measure of Gaelic poetry is essentially alien to the nature of English, which falls more readily into line of eight syllables. With few exceptions Sigerson's versions successfully reproduce this measure, whenever the text so requires. The perfection and diversity of the Gaelic verse forms precluded their illustration in every case, but the volume contains many examples of this elaborate verse structure, with its internal rhymes and alliterations, its consonant and assonant rhymes. This complicated technique is abundantly displayed in the course of translation, and testifies to the age and development of Gaelic culture.

In this connection reference must be made to the Introduction, which displays Sigerson's mastery of his subject and his wide scholarship, and, being in the form of a commentary, adds so much to the value and interest of his work. He discusses, for example, the claim of Irish literature to have created a system of versification absolutely different from that of Greece and Rome, and is able to illustrate his thesis by the first poem of the anthology, the extremely ancient incantation of the Druid-poet Amergin. The translation brings out exactly the rhyme of the text, which demonstrates the existence of rhyming verse in Ireland at a time when such forms were, so far as we know, undreamt of in other countries. Then follows the *Triumph Song of Amergin*, which appears to be an early instance of blank-verse, whose invention must also be ascribed to the Gaelic genius. The poems representing the Cuculain period deal entirely with those incidents and stories whose beauty and significance had been revealed by the sympathetic imagination of Standish O'Grady. *Deirdre's Lament for the Sons of Usnach*, the relations of Cuculain and Ferdial, and other features of the

Red Branch History had become part of the material of a new generation of poets, since the publication of the *Bardic History*. It is interesting, therefore, to study in Sigerson's versions the technique of the contemporary poetry relating to this subject. O'Grady had given the content and the spirit of bardic literature, it remained for Sigerson to analyse its form, and reproduce its structural characteristics. In *Cuculain's Lament for Ferdial* for example, we see how the bards employed the burthen, a form which only came into English verse at a late date. Similarly with many other metrical inventions generally believed to be of comparatively recent origin. These admirable translations reproduce the numerous metrical characteristics of Gaelic literature, whose diversity indicates how highly developed was the art of versification in ancient Ireland.

Bards of the Gael and Gall, while emphasising the technical achievement of Irish poetry, does not sacrifice the poetic substance to the metric shadow. When the bards had obtained such command over the instruments of their craft, they were necessarily tempted at times to indulge in soulless exercises in technique, the metrical gymnastics which we associate with the poetry of the *Précieux* and the fashionable *ruelles* of seventeenth-century Paris. Some of the effects cited by Sigerson remind us of the *pointes* and *concetti* beloved of the Hotel Rambouillet, but as a rule he concerns himself only with such forms as were destined to be permanent factors in the development of European poetry. At the same time he traces the growth of those traits which have since been identified so completely with Celtic verse. From Amergin's Chant to the present day, the same feeling for nature, with its underlying suggestion of pantheistic sympathy, is noticeable, and this unity of sentiment is rightly emphasised and illustrated in the comprehensive sweep of Sigerson's anthology.

Interesting, too, is the manner in which he explains the origin of the melancholy that pervades Irish poetry, and has so long been accepted as its dominant characteristic. In the dirges of Oisin lamenting the death of the Fianna we hear for the first time the note of "Celtic sadness" of which so much has been written. Oisin, the last of the great pagans, mourns the departure of his companions, and the disappearance of all they stood for, in the rising influence of Christianity. The dialogues of Oisin and Patrick remain as the expression of the eternal conflict between the heroic and the Christian ideal. If the mournful note was first heard in the lamentation of paganism when displaced by asceticism, it is to the same cause that we must ascribe the prevalence of a certain tone of sadness in more recent times. The most distinguished of the modern Irish poets have all been on the side of Oisin, they have made the same protest, and their work is tinged by regret for the joylessness of an age unfit to be compared with the great age of which the bards sang. They have been transported by the force of imagination and sympathy to this heroic world peopled with the noble figures and lordly ideals of Celtic civilisation. Filled with the beauties of this dream-world, once a reality, their minds dwell in sadness upon the altered destiny of the race, whom they ceaselessly exhort to return to the path which will lead, as of old, to the unfolding of the perfect flower of national and spiritual greatness.

From the fifth to the ninth century Ireland was the guardian of European civilisation, fostering the arts, and sending teachers to all parts of the Continent. Sigerson's work in *Bards of the Gael and Gall* possesses, therefore, an interest extending far beyond his immediate hearers. Those who have studied European literatures may learn through his exact versions from the Gaelic the precise nature of the debt of other nations to Irish culture. He shows how the verse forms of Gaelic filtered through to the Continent, as a result of their introduction into the Latin hymns and the *Carmen Paschale* of Sedulius, the first great Christian epic. The early saints whose hymns, for all their Latin, betrayed the Gaelic influence in the vowel end-rhymes, and systematic alliteration, were the disseminators of a new literary tradition, a system of versification entirely independent of Greek and Roman influences. While many of the Gaelic verse-forms proved immediately adaptable to the exigencies of the Latin language, and in due course to its derivatives, others have always remained the peculiar possession of the tongue in which they were originally conceived. Few poets in English have habitually exercised all the forms that Sigerson has used in the illustration of his text. The diversity of these, however, shows how far an Irish writer can succeed in expressing native forms in a foreign language. At the same time, they afford an explanation of the metrical characteristics and peculiarities of all Anglo-Irish poetry. The love of recurrent and interwoven vowel sounds, and the assonances of the modern poets, are simply the survival in the English-speaking Irishman of the verse traditions of his race. In *Bards of the Gael and Gall*, George Sigerson has combined an anthology which, while substantiating the claim of Ancient Ireland to be the "Mother of Literatures," vindicates, above all, the right of her own sons to turn to her for their literary education.

Other nations have at one time regarded Ireland as their teacher, and preserve in their literature some of the fruits of her instruction. All the more, therefore, may we expect to find the Irish nation cherishing her teaching, imitating her models, and striving to produce a literature in harmony with the great traditions she created.

DOUGLAS HYDE

It will be the duty of the historian of the Gaelic Movement in Ireland to render justice to the achievement of Douglas Hyde, whose life has been devoted to the restoration of the Gaelic language and literature. In a study of the Literary Revival, concerning itself solely with Anglo-Irish literature, there can be no question of even attempting to give adequate consideration to his work. In a sense, Hyde represents a tendency opposed in principle, if not in fact, to the creation of a national literature in the English language. In a famous lecture delivered to the Irish National Literary Society in Dublin, shortly after its foundation, he pleaded for "the necessity of de-Anglicising Ireland," and his constant purpose has been to effect the object which he defined on that occasion. He has been the organiser of a vast propaganda on behalf of all that is Irish, music, literature, games and customs of every kind. He was careful in 1892 to explain that work of de-Anglicisation was not "a protest against imitating what is best in the English people," but was "to show the folly of neglecting what is Irish, and hastening to adopt, pell-mell, and indiscriminately, everything that is English, simply because it *is* English." Since then, however, his more enthusiastic disciples have swept away these limits, and have championed everything that is Irish, simply because it *is* Irish. Consequently, they incline to view with suspicion the growth of Anglo-Irish literature, on the ground that it is written in an alien language, and has, in some cases, been primarily addressed to the British, rather than the Irish public. Language, it is argued, is the sign and symbol of nationality, and there can be no literature expressive of Irish nationality which is not composed in the Irish language.

Whether Hyde himself is entirely in agreement with this application of his teaching, it is impossible to say. If we may accept the statements of competent critics, his best work, plays, poems, and fairy tales, has been in Gaelic, while such of it as has been conceived in English is devoted to the history and vindication of the claims of Gaelic literature. Exception must be made of the three original poems published in 1895, together with some verse translations, under the title *The Three Sorrows of Story-telling*. The first of these, *Deirdre*, was a prize poem, which obtained the Vice-Chancellor's prize in Dublin University, and possesses all the merits and defects peculiar to that order of composition. The same may be said of the other two stories, *The Children of Lir*, and *The Fate of the Children of Tuireann*, which were written about the same time. Perhaps the most significant feature of *Deirdre* is that a poem upon an essentially Irish theme should have been presented and found favour in a University which, at that time, was definitely hostile to de-Anglicised Ireland and, in the person of two of its most distinguished professors, had publicly expressed its contempt for the ancient literature of the country. In the same year, however, Hyde published his *Story of Gaelic Literature*,

an admirable sketch, which was elaborated and ultimately appeared in 1899 as *The Literary History of
Ireland*. This is Hyde's most important original
work in English. For the first time a connected
and adequate survey had been made of literary
evolution of Gaelic Ireland. Hitherto Gaelic literature had only secured a few incidental pages or
chapters in the works of such Irish antiquarians as
O'Curry, for the necessarily rough and imperfect
catalogues of Bishop Nicholson in the early part
of the eighteenth century, and of Edward O'Reilly
at the beginning of the nineteenth, can hardly be
described as histories in the proper sense of the term.
Hyde's book was the first of its kind and, apart
from its value to the student of Gaelic literature,
was a fine piece of propaganda. With such a demonstration of the diversity and importance of the old
literature, it was no longer possible to dismiss the
claims of the Language Movement. Hyde answered,
once and for all, the objection of his more educated
opponents that the Irish language did not repay
study because it had no literature. *The Literary
History of Ireland* placed within the reach of the
general public the facts which had previously been
vaguely admitted, or denied from hearsay. After
its publication very little was heard about the "bar-
barians" who were supposed to have constituted
Gaelic Ireland, and whose literature was alleged to
be disgusting or negligible.

Against the specific claim of many of Hyde's
adherents, that Anglo-Irish literature is a contradiction in terms, we may set the fact that their
leader was one of the early vice-presidents of the
National Literary Society, which he worked so hard,
with many others, to found, and that neither this
Society nor the Irish Literary Society in London,

was created solely with a view to fostering Gaelic literature. At the same time, it must be admitted, the principle of the Language Movement certainly seems to authorise the conclusions which enthusiasts have drawn from it. If language be accepted as the criterion of nationality, then the Literary Revival is condemned as un-national, and Anglo-Irish literature becomes simply a phase of English literature. This view represents the point at which two extremes of criticism meet. The English critics who refuse to admit the claim of Anglo-Irish literature to speak for a distinct and separate tradition from that of England, and the Irish critics who are so possessed by a sense of nationality that they cannot allow their English-speaking countrymen to come forward as representing the national spirit. On both sides there is an over-emphasis of the importance of the English language, as if that were the determining factor. But those who persist in regarding literary Ireland as a province of England are no less mistaken than those who believe that Ireland loses her identity once she accepts the English language. The striking difference between the Anglo-Irish literature of the Revival, and the Anglicised Irish literature which has always existed outside it, is sufficient proof that both views are mistaken. Ireland has produced writers whose work reveals nothing of their country but a certain note of provinciality; they have been simply imitators of England. She has also given to English literature writers like Burke and Swift who have been lost to Ireland, who have been no more hers than have any of the great names in the literary history of England. In neither case is there any justification for the generalisations of the two classes of critics already mentioned.

So long as Irish legends and stories, traditions and customs are cherished, so long will the feeling of nationality endure. It was precisely the desire to rescue and preserve these things which gave birth to the Revival. It is, therefore, absurd to pretend that the new literature, which has done so much in this direction, is not national. It is, however, equally true that the Gaelic Movement, which has coincided to a great extent with the Revival, has played a very important part in the development of Anglo-Irish literature. Many of the younger poets have been drawn into the Language Movement, while those who have not directly participated, have been indirectly influenced by it. The general impulse towards Irish sources has been greatly strengthened by the propaganda of Douglas Hyde and the Gaelic League, of which he is President. So long as the League exists we may be sure that no effort will be wanting to protect all that is most truly Irish in the life of the country. Whether it can do more than postpone for a while the ultimate disappearance of the Gaelic language is a question which we are not now called upon to discuss.

For many reasons it is to be hoped that the energy and optimism of Hyde will be justified. The endurance of Gaelic constitutes, as it were, a reserve of literary vitality, where our writers may renew themselves, by imbibing afresh from the very sources of the national spirit and tradition. The obliteration of all Gaelic traces would probably weaken the forces of Anglo-Irish literature and leave it open to the process of Anglicisation. Where there is no national spirit capable of moulding the literature of the country in its own image, no tradition springing up from the roots of the nation, resistance is impossible. The race whose language is used inevitably dominates. It is highly probable that the general public is quite uncertain which of its favourite novelists and poets are English and which are American,—the difference is not always obvious.

In this respect Ireland is in a position somewhat similar to that of Belgium. If some French critics prefer to consider Brussels as the centre of a provincial literature, others have recognised the literary nationality of Belgium. They see in the work of a Verhaeren the presence of elements entirely different from those that characterise French poetry. The spirit of Belgian literature expresses a tradition far removed from that of France. The presence of Walloon and Flemish are sufficient to guarantee the immunity of Belgian traditions, and to safeguard the nationality of those who write and speak French. Like Gaelic in Ireland, they exercise an influence upon Franco-Belgian literature which cannot be overlooked. Yet Belgium also has her champions of nationality, who fear that the French language is incompatible with the national spirit. In both countries the obvious solution of the difficulty is the recognition that they are bi-lingual. There is no necessary conflict between Gaelic and Anglo-Irish literature, they are complementary, not antagonistic. Whatever reproaches the more ardent Gaels have made against those Irish writers whose medium is English, the latter have never retaliated. They admit to the full all the claims of the older language, and they have constantly acknowledged their obligations to Gaelic literature. They only plead for the right of co-existence.

In addition to the material derived from the old Gaelic literature, the Revival has found in the folk-lore and folk-songs of the peasantry a valuable deposit of literary ore which was in danger of being lost owing to the disappearance of Gaelic. This vast unwritten literature was cherished solely by the Irish-speaking country folk, and the diminution of the latter threatened it with oblivion. It was natural that Douglas Hyde, having set himself to restore the Gaelic language, should have been keenly sensible of the value of these songs and stories, which contained, as it were, the sparks of the tradition which he was endeavouring to fan into flame. He began at an early date to collect Gaelic folk-lore, and rapidly established a reputation as the foremost authority in this branch of Irish literature. As a folklorist he has exercised a very special influence upon the Literary Revival. Like his first volume of folktales, *Leabhar Sgeuluigheachta*, published in 1889, most of his work has been written in Gaelic, for the force of personal example has been conspicuous in his propaganda on behalf of the Language Movement. In order, however, to reach those less proficient than himself, he adopted in many cases the plan of giving parallel versions, Irish on the one side and the English translation on the other. *Beside the Fire*, the *Love Songs of Connacht* and the *Religious Songs of Connacht* were published in this fashion, and it is these three works which must directly affect the development of Anglo-Irish literature. This is not the place to consider Hyde's achievement in Gaelic, but his translations in the three volumes referred to have a significance which must command attention in any study of the Literary Revival.

Prior to 1890 various efforts had been made to preserve something of Irish folk-lore, but it was not until the appearance in that year of *Beside the Fire*, that any serious contribution in the English lan-

guage was made to the subject. As far back as
1825, Crofton Croker had published *Fairy Legends
and Traditions of the South of Ireland*, a work whose
literary charm has been widely recognised, but whose
scientific value is as slight as that of the collections
of Kennedy, Lady Wilde and Curtin, which succeeded it. In none of these is it possible to discover
the sources from which the stories have been collected, nor can one be certain how far the originals
have been followed, and to what extent the ground-
work has been elaborated by the authors. The
folk-tales suffered in many ways by this treatment.
Their origins were lost, and they became dissociated
from the soil from which they sprang by the fact
that interest inevitably shifted from the stories
themselves to the manner and style of their narration. As Hyde pointed out, it was essential that
folk-lore should not be divorced from its original
expression in language. It is easy, therefore, to
understand why his first *Book of Folk Stories* (*Leabhar
Sgeuluigheachta*) should have appeared in Irish, for
it is in the old language that the folk-tales and songs
are remembered. Except in those districts where English displaced Irish at such an early date that education and reading had not time to thrust themselves
between the people and their spoken literature, the
Gaelic stories did not pass into the new language.
Consequently the rapidly declining population of
native Irish speakers constituted the source of Hyde's
researches.

In *Beside the Fire* he gives, in addition to translations of portions of *Leabhar Sgeuluigheachta*, a
number of Connacht folk-tales, in the original Irish
of the narrators, with a parallel version in English.
In this way Hyde initiated a new method of collecting and preserving Gaelic folk-lore. His stories are

not at all modified by him, but are transcribed as he heard them, the circumstances under which each tale was obtained being included in an appendix. The same treatment was adopted by William Larminie, whose *West Irish Folk-Tales and Romances* was published in 1893, and did for the coast of Connacht and Donegal what Hyde had done for the inland portion of the first-mentioned province. Larminie did not always give the Irish text, but in the cases where he did so, his work had the additional value to students of Gaelic, of reproducing phonetically the dialect of the speaker.

The desire for accuracy which prompted Hyde to reproduce the original language of the Gaelic folk-tales, and the consequent method of giving parallel translations, are factors of greater significance than might at first sight be imagined. This constant juxtaposition of Irish and English has profoundly affected the form of modern Anglo-Irish literature. Instead of the haphazard, and usually quite false, idioms and accent which at one time were the convention in all reproductions of English as spoken in Ireland, the Literary Revival has given us the true form of Anglo-Irish, so that our literature represents perfectly the old Gaelic spirit in its modern garb. This great change has been brought about by two complementary influences. The restoration of the Irish language has reaffirmed the hold of Gaelic upon the mind of the people, and emphasised the modifications of English as moulded by the Irish idiom. At the same time the scientific care with which Hyde and the translators have sought to render exactly the Anglo-Irish equivalents of their texts has tended to fix more effectively and more precisely the language of an English-speaking, but essentially Gaelic race. *Beside the Fire*, so far as it is written in English, is a careful study of that language as it is used under the limitations and modifications imposed by the older tongue. In the preface Hyde expresses his desire to avoid literal translation, and his determination to introduce only such Gaelic idioms as are ordinarily introduced into their English by the people. Within these limits he has succeeded in giving the true Irish flavour to his translations, he avoids all tenses not found in Irish, and by using those similarly wanting in English, as well as the phrases commonly substituted for the unfamiliar tenses, he produces a pleasant sense of reality. This book is as far from the imaginary and ludicrous English of the traditional Irishman, as from the stilted and artificial, or too literary, style of its predecessors. It is the first attempt to render the folk-literature of Ireland in the true Anglo-Irish idiom, and marks the beginning of an influence which Hyde's later work has done so much to strengthen.

The introduction of Anglo-Irish speech into literature dates from an earlier period than that which saw the birth of the Celtic renascence and the Literary Revival. The early nineteenth-century novelists, Charles Lever, Samuel Lover, Gerald Griffin and the Banims, had used this speech, mainly as the vital part of the equipment of the "stage Irishman," whom they invented. In this respect, however, exception must be made of William Carleton, that isolated and distinguished figure in the literary history of Ireland. He looked upon his country with the eyes of a true Celt, and if his fine studies of country life have constituted him the greatest novelist in Irish literature, it is because they are characterised by a degree of verisimilitude and penetration far beyond that attained by his contemporaries just mentioned. The completeness and realism of Carleton's work naturally involved the proper use of the language of the people whom he described so faithfully. Nevertheless, the more popular writings of Lever and Lover predominated in the public mind,—for Carleton has never received his due measure of appreciation—and Anglo-Irish became associated with comic situations and cheap buffoonery. It has been the distinction of the literature of the Revival that it has here effected a complete dissociation of ideas. It has killed the traditional stage Irishman—although some of our novelists, as will be seen, are intent upon reviving him—and with him has disappeared his language. In freeing Anglo-Irish from the vulgarities and absurdities which clung to it, and restoring it to the dignity of normal human speech, Douglas Hyde performed a service no less valuable to literature than his work for the preservation of Gaelic. For there can be little doubt that this great change is due, for the most part, if not entirely, to the example of Hyde. He was responsible for the methodical association of the ancient language with the English that has accompanied or replaced it in the mouth of the people. This constant conjunction, in addition to emphasising the influence of the one language upon the other, tended to make the reproduction of the Anglo-Irish idiom more accurate. Less attention was paid to the more superficial matter of variations in vowel sounds, which to the older writers was the beginning and end of peasant speech, and more care was taken to note the structural differences, the grammar and rhythm of English as passed through the Gaelic mould.

Beside the Fire, while it showed the author's preoccupation with the scientific use of Anglo-Irish, did not contain the elements necessary for so complete

a transfiguration of this speech as the Literary
Revival has witnessed. What was there suggested,
and very cautiously outlined, did not wait long for
complete realisation. In 1893, *The Love Songs of
Connacht* came as a double revelation, first, of the
beauties of folk-poetry, and, secondly, of the charm
of Gaelicised English. Adopting the same methods
as when collecting the prose-tales published three
years before, Hyde had obtained from the lips of the
Connacht peasantry, and from old manuscripts
hitherto neglected, a number of charming folk-songs
in danger of being lost. *The Songs of Connacht*
originally appeared in serial form in *The Nation*, and
later, in *The Weekly Freeman*, the first chapter being
published in 1890. There were seven chapters entitled, respectively, *Carolan and his Contemporaries,
Songs in Praise of Women, Drinking Songs, Love
Songs, Songs Ascribed to Raftery* and two chapters of
Religious Songs. Of these, only Chapters IV, V, VI
and VII were translated and published in book form.
A concluding chapter containing *Keenes and Laments* was to have completed the work, but so far it
has never been published. This work attaches to
that of Sigerson's *Poets and Poetry of Munster*, in
that it performs for Connacht the same service as
the older work did for Munster. Continuing the
method initiated by Sigerson, Hyde attempts in
more than half of these translations to reproduce the
rhyme and metres of the original Gaelic. His verse
renderings are frequently very beautiful, and,
although his best poetry has been written in Gaelic,
these translations prove that he can use the English
language with real skill and delicacy. *The Love
Songs of Connacht* were supplemented some years
later by *Songs Ascribed to Raftery* in 1903 and in 1906
by *The Religious Songs of Connacht*. These volumes

represent a most valuable treasury of folk-poetry, and will rank with the work of Mangan and Sigerson as the repository of the best that could be saved of the old Gaelic tradition while still living. The gathering of these portions of a great heritage was the saving of the still smouldering ashes from which a new flame could be kindled.

Important, however, as is this aspect of Hyde's work, these Connacht songs have a special significance for the student of contemporary Anglo-Irish literature. Here he will find the source of what has come to be regarded as the chief discovery, and most notable characteristic, of the drama of the Literary Revival, the effective employment of the Anglo-Irish idiom. In his verse Hyde approximates, in spite of himself, to the style of the orthodox translators who preceded him, and excellent as is this part of his work, it is not to be compared, either in beauty or importance, with the prose translations, which are frequently substituted for rhymed versions, and sometimes accompany them. These are his finest and most original contributions to Anglo-Irish literature, and have proved to be the starting point of a new literary language. Casting aside the hesitations which restricted him in his English rendering of *Beside the Fire*, Hyde translated his *Songs of Connacht*, not into formal English, with here and there a Gaelicism, but into the language nearest the form and spirit of the original, the English of the country people, in whose speech the old Gaelic influences predominate. Both his own prose commentary and the text are rendered in this idiom, and the freshness and vigour of the one, coupled with the poetic charm of the other, demonstrated at once that a new medium of great strength and flexibility lay to the hand of Irish literature:

"If I were to be on the Brow of Nefin and my hundred loves by my side, it is pleasantly we would sleep together like the little bird upon the bough. It is your melodious wordy little mouth that increased my pain and a quiet sleep I cannot get until I shall die, alas!"

"If you were to see the star of knowledge and she coming in the mouth of the road, you would say that it was a jewel at a distance from you who would disperse fog and enchantment." (*Love Songs of Connacht.*)

Such passages abound in these translations, and are obviously the forerunners of the eloquent, rhythmic phrasing now identified with the style of J. M. Synge. Under Hyde's guidance, he achieved in this speech effects which have consecrated the Anglo-Irish idiom as a vehicle of the purest poetry. The extravagant, amorous speeches of *The Playboy of the Western World* are obviously contained, in their essence, in Hyde's versions.

"If you were to see the sky-woman and she prepared and dressed
Of a fine sunny day in the street, and She walking,
And a light kindled out of her shining bosom
That would give sight to the man without an eye.
There is the love of hundreds in the forehead of her face,
Her appearance is as it were the Star of Monday,
And if she had been in being in the time of the gods
It is not to Venus the apple would have been delivered up."

If we did not know the above to be a verse from the *Songs of Raftery* we might easily imagine that it was a fragment of *The Playboy*, Christy Mahon's, eloquence.

The name of Douglas Hyde has naturally been more prominently associated with the Gaelic Movement than with the Literary Revival. As a Gaelic writer he has attained a distinction which considerably enhances the force and value of his propaganda. The Revival, however, must always count him a powerful influence. It has derived strength and support from the collateral effect of Hyde's labours for the restoration of Gaelic, and to his direct collaboration it owes in part, if not entirely, some of its most fortunate achievements. The fundamental importance of the *Songs of Connacht* in the evolution of our contemporary literature has been insufficiently understood by the general public. Once Hyde had set the example, the possibilities of Gaelic-English were realised by the other writers, and greater credit has fallen to the better-known work of his successors. Lady Gregory, notably, employed his method in *Cuchulain of Muirthemne* and *The Book of Saints and Wonders*, with such effect that it is frequently forgotten how O'Grady preceded her by a quarter of a century, in the field of legend, and Hyde by ten years, in the use of Anglo-Irish idiom. It is interesting, therefore, to refer to the testimony of W. B. Yeats, who wrote some fifteen years ago, when Douglas Hyde was helping to create an Irish theatre:

"These plays remind me of my first reading of *The Love Songs of Connacht*. The prose parts of that book were to me, as they were to many others, the coming of a new power into literature. . . . I would have him keep to that English idiom of the Irish-thinking people of the West. . . . It is the only good English spoken by any large number of Irish people to-day, and one must found good literature on a living speech."

If peasant speech has now become an accepted convention of the Irish theatre, it is because the younger dramatists have confined themselves almost exclusively to the writing of peasant plays, both these mutually dependent facts being due to the prestige conferred upon the *genre* by Synge. His plays removed this speech from all the associations of low comedy and buffoonery which clung to it, and established the dignity and beauty of Anglo-Irish. While he consummated the rehabilitation of the idiom, the process had been definitely inaugurated by Douglas Hyde. *The Love Songs of Connacht* were the constant study of the author of *The Playboy*, whose plays testify, more than those of any other writer, to the influence of Hyde's prose. In thus stimulating the dramatist who was to leave so deep a mark upon the form of the Irish Theatre, Douglas Hyde must be counted an important force in the evolution of our national drama. Without injustice to the labours of W. B. Yeats, it may be said that the success of his efforts would not have been complete but for Synge. Had it not been for Hyde, the latter's most striking achievement might never have been known.

CHAPTER IV

THE TRANSITION

WILLIAM ALLINGHAM. THE CRYSTALLISATION OF THE
NEW SPIRIT: THE IRISH LITERARY SOCIETIES

DURING the first half of the nineteenth
century, the intellectual energies of Ireland were so absorbed by the political
struggle that literature had no existence,
except in so far as it ministered to the cause of
nationalism in politics. The writers of *The Nation*
were, as has been stated, patriots first and poets
after, although Davis's writings reveal in him the
desire to effect an awakening of the Irish spirit
which would be intellectual and literary as well as
political. In time the Young Ireland movement
was succeeded by the Fenians, whose journal *The
Irish People* became a centre of politico-literary
activity analogous to *The Nation*. Its editor, John
O'Leary, had a fine feeling for letters, but the circumstances of the period inevitably favoured the
production of literature in which political values
were substituted for artistic. The poetry of the
Fenian movement is at its best in the work of Charles
J. Kickham, John Keegan Casey and Ellen O'Leary.
It has a special interest in the history of the Revival,
for instead of the vehement rhetorical passion of the
Young Irelanders we find a plaintiveness, a sad
idyllic note, which suggest the transition to the manner of the contemporary Irish poets. It is not with-

out a certain significance that O'Leary, on his return from exile, should have actively supported the revolt of the new generation, against the political and oratorical vehemence of the Young Ireland tradition.

It was not until the last quarter of the century that there was any concerted literary activity entirely independent of political purposes. We have seen that prior to that time individual poets had worked apart from the popular literary movements of their day, and, while avoiding the political nationalism of the latter, had contrived to give to their work the imprint of Irish nationality, in the deepest sense. The most important of these was Ferguson, who was not identified with either *The Nation* group or the poets of the Fenian movement. The position of his contemporaries Aubrey de Vere and William Allingham was somewhat similar; they too were working upon Irish themes, and ultimately found in the Gaelic legends some of the material of their art. Their work, however, is English rather than Celtic in spirit, and hardly belongs to the new literature. For that reason Ferguson, not de Vere, is the herald of the Revival, although the latter's *Inisfail* was published four years earlier than *Lays of the Western Gael*, and his *Legends of St. Patrick* coincided with the appearance of *Congal*, in 1872. Allingham at times came nearer to the Irish tradition than de Vere who, though he survived both Ferguson and Allingham, and lived to witness the first fruits of the renascence, remained fundamentally an English poet of the Wordsworthian line. As early as 1864, one year before Ferguson's *Lays*, Allingham had published *Laurence Bloomfield in Ireland*, for whose "flat decasyllabics" the author had justly but little hope of success. It is said that this poem first awakened Gladstone's interest in the agrarian problem, as it existed in Ireland. But the "epic of the Irish Land Question" gains nothing by reference to the judgment of one whose enthusiasms, so far as contemporary literature was concerned, must often have been a shock to his admirers. More successful were the songs and ballads which at once became popular with the people of Allingham's native Ballyshannon. Some of these appeared in *The Music Master* in 1855, and from the preface it appears that certain of them were actually printed and circulated in the traditional ballad-sheet form. Such songs as *The Winding Banks of Erne* and *Kate of Ballyshanny* are far more perfect of their kind than any of the author's longer Irish poems. The proof of their success resides in the fact that they have become familiar throughout the countryside.

Allingham wavered always between the two traditions, and were it not for his ballads, he would not find a place in the history of Anglo-Irish literature. He had an entirely English distrust for the Anglo-Irish idiom, in spite of his desire to write popular songs. He recorded his pleasure at hearing his songs sung by the girls at their cottage doors in Ballyshannon, nevertheless he shrank from using the phraseology natural to that form of composition. He actually complains that "the choice of words for poetry in Irish-English is narrowly limited," without realising that this absence of variety was due solely to his own fear of departing from the conventional diction of literary English. Now that Hyde, Synge and the younger poets have shown the effects that may be obtained by the use of that idiom, it is difficult to sympathise with Allingham's apologies for the occasional employment of it. His failure to perceive the beauties of a medium he had evidently tried to wield stamps him as quite out of touch with the current of modern Irish literature. He could, however, hardly have been otherwise. As editor of *Fraser's Magazine* he was more intimately associated with the literary life of England than of Ireland. His close friendship with Carlyle, Tennyson, and with the Pre-Raphaelites, influenced him more than anything in his own country. There was then no centre of literary activity in Ireland to which he might turn. He was the last of the scattered, isolated, Irish poets, who essayed to cultivate something of the national tradition, while unable to join the politico-literary groups of their time. That Allingham did not succeed in this respect as Ferguson succeeded, was natural. He had none of the latter's knowledge of Gaelic antiquity, and had not deliberately renounced the chance of securing recognition as an English poet by devoting himself to Irish legendary and historical themes. In spite of a typically West Briton fear that an Irish Parliament would make Ireland not so "homely as Devonshire," Allingham was attached to his country. Whenever he was inspired by the love of his native home, Ballyshannon, his verse revealed the temperament and spirit of his race. Neither his political and religious alienation, nor his English *milieu* could obliterate these. It is by such songs that he is remembered in the history of Anglo-Irish literature.

The death of William Allingham in 1889 coincided with the beginning of a new phase in the literary evolution of Ireland. The collapse of the Parnell movement brought about a slackening of political pressure which enabled the intellectual forces to emerge that had been germinating and gathering strength during the early Eighties. The first volumes of various young poets had just been published (Katharine Tynan's *Louise de la Vallière* and *Sham-*

rocks, W. B. Yeats's *Mosada* and *The Wanderings of Oisin* and William Larminie's *Glanlua*) and had secured an amount of attention that would have been impossible in the years of strenuous politics. Both in Dublin and in London groups of writers were forming for the purpose of fostering Irish literature, and the idea of literary, as distinct from political, nationalism was taking shape in the minds of a new generation. The example and enthusiasm of O'Grady had turned the poets to the sources of nationality, and for the first time there was a deliberate concentration of effort upon the foundation of a new literature which would carry on the traditions of the old. At last the time had come when a concerted move was possible, by joining the two elements which had heretofore remained apart. So far, the division of Irish writers has been into two categories. On the one hand those who banded together for political purposes, with patriotic verse as an accidental or incidental accompaniment. On the other, the more or less isolated individuals who strove to renew the Celtic spirit, but whose common endeavour failed to bring them together, although it excluded them from the existing politico-literary groups. Now we enter upon a new period when, with the elimination of purely political partisanship, and the substitution of a broad sense of nationality, there came a conscious unity of purpose. Associations were formed of a non-political, intellectual, yet national, kind. This co-operation of nationalism and literature, outside of politics, resulted in the renascence known as the Irish Literary Revival.

The definite crystallisation of the movement of cohesion was the creation in 1892 of the Irish Literary Society in London and the Irish National Literary Society in Dublin. The first steps were taken in

London, where the Southwark Irish Literary Club was founded in 1883. During the time of political stress this club had contented itself, like others of its kind, with attending to the education of the Irish children of South London. As the years went on it became evident that a more direct preoccupation with literature would have some chance of success, and the Club organised itself on lines more similar to those afterwards adopted by the Literary Societies. Lectures were delivered on Irish subjects, the work of Irish poets was collected and published, and a general effort was made to stimulate the interest and activities of Irish readers and writers. New talent was encouraged by the institution of "original nights," when members had to contribute material from their own resources. Some of the members subsequently presented their work to the public and met with a favourable reception. Probably the most important of these was F. A. Fahy, whose *Irish Songs and Poems* appeared in 1887, after having served as his contributions to many "original nights." As popular poetry this book has enjoyed wide success, but the author is more important to the present history as being the pioneer who prepared the way for the Irish Literary Society. It was he who worked so hard in the early days of the Southwark Junior Literary Club, and effected the various transformations which made of that modest institution a literary centre for Irishmen in London, until the transition to the Irish Literary Society was inevitable and almost imperceptible.

The Southwark Literary Club had been in existence some years while a corresponding group was forming in Dublin. In 1888, the Pan-Celtic Society was created, but its membership was more restricted than that of the London Club, for only those could

join who had made some original contribution to
Irish literature, or who had a literary acquaintance
with the Irish language. Douglas Hyde, George
Sigerson, John Todhunter and A. P. Graves, may be
mentioned as the more important of those who initiated the Society, together with a number of writers
of varying note, from Rose Kavanagh, Ellen O'Leary
and John O'Leary to Gerald C. Pelly, A. F. Downey
and M. D. Wyer, the three real founders, whose
names have lapsed into obscurity. Most of these
early members contributed to *Lays and Lyrics of the
Pan-Celtic Society*, an undistinguished volume which
appeared in 1889 and was far from revealing the
promise of the literature at that time in preparation.
The Pan-Celtic Society is interesting because of its
intentions rather than of its actual achievement.
The conditions of membership indicated a more
deliberate attempt to carry on the work of the
Revival, by uniting only those who were actively
aiding the creation of a new literature. The inclusion of those possessing a knowledge of Irish may be
regarded as part of this intention, inasmuch as the
tapping of Gaelic sources was an essential. At the
same time it may be considered as the germ of the
idea afterwards elaborated by Douglas Hyde in the
foundation of the Gaelic League.

Now that the same current was working simultaneously in Dublin and London, the principle of co-
operation for literary objects was definitely and
practically established. There was a constant inter-
change of men and ideas between the societies in
both capitals. In London the Southwark Club was
attracting the young writers; W. B. Yeats had lec-
tured, and Katharine Tynan, John Todhunter,
Douglas Hyde, and others, had found their way to
the meetings. This influx of original talent led to

certain changes and modifications. Lecturing ceased
to be the mainstay of the Club, there was a growing
conviction that more attention should be given to
the production of new work, and the publication of
older writers whose names were being forgotten by a
generation unfamiliar with the periodicals to which
they contributed. In 1891, a meeting took place at
the house of W. B. Yeats. T. W. Rolleston, Todhunter
and other members of the Southwark Club were
present, and a scheme was discussed whereby the
Club might be transformed into a more efficient
medium for the cultivation and spread of Irish literature. The result was seen in the following year
when the Irish Literary Society and the Irish National Literary Society came into existence. The
London Society soon gathered together the best of
the Irish poets, Lionel Johnson, Stopford Brooke,
Alice Milligan, Katharine Tynan, John Todhunter.
To these we may add the names of some of the
better-known members of the Dublin Society: Sigerson, Hyde, Standish O'Grady, Yeats and William
Larminie. A glance at these names is sufficient to
show that in the year 1892 the two Societies were
representative of contemporary Anglo-Irish Literature, and that they contained the forces to which we
owe the Literary Revival. For a few years after
the inauguration of the Irish Literary and Irish
National Literary Societies, it was permissible to
speak of a literary "movement" in Ireland. This
unity and homogeneity of Irish intellectual activity
lasted long enough to impose the conception of a
national Anglo-Irish literature, but the process of
disintegration was too rapid to justify the application of the word movement to its later phases.

The main purposes of these Societies was to foster
the new growth of Irish literature by means of lec-

tures on Celtic subjects, and by the publication of
the work of writers hitherto neglected, as well as of
the younger men who were beginning to make themselves heard. Some of these early lectures are most
excellent propaganda, and constitute, in their printed
form, documents of some importance in the history
of contemporary literature in Ireland. In Dublin,
the inaugural address, *Irish Literature: its Origin,
Environment and Influence*, was delivered by George
Sigerson, who gave in brief outline a survey of the
material which he developed and illustrated later in
Bards of the Gael and Gall. This fine résumé was
particularly well chosen in the circumstances, for it
was at once a reminder of Ireland's past literary
greatness and an indication of the direction in which
her future must evolve. The following year, 1893,
saw the inauguration of the London Society by a
lecture from Stopford Brooke on *The Need and Use
of Getting Irish Literature into the English Tongue.*
While estimating the importance of ancient literature, the lecturer vindicated the right of Anglo-
Irish literature to be regarded as its successor. As
he pointed out, the use of the English language need
not necessarily hamper the expression of the Celtic
spirit nor interfere with the continuance of Gaelic
traditions. In order, however, that this might be
so, it was imperative that Anglo-Irish writers should
work upon the material bequeathed to them by
their Gaelic ancestors. Amplifying this point, the
lecturer demonstrated the importance of the work
of translation and popularisation by which the
legendary and historical past could be brought before
the public. He defined the most essential tasks, as
the translation of the Gaelic texts, the moulding of
the various mythological and historical cycles into an
imaginative unity, after the fashion of Malory, the

treatment in verse of the isolated episodes and tales relating to the heroes of the supernatural and heroic world, and, finally, the collection of the folk-stories of Ireland. In these four branches he predicted that the sources of a literary renascence would be found. The results which are now traceable to the efforts of O'Grady, Sigerson and Hyde are proofs of the wisdom of Stopford Brooke's recommendations. Indeed, at the present time, it is difficult to re-read his lecture without feeling that it is a complete manifesto of the principles and aims of the Literary Revival.

While lectures from Standish O'Grady, Douglas Hyde, W. B. Yeats, Lionel Johnson and others, made this part of the programme a success, the Societies were less fortunate with the other important branch of their undertaking. It will be remembered that when Yeats and his friends reconstituted the Southwark Literary Club the publishing of Irish books was a most essential feature of their plans. This idea was ultimately half realised, but not until it had provoked a scission in the newly-formed ranks of Irish literature. The early lectures must be counted as among the most useful contributions to the Literary Revival, and those that have been preserved are valuable documents to the student of its history. To the addresses already mentioned may be added Hyde's *Necessity of De-Anglicising the Irish Nation*, and Lionel Johnson's *Poetry and Patriotism*, which have been given to the public in book form. Not so successful, however, was the series of books for which the Irish Literary Society was indirectly, at least, responsible. Published as "The New Irish Library," under the editorship of the first President of the Society, these books by no means corresponded to the needs of Irish writers as originally and rightly defined by those who met at Yeats's house in 1891. There was no attempt to encourage unknown talent and consequently none of the works chosen represent new names that have since become famous. In fact, apart from O'Grady's *Bog of Stars* and Hyde's *Story of Early Gaelic Literature*, the "New Irish Library" contains no new work of any significance in the Literary Revival. Ferguson's *Lays of the Red Branch* was available in another form, and the remaining volumes bear no relation to the new literature that was being written.

The cause of this failure was the conflict which arose out of the difference of opinion between two generations as to what national literature really should be. On the one side were the young writers of whom Yeats was the spokesman, representing the future; on the other was Sir Gavan Duffy, who belonged to the past. The friend of Davis, and one who had, consequently, participated in the only previous attempt to effect an intellectual awakening in Ireland, Gavan Duffy was, of course, an exponent of the ideas of *The Nation* school, of which he was the survivor. His election to the Presidency of the Irish Literary Society was doubtless imposed by the prestige attaching to one who had helped to make Irish history. His young admirers had the superstitious respect of youth for old age. Generous as were their sentiments, they inevitably redounded to the discomfort of a Society bent upon innovation. The President's conception of Irish literature was exactly opposed to that of the new generation, his standards were those of the politico-literary groups of his youth. In the Irish press, W. B. Yeats fought on behalf of his contemporaries, and in various articles and lectures defined the claims and principles of nationality, as opposed to political nationalism, in letters. The controversy over the publication of "The New Irish Library" is a specific incident in the continuous fight of the younger writers against the literary ideals of the old school. It is only necessary to re-read the contemporary utterances, such for example as Lionel Johnson's *Poetry and Patriotism*, to see how sharp was the conflict between the new and the old. It was the eternal clash of youth and old age with the usual results. At first deference to years, actually or supposedly fruitful of experience, the incurable optimism which makes the young hopeful of the co-operation of their elders, and finally, the realisation of an abyss between the two, into which one or other falls in the attempt to cross the bridge of compromise.

So far as "The New Irish Library" was concerned, Gavan Duffy's ideas carried the day. Instead of work which might now be considered as the first offerings of the Revival, he selected, for the most part, waifs and strays of the Young Ireland Movement, or writers of slight interest beyond the generation of 1848. Those who should have been included published their work elsewhere, affirming the new spirit, and confirming the tendencies which are now recognised as the basis of national literature. At the same time this early split has had a decided effect. It is probably because of this rift that Irish literary effort never attained for long a sufficient degree of concerted action to warrant its being termed a "movement." Without underestimating the work accomplished by the Irish Literary and the Irish National Literary Societies, it may be said that they have not fulfilled the rôle originally assigned to them.

The "spirit of *The Nation*" element has somehow preponderated, and the best work of the Revival has been created outside of them. Many of the finest writers are not associated with either Society, unless purely formally, in the case of some of the older names. While they have not remained strangers to any manifestation of intellectual activity, they have usually been witnesses *after* the fact. With a huge membership they make no pretence of having a majority creatively interested in literature. The dramatic movement, though begun under the auspices of the Irish Literary Society, soon drifted away as a separate organisation, as, before it, the Gaelic Movement had engendered the Gaelic League. Thus neither Gaelic nor Anglo-Irish literature centres about these Societies, which are content to be informed of what is happening in either branch by the lecturers whom they invite from time to time. Nevertheless they have adapted themselves to the moderate part circumstances have called upon them to play. In London particularly the Irish Literary Society still subserves its most useful and original purpose, as a meeting place for all concerned with Irish literature. In Dublin the presence of smaller groups of writers makes this need of a common centre less felt. In both cities the Societies maintain the necessary current of sympathy between those at the head of the literary stream and those who are nearer the mouth. If they do not constitute a "movement," they idnicate, at all events, a consciousness of literary identity. "A literary movement," says a well-known Irish poet, "consists of five or six people who live in the same town and hate each other cordially." This *boutade* provoked by the constant references to "the Irish Literary Movement," is as close to the facts of Irish experience as the exaggeration of paradox will permit. So long, however, as our Literary Societies exist they will supply a register of our belief that there *is* an Irish, as distinct from an English, literature, though it cannot be enclosed in the terms of a movement.

CHAPTER V

THE REVIVAL

POEMS AND BALLADS OF YOUNG IRELAND. J. TOD-
HUNTER, KATHARINE TYNAN, T. W. ROLLESTON,
WILLIAM LARMINIE

RELIEF from politics has been the condition precedent of intellectual, as well as of economic, progress in Ireland. Then only has it been possible to divert intellectual energies into the broader channels of social reconstruction. The "first lull in politics" postulated by W. B. Yeats, slight though it was, proved sufficient to permit a certain intellectual expansion, whose outward and more material manifestations have been noticed in the last chapter. This sense of unity and cohesion, which resulted in the creation of the Literary Societies, was, of course, for some years a strong undercurrent awaiting a propitious moment to rise to the surface. This period of waiting, while the seeds of a new literary ideal were germinating and spreading, was not barren of fruit of a certain maturity. Under the editorship of T. W. Rolleston, *The Dublin University Review* was publishing work of a distinctive kind, notably that of W. B. Yeats, while *The Irish Monthly* was for some time the meeting place of many young poets since prominently identified with the Literary Revival. Apart, however, from these individual activities must be considered *Poems and Ballads of Young Ireland*, which in 1888 announced the co-operative, con-

certed nature of the effort of the younger generation
to give a new impulse to Irish poetry.

This slim little book, in its white buckram covers,
will always be regarded with special affection by
lovers of Irish literature, for it was the first offering
of the Literary Revival. Here are associated as
collaborators the names of those who have established the claim of Ireland to be adequately expressed in the English language. George Sigerson
contributed one poem, as the representative of the
pioneers, but the bulk of the volume is the work of
the younger writers—Douglas Hyde, T. W. Rolleston, W. B. Yeats, Katharine Tynan, Rose Kavanagh
and John Todhunter. The last-mentioned, though
a contemporary of Sigerson, must be regarded as a
newcomer so far as Irish poetry is concerned, his
earlier work deriving no inspiration from national
sources. Some crudities of rhyme are noticeable in a
few of the poems, though principally in those of the
minor contributors, who have never taken a very
high place among the poets of the Revival. The majority of the contributions show a singular sureness
of grip and a maturity of talent, remarkable in the
verse of beginners. Such poems as Yeats's *King
Goll* and *The Stolen Child*, Todhunter's *Aghadoe* and
The Coffin Ship, possessed qualities of emotion and
execution which have since entitled them to rank
with the best that these writers have done.

Whatever be the merits and defects of each poem,
the volume as a whole represents a high level of
workmanship. But it is not so much for that reason,
as on account of its freshness and promise, that *Poems
and Ballads of Young Ireland* must be counted as
an historical document. Here and there are verses
inspired by the old spirit of rhetoric and aggressive
patriotism, but the book is essentially a harbinger

of the new tradition in Irish poetry. Douglas Hyde's *From the Irish* and *St. Colum-Cille and the Heron* have their basis in those Gaelic songs whose revelation has become our debt to him; in *The Flight of O'Donnell*, T. W. Rolleston's theme was that which had seized about the same time the imagination of O'Grady, and gave us the spirited romances, *Red Hugh's Captivity* and *The Flight of the Eagle*. Yeats showed at once his preoccupation with the legends and fairy stories of the countryside, while Todhunter even advanced to the point of making Anglo-Irish the effective and pathetic medium of tragic speech. Titles such as *Bresal's Bride* and *The Dead at Clonmacnois*, were indicative of the return to the heroic age and to the legendary material in which Standish O'Grady had stimulated such an interest. In short, the themes of this first non-political association of Irish writers are intensely Irish, yet, with two or three exceptions, they are entirely dissimilar from those that inspired the singers of the '48 movement, or the Fenians, who are here represented by Ellen O'Leary. Even her contributions have more of the plaintiveness than of aggressiveness which have been noted as the characteristics of the school to which she belonged. *Poems and Ballads of Young Ireland* is patriotic, but patriotism in the old sense did not inspire these writers. For political history they substituted legends, fairy tales, the spiritism of the Irish countryside, and so doing they indicated broadly the lines upon which contemporary poetry has developed.

JOHN TODHUNTER

Of those who collaborated in *Poems and Ballads of Young Ireland* Todhunter was, with Sigerson, the representative of an older generation. Although born in the same year as the latter, he was the oldest and most experienced writer of the group. While Sigerson's first book, *Poets and Poetry of Munster*, appeared in 1860, it was not until 1897 that *Bards of the Gael and Gall*, his second contribution to literature, appeared. Todhunter, on the other hand, though he began later, in 1876, with *Laurella and other Poems*, had half a dozen volumes to his name when *Poems and Ballads of Young Ireland* was published. His *Study of Shelley* in 1880, followed by *Forest Songs* in 1881, had established his position as a poet and critic of some importance, and three tragedies, *Alkestis*, *Rienzi* and *Helena in Troas*, had secured him the approbation of competent judges of classical literature. None of this work, however, bore any trace of the author's nationality, and it was not until he was caught in the movement which created the Irish Literary Society, that Todhunter turned his attention to Ireland. Later he was one of the Irish poets with W. B. Yeats, Lionel Johnson and T. W. Rolleston, who joined the gatherings at the "Cheshire Cheese," and shared in the production of the *Book of the Rhymers' Club*.

John Todhunter's first book of verse upon Irish themes, *The Banshee and other Poems*, was published in 1888, and was dedicated "To Standish O'Grady, whose epic *History of Ireland* first gave me an interest in our bardic tales." This is probably the earliest public record of the position of O'Grady in the Revival, and it expresses the obligation not only of Todhunter, but of all the Irish poets who followed him. It is, perhaps, of special significance coming from one whose mind had been moulded by very different influences. That a writer whose talent had already matured should have been influenced by the

Bardic History to the extent of discovering in himself an entirely new vein of poetry, is no slight evidence of the fascination exercised by O'Grady upon the poets of that time. In Todhunter's case it was hardly to be expected that his work should be completely transformed, he could only react to the new stimulus within the limits permitted by previous formative influences. The younger men, however, whose minds were fresh, succumbed more completely to the contact with this epic imagination.

The Banshee and other Poems is undoubtedly Todhunter's most successful book of Irish verse. It is the most important, for the later volume, *Three Bardic Tales*, which appeared in 1896, is simply a reprint of *The Doom of the Children of Lir* and *The Lamentation for the Three Sons of Turann*, supplemented by the third "sorrow of storytelling," *The Fate of the Sons of Usna*. In their last form these poems have a homogeneity that was absent from the previous collection. On the first occasion the symmetry and harmony of the book were disturbed by the addition of "other poems," mostly of a commonplace, English type, whose banality only added to the incongruity of their appearance in such surroundings. Contrary to what would appear to be the popular assumption of many critics, no claim has ever been made for the perfection of Irish verse as such. It is merely suggested that Irish poetry should be Irish, whether it be good or bad. The banal poems of many West British Irishmen are exasperating to their countrymen, not because Irish banality is superior to the English variety, but because the latter, in the work of another nation, becomes doubly feeble and imitative.

The finest of Todhunter's Irish poems is that which gave its name to the volume of 1888. *The Banshee,* though less ambitious than any of the bardic versions, together with the verses reprinted from *Poems and Ballads of Young Ireland*, will be remembered by many who have failed to enjoy the poems derived from legendary sources. The latter, in spite of occasional passages, leave the reader cold. The *Three Bardic Tales* correspond in substance to Hyde's *Three Sorrows of Storytelling*, which dates from about the same time, though two of Todhunter's versions were published before Hyde's little book appeared in 1895. In many respects Hyde's renderings are more pleasing than those of the older poet. Todhunter's rhymeless alexandrine quatrains in *The Doom of the Children of Lir* are, for example, more tiresome than the "orthodox English Iambics" of Hyde's poems on the same subject. *The Fate of the Sons of Usna*, a very lengthy, elaborate treatment of the greatest of the old romances, will not bear comparison with Ferguson's less complete rendering of the Deirdre saga, nor with the numerous poems which this popular theme has given the Revival. Here again Todhunter's rejection of rhyme, even in the lyrical passages with which the narrative is interspersed, militates against the enjoyment of the poem; Deirdre's *Farewell to Alba* and *Lament for the Sons of Usna* are infinitely more touching in Ferguson than in Todhunter. In the preface to *The Banshee* the author was able to claim a certain novelty for his *Lamentation for the Sons of Turann*. Of the "three sorrows of storytelling" this has proved the least attractive to the Irish poets, and in 1888 Todhunter was the first to make it the subject of a poem in English. When he reprinted it, however, in 1896, its isolation had been challenged in the previous year by Douglas Hyde's volume already mentioned. Like the *Story of the Children of*

Lir, that of the *Children of Turann* belongs to the mythological cycle, and is separated by several hundred years from the heroic cycle of which Deirdre is a part. Hyde alone among the poets has sought to give an adequate account of this interesting mythus. He relates how Lugh, while endeavouring to free the Tuatha De Danaan from the levies of the Formorians, sent his father to his death at the hands of the three sons of Turann. Upon the latter he therefore imposed an eightfold blood-fine, or eric, as it was called, six parts of which they were able to obtain. Lugh's last two demands, however, they forgot, because of a spell he cast upon them. Having secured the greater part of the ransom, Lugh sent the three to fulfil the remaining conditions, and in accomplishing this they lost their lives. Turann, on learning the fate of his sons, made a great lamentation over their bodies and then fell dead beside them. While Hyde recounts the whole story, Todhunter takes it up at the point where the father stands by the corpses of his sons. His poem relates briefly the circumstances of their death, but is really an elaborate *caoine* of the typical Irish kind. That is to say, it is typical so far as its division into elegiac strophes was suggested by the form of the Ulster *caoine*, and in its recapitulation of the life and virtues of the dead. In manner and spirit, on the other hand, the poem is not Celtic, and does not reach the note of tragic intensity of *The Coffin Ship*. Here the wail of the mourner is caught and rendered with fine pathetic realism.

Todhunter's greatest success has been in these shorter poems, which first appeared in *Poems and Ballads of Young Ireland*. His versions of the bardic tales, though they testify to the influence of O'Grady upon the literature in formation, do not in themselves constitute a very notable contribution to Anglo-Irish verse. The absence of rhyme in his lyrical measures, his frequent lapses into purely prosaic diction, are defects in his longer poems which are not compensated by the occasional lines showing something of the wild energy befitting the heroic stories. This lack of rhythm is all the more notice-able in a poet who has shown himself particularly susceptible to melody and has, in *Sounds and Sweet Airs*, for example, transferred into verbal music the emotions awakened by the hearing of Chopin, Bee-thoven and other composers. The fact is that the last-mentioned book probably represents more truly Todhunter's poetic faculty. He was drawn to Ire-land too late, when his talent had already ripened, and he could not break away from the influences that had moulded him during fifty years. Although he was one of those who helped to make the Irish Lit-erary Society, his participation in the Literary Re-vival was deliberate rather than instinctive. In support of this, it is only necessary to observe that since the publication of *The Banshee* in 1888 and the creation of the Literary Societies in 1892, Tod-hunter's work has not been related to Ireland or inspired by the Irish spirit. His *Life of Sarsfield* in 1895 can scarcely be regarded as creative literature, while two of the *Three Bardic Tales* were reprinted from the first collection of Irish poems, and the third, though not published in 1888, dated from that time. In short, once the first inspiration and enthusiasm of the Revival had spent themselves in him, Todhunter reverted to the tradition in which he had been educated. He wrote in England for the English public, and ceased to be any more rep-resentative of his country than George Bernard Shaw, with whom, indeed, he shared the honours in 1893, when *The Black Cat* was produced by the Independent Theatre Society, shortly after the production of *Widowers' Houses*. It is true that *The Land of Heart's Desire* was performed a year later under the same auspices, but while Yeats's play was Irish, and owed its appearance in England to circumstances which the Irish National Theatre has since altered, Todhunter's was a work which naturally called for the attention of those interested in fostering English literary drama. The one play was transplanted, the other was in its native element.

It is greatly to the credit of Todhunter that, in spite of his surroundings and training, he should have understood the new spirit that was at work in Anglo-Irish literature, and which tended to eliminate the Anglicised Irish poets of which he was a survivor. He might easily have remained indifferent, like his friend, Professor Dowden, whose abstention from all demonstrations of sympathy was open to the suspicion of *parti pris*—a suspicion confirmed since the publication of his correspondence. Nothing could have been more natural than that Todhunter, like Dowden, should have become imbued with the distrust of everything un-English in Irish life, once so prevalent in the University at which both were educated. Instead, however, of boasting that he had never allowed Irish ideals to interfere with his devotion to those of England, Todhunter placed himself in contact with the stream of ideas that was flowing into Anglo-Irish literature from the very sources of national culture. He did not—he could not—wholly de-Anglicise himself, but at all events he succeeded for a time in seeing Ireland with the eyes of an Irishman.

KATHARINE TYNAN

Very different were the results of the influence exercised by the Revival upon Katharine Tynan. Although one of the youngest of those who collaborated in *Poems and Ballads of Young Ireland*, she was already the author of two books of verse which had indicated her as a poet of more than average promise. Seldom has the first effort of a beginner met with such encouragement as greeted Katharine Tynan's *Louise de la Vallière and other Poems* in 1885. Until the publication of this little volume, the author was known principally to the literary circles in Dublin where the new spirit was stirring. She was a constant contributor to *The Irish Monthly*, a review which, in the Eighties and early Nineties, afforded an opening to a surprising variety of Irish poetry, from semi-patriotic, semi-devotional verse, of a very minor, local kind, to the work of W. B. Yeats, and even of Oscar Wilde, and including between these extremes, such writers as Katharine Tynan, Alice Furlong and Rose Kavanagh. With *Louise de la Vallière*, Katharine Tynan attained at once to a popularity which she has never ceased to enjoy, but which has not been entirely to her advantage.

It is not easy to understand why what she herself describes as a "very-much derived little volume" should have had a fate so different from that of the first work of so many young poets. *The Dead Spring, Joan of Arc, King Cophetua's Queen* and many of the other poems, are obviously inspired by the Pre-Raphaelite movement, and cannot be said to reveal anything of the poet's personality. On the other hand, two sonnets on *Fra Angelico at Fiesole*, though perhaps derived from the same source, are more characteristic of Katharine Tynan's later manner.

They have something of the innocent tenderness, the devotional sensitiveness to external beauty which are associated with her best work. These elements are more clearly present in such a poem as *An Answer*, which, in its absence of word-painting after Rossetti, foreshadows more precisely the style of much of her subsequent poetry. The promise of this volume would have been imperfect, however, had the note of nationality been absent. Beautiful as are some of the poems already mentioned, they could not have warranted the general recognition of Katharine Tynan as the singer of a distinctively Irish song. The Pre-Raphaelite tinge of *Louise de la Vallière* made the book one which might have been written by a young disciple of Rossetti, were it not for the five poems—the most stirring of all—whose theme was patriotic or national. The best of all these is *Waiting*, in which the legend is related of Finn and his warriors, who lie in a frozen sleep in a cavern of the Donegal mountains biding the time when they shall come forth to do battle for Ireland, at the hour of her redemption. The element of mystery is here combined with a living patriotism which give to this poem a thrill of reality contrasting with the rather imitative echoes of the verses of more commonplace inspiration. The lines on the death of A. M. Sullivan, entitled *The Dead Patriot* and *The Flight of the Wild Geese*, though less remote in their subjects, are not more intensely felt than this poem of legend. They, too, are infused with the emotion which is necessary to the creation of genuine poetry.

In her second volume, *Shamrocks*, published in 1887, we find Katharine Tynan occupied more frequently with Celtic themes. The first and longest poem, *The Pursuit of Diarmuid and Grainne*, was one of the earliest attempts to make use of the

Ossianic material in Anglo-Irish poetry. Though it is spoiled by rather conventional diction, there are many charming pictures which give to it an interest other than that necessarily attaching to the early poetry derived from legendary and historical sources. *The Story of Aibhric* and *The Fate of King Feargus* also witness to the poet's increased attention to Gaelic subjects since the publication of *Louise de la Vallière*. The religious feeling so noticeable in Katharine Tynan's work comes out very definitely in this volume. *St. Francis to the Birds* is one of her best and most characteristic impressions of that simple piety which imbues so much of her verse, and has again and again drawn her to the gentle figure of Assisi. *Ballads and Lyrics*, which followed in 1891, contained several poems relating to St. Francis, but none of these is superior to the first. This book, however, represents more adequately all the phases of the poet's talent, and shows a great advance upon its predecessors. There is a more pronounced individuality in this work than heretofore, and many of her previous themes are here rehandled with a surer touch. The opening verses, *The Children of Lir*, are far superior to the preliminary treatment of the same subject in *The Story of Aibhric*, already mentioned. Christian and pagan folk-lore are the basis of most of this volume, *Our Lady's Exile, The Hiding-Away of Blessed Angus, The Fairy Foster-Mother* and *The Witch* are typical poems of a kind Katharine Tynan has familiarised in many later books. They combine those two striking traits of Irish peasant character: an unlimited faith in the possibilities of witchcraft together with a profound belief in the more picturesque legends of Catholicism.

Ballads and Lyrics is Katharine Tynan's most

representative, and probably her best volume, as it is certainly that which bears most distinctly the Celtic imprint. *Cuckoo Songs*, published in 1894, suffers, by comparison, owing to a certain monotony due to the predominance of the devotional element, nor did the author recover the variety of *Ballads and Lyrics* in the four years' interval that preceded the publication of *The Wind in the Trees*. Here, the sub-title, "A Book of Country Verse," announced a certain limitation of scope. The entire volume is devoted to a series of intimate impressions of external nature, of the beauties of leaf and flower, all conceived in the vein of simple, loving admiration which has made her the sympathetic interpreter of mediæval Catholicism. In spite of the charm of such pictures as *Leaves*, *The Grey Mornings*, the volume can hardly be said to mark any progress, unless it be in a more careful technique. This halt in the development of Katharine Tynan's talent may be due to the fact that she has been too prolific for one whose gift is manifestly of slender proportions. Had she written but three volumes, they would easily have held the best of her inspiration. Using the word in its best sense, we may describe her as an essentially minor poet, though a minor poet of the first rank. Narrative verse was not her forte and she abandoned it early for lighter forms. Her themes have constantly been those of minor poetry, the birds and flowers of the countryside, the green fields and in general the simpler emotions derived from nature. She has treated these subjects with frequent delicacy and skill, and to them she owes her greatest successes. Nevertheless, she has continued to publish regularly books of this unsophisticated verse, each resembling its predecessor, alike in form and content. This inability to understand how rapidly such a vein becomes exhausted has resulted in the swamping of much good work by such volumes as *New Poems*, to mention one of the more recent, where there is hardly a line that could not have been written by the average young lady and gentleman with a facility for rhyme. It is difficult, when reading her later verse, to remember that until the arrival of W. B. Yeats, Katharine Tynan was held to be the young poet of the greatest promise in Ireland. In her first three or four volumes she did respond to the reasonable hopes which were rightly entertained of the author of *Louise de la Vallière*, even though she could never wholly justify the laudatory phrases with which that little book was received.

If her poetry has suffered by being subjected to the same exploitation as her prose, Katharine Tynan is none the less an interesting figure in contemporary literature. She is almost unique in that she is the only writer of any importance whose Catholicism has found literary expression. Reference has previously been made to the famous discussion of Oisin and St. Patrick, the clash of Paganism and Christianity, and to the fact that the Irish poets have almost unanimously declared themselves on the side of the former. It is certainly remarkable how completely the better Catholic writers have effaced their religion from their work. That is not to say they have deliberately suppressed their beliefs, or that the others have openly declared their hostility to the Catholic Church. The fact is simply that one class has been frankly pagan, and, as a rule, mystic, while the other has in no way been inspired or influenced by the teaching to which it assents. It is significant, for example, that so precious an anthology of Catholic folk-poetry as *The Religious Songs of*

Connacht should have been compiled by a Protestant. One would naturally expect that a task of this kind would have appealed to one of the Catholic poets, whose identity of belief and sympathy would specially qualify him to act as an interpreter. But apart from the most minor poets, Katharine Tynan alone reflects that attitude of Catholic Ireland in her verse. Outside of Ireland, Catholicism has been an æsthetic influence. Continental critics have come to regard the Catholic Church as a fosterer of the arts, and many ingenious conclusions have been drawn from the contrast between the artistic imaginativeness of the Latin and Catholic races, and the joyless materialism and ugliness of the Teutonic and Protestant countries. France, especially, has afforded interesting instances of the intimate artistic relations between the Catholic Church and literature. The French Protestant has invariably a certain heaviness, a lack of suppleness and vivacity which distinguish his writing from that of the majority who are untouched by the Lutheran heresy.

Ireland presents a problem for the champions of neo-Catholicism, for there they will find little to support their enthusiasm for the older Church, as a refuge from the democratic mediocrity, and intolerant freedom, of the most Protestant sections of Protestantism. It is impossible to conceive of a Huysmans or a Verlaine being converted to Irish Catholicism. The "*grands convertis*" had a conception of religion entirely remote from the philosophy of Catholic Ireland, whose artistically barren soil could never produce a Chartres Cathedral, while its inhabitants would view with horror such a "convert" as the author of *La Cathédrale*. Irish ecclesiastical architecture is, as a rule, as unrelievedly dull as that which we associate with the extremer forms of Protestantism.

The externals of Irish life immediately demonstrate how slight is the artistic influence of Catholicism in Ireland. Irish Catholics have none of the easy tolerance and freedom of religious majorities elsewhere, but have the narrowness and hardness of a small sect. All the repressive measures of puritanism are heartily enforced, in emulation of the efforts of the Protestant minority. In short, the Protestantism of the Irish Catholic is such as to deprive the Church of precisely those elements which are favourable to literary and intellectual development, and have rallied so many artists to her support. Nor have those peculiar qualities of genuine Protestantism been substituted, to which the Northern races owe their most characteristic virtues. As a result, the Catholic Irishman does not find in his religion the spiritual emotion and the æsthetic stimulant necessary to the creation of a work of art. Consequently, his inspiration has been drawn from sources independent of his religious beliefs.

The foregoing may seem to preclude the possibility of there being even one truly Catholic poet, and to be completely disproved by the existence of such an anthology as *The Religious Songs of Connacht*. The contradiction is, however, more apparent than real; the old antagonism of bard and saint, of which the historians have written, still lingers obscurely in Ireland, and it has been seriously contended that the Catholic Church is an exotic. Nevertheless the people, and more particularly the peasantry, have associated the bardic divinities and heroes with the saints and wonders of Christianity. Sacred and profane legends have become so identical a part of the belief of the rural population that the one has infused the other with a certain breath of poetry. In the large cities a deliberate effort has been made to find a spiritual background for Irish life, and, as we shall see in a later chapter, with most interesting results. In the country towns, unfortunately, this has not been the case, and the spiritual death that hangs over them is obviously due in part to this failure of Catholicism to become properly assimilated. In the remoter Irish-speaking districts, however, what was conscious in the cities has been instinctive, and a certain folk-poetry has grown up. The presence of the Gaelic language guaranteed the survival of the bardic tradition, and the heroic figures of antiquity naturally amalgamated with those of sacred history. Where the Celtic flame had not been extinguished poetry was possible. The ancient tongue had the associations lacking in the speech of the provincial towns, and only recovered by the concerted move of a few more cultivated groups in the cities. The latter, being more deliberate, were naturally more radical in their return to the origins of nationality and of national literature, and quickly dissociated the fundamental traits of the Celtic spirit from the extraneous agglomerations of Catholicism. Hence on the one hand, *The Religious Songs of Connacht*, and on the other, the poetry of A. E., W. B. Yeats and the writers associated with them.

Katharine Tynan, though also associated, to some extent, with the group of poets last mentioned, remained uninfluenced by the revolt which led them to the very sources of Celtic spirituality. She remained undisturbed in her acceptation of the simple teaching of the Catholic Church, and it is just in so far as she approximates to the attitude of the country people that she is a Catholic poet. One does not find her expressing the profounder aspects of Cathol-

icism, the exaltation and rapture of belief, for
these belong to a more emotional and intellectual
religion than that of the Irish Catholic. In Ireland
the folk-lore conception of Catholicism is the most
prevalent, as they know who have essayed to raise
the theological level to that of France or Italy.
Modernism is a problem which we have not yet
faced. In the realm of folk-lore, at all events, is witnessed a certain reconciliation of the antagonistic
bardic and Christian elements. Katharine Tynan's
verse, therefore, voices that naïve faith, that complete surrender to the simpler emotions of wonder
and pity, which characterise the religious experiences
of the plain man.

Her delight in St. Francis is typical of her general
manner. She never touches the speculative depths
of such Catholics as Pascal, the doubts and ecstasies
of the great believers are not hers. She sees nature
with the eyes of devout reverence, and in her tender
descriptions of all the small creatures of God, her
love for the old or the helpless, she excels in conveying a sense of child-like admiration for and confidence in the works of an Almighty Power. Her
Rhymed Life of St. Patrick accurately reproduces the
popular view of the saint, widely different as that is
from the facts. The little book of six miracle plays
published in 1895 is another of her best-known works
devoted entirely to religious subjects. Here, however, there is a rather too careful simplicity, giving
an air of artificiality not usual, for spontaneity is a
noticeable feature of her devotional outpourings.
But it must be said that here also she has failed to
exercise any restraint. Her numerous contributions
to magazines of piety are rarely suitable for republication. The devotional side of Katharine Tynan's
work is quite adequately represented by a selection

from her religious verse, such as that which has recently appeared under the title, *The Flower of Peace*.

Interesting though she may be as the only important Catholic poet in Ireland, Katharine Tynan will hardly rank with the best writers of the Literary Revival. For the reasons we have seen, Irish Catholicism is necessarily a shallow vein of inspiration, and even at best, it has not created, and cannot create, great poetry. In the special circumstances just described, it has inspired folk-poetry that has many beauties, but the power of *The Religious Songs of Connacht* loses by transposition. There is more of the poetic essence in Douglas Hyde's collection than in Katharine Tynan's many volumes. Nevertheless, she has written more verse than any of her contemporaries, with the possible exception of W. B. Yeats, and this, notwithstanding the incredible list of fiction with which she has endowed the circulating libraries. In Yeats's case the volume of writing is distributed over a wide range of subject and has been constantly revised. When Katharine Tynan, with a fraction of the poetic material, has spread it over so many pages, it is not surprising her work should be thin. *Irish Poems*, published in 1913, contains a selection from the best of her more recent poetry. If we are to judge her by this volume, we must forget all the inferior verse, all the book-making, which is doubtless inevitable, so long as commercialism is the master instead of the servant of art. This is all the more easy, as she has here collected a sufficient number of beautiful poems to ensure her remembrance by all who care for the unassuming songs of a poet whose voice has so often sung the fragrance of the country, and the charm of natural beauty.

T. W. ROLLESTON

There is a certain similarity between the position of T. W. Rolleston and that of John Todhunter in the history of the Revival. Both were already well-known in a different sphere of literature when they joined the group of *Poems and Ballads of Young Ireland,* and neither continued very long to write poetry of a distinctively Irish character. Like Todhunter, Rolleston was attracted to Irish literature by the example of Standish O'Grady, although he was definitely engaged upon work of a very different kind, having become known prior to 1888, as a critic of Walt Whitman and Epictetus. He did not, however, publish an independent volume of verse until comparatively recently, when *Sea Spray: Verses and Translations* appeared in 1909. While it contains some of Rolleston's early verse, this book can hardly be described as a typical collection of modern Irish poetry. With Todhunter and Yeats, he collaborated in both series of *The Book of the Rhymers' Club,* and this association seems to have Anglicised his verse as effectively as it did that of Todhunter, for, of the Irish poets who met at the "Cheshire Cheese," Yeats alone preserved his national identity.

The Dead at Clanmacnois and *The Grave of Rury* are poems which awake a regret that their author should have so soon forsaken Celtic sources, but it is certainly better that he should have done so, than have continued to write when the freshness of inspiration had left him. He has preferred to give the anthologists a few verses whose charm is undeniable rather than to submerge his talent in a mass of feeble poetry. It is as a prose writer that he has rendered most service to the literature of his country, which is indebted to him for *Imagination and Art in Gaelic*

Literature (1900), *The High Deeds of Finn* and *Myths and Legends of the Celtic Race* (1911). For the present we may note that Rolleston's failure to realise such hopes as were raised by his contributions to *Poems and Ballads of Young Ireland* does not in any way lessen the value of his work at this early period. He worked energetically with those who created the Irish Literary Society, of which he was the first Secretary, and whose success was due in a great measure to his help.

At an earlier date he had established a claim upon lovers of Irish poetry by his editorship of *The Dublin University Review*. He was responsible for the growth of that periodical into something very different from what might have been expected from its title. The review, however, was not connected with the institution after which it was named, and became, in Rolleston's hands, a centre of national ideas and Irish culture. These pages saw the publication of the first important poems of W. B. Yeats, *The Island of Statues* in 1885 and *Mosada*, the following year, in addition to several shorter poems by the same writer. *The Dublin University Review* died shortly afterwards of that pecuniary malnutrition which has so often been the lot of Irish reviews, however well nourished they may have been intellectually. In the present instance Rolleston was able to face extinction in the satisfaction of knowing that he had done well by the new literature in Ireland. By sheltering the work of W. B. Yeats he assisted the Revival more materially than any original effort could possibly have done. Rolleston's work about this time was not confined to the literature of the future. He was responsible for the appearance of a volume of Ellen O'Leary's poems, and also a selection from the work of Thomas Davis, which has been re-issued in more elaborate form, as one of the recently instituted series, "Every Irishman's Library." In thus rendering accessible some of the better work of the older school he increased the obligation of Irish readers to his editorial activities. It is, therefore, for his practical and critical services that he is remembered in the history of the Irish Literary Revival. As joint editor of the *Treasury of Irish Poetry* he has helped to produce an Anthology which is still indispensable to the study of Anglo-Irish literature. Since its publication in 1900 our poetic "treasury" has been enriched by many new names. But were a new, enlarged, edition to be brought out, this book would strengthen a position as yet unchallenged by any of the numerous collections of Irish poetry that have followed it.

WILLIAM LARMINIE

Although he did not contribute to *Poems and Ballads of Young Ireland*, William Larminie may be counted as one of those early poets whom we have described as the vanguard of the Revival. *Glanlua and other Poems* appeared in 1889, a date marking, as we have seen, the beginnings of modern Irish poetry. Larminie was unlike the contemporary poets we have mentioned in that he neither belonged to the young generation of Katharine Tynan and W. B. Yeats, nor had he the literary experience of Todhunter or Rolleston, to whom his years approximated him. He began to write at an age considerably in advance of that of the other beginners, for he was forty when *Glanlua* was published. This fact is a testimony to the potency of the influences that stirred the intellectual waters of Ireland during the early years of the Revival. Todhunter furnished us with an instance of an older writer having been led to alter both the form and content of his work by the spell of nationality. Larminie, however, is more interesting, inasmuch as he seems to have discovered himself in the general literary awakening of the time. It was, perhaps, not easy for a writer of some maturity like Todhunter to cultivate a new style, and to abandon, even temporarily, the traditions he had followed with success. It must have been even more difficult for Larminie to answer suddenly the call to letters.

What was re-creation in Todhunter was a veritable creation in Larminie, whose literary faculties had lain dormant. This quickening of the poetic spirit was due, once again, to the revelation of bardic literature. Larminie's verse is informed throughout by the Celtic spirit of legend and mysticism, and few of his poems find their inspiration outside of Ireland. The title-poem of his second volume, *Fand and other Poems*, published in 1892, was, like *Glanlua*, derived from the history of the Red Branch. While the former book contained only three poems in addition to *Glanlua*, the latter is more substantial, and more representative of the author's talent. Besides *Fand*, it contains *Moytura*, equally based upon bardic material, and Larminie's most ambitious effort. Unlike the younger poets of the time, he was attracted to narrative rather than lyric poetry, for the bulk of his verse is contained in the three long poems named, *Glanlua*, *Fand* and *Moytura*. At the same time he has written some lyrics of great charm; *Sunset at Malinmore, Consolation* and *The Finding of Hy Brasil* may be cited amongst the best of the very few shorter poems Larminie has left.

Fand and *Moytura* possess an interest for the student of Anglo-Irish poetry not shared by *Glanlua*.

While the latter is written in regular rhymed verse, the former are in the nature of a metrical experiment. Larminie had devoted some time to the study of the development of metrics and, although it was not until a couple of years later that he publicly formulated his theory, he experimented in this volume of 1892. Briefly his contention was that assonance, being prior to rhyme, as is evident from early Gaelic poetry, might be substituted, especially where the rhyme is either purely visual or inaudible. In *Fand and other Poems* assonance is systematically employed, in both regular and irregular forms. This tradition of Gaelic literature has left its mark upon the verse of many living Irish poets. Whether consciously or unconsciously, the work of W. B. Yeats and A. E. is frequently assonantal, but Larminie is the only poet, apart from the translators, who deliberately had recourse to this form. It is not merely occasionally, but throughout an entire volume, that he uses assonance.

The experimental character of his verse undoubtedly contributed to his failure to secure popular recognition. The story of Cuchulain and Fand, which corresponds and contrasts so interestingly with the legend of Venus and Tannhäuser, is a theme which should naturally engage the attention of a poet sensible of the beauties of Celtic literature. In *Fand*, Larminie handled the subject with great sympathy, but the irregularity of his verse precluded him from reaching the imagination of the general public. *Moytura* similarly was limited in its effectiveness, though to a lesser extent, by the strangeness of its forms. Here the great struggle between the Tuatha de Danaan and the Formorians lends itself more easily to popular treatment. There are more opportunities for achieving those effects of language, those pictures evoked by words full of colour and music, which are generally held to constitute poetry. This legendary battle of the Celtic deities, symbolising the victory over darkness of the powers of light, is unfolded in a narrative of great imaginative strength. The reader is caught by an excitement which enables him to forget the unfamiliar metres, elsewhere more noticeable, because unrelieved by any verbal charm.

Without subcribing to Verlaine's "*de la musique avant toute chose*," we may reasonably demand that poetry possess some musical quality. Thè frequent error of mistaking mere sound for poetic beauty springs from the just and instinctive belief that verse should strike the ear by some obvious, artistic quality absent from prose. It is claimed for English poetry that it does not rely upon the ear for its effects, but is addressed primarily to the mind and to the spirit. This seems to be the point of departure of that criticism which constantly assures us of the superiority of English over French verse. The superstition that French is the language of prose, and English the language of poetry, has gained wide acceptance from the authority of Matthew Arnold. His well-known dictum has been repeated by all English-speaking critics of French poetry, although it was a generalisation as hasty as that in which he belauded the excellence of the so-called "journeyman work of literature" in France.

Arnold's theory regarding French poetry has no apparent basis beyond the fact that the latter must be, above all things, musical; no elevation of thought, nor depth of spirituality being sufficient to make inharmonious verse pass for poetry. Because of the manifest beauties of French prose Arnold assumes it must be the medium in which the French language attains its highest achievements. But the prose of France is the direct outcome of her verse, the beauty of Pascal being intimately related to the beauty of Racine. It is strange, moreover, that Arnold's generalisation has been accepted precisely by those who hold that the English Bible is unique. The existence of the Authorised Verson is surely an external vindication of the claims of English prose, and a fundamental invalidation of Arnold's theory. In the absence of any French prose surpassing that of the Bible a doubt is permissible as to the necessary inequality of the claims of English and French poetry.

This digression has not led us as far away from our subject as may appear, for Larminie supplies, in a minor way, an illustration of the point at issue. If a philosophy and a spiritual message are more essential to poetry than verbal music, then the author of *Moytura* should have secured the attention bestowed upon his contemporaries. It would be wrong to suggest that he lacks charm, for few will deny, once they have mastered his rhythms, that he has skill and imagination enough to hold the attention. But by no means can he be described as a master of fine language, he is far too often preoccupied by the thought itself to elaborate scrupulously its expression. There is a dignity and elevation, rather than beauty, in his verse, while its originality is evident. These qualities, however, were inadequate to the task he had undertaken, and to which he probably sacrificed a measure of success. In order to impose his theory of assonance as a substitute for rhyme, something more was required.

Plausibly as he argued, in *The Development of English Metres*, against the use of worn-out or useless rhymes, the ultimate test of his case was his verse. Could he in practise show any pleasing and acceptable improvement upon the forms he wished to displace? Here, unfortunately, he demonstrated, not that hackneyed rhymes were desirable, but that disagreeable assonance was not preferable. His proposals might have had more success had they come from a poet skilled in the use of language, and in command of a perfect technique. Larminie's poems lack artistry, they are often harsh, and while their spiritual worth attracts, their form repels. It is, nevertheless, an interesting commentary upon the alleged English predilection for substance rather than form in poetry that, when the essentially musical, unreflective work of many contemporary Irish poets was greeted in England with enthusiasm, Larminie was hardly known outside his own country.

An early death prevented Larminie from realising his literary powers to their full extent. Whether he would have continued to write verse, and ultimately have given us a volume of poetry adequately representative of its legendary sources, must remain a matter of conjecture. Reference has been made in a former chapter to his *West Irish Folk Tales and Romances*, a work which shows how deep was his interest in the remnants of Ireland's Gaelic heritage. A poet who added a wide acquaintance with the Irish language to the living Celtic tradition preserved in it, clearly enjoyed an advantage shared by none of his contemporaries. Here, if ever, was a combination that might have given Anglo-Irish literature an epic. But indications seem to point to a determination in Larminie to forsake poetry. His first prose work, above referred to, was published in 1893, a year after *Fand*, and from that date until his death in 1900, he was engaged principally in critical work. This changed activity during the last years of his life, having regard to the fact that he died leaving an unfinished study of Scotus Erigena, suggests that he intended to seek in prose the success his poetry had denied him. In sharp contrast to William Larminie stands the poet who now claims attention and whose first important volume, *The Wanderings of Oisin,* appeared the same year as *Glanlua.*

CHAPTER VI

WILLIAM BUTLER YEATS: THE POEMS

FOR many years W. B. Yeats was the most widely-known name in contemporary Irish literature, and it was not until the success of J. M. Synge that his predominance was challenged. Even then, however, the great difference in the work and manner of the two writers resulted in there being but a slight modification in the popular estimate of Yeats's importance. To many people he was, and is, synonymous with the Irish Literary Revival, of which they believe him to be the beginning and the end. As we have seen, not Yeats, but O'Grady, was the beginning of the Revival, and, as will be shown, very little of the work done by Irish writers during the past decade, or more, is traceable to the former. In attempting to delimit the influence of Yeats there is no intention to belittle what he has done, nor to deny that such an influence exists. He has certainly affected the course of the Revival, more especially in the first years of its existence, and is mainly responsible for the ultimate development of the Irish Theatre, but in neither instance has his rôle been that popularly attributed to him. At first his influence upon his contemporaries was undeniable. He induced them to abandon their politico-literary idols, and his own example served at once to enforce his arguments. His work not only exposed the weakness of the popular models, but at the same time attracted serious attention to the poetic awakening in Ireland. But this direct impulse was not sufficiently enduring to substantiate the claim that all our modern poetry comes from Yeats. In the theatre he has not at all moulded the form of Irish drama, for his plays have found no imitators, and remain separate and utterly distinct from the work of the other playwrights. Nevertheless, his presence has been a factor of some weight in the evolution of the Revival. Poet, dramatist, storyteller and essayist, he commands attention in almost every department of literature, and the mere bulk and diversity of his writings, apart from their intrinsic excellencies, are sufficient to ensure him a position of the first importance in any survey of Ireland's literary activities during the past quarter of a century. But he began as a poet, and a poet he remained essentially and at all times. His poetry will, therefore, be the first and main subject of our consideration, for by that his position must be estimated in the world of Irish letters.

LYRICAL AND NARRATIVE POEMS

It is only necessary to compare the four poems contributed by Yeats to *Poems and Ballads of Young Ireland* with those of his collaborators, to realise how vastly superior he was both to his young contemporaries and to the older writers represented. *The Madness of King Goll* and *The Stolen Child*, the former one of the finest poems Yeats has written, show a remarkable delicacy and maturity of craftsmanship in a young man of twenty-two. Their respective themes, drawn from legend and fairy lore, presage, moreover, the lines along which the poet developed his greatest successes. They have that glamour and sense of mysterious reality which

are peculiar to Yeats's verse at its best, and haunt
the memory like a subtle, intellectual perfume. The
legend of King Goll is one which the poet is able to
interpret in the spirit of true Celtic mysticism. The
old king who, in his madness, hears the voices of
superhuman presences in the crying of the wind and
the rolling of the waters, who feels the breath of the
elemental powers, and the tramping feet of super-
human beings—all the mystery of nature as sensed
by the Celt is rendered with extraordinary skill and
verbal felicity. The refrain:

"They will not hush, the leaves a-flutter round me, the beach
leaves old."

is not easily forgotten. This poem, and those that
accompanied it, are the true forerunners of the
poetry which has established the position of W. B.
Yeats in contemporary literature. Their publication, however, did not represent the first appearance of his work in book form. Yeats began with
Mosada, a twelve-page brochure, published in 1886,
but neither this, nor *The Island of Statues*, its predecessor in the pages of the *Dublin University Review*,
can be regarded as announcing the poet we have
come to know. They are not so closely related to his
maturer and characteristic work as the contributions to *Poems and Ballads of Young Ireland*. They
were written while the poet was still searching for
the direction in which lay the finest flowering of his
talent. "When I first wrote," he says, "I went here
and there for my subjects as my reading led me, and
preferred to all other countries Arcadia and the India
of romance." To this period of uncertainty belong
The Island of Statues, *Mosada*, and *The Seeker*, three
poems which have not been included in any volume
of Yeats's collected works since 1889, when he re-

published them in *The Wanderings of Oisin*. They
were written at a time when the poet had not yet
realised that Ireland was to be the source from
which he would derive his surest inspiration. Neither
the mediæval Spain of *Mosada*, nor the Arcady
of *The Island of Statues*, gave him the setting and
atmosphere in which his genius could find its characteristic expression. Yeats was still too young
to shake off the domination of Spenser and Shelley,
whom he admired so deeply that he had to complain
of his verses being "too full of the reds and yellows
Shelley gathered in Italy." Hence we find Ireland completely absent from these early poems,
though their themes were not such as to preclude
the hope of finding equivalents in the world of Irish
romance. It is to the best of the three, *The Island of
Statues*, that he probably alluded when he said: "I
had read Shelley and Spenser, and had tried to mix
their styles together in a pastoral play which I have
not come to dislike much." This "Arcadian Faery
Tale in Two Acts," with its reminiscences of Shelley,
and its Spenserian mould, certainly corresponds to
Yeats's reference. In spite of this frank admission
of imitation, an imitation which would in any case
be expected in a young writer of nineteen years, *The
Island of Statues* is far from being weakly imitative.
It has an originality which is not weakened by the
poet's consciousness of his models, and which
indicates undoubted power. As has been stated, this
early work does not reveal the poet we now know
Yeats to be. That is to say, the national element
is not pronounced in the three poems, which date
from a time when he was as yet uncertain of the
direction to which he should turn. The statement
obviously does not imply that it is impossible to
recognise in *Mosada*, or its predecessors, the author

of *The Wanderings of Oisin*. His first verses have many qualities in common with those of later years; the differences are of degree and of subject, rather than of manner and form. They have, above all, that music and beauty which were ultimately so exquisitely heightened when the voice of Celtic Ireland sang in his verse:

> Thou shalt outlive thine amorous happy time,
> And dead as are the lovers of old rime
> Shall be the hunter-lover of thy youth.
> Yet ever more, through all thy days of ruth,
> Shall grow thy beauty and dreamless truth. . . . .

Such lines as these bear the imprint of the spirit by which Yeats's best work is informed. But the only part of *The Island of Statues* that he has preserved is that little lyric *The Cloak, the Boat and the Shoes*, and even this he has slightly emended, with that fastidiousness which has prevented him from reprinting many of his early poems, and has effected such great changes in the later editions of all his works.

When, after four years of poetical activity, Yeats offered his first collection of verse to the public, in 1889, he was evidently progressing towards the realisation of his powers. Both in choice of subject and in style *The Wanderings of Oisin and other Poems* marks an advance sufficient to warrant its being described as a representative volume. In essence most of his later work is here, and, as the book contained all his poetry up to that date, it is usually regarded as the beginning of W. B. Yeats. It has, indeed, been made by many the point of departure of the Revival, but there is evidence that this is not the case. Granted that Standish O'Grady is the source, it will easily be seen that *The Wanderings of Oisin* was not the first stream of poetry to issue from him. Larminie's *Glanlua*, and Todhunter's *Banshee* were the contemporaneous products of the same impulse as gave birth to Yeats's volume. Since O'Grady had sent the young generation to the roots of national culture a number of new writers were at work, and the year 1889 saw their emergence from obscurity. Hyde's *Leabhar Sgeuluigheachta*, which heralded the Gaelic Movement, appeared in the same years as *The Wanderings of Oisin*, and 1889 is, therefore, a date of some interest to students of contemporary Irish literature. The time had come for the realisation of various ideas and ideals which were stirring in Ireland, hence the almost simultaneous appearance of a number of writers representing or emphasising new tendencies. But neither Yeats nor Larminie nor Todhunter can be regarded as originating any movement, inasmuch as they themselves were the outcome of a movement already initiated.

Without admitting the wider claims made on behalf of *The Wanderings of Oisin*, we may justly consider it as the beginning of Yeats's career. The title poem itself sufficiently indicates a definite orientation towards national poetry, instead of the vague romances of Arcady and Spain with which the poet was at first engaged. The latter, it is true, find here their first and only republication, but the volume, in the main, is distinctly Irish. Yeats was an early champion of Ferguson against the rhetorical school and, during the first years of the Literary Societies, he had constantly to assail the theory that *The Nation* poets were unimpeachable models for all who desired to write Irish poetry. As far back as 1886 he wrote in the *Dublin University Review*, urging the merits of Ferguson, whom he recognised as the true precursor of the new spirit. This discipleship explains in some measure *The Wanderings of Oisin*. Although there is no trace of Ferguson in

Yeats's style, he played, nevertheless, an important part in the literary education of the young poet. It was doubtless his study of Ferguson that prompted him to essay an epic poem upon an Irish subject, and to give, in *The Wanderings of Oisin*, the measure of his genius. From Ferguson and Allingham Yeats learned what Irish poetry could be made, once the political note was softened or entirely silenced. "If somebody could make a style," he wrote, "which would not be an English style, and yet would be musical and full of colour many others would catch fire from him." This was the thought which turned Yeats from Spain and Arcady to Ireland, and in his volume of 1889, we find him in the act of realising his ideal of national poetry. An artist in words, he had an advantage over Ferguson, whose conception and aims were lofty, but whose craftsmanship was unequal. Having been roused by O'Grady's prose, Yeats was able to bring to the old legends an admiration equal to Ferguson's, but a sense of artistry and a temperament unknown to the older writer. He constantly exhorted his contemporaries to chasten their enthusiasm for the crude outbursts of aggressive patriotism, for, as he pointed out, "if more of them would write about the beliefs of the people like Allingham, or about old legends like Ferguson, they would find it easier to get a style."

The first edition of *The Wanderings of Oisin* differs materially from the version published in the collected volume *Poems*, of 1895. The latter, though subsequently emended here and there, is substantially the poem as it appeared in its final form in later editions. Even in its original form the poem could not but be a revelation of the poetical possibilities of the new Irish literature. Starting from the idea of the clash of Paganism and Christianity, which had appealed so often to the poets of old, Yeats succeeded in creating something which was as truly in harmony with the Celtic spirit as it was expressive of himself and the generation he announced. The tale relates Oisin's departure for the magic faery land, where with Niamh he dwells for three centuries, first in the Island of Dancing, then in the Island of Victories, and finally in the Island of Forgetfulness; the framework of legend is preserved, but the content is an expression of personality, where the past is blended subtly with the present. Ferguson, familiar as he was with the legends and mythology of Ireland, failed somehow to infuse the warmth of reality into his reconstructions of antiquity; his poems, like those of Todhunter, and others who have treated of the legendary subjects, do not give the sense of intimacy needed to transport the reader. Their efforts are somewhat too deliberate; one feels that they have approached the heroic and fairy lore of Ireland as they would the myths of Greece and Rome, and their work is frequently no more convincing than the "classical" tragedies which engage the attention of so many young poets. It was Yeats's distinction that from the first he created the impression of an intimate harmony between himself and his subject. With a singular imaginative power he was able to obtain the freedom of a region of Celtic legend and romance which more painstaking scholars had surveyed without ever apprehending its true atmosphere.

It is hardly necessary to state that Yeats did not attain at once to the almost perfect understanding of the spirit that moved in him, and demanded to be clothed in words adequate to its origins and traditions. "It was years," he admits, "before I could rid myself of Shelley's Italian light." In other words, a severe literary discipline was necessary before he

could give to Irish subjects a mind sufficiently free
from English influences to permit of a true congruity between style and matter. The difficulty
which presented itself is one necessarily familiar to
Irishmen since the days when their language was
suppressed with the object of extinguishing their
nationality. Although this object has not been
achieved, except with a certain minority whose
national sense is atrophied or perverted, the dis-
placement of Irish by English has tended to place a
veil between the people and their own literature and
culture. The writer who wishes to see his country
reflected in his work must break through this veil of
English, and generally, in doing so, he carries with
him some remnants of the obstacle through which he
has passed. Afterwards his success is measured by
the extent to which he is unhampered by these foreign elements that cling to him. This experience
fell, of course, to Yeats who was obliged to consecrate himself to the task of eliminating from his style
those qualities he knew to be un-Irish, and therefore
unsuited to the poetry that came to him from
national sources.

It is interesting to compare the earlier and later
editions of Yeats's work, and to see him in the very
act of pruning his style of all rude or incongruous
elements. The passage in which Oisin describes his
meeting with Niamh may serve as an example. The
1889 edition reads:

And Bran, Sgeolan and Lomair
Were lolling their tongues, and the silken hair
Of our strong steeds was dark with sweat,
When ambiing down the vale we met
A maiden on a slender steed,
Whose careful pastern pressed the sod
As though he held an earthy mead
Scarce worthy of a hoof gold-shod,

For gold his hoofs and silk his rein,
And 'tween his ears above his mane
A golden crescent lit the plain,
And pearly white his well-groomed hair.
His mistress was more mild and fair
Than doves that moaned round Eman's hall

. . . . .

Her eyes were soft as dewdrops hanging
Upon the grass-blade bending tips,
And like a sunset were her lips,
A stormy sunset o'er doomed ships.
Her hair was of citron tincture
And gathered in a silver cincture;
Down to her feet white vesture flowed
And with the woven crimson glowed,
Of many a figured creature strange
And birds that on the seven seas range.

. . . . .

This early version contains many passages of undeniable charm, and these few verses are sufficient to
give an idea of its strength and weakness.   But the
revised version of 1895, which has not undergone
very important modifications since, shows a wonderful transformation.

Caolte, and Conan, and Finn were there,
When we followed a deer with our baying hounds,
With Bran, Sgeolan and Lomair,
And passing the Firbolgs' burial mounds,
Came to the cairn-heaped grassy hill
Where passionate Maeve is stony still;
And found on the dove-gray edge of the sea
A pearl-pale, high-born lady, who rode
On a horse with a bridle of findrinny;
And like a sunset were her lips;
A stormy sunset on doomed ships;
A citron colour gloomed in her hair,
But down to her feet white vesture flowed
And with the glimmering crimson glowed
Of many a figured embroidery.

. . . .

The entire description now occupies a third less of its original compass. The unconvincing images and similes have disappeared, while the essential colouring is retained by the more natural application of the adjectives "pearl-pale and dove-gray." Nothing has been omitted in the re-writing that we could have wished to see preserved. With a sure sense of art, only the irrelevant has been rejected, for a more timid or less sensitive hand might have hesitated at the boldness of

> "And like a sunset were her lips
> A stormy sunset on doomed ships;"

Significant too, as illustrating that harmony between the true self of the poet and his subject, is his simultaneous achievement of two results. He might have emended the poem in obedience to the suggestions of a well-developed sense of poetic values, but at the same time have lessened or destroyed its inner qualities. On the contrary, this elevation of form resulted in a heightening of the Celtic note. Surely no more striking demonstration was possible of the real and subtle relation of form and content. Here, obviously, was no mere manipulation of local colour formulæ. The nearer Yeats approaches to the perfect expression of his thought, the more finely he attunes his instrument, the more national becomes his song.

The Countess Kathleen and Various Legends and Lyrics, in 1892, revealed a more exclusive preoccupation with Ireland than the preceding volume. There is not a line in the book that is not instinct with the spirit of nationality, yet anything more different from what had hitherto been accepted as the typical collection of Irish national poetry it would be difficult to conceive. Perceiving this, yet conscious that his verses were none the less the expression of his country, Yeats voices his conviction in the fine *Apologia* which is now so familiar:

> Nor may I less be counted one
> With Davis, Mangan, Ferguson,
> Because to him who ponders well
> My rhymes more than their rhyming tell. . . .

These poems belong to the period when Yeats was a member of the Young Ireland Society, and when, though fighting against the undue regard in which Davis and his school were held, he desired, like them, to write "popular poetry." Although convinced of the superiority of Mangan, and of Ferguson especially, he nevertheless tried to convince himself that the popular patriotic poets wrote well, and to improve upon the tradition they had created. The most successful of these attempts are the ballads, *Father Gilligan*, *Father O'Hart* and *The Lamentation of the Old Pensioner*. These, like the songs, *Down by the Salley Garden* and *The Meditation of an Old Fisherman*, from the previous volume, are the result of direct contact with the country people, and may fairly claim to be as "popular" as is possible for Yeats. The author has suggested in later years that these poems are trivial and sentimental, weaknesses he ascribes to the fact of their being "imitations." But to many they will possess a charm and spontaneity preferable to the laboured obscurities of his maturity.

Distinct from the verses inspired by country lore are those which have their roots in the heroic age. Here it is possible to see the influence of Ferguson driving the poet to the libraries, where he could satisfy the appetite awakened by O'Grady for the ancient sagas. *Fergus and the Druid* and *The Death*

of Cuchullin are fragments in the Fergusonian manner—for Ferguson invariably confines his treatment
to some slight incident rather than to a sequence of
episodes from the heroic cycles. Yeats, however, is
able to supply the element of beauty whose absence
made Ferguson's work so frequently colourless. The
latter held his reader to the interest of the subject
in itself, whereas the former compels attention by
the art of his verse. One forgets the fragmentary
theme in order to enjoy the expression of the poet's
thought. Ferguson could not have written:

> A wild and foolish labourer is a king,
> To do and do and do, and never dream.

The lines are a formula of Yeats's attitude towards
life. Even less likely is the author of *Congal* to
make us lose sight of his subject in order to admire
the thought.

> I see my life go dripping like a stream
> From change to change; I have been many things—
> A green drop in the surge, a gleam of light
> Upon a sword, a fir-tree on a hill,
> An old slave grinding at a heavy guern,
> A king sitting upon a chair of gold. . . .

Fergus and the Druid is as great an advance upon,
say, Ferguson's *Abdication of Fergus MacRoy*, as the
ballads mentioned were upon those of Davis and his
followers. Less successful is *The Death of Cuchullin*,
which deals with that intensely tragic situation of
Irish legend, the slaying of Cuchullin by his father,
who is ignorant of his son's identity. The tragedy
is lost in the poem, nor are there any touches of personality to compensate for the author's failure to
catch the proper note. Conscious, no doubt, of
this ineffectiveness, Yeats later returned to the subject in the one-act play, *On Baile's Strand*. Here,

at all events, the conception is more adequate. How far he has succeeded in capturing the tragic mood, we shall see when examining his dramatic work.

From 1892 until 1899, there was a pause in the poetic activity of Yeats. During that period he did not produce a new book of verse, contenting himself with publishing in 1895 his first volume of collected poems. This contained but one poem which had not already appeared in book form, and a re-writing, under the title, *A Dream of a Blessed Spirit*, of a song from *The Countess Kathleen*, not retained in the second and later versions of that play. Beyond rewriting and emending certain early poems, the author made no additions to his lyrics until 1899, when he published *The Wind Among the Reeds*. This very slender volume, whose text is almost submerged in explanatory notes, indicated that the seven years which went to produce it could not have been wholly consecrated to verse. They were, in point of fact, the years in which Yeats wrote most of his prose work, apart from that connected with the Irish Dramatic Movement. As editor of Blake, critic of the numerous works being written under the first impetus of the Revival, and author of *The Celtic Twilight* and *The Secret Rose*, the poet of *The Countess Kathleen* had been fully occupied in that interval which preceded *The Wind Among the Reeds*. He did not merit the reproaches of the critics who, on its appearance, complained that the book was small, and regarded it as evidence of inactivity.

While apparently unsubstantial, *The Wind Among the Reeds* was Yeats's most serious lyrical work, at least in intention. It was written under the influence of the author's recent study of Blake, and at a time when he was engaged in those mystical speculations of which *The Secret Rose* and *The Tables of*

the Law were the earlier expression.   Aedh, Hanrahan and Michael Robartes are transferred from the
former work and become the personages of many of
these poems, where they retain at the same time
their original symbolical significance.   This movement in the direction of symbolism began to define
itself when Yeats gave to a number of poems from
The Countess Kathleen the sub-title *The Rose*, on the
occasion of their republication in 1895.   These poems
were written under the growing influence of a mysticism which was separating him from the young poets
who had grown up with Yeats in the revived tradition of Irish literature.   Already in 1892 he felt
that he was going beyond the goal set by his contemporaries, and those of their predecessors whom they
had elected to follow.   Thus he wrote in the Apologia
addressed to Ireland:

> Know that I would accounted be
> True brother of that company
> Who sang to sweeten Ireland's wrong,
> Ballad and story, rann and song;
> Nor be I any less of them,
> Because the red rose-bordered hem
> Of her whose history began
> Before God made the angelic clan,
> Trails all about the written page. . . .

The "red rose-bordered hem" is the *Leitmotiv* of
Yeats's thought at this time.   It emerges more definitely in *The Rose*, is emphasised in *The Secret Rose*
and *Rosa Alchemica* and culminates in *The Wind
Among the Reeds*, with which the personages and
fundamental teaching of the former stories are
interwoven.

Eternal Beauty, which is the poet's quest, is symbolised for him by the Rose, and thus he gave that
title, in 1895, to the poems which were the pathway

leading him in the direction of his ideal. It is not difficult to see in such verses as *The Two Trees* the transition to *The Wind Among the Reeds,* where the highest point of progress is reached. The book is probably the most complete expression of Yeats. It is the most characteristic, for all his faults and most of his virtues are developed to a maximum, so that it has become, as it were, the quintessence of Yeats, where friend and foe alike seek the justification of their admiration and hostility, respectively. It is significant that *The Wind Among the Reeds* has remained throughout all subsequent editions unaltered from the form of 1899. Unlike its predecessors, the volume has not undergone those constant modifications and emendations which have made the variations in Yeats's work almost notorious. It seems as if the technical perfection of the first edition has, for once, satisfied the author. It has happened, more than once, that sympathetic criticism has had to protest against the poet's fastidiousness, but on this occasion Yeats's own estimate of his work has coincided with that of his critics. Whatever objections have been levelled against *The Wind Among the Reeds,* it has been recognised as a final demonstration of the author's command of his craft. A volume which opens with *The Hosting of the Sidhe* cannot but draw forth the praise of those who have responded to the call of the Celtic element in literature:

> The host is riding from Knocknarea
> And over the grave of Clooth-na bare;
> Caolte tossing his burning hair
> And Niamh calling: Away, come away:
> Empty your heart of its mortal dream.

The Wind Among the Reeds contains many verses like these, yet the cumulative effect of the book is

unfavourable to all but the few—or is it the many?—
who profess to find in Yeats's overweighted symbolism the exposition of a profound creed. In spite
of the general protest against the numerous poems
involving voluminous explanatory notes, and the
absolute obscurity of several, this is the collection
of verse which has established the author's claim
to the title "mystic poet." The prose works preceding it, already referred to, constitute a more substantial effort to establish that claim, but *The Wind
Among the Reeds* is the first mature expression of
Yeats's mysticism in verse. It marks the maturity
of his technique, the end of his career as purely lyric
poet, and the beginning of a phase in his evolution
with which he has come to be popularly and completely identified. Yet, it is doubtful, with all its
paraphernalia of occultism, its display of mystic
lore, if the book is one in which the authentic voice
of the mystic is heard.

Mysticism is, above all, intellectual, when it is not
charlatanism. Vision comes only as the reward of
severe mental discipline, after study as rigorous as
that demanded by any of the so-called "exact"
sciences. But there is no trace of this in Yeats,
who cannot properly be described as an intellectual
poet. His appeal is primarily sensuous. None can
charm the ear more delicately, or please the eye
of imagination more skilfully than the author of
Oisin. It is improbable that he has ever mastered
the science of mysticism as he has mastered the
science of verse. So long as the mind surrenders
to the heart, thought to emotion, Yeats carries the
reader with him. A typical illustration is that
wonderful lyric *The Rose of the World*, one of the
earliest pages about which trails "the red rose-bordered hem":

Who dreamed that beauty passes like a dream?
For these red lips, with all their mournful pride,
Mournful that no new wonder may betide,
Troy passed away in one high funeral gleam,
And Usna's children died.

.   .   .   .   .

Bow down, archangels, in your dim abode:
Before you were, or any hearts to beat,
Weary and kind one stood beside His seat;
He made the world to be a grassy road
Before her wandering feet.

The last verse empties the poem of all intellectual
content. It is impossible to know who is "weary
and kind," for the adjectives are inapplicable to any
being conceived by the preceding verses. One cannot imagine Eternal Beauty as ever having been
"weary and kind," and, assuming the allusion to be
some living woman, it is equally inconceivable that
she should have existed "weary and kind," in the
region of time and space considered by the poet. It
would be easy to cite other instances of this inconse-
quence in Yeats's thought, and when we shall have
considered his prose writings, it will be seen that
these incongruities are not due to the exigencies of
rhyme. Not poetic licence, but a fundamental misconception of mystic doctrine, is the explanation.

Mysticism to Yeats is not an intellectual belief,
but an emotional or artistic refuge. His visions do
not convince us, because they are obviously "literary" rather than spiritual. The concepts which
are realities to Blake, or to Yeats's contemporary,
A. E., are to him symbols, nor do they strike the
reader as being anything more. Of symbolism—
even mystic symbolism—there is plenty, but of
mysticism hardly a trace. In the earlier poems there
is more evidence of genuine mystic feeling than in
The Wind Among the Reeds and its successors. Since

1899 the poet has been almost completely merged in the dramatist, but three very slim collections of lyric verse have appeared at long intervals, *In the Seven Woods* (1903), *The Green Helmet and other Poems* (1910) and *Responsibilities* (1914). All three continue the manner of the 1899 volume, but *The Wind Among the Reeds* remains, nevertheless, the culminating point of progress in the direction of mystic symbolism. Beyond it no advance can be made. It is, therefore, needless to say that, in attempting to go further, the poet has come to a standstill. In *The Green Helmet and other Poems* he cries:

> The fascination of what's difficult
> Has dried the sap out of my veins. . . .

Although the reference is more particularly to his experiments with the theatre, the lines are appropriate to more than the plays of the later Yeats. Symbolism has been both a good servant and a bad master, for at one period it had vanquished the poet. When we were asked in *The Wind Among the Reeds* to remember that "Hanrahan is the simplicity of an imagination too changeable to gather permanent possessions, or the adoration of the shepherds; and Michael Robartes is the pride of imagination brooding upon the greatness of its possessions, or the adoration of the Magi; while Aedh is the myrrh and frankincense that the imagination offers continually before all that it loves"—it was clear that the symbol had become more to Yeats than the thought. In 1899 criticism was indignant at the obscurities of the celebrated, *Mongan Laments the Change that has come upon Him and His Beloved*, but in 1903 *In the Seven Woods* contained a similar piece of ingenuity, *The Rider from the North*, while *The Grey Rock* in *Responsibilities* surpasses both in its wealth of

enigma. Yeats has abandoned the hope of disarm-
ing hostility by notes, as in *The Wind Among the
Reeds;* his allusions and symbols are now left for the
few who can read as they run. In this he is wise, for
it is doubtful if such a glose as that quoted concerning Hanrahan, Robartes and Aedh, will be of any
help to the uninitiated in their attempt to appreciate the poetry. But it is equally doubtful if the
existence of such poems as those mentioned is any
more justified because to some the symbols are as
familiar as to the author.

It would be unjust to suggest that Yeats's later
poems grow increasingly obscure, and perhaps unintentionally that is the impression left by what has
been said. While it is true that *In the Seven Woods*
and subsequent collections mark no advance on
The Wind Among the Reeds, they contain work which
is equal to the best Yeats has written. The specifically symbolic-mystic poems are inevitably what
was to be expected, but the author has still his
artistry, the verbal magic, and the technique which
made *The Wind Among the Reeds* an achievement.
The return to the themes of Irish legend in *The Old
Age of Queen Maeve* and *Baile and Aillinn;* the *Song
of Red Hanrahan* and *The Withering of the Boughs*
made *In the Seven Woods* a volume precious to those
admirers of Yeats whose passion for the allusive
and elusive was within bounds. This, with *The
Green Helmet and other Poems* and *Responsibilities,*
would make a book to be placed beside *The Wind
Among the Reeds.* The most recent volume, particularly, is interesting, as sounding the note of actuality.
The Grey Rock and *The Two Kings* are here, of
course, to remind us that Yeats is unrepentant, but
the majority of the poems in *Responsibilities* are as
free from the defects of elaborate symbolism as

Yeats's early work. They are written out of the experience gained from years of controversy and struggle in the practical world on behalf of an ideal. Some are directly inspired by incidents connected with the Irish National Theatre propaganda, others bear upon certain notorious episodes of Ireland's artistic history, and these contemporaneous utterances bring the poet from the dream-world to everyday life, with most happy results. There is a firmness and directness of outline which are not usually associated with the poetry of Yeats. He has freed himself from the preoccupations of symbolism only to gain in beauty and energy what he has lost in vagueness and mystery. Who will not prefer *September*, 1913, with its passionate cry:

> Romantic Ireland's dead and gone,
> It's with O'Leary in the grave.

to those overcharged memories of diligently acquired mysticism?

Regret has frequently been expressed that Yeats should have almost forsaken lyric poetry, after the publication of *The Wind Among the Reeds*, in the year which saw the beginning of the dramatic movement, whose existence has absorbed him. The theatre, it is contended, has robbed us of great poetry. Apart from the effectiveness of Yeats's participation in the movement to found a National Theatre, there is much to be said against this contention. Yeats has not failed to exercise such influence as was inherent in his work upon Irish literature. As the bearer of a poetic standard as lofty as it was national he has fulfilled his part. His work has called forth more imitators in England than in his own country, but it has been indirectly an important factor in the development of contem-

porary Irish poetry. Had the drama not called him
away in 1899, it is possible that his value as a lyric
poet might have diminished, for the volume published in that year did not afford any hope of further evolution along the same lines. Mature in its
technique, *The Wind Among the Reeds* could only
have given promise for the future in its substance,
but as we have seen the content is as imperfect as
the form is perfect. The encroachment of a too
weighty symbolism, and the elaboration of the purely
picturesque, occult, elements of mysticism, threatened to lead to repetition and sterility.

For a time, indeed, as the poet wrote, it seemed
as if "the fascination of what is difficult" had "dried
the sap" out of his veins, but gradually there has
come into the poems of his maturity a note of cold,
austere beauty, which fittingly replaces, with the
advancing years, the magical glamour, the prodigal
loveliness of his early poetry. The whole section of
lyrics dated 1904–1919 in his most recent volume of
Selected Poems, published in 1921, is full of fine
things which compensate, to some degree, for the
drastic elimination of almost two-thirds of the work
of the ten years from 1889 to 1899. For example,
When Helen Lived:

> We have cried in our despair
>   That men desert,
> For some trivial affair
>   Or noisy insolent sport,
> Beauty that we have won
>   From bitterest hours;
> Yet we, had we talked within
>   Those topless towers
> Where Helen walked with her boy,
>   Had given but as the rest
> Of the men and women of Troy,
>   A word and a jest—

and *No Second Troy:*

> Why should I blame her that she filled my days
>   With misery, or that she would of late
> Have taught to ignorant men most violent ways,
>   Or hurled the little streets upon the great,
> Had they but courage equal to desire?
>   What could have made her peaceful with a mind
> That nobleness made simple as a fire,
>   With beauty like a tightened bow, a kind
> That is not natural in an age like this,
>   Being high and solitary and most stern?
> Why, what could she have done being what she is?
> Was there another Troy for her to burn?

The skilful economy of words, the almost conversational tone, have led English critics to speak of the exhaustion and tenuousness of Yeats's later work. What one feels is the self-disciplined austerity, the restraint of a poet in his maturity, who is perhaps a little too conscious of the generous sins of his youth. If the freshness of those colourful early poems is gone, here is the deep mellowness of one who cries:

> I am worn out with dreams;
>   A weather-worn, marble triton,
> Among the streams;
> And all day long I look
>   Upon this lady's beauty
> As though I had found in a book
>   A pictured beauty,
> Pleased to have filled the eyes
>   Or the discerning ears,
> Delighted to be but wise,
>   For men improve with the years.

CHAPTER VII

WILLIAM BUTLER YEATS: THE PLAYS

IT is customary to deplore the loss to Irish poetry which has resulted from the absorption of Yeats by the theatre. It should not, however, be forgotten that this interest in drama did not come to him as a later phase. His first published work, which appeared in *The Dublin University Review* in 1885, was *The Island of Statues: An Arcadian Faery Tale in Two Acts*, followed in 1886 by *Mosada, a Dramatic Poem*, both of which indicate a certain leaning towards the dramatic form of writing. Neither was written, of course, with a view of being produced upon the stage, but, though subsequent practical experience has given the author some command of the technique of the theatre, those early poems are not so widely removed from the later plays as might be imagined. The dramatic element being usually subordinate to the poetic, the young poet is still plainly visible in the more experienced playwright. The development of Yeats as a dramatist is intimately connected with the development of the Irish National Theatre, but it is hardly correct to say that the latter is responsible for the former. The rise of the Dramatic Movement in 1899 coincided with the culmination of his lyric efforts in *The Wind Among the Reeds*, but, as has been suggested in the previous chapter, the relative inactivity which ensued may be attributed to another cause. The creation of a national theatre did

145

not so completely absorb the lyricist as is usually asserted. If Yeats devoted himself with such intensity of purpose to the work of the theatre it was because he felt that there he would find opportunities to develop, rather than in the direction he had hitherto exclusively followed.

The Dramatic Movement was the occasion, not the cause, of the second phase of Yeats's evolution. The dramatic instinct was in him from the beginning. *The Countess Kathleen* was written in 1892, seven years before the foundation of the Irish Theatre, while the first of his plays to be performed was *The Land of Heart's Desire*, produced in London as early as 1894. In its earlier form *The Countess Kathleen* differs greatly from the version published in the *Poems* of 1895, which has remained practically unchanged. The former was apparently not conceived as a stage production, and reads like a dramatic poem rather than a play. In 1895, however, the loosely-knit "scenes," into which it was divided, became "acts," and by a process of expansion and excision the work was lengthened and strengthened at the same time. Yet this strengthening has not constituted it a drama, in any acceptable sense of the term, for Yeats has succeeded in enhancing the dramatic quality of his work only in so far as he has added to its poetic strength. The *Countess Kathleen* is a more perfect poem now than when first conceived, but in the theatre it is as unconvincing as ever. The theme of sacrifice, of the woman who sells her soul to the demons that her people may not traffic theirs, is obviously one for the dramatist, but Yeats has been unable to grasp it. There is not a dramatic incident in the whole play, the tension is loose, and the action so diffuse that the supreme moment of Kathleen's sacrifice passes almost unnoticed. Failure to express the dramatic intensity of the situation must be attributed to that fundamental weakness in the poet which almost invariably deprives him of the effects which a skilled dramatist would achieve. That he sensed the possibilities of the theme is evident from the manner in which he altered the first version. The death of the Countess Kathleen and her assumption into Paradise afforded a dénouement to which the later versions are immeasurably more adequate than that of 1892. But, characteristically, the improvements are literary rather than dramatic. The poet's judgment was sure enough to enable him to preserve all the finest lines of the early play, and in closing the drama he uses them with heightened effect. If the Angel's song, *All the Heavy Days are Over*, is omitted, we find it elsewhere in Yeats's lyrics as *The Dream of a Blessed Spirit*, with the last verse altered by a veritable inspiration. In return, are substituted those lovely lines:

> Bend down your faces, Oona and Aleel:
> I gaze upon them as the swallow gazes
> Upon the nest under the eave, before
> He wander the loud waters. . . .

with which Kathleen takes leave of her companions. What added force, too, is given to the well-known verses of the original play:

> The years like great black oxen tread the world
> And God the herdsman goads them on behind,
> And I am broken by their passing feet.

Instead of being uttered almost in the void by Oona to "a young peasant," these lines are now the comment of a mother upon the loss of her child. They close the drama upon the deeper note of tragedy.

Yeats has so frequently and so materially revised his plays that they may be considered without insistence upon chronological sequence. Radical changes in rewriting deprive many of them of their priority. Title and theme may belong to an early date, but a new edition often means a new play. It would be superfluous to preserve the form of chronology when the essentials are lacking. In 1914, for example, *Responsibilities* contained a version of *The Hour Glass* differing from that of 1903 in such a manner as to render unnecessary any attempt to treat the play as belonging to one period rather than the other. It will, therefore, be most convenient to divide the dramatic works of Yeats into groups. On the one side are the plays whose material is derived from the myths and legends of the Heroic Age, on the other those of one act, inspired by peasant and fairy lore. As the latter attach themselves in manner, at least, to *The Countess Kathleen*, they call for attention at this point. Since the Heroic dramas mainly belong to the latest period of the poet's activities, departure from the strict chronological order will not distort the general picture of Yeats's development as a dramatist.

The Land of Heart's Desire, *Cathleen ni Houlihan*, *The Hour Glass* and *The Pot of Broth* are the most popular contributions Yeats has made to the Irish theatre. *The Land of Heart's Desire* is, as it were, the complement of its predecessor, *The Countess Kathleen*, in that it illustrates the strain of paganism which is as surely a part of Celtic folklore as the piety of which the former play is an expression. Yeats's peculiar skill in handling fairy themes was manifest from the first, when he contributed *The Stolen Child* to *Poems and Ballads of Young Ireland*, and in *The Land of Heart's Desire* he demonstrated

his power to elaborate such themes without destroying their delicate simplicity. The story of how the
fairy child stole away Maire Bruin, the young bride,
is typical of the many romances which the peasant
mind has created out of the doings of the Good People
in Ireland. To Yeats these fairy tales have become,
as they doubtless originally were, symbols expressing
the aspirations of the soul; he gives to them a
spiritual significance which heightens their charm,
while preserving the sense of *naïveté* in which they
survive throughout the Irish countryside. *The Land
of Heart's Desire* is a perfect example of the poet's
intimate sympathy with these remnants of Celtic
mythology. The realism of Bridget and Maurteen
Bruin's terror and awe before the fairy visitor, the
combination of childlike superstition and deep
mysticism with which the play is informed, produce
the happiest effect. Maire's response to the call
of the Sidhe is, for the reader as for the author, an
act of obedience to the mysterious forces that draw
men out of themselves into the transcendental world
of the spirit. The poet here expresses the emotion
which dominates so much of his work and is so powerfully suggested in *The Hosting of the Sidhe*.

Withal, the primitive framework of the little drama
remains unspoiled, the meaning does not obscure
the action and is not obscured by it. Yet it is the
only fairy play which Yeats has written, in spite of
the fact that no other play of his has been so frequently performed. Probably the poet has found
that such themes do not lend themselves to dramatic
form. *The Land of Heart's Desire* is more devoid
of dramatic incident than even *The Countess Kathleen;* both are essentially poems. Whatever elements of drama the latter may contain are unexploited, but the former contains no such element at

all. Countess Kathleen's sacrifice is potentially dramatic, the struggle between Father Hart and the fairy for the soul of Maire Bruin has not the semblance of drama. So completely is the symbolism understood, so naturally is the situation felt, that the question of conflict does not rise. The question was raised, it is true, by contemporary objectors who professed to be horrified that the crucifix should be removed by the priest at the request of the Pagan child. These were the same primitive moralists who raised an outcry against *The Countess Kathleen,* on the ground that the selling of Kathleen's soul to the demons was heresy, and a libel upon the Irish people, while the trampling under foot of a shrine was pronounced sacrilegious. These evidences of rudimentary theology have long since been forgotten, though they were remembered in connection with similar outbursts against J. M. Synge. Most people are content to remember *The Land of Heart's Desire* as a beautiful poem, for such it is. Precisely the absence of dramatic emotion enables the reader to appreciate undisturbed the lyrical beauty with which the play is so richly endowed.

There is a certain irony in the fact that Yeats's most successful play, from the point of view of the theatre, should be one he has never had to revise, and which is written, not in verse, but in prose. *Cathleen ni Houlihan* was performed in 1902 by W. G. Fay's Irish National Dramatic Company in Dublin, and was the first of those folk-dramas with which the Irish National Theatre has become identified. As we shall see in a later chapter, this Dramatic Company was the embryo of the Irish National, as distinct from the short-lived Irish Literary, Theatre. Thus, Yeats's greatest dramatic

success coincided with the inauguration of the Movement which has given Ireland a national drama.
The play was favourably received at the outset, and
its appeal has never failed.   To the already unique
circumstances connected with it, therefore, must be
added the fact that, alone of Yeats's work, *Cathleen
ni Houlihan* commands the admiration of all sections
of Irish opinion.   The now familiar story of Cathleen
ni Houlihan's sudden appearance to Michael Gil-
lane on the eve of his wedding, in the tragic days of
1798, when "the French were on sea," and the hopes
of Ireland were high, needs no recapitulation.
Michael hears the voice of his country in the appeal
of the Poor Old Woman, and no Irish audience could
fail to thrill in response to that call.   The tragedy
of the young man's instant surrender, his forsaking
of home and those dear to him, stir the emotions,
for is this not the tragedy which underlies and en-
nobles all patriotism.   Here the symbolism of Yeats
is seen to its advantage, for the very absence of
specific local incidents raises the drama to the plane
of the eternal verities.   Noble and austere, but with
none of the coldness of the abstract, *Cathleen ni
Houlihan* is infused with the warmth and passion of
poetry and life.

The Pot of Broth is often referred to as the only
farce Yeats has written.   It is a retelling of the
popular folk-tale which relates how a crafty tramp,
by dint of much "blarney," succeeds in tricking a
miserly housewife.   While he envelops her in a cloud
of verbosity and compliment, he obtains the ingredients for a pot of broth, which he had undertaken to provide out of the magic properties of a
stone.   Engrossed in the man's conversation she
fails to observe what is happening, and is left happy
in the possession of the stone of whose magic she is

persuaded. It is an amusing trifle, but there is no trace of Yeats's style in it. There is, on the contrary, every indication that Lady Gregory was the writer. The slightness of the subject, the droll short sentences, and the grotesque loquacity of the tramp, are now familar characteristics of Lady Gregory's comedies and farces. Except for a certain restraint, not visible in the verbal and other exaggerations of such plays as *The Jackdaw* and *Hyacinth Halvey*, the part of Yeats in *The Pot of Broth* is almost indiscernible. It was written by Lady Gregory in collaboration with the poet, in order to supply the need of the newly inaugurated National Theatre for folk-plays. It is significant that Yeats omitted it from the eight-volume edition of his collected works published in 1908. Irish legend furnished the material of *The Hour Glass*, a morality, which was performed for the first time in 1903. During the nine years which elapsed before the production of the revised version in 1912, Yeats had acquired a keener sense of the theatre, and the new play, as published in 1914, is a more convincing conception than the original. Not only is the metrical form more appropriate than the earlier prose, but the structural alterations have strengthened the play intellectually. As Yeats confesses, there was a charm in the naïve legend of the Wise Man who, having destroyed the faculty of belief in the community about him, finds salvation in the wisdom of Teigue, the fool, who alone remained untouched by the breath of scepticism. But on the stage this charm was threatened by an appearance of platitude. As now conceived, *The Hour Glass* escapes this dilemma, and is at the same time more true to the poet's own philosophy.

The unfolding of the drama is more skilful than in the early version. The refusal of the Wise Man's pupils to admit that remnant of faith which would save him from eternal punishment is brought out in a satisfactory manner; the part of the Fool is devised with a clearer sense of proportion. There was something too mechanical in his former rôle, his relation to the discussion of the teacher and his pupils was forced and arbitrary. By subordinating this part, the dénouement in particular has been strengthened. Instead of being enlightened by the inadvertent confession of Teigue, the Wise Man dies in ignorance of the precise extent of the Fool's belief. With finer effect Yeats shows him accepting the Eternal Will and dying confidently in the conviction of an ordered Destiny. The play still closes on the same scene in which the Angel receives the soul of the philosopher and bears it into Paradise. There was, however, something false in the manner of this consummation. That the Wise Man should accept the artless wisdom of Teigue did not appear probable. For this *naïveté*, so unconvincing in the theatre, Yeats has substituted a more fitting conclusion. Recognising submission as the secret of the Fool's salvation, the Wise Man is reconciled to the will of God. In obedience to intuition he finds the revelation of truth. *Where there is Nothing*, like *The Pot of Broth*, was excluded from the Collected Edition of Yeats's works. But the former has been more decisively repudiated than the latter, inasmuch as *The Pot of Broth* has frequently been reprinted, even since 1908. On the other hand, *Where there is Nothing* has never appeared since its first publication in 1903. When collecting his work for the complete edition, Yeats selected the version written with Lady Gregory, entitled *The Unicorn from the Stars*. From an explanatory note it appears that the earlier play was also written with Lady Gregory's assistance. In fact, three people collaborated, and it was written in a fortnight, to "save from a plagiarist a subject that seemed worth the keeping till greater knowledge of the stage made an adequate treatment possible." As in most of his later prose work, evidence of Lady Gregory's collaboration was not wanting in *Where there is Nothing*, but in *The Unicorn from the Stars* hers is the dominating presence, so that the play belongs to her rather than to Yeats, whose original idea alone remains.

The idea of Paul Ruttledge's revolt against convention; how he allies himself with vagrants to overthrow the social laws of respectability and eventually, by seductive heresy, draws with him a section of the Church to the overturning of dogma, only to die at the hands of an outraged community—such a theme was, indeed, "worth the keeping." Unfortunately, neither the three collaborators, in the first instance, nor the two, in the second, have succeeded in exploiting it. If anything, *Where there is Nothing* is superior to *The Unicorn from the Stars*, for there, at least, Yeats was able to suggest the conditions which produced Ruttledge's revolt. The play is chaotic, fragmentary, a mere scenario, in a sense, despite its length, which exceeds that of any other play by the same author. But it contains the elements of drama; the situation is clearly determined and demands but a little careful elaboration and pruning. It is, therefore, a matter of regret that, when Lady Gregory undertook the subject, the *venue* of the play should have been so completely altered. The brooding young "heretic," whose rebellion was so natural, becomes the coach-builder, Martin Hearn, who emerges from a cataleptic trance seized with a spirit of revolt, as a result of a vision when in that state. It is difficult to appreciate exactly the nature of the revelation which Hearn brings back with him from his trance, and the motives of all his subsequent actions remain, consequently, dubious and unconvincing. The very conditions of his life take away from the effect of the change in him, whereas Paul Ruttledge, the wealthy young idler, was admirably conceived. His desire for the unorthodox, his excess of zeal in embracing heresy, were the natural reactions of a man in his position with such a temperament. When he does fall into a trance the scene is not only convincing, but adds materially to our understanding of the situation. In short, *Where there is Nothing* justifies Yeats's original belief in the merits of the subject. *The Unicorn from the Stars* belies it. The "greater knowledge of the stage," evident in the dialogue, has made "an adequate treatment" impossible.

The first of the mythological and legendary dramas is *The Shadowy Waters*, which was begun as early as 1897, and appeared in 1900. No play of Yeats has been more often revised than this, and one is not surprised to learn that he prefers it to any of the others. As first staged in 1904, it differed considerably from the version published in 1900, and it was again rewritten for publication in 1906. The latter text has been retained, but it is condensed and altered in the acting edition, verse and prose being used, instead of blank verse throughout. This modification detracts noticeably from the charm of the play, and is a practical admission of its unsuitability to the demands of the theatre. But the beauty of *The Shadowy Waters* is so essentially poetic, that its qualities as drama are easily forgotten. One reads it, as one reads *The Wanderings of Oisin*, for the sake of its mood, the elusive mystery of its atmosphere, the delicacy of its expression.

The dramatic claims of the play may be said never

to have existed; from the earliest to the latest version the theme remains fundamentally incapable of dramatic expression. Forgael's quest for the Absolute symbolised by imperishable love; his meeting with Queen Dectora, who offers him the love of mortals, ephemeral and unsatisfying to the soul whose pursuit is the eternal, and finally their union in the spirit, when Forgael convinces her of the reality of his dream—such is the framework which the poet has clothed with beautiful imagery of thought and language. Plot and setting are vague and impalpable, it is impossible to convey the meaning of the poem within the exigencies of the theatre. For it is a poem and nothing else, a fact which explains the fondness of Yeats for this play above all others. The instinct of the poet, which always predominates in him, has kept him faithful to the theme wherein he finds the truest expression of himself. Many years of constant preoccupation have made *The Shadowy Waters* a reflection of the poet's intimate thoughts. How often in the lyrics have we heard him utter the cry of Forgael!

> Could we but give us wholly to the dreams,
> And get into their world that to the sense
> Is shadow, and not linger wretchedly
> Among substantial things.

The theme of *The Shadowy Waters* is the *Leitmotiv* of Yeats's poetry.

The King's Threshold has been regarded as a sort of personal manifesto, though it reveals less of Yeats's attitude towards life than *The Shadowy Waters*. The reason why it has been identified more closely with the poet's personality is too obvious to merit undue emphasis. From the old Irish prose Romances Yeats has selected the story of the demands made by the poets at the court of King Guaire of

Gort. The play relates how Seanchan, the Chief Poet of Ireland, starves on the royal threshold rather than be deprived of his right to sit at the King's table. The temptation to see in Seanchan the embodiment of Yeats's own claim on behalf of poetry was too great to be missed. The adversaries of the National Theatre movement eagerly seized upon the material offered for some cheap sarcasm. Yeats's treatment of the old romance, his vindication of Seanchan, were held to be simply the outcome of his own arrogance. As *The King's Threshold* was produced at a time when the hypermoral patriots were beginning their campaign against Synge, it had the air of being a challenge, and, like most of Yeats's challenges to popular prejudice, it drew forth the inevitable stream of stereotyped abuse. Nowadays it is difficult to understand the offensiveness of the various plays which have excited the wrath of supersensitive Gaels.

The King's Threshold, in particular, is the last play one would suspect of arousing animosity. That Yeats should sympathise with the demand of the old Irish poet, that he should wish to uphold the dignity of his craft is natural, but it is labouring an obvious identity of feeling to suggest that this play is Yeats's *apologia*. It lacks, for one thing, the finish which might be expected in the utterance of a poet who has always brought perfect craftsmanship to the expression of his personal emotions. Although it has been almost completely rewritten since its first publication in 1904, it does not show traces of greater perfection. The structure of the play remains unaltered in essentials, but precisely the unessentials have been revised to the detriment of the original. The comic parts of the mayor and the cripples are now expanded in a manner quite unknown to the first edition. They do not ring true, somehow, and arouse the suspicion of being, as it were, interpolated at the suggestion of another. Their foolery seemed more natural in its earlier form than now, when it reminds us too sharply of the popular farces in which "Kiltartan speech" provides the staple amusement. *The King's Threshold* retains many of the beauties of its original conception, which adhered closely to the plan of Edwin Ellis's *Sancan the Bard*. This forgotten play, to which Yeats acknowledges his indebtedness, was published in 1895, and has but little interest, except as showing how far he has surpassed his friend in the interpretation of Gaelic legend. Structurally *Sancan the Bard* and the first version of *The King's Threshold* are almost identical, and the superiority of the latter is a demonstration of the natural advantage enjoyed by an Irishman in his treatment of an Irish theme. The sense of drama is neither more nor less than that to which Yeats has accustomed us, the poetic appeal dominates the dramatic, but whenever the former weakens, the latter is insufficient to bear the burden of interest. *Sancan the Bard*, equally devoid of dramatic quality, also lacks both the spirit and the poetry which compensate for this defect in Yeats's play. For all its revision, however, *The King's Threshold* has evidently not been dreamed and redreamed like *The Shadowy Waters*, which is undoubtedly the most intimate reflection in dramatic form of the poet's thought.

In the last chapter it was stated that the poem entitled *The Death of Cuchullin* failed to realise the poignancy of the episode in which the warrior, having unwittingly slain his son, dies battling with the waves. After an interval of more than ten years Yeats returned to the subject. *On Baile's Strand*

was published in 1904, in a form no less undramatic
than the poem of 1892. But two years later the
play was revised, and so strengthened as to be among
the best work Yeats has contributed to the theatre.
Not that the revision has enabled him to exploit
fully the tragedy of Cuchulain's encounter with his
son. The situation is one which gives scope to the
employment of the greatest tragic effects, for the
story contains all that Aristotle postulated as essential to the plot of tragedy. But Yeats does not seem
able to take advantage of the elements already presented to him by the subject itself. The classical
combination of the inevitable with the unexpected is
wanting, while the moment of recognition is inade-
quately prepared. Nevertheless, he has corrected
some very serious mistakes in this connection.
Formerly the identity of Cuchulain's son was blurted
out early in the play, instead of being suggested
by hints and half-revelations, while the necessity
for Cuchulain's combat with the stranger was not
contrived as clearly and naturally as in the present edition. Consequently, there was no suspense in the original play, no emotion arising
out of fear and pity in the presence of the inexor-
able.

As it now stands, *On Baile's Strand* is convincing,
though none of the effects are prepared and heightened, as they must be if we are to witness high
tragedy. The tragic knot, if it might be strengthened by greater tension, is not at least untied until
the last moment, whereas at first it was cut by the
pointless garrulity of the Blind Man and the Fool,
who supply the tragi-comic relief. Many fine passages have been added in the rewriting, as when
Cuchulain recalls her who was to be the mother of
his unknown child:

> . . . Ah! Conchubar, had you seen her
> With that high, laughing, turbulent head of hers
> Thrown backward, and the bow-string at her ear

On Baile's Strand is an instance, not only of Yeats's increased sense of dramatic fitness, but also of the occasional reward which his desire for revision brings to him. Reference has already been made to the attraction exercised by the story of Deirdre upon the Irish poets since Ferguson. It is, therefore, rather strange that Yeats should not have dramatised the subject until comparatively late. One would have thought that *Deirdre* would be among his first contributions to the National Theatre, whereas it is the second last play he has published. It is true, A. E.'s drama of that name was written expressly for the Irish National Dramatic Company in 1902, and was the first offering of the then embryonic National Theatre. But the mere question of precedence can have but little weight in a case where originality was possible only in the treatment and mode of expression. Deirdre has been to the Irish dramatists what Iphigenia was to the Greek poets. As Æschylus, Sophocles and Euripides were not afraid to challenge comparison in their handling of an identical theme, so the three chief figures of the Literary Revival have interpreted the legend of Deirdre. For the moment we are concerned with Yeats, to whom we shall return at a later stage, when the occasion demands contrast and comparison with A. E. and Synge, in their treatment of this subject.

Yeats's *Deirdre* does not suffer from being read beside the others. Its tardy appearance is more probably due to his desire for greater practical experience of the theatre, before essaying to re-create from material already so familiar. The result is a play which is as skilfully presented as the limits of

Yeats's technique will permit. In view of the tendency to diffuseness which has been noted, it was wise to concentrate upon the crisis of Deirdre's story, and to make of it one act. By the introduction of the musicians, who play the rôle of a Greek chorus, he is able to give in outline the history of the events which preceded the return of Naisi and Deirdre to the house of Conchubar. The use of the chorus is admirable, dramatic tension is at once produced by this swift narration of what would otherwise have dragged vaguely and nervelessly, destroying the tragic expectancy with which one should follow the final unfolding of the fateful history. The shadowy dream-world in which Yeats invariably casts the action of his plays could not have failed to deprive *Deirdre* of its essential humanity. Whereas the musing song of the musicians puts us in possession of the facts necessary to the understanding of what follows, and is, at the same time, wholly in keeping with the peculiar rhythm of the poet's mind. Effective, too, is the participation of the musicians in the action of the drama, notably the lovely song of Queen Edain, as Deirdre enters.

All the details of construction show a marked advance in Yeats's command of stage effects. The furtive swarthy figures seen in the background strike a sinister note, the atmosphere is charged with suspicion and treachery, so that the ensnaring and murder of Naisi strike, at last, an audience prepared by the dramatist's skill to receive a full impression of horror. It is rare that Yeats is so successful in awakening the proper emotions by the action itself. More usually the spectator must transport himself into the far-away mood of the poet, before he can experience to the full the meaning of the words and gestures which are but an approximate realisation of the author's intention. Nevertheless, *Deirdre* is still an essentially "Yeatsian" drama, the figures are those of a dream, for all the conviction they derive from the setting. Were it not that the subject is the crisis of a tragedy, Deirdre, Naisi and Conchubar would be but the poetic expression of a symbolist's reverie, as he turns the pages of Ireland's legendary history.

Since 1908 Yeats's dramatic work has been that of revision, for *The Green Helmet*, published in 1910, is a versified form of *The Golden Helmet*, which appeared in 1908. The play is but a trifle, and should be read as an introduction to *On Baile's Strand*. Founded on the old Irish story, *The Feast of Bricriu*, it relates how Conall and Laegaire were humiliated by the Red Man, a Spirit from the sea, who inflicted, by demoniacal arts, the stigma of cowardice upon those warriors. The hero Cuchulain is able, by his traditional courage, to defeat the supernatural visitant, and is rewarded with the golden helmet, which confers upon him the championship whose history was the greatest theme of bardic song. *The Green Helmet* is the only farce of its kind that has been produced; for the first time the great figures of the Heroic Age are presented in an attitude other than that of lofty nobility, with which tradition has associated them. There is interesting satire in the interplay of jealousies and petty quarrels, when the Red Man leaves the helmet to arouse dissension amongst those who claim it. Cuchulain's wife, Emer, his charioteer, Laeg, and the wife of Laegaire, provide comedy which has a special significance in Ireland, where the spirit of faction symbolised has never wanted supporters. Perhaps it was the element of grotesqueness and comedy which prompted Yeats to essay a form of verse entirely unlike that of his other plays. The ballad metre of *The Green Helmet* cannot be regarded as so happy an innovation as the introduction of humour into a play of the Heroic Age. The prose of *The Golden Helmet* did not demand such a change, and ought to have been retained, if the poet felt that his work could not be versified within the limits of the verse forms most adapted to the theatre.

When Lionel Johnson suggested that Yeats wrote for the stage in order to hear his verse spoken, he was right. The statement does not envisage all the facts of the case, it ignores the relation of Yeats to the Dramatic Movement, but in so far as it considers the purely personal side of his dramatic activities, it is more than a half truth. The dominant motive in Yeats's mind at the time of writing seems invariably to be the attainment of artistic perfection of language. His commentaries on his own and other plays, his experiments with the psaltery, all indicate a preoccupation with the vocal effects of poetic drama. Whenever he considers the performance of a play his chief concern is for the music of the words and the picturesqueness of the setting. The movements of the actors do not engage his attention, except it be to see that they are reduced to a minimum.

In the long course of experiment which has constituted the relation of W. B. Yeats to the theatre he has now arrived at the point of seeking an escape from that defiant institution, and in the Anglo-Irish Noh play he professes to have found salvation. He has got far away from the folk play that would "uplift the man of the roads" in the collection of *Four Plays for Dancers*, but he declares he has discovered at last the solution of the problem presented to him as a poet-dramatist by the modern stage.

My blunder has been that I did not discover in my youth that my theatre must be the ancient theatre made by unrolling a carpet, or marking out a place with a stick, or setting a screen against a wall. Certainly those who care for my kind of poetry must be numerous enough, if I can bring them together, to pay half a dozen players who can bring all their properties in a cab and perform in their leisure moments.

At the Hawk's Well was produced in accordance with the Noh tradition, the players wearing masks and "sitting against a screen covered with some one unchangeable pattern." It is they who "describe landscape or event, and accompany movement with drum or gong, or deepen the emotion of the words with zither or flute." The stage is a platform surrounded on three sides by the audience, the movements are founded on those of puppets, and song and dance alternate with speech.

In *Four Plays for Dancers* he has partially redeemed his promise to complete a "dramatic celebration of the life of Cuchulain planned long ago," of which the *Hawk's Well* was the first part. *The Only Jealousy of Emer* is a further episode in the Cuchulain series, and may be described as a sequel to *On Baile's Strand*. It is a subtle and tenuous drama, whose scene is laid in a fisherman's hut where, after he had rushed into the sea on learning that his unknown antagonist was his son, Cuchulain's lifeless body has been brought. His wife Emer has called his mistress, Eithne Inguba, to see if her love can call Cuchulain back to life. He has been lured by a Woman of the Sidhe, and only by a renunciation of their ultimate hope of reconciliation can Emer restore her husband to this world. The Noh form is peculiarly adapted to the suggestive beauty of the poetry in which the dramatic conceptions of Yeats develop. Heightened by the conventions of movement, the gestures of the Noh performers, his effects are secured in a manner impossible on

the ordinary stage, where the author's own dissatisfaction is only too often shared by the public. The
oft revised and never satisfactory *Shadowy Waters*
might be re-written in the Noh manner with results
heretofore unachieved.

With *The Dreaming of the Bones* there enters—to
the Irish mind, at least—an element of regret that
an exotic form should have been allowed to hamper
a theme peculiarly national. In the meeting between a young man escaping from the Dublin Rising
in 1916 and the shades of Dermot and Devorgilla,
whose love betrayed Ireland, Yeats had a situation
which demanded other treatment. Moving and
beautiful as the poem now reads, one's fancy dwells
upon its potentialities as a play to set beside *Cathleen ni Houlihan*, and one is tempted to clamour for
what might be, instead of considering what is . . .
irrevocably, so far as the creative impulse is concerned, for these Anglo-Irish Noh plays are the creatures of a mood. Yeats refers to them more than
once as a passing phase of experimental effort, but
they are definite evidence of a revolt against the
mechanism of the modern stage, however intellectual
it may become. Yet, while we may welcome any
theory which seems to provide him with the necessary stimulus to write poetic plays, it is clear that
the drama cannot be restored to dignity by a nega-
tion of the material framework of its existence.
Theatre reformers move towards a species of dramatic Nirvana, eliminating scenery, actor, audience.
When there are no playgoers to be bored by impossible plays, no dramatists to be subordinated to
scenic effects, and no actors to interfere with the
poetry of ideal speech, then we shall witness the eu-
thanasia of the Higher Drama.

CHAPTER VIII

W. B. YEATS: THE PROSE WRITINGS

IN addition to the four plays that are not written in verse Yeats has formally acknowledged a large body of prose work. Of the eight volumes comprising the Collected Edition, four are devoted to verse and as many to prose. Since 1908 some slight additions to the latter must be made; *J. M. Synge and the Ireland of his Time*, which appeared in 1911, and was included the next year in *The Cutting of an Agate*, a miscellaneous collection of essays, published in New York. Finally, a chapter of autobiography has just recently been added to these, *Reveries over Childhood and Youth* (1916). Thus, in half a dozen volumes will be found the various prose writings which we shall now consider in chronological order.

Although he wrote at an earlier date in the Irish reviews on behalf of the new literature which was making Ferguson and O'Grady its starting-point, it was not until 1887 that Yeats began seriously to give his attention to prose. In that year he moved from Dublin to London, where the need and opportunity of journalistic activity arose. In 1889 he had begun to contribute to *The Scots Observer* those sketches which, with subsequent contributions to *The National Observer*, formed the bulk of his first important volume of prose, *The Celtic Twilight*. This, however, was not the first prose book to appear above Yeats's name. As editor, he was responsible for no less than four collections of Irish stories, *Fairy and Folk Tales of the Irish Peasantry* (1888), *Stories from Carleton* (1889), *Representative Irish Tales* (1890), and *Irish Fairy Tales* (1892)—all of which served to prepare the way for his own entrance into the same field.

This did not occur, however, immediately, for *The Celtic Twilight* was preceded by the pseudonymous *John Sherman and Dhoya*, which appeared in 1891 over the name of "Ganconagh." *Dhoya* is a slight folk-tale *pastiche*, suggestive of the more familiar stories which were to follow, but without the qualities that have enabled the latter to survive. *John Sherman*, on the other hand, is unique, as being the only work of fiction, in the ordinary sense, which Yeats has published. It is little more than a novel-ette in size, but within those limits the author has packed more careful observation and analysis than are found in many novels of greater pretensions. John Sherman's life in the country town of Ballagh, his visit to London and return to his native Sligo are probably autobiographical to a large extent. Particularly happy is the picture of Sherman's circle in Ballagh; the man himself and Mary Carton are admirable illustrations of character moulded by the apparently narrow conditions of Irish provincial life, where, nevertheless, a sense of the profundity of life comes from a slower and more reflective existence than is possible in the rapidly-moving social and industrial centres. The contrast between Ballagh and London, between Mary Carton and Margaret Leland, is a synthesis, so to speak, of the differences which separate Irish from English conditions. The disinterested contemplation of life is more easily found in a country where, from one cause and an-other, leisure is not the prerogative of wealth. The story has the most immaterial of plots, and hinges entirely upon the clash of the dreamy, introspective Sherman with the hard facts and superficialities of London life. It is cast in a restrained and very minor key, but has all the interest of a more crowded and eventful narrative. In the creation of atmosphere and the characterisation of types the chief merit of *John Sherman* must be sought. So well has Yeats sketched in his background, so successfully has he preserved the analysis of his characters, that one regrets the isolation of this story. Had the Literary Revival produced a novelist, we should have expected him to make this book a point of departure. Whether Yeats himself could have progressed further in this direction must remain a matter of conjecture. *John Sherman* was written so directly out of the author's own experience that it would have been unwise to insist upon its promise for the future. That Yeats felt it to be a part of him that was long since dead seems to be indicated by his hesitation in publicly claiming it as his own. It was not formally incorporated into the body of his work until 1908, when it at last figured in the Collected Edition.

The Celtic Twilight was published in 1893, and reissued in 1902 with seventeen additional chapters. This collection of fairy-lore is perhaps the best book of prose Yeats has written. If the title provided journalists with a phrase which still serves to belabour the author, the work itself furnished some interesting data as to the formative influences to which he was subjected in his youth. Compiled from the stories heard by Yeats when he wandered over the countryside of Sligo and Galway as a young man, *The Celtic Twilight* is a compendium of the Celtic folk literature still living in the memory of the people. Most of the tales are but slightly elaborated, they are free from all comment, and present, therefore, an interesting picture of the imaginative life of Celtic Ireland. The book is concerned, of course, solely with the attitude of the people towards what we term the supernatural, the spirit world that is about us. In a series of sketches Yeats illustrates how intimate is the relation between the visible and invisible world in the minds of the peasantry who have preserved intact the faculty of belief and vision. To them every hillside and forest is filled with mysterious presences who may at any time reveal themselves. Not all are like the man of whom we are told the complaint: "By the cross of Jesus! how shall I go? If I pass by the hill of Dunboy old Captain Burney may look out on me. If I go round by the water, and up by the steps, there is the headless one and another on the quays, and a new one under the old churchyard wall. If I go round the other way, Mrs. Stewart is appearing at Hillside Gate, and the devil himself is in the hospital lane." For him the world was full enough of spirits, but they were not of a kind to which he felt attracted. This is not the usual attitude, as Yeats points out. His stories, in the main, depict people who have contrived the most friendly relations with the super-human. The fairies and spirits that haunt them are no longer objects of fear; they are part of everyday life and on occasion may come to ask a favour or to render one.

So impressed is the author by this pleasant intercourse that he is impelled to write *A Remonstrance with Scotsmen for having soured the disposition of their Ghosts and Faeries*, a charming piece of humour, in which Scotland and Ireland are contrasted in their treatment of sprites and goblins. "You have discovered the faeries to be pagan and wicked. You would have them all up before the magistrate. In

Ireland warlike mortals have gone amongst them in their battles, and they in turn have taught them great skill with herbs. . . . In Scotland you have denounced them from the pulpit. In Ireland they have been permitted by the priests to consult them on the state of their souls." *The Celtic Twilight* is simply a detailed picture of the happy state of affairs which prompted this *Remonstrance*. It describes a world in which the natural and the supernatural, Christianity and Paganism, are so closely allied that they blend into a special and characteristic *Weltanschauung*. Maeve and Angus are still visible in this twilight of the Celtic imagination, where the traditions of another time and another creed have not yet been effaced. "We," writes Yeats, "exchange civilities with the world beyond," and he reproaches Scotsmen with having allowed theology to break such intercourse in Scotland! It is just this "exchange of civilities," the sense of fellowship with Nature, which has moulded the character of Irish literature. Only the existence of a highly sensitive imagination can account for the continued exercise of this faculty of vision, commonly identified with the superstitions of primitive races. *The Celtic Twilight* does, at times, appear to countenance too readily the less spiritual manifestations of belief, but, for the most part, the theories suggest imaginative strength rather than credulous weakness. That they should be the substance of the young poet's note-books is a fact which helps to explain the direction in which his own imaginative life expanded. When he set himself deliberately towards the goal of national culture his intellectual impulse had been strengthened by the emotional experiences of this early intercourse with Celtic Ireland.

In 1897 Yeats published *The Secret Rose* and *The*

Tables of the Law and the Adoration of the Magi, a collection of stories foreshadowing *The Wind Among the Reeds*, which presented in 1899 the quintessence of the mysticism here illustrated in prose. The homogeneity of the stories is such that the smaller book may be counted a part of the larger, *The Secret Rose*, which is rightly regarded as the complete expression of Yeats's attitude towards the spirit world. Since its first appearance the author has more than once separated and rearranged the contents. Thus, in 1904 the *Stories of Red Hanrahan* were published independently of the remaining text of *The Secret Rose*, and have not been restored to subsequent editions. In their latest guise they appear in one volume, but without the original unity of title, as *Stories of Red Hanrahan, The Secret Rose* and *Rosa Alchemica*. Except in so far as this 1913 edition brings together again material which should never have been broken up, its *raison d'être* is far to seek. Few who are familiar with the earliest form will approve of the latest versions, where Kiltartan speech is substituted for the delicate prose in which the stories were first written. The desire to be "in the tradition of the people among whom he, or some likeness of him, drifted and is remembered" was the reason given by the author for rewriting *Stories of Red Hanrahan*, which was the beginning of the process which has resulted in a remoulding of the entire series. As published in 1897, *The Secret Rose* admitted of a certain simplification of content, if not of form. The selection of the Hanrahan stories in 1904 for a simplified retelling might have been counted as an improvement, had the matter been reduced to its essential elements and freed from a too insistent preoccupation with occult effects. The mere introduction of peasant idiom cannot, however, be regarded as compensation for the loss arising out of a mistaken conception of the need for simplicity. In the American edition of this volume the process of simplification has shorn even *The Secret Rose* of many beauties unspoiled by revision in the English publication. The substance of *The Secret Rose* and kindred stories is akin to that of *The Celtic Twilight*, in that both works are an attempt to portray visionary Ireland. Fairy lore and legend are again put under contribution, and are woven into a delicate fabric by the imagination of the poet. But the earlier work is concerned with the simpler visions of the peasant mind, whereas *The Secret Rose*, as its very title indicates, is influenced strongly by the doctrines of the intellectual mystics, those whose beliefs are something more conscious and reasoned than the native, instinctive mysticism of the Celtic countryside. The commentator of Blake, the disciple of Sar Péladan, is now in evidence. His form has become more impeccable, his style is wonderfully adapted to the thought of the narrator, but his former simplicity of manner has disappeared. The naïve, artless stories of *The Celtic Twilight* are transformed by a mind that has been fed on Boehme and Swedenborg. Many, however, such as *Rosa Alchemica*, are the direct product of the author's studies of the occult.

Regarded as "tales of mystery and imagination," *Rosa Alchemica* and *The Tables of the Law* have an interest which quite justifies their existence. They are written with great skill; the atmosphere of the supernatural, and an evident acquaintance with the paraphernalia of alchemy and occultism, combine to give an impression of mystery and reality which successfully appeals to the reader. Similarly, in the narratives drawn from Irish legend, Yeats utilises to their advantage the knowledge of mystic teaching and cabalistic formulæ which he had gleaned from various sources. Coupled with the peculiar style, at once highly artificial and very simple, in which the stories are told, these elements of mysticism complete the special charm of *The Secret Rose*. They correspond in his thought to the studied simplicity of his style, both are the product of an artifice, and are so complementary as to make the book a consummate piece of artistry. One has only to compare *Red Hanrahan* in its recent Kiltartan garb with its original appearance to see how inseparable are form and matter in the original volume, *The Secret Rose*. To make the stories convincing in peasant speech they must be emptied of all the esoteric content which harmonised with the mood and language of their first telling. To some extent this was done when the Hanrahan stories were published separately in 1904, but they have not been reduced to the essentials whose directness and simplicity of outline would permit of their being rewritten "nearer to the mind of the country places." Hanrahan is still, as the poet conceived him, "the simplicity of an imagination too changeable to gather permanent possessions." Symbolism of this kind does not seem congruous with the dialect of Kiltartan. Douglas Hyde's *Casadh an tsugáin*, treating of one of Yeats's Hanrahan episodes, is better calculated to reach the folk imagination than the belated simplifications of *The Secret Rose*.

It is not until the mysticism of the book is examined from an intellectual point of view that one fully realises how fundamentally literary it is. Not for nothing are form and content so necessary to one another. What was stated of *The Wind Among the Reeds* is true of *The Secret Rose*, their mysticism is decorative, or at best symbolic, and must not be interrogated too closely for a revelation of doctrinal certainty. Yeats has heard the mystic messages of Blake and Boehme, but he does not appear to have correlated the various teachings of his masters into any coherent body of belief. While he himself may find a personal satisfaction in a certain wavering and nebulous theosophy, his own utterances are hardly sufficiently substantial to help the uninitiated. The transcendental common-sense of the true mystic cannot but be shocked at Red Hanrahan's vision in which the lovers had "heart-shaped mirrors instead of hearts, and they were looking and ever looking on their own faces in one another's mirrors." This is obviously no mystic's vision, but simply the conceit of a poet, a symbol not without literary charm. More fundamental is the weakness revealed by such an allusion as that, in *Rosa Alchemica*, to beings "each wrapped in his eternal moment, in the perfect lifting of an arm, in a little circlet of rhythmical words." The eternal moment does not come to the mystic in another's conception of him, and "the perfect lifting of an arm" has no other sense but that it is a purely external idea of perfection as seen by another. Mysticism teaches that the eternal moment is one of self-realisation, it is subjective not objective. The highest moment of a man's life is fixed by himself, and cannot be a beautiful gesture, which is felt to be such only by an onlooker. These two points, which might be multiplied by reference to other stories, illustrate precisely the two aspects of Yeats's mysticism. It is either symbolism or ornament. The visions of others have supplied him with rich material for his art, which is essentially external. A "circlet of rhythmical words," a beautiful movement of the body, these are things upon which his poetic imagination seizes, and who will deny that he has thereby achieved effects of great beauty?   Whatever of mysticism he possesses is far more closely related to the fairy beliefs of the people than to the intellectual doctrines of the great mystics.   There is a note of sincerity, therefore, in *The Celtic Twilight* which one misses in the more elaborate stories of *The Secret Rose*.   But the latter is the more finished work from the point of view of technique.   In this it resembles *The Wind Among the Reeds*, the product of the same mood and similarly more perfect in its art than the poems which preceded it.   Just as many prefer the verse prior to 1899, so they will put *The Celtic Twilight* above its successor.   It is useless to seek, in either *The Wind Among the Reeds* or *The Secret Rose*, any intelligible statement of mysticism.   Both are primarily the work of an artist rather than a thinker, and may be enjoyed to the full as such.   They are rich in beauty of style and abound in evidences of a sensitive yet powerful imagination.   As contributions to the literature of fantasy and symbol they have a value transcending that which must always entitle them to a high place in the history of the Literary Revival.

The essays of Yeats, though numerous, have been only in part reprinted.   The early years of journalism in London saw him engaged in a great deal of journeyman work—prefaces to editions and anthologies of Irish authors, book reviews and the like— which he has allowed to remain uncollected.   All this writing was good propaganda, and had considerable influence in defining and asserting the position of modern Anglo-Irish literature.   If it does not find a place in the list of his published works, the fault must be attributed to the necessarily ephemeral nature of most journalism. Nevertheless not all of this propagandist work has been rejected, as may be seen from the essays included in the Collected Edition of Yeats's works.

The earliest and most important book of essays, *Ideas of Good and Evil*, was published in 1903, and was followed in 1907 by *Discoveries*, a much smaller collection, issued semi-privately by the Dun Emer Press, now known as the Cuala Press, and conducted by a sister of the poet. This mode of publication was adopted for the subsequent volumes of prose, *Poetry and Ireland* (1908) and *J. M. Synge and the Ireland of his Time* (1911). But so slight are all three that they have been incorporated with some other essays into the volume, *The Cutting of an Agate*, which was published in New York in 1912. Upon this book, and *Ideas of Good and Evil*, rests the claim of Yeats to be considered as an essayist. They contain all the essays included in the Collected Edition, except the articles from *Beltaine*, *Samhain* and its supplement, *The Arrow*. These publications, which ran respectively from 1899 to 1900, and from 1903 to 1908, are evidence of the energy and enthusiasm with which Yeats forwarded the Dramatic Movement, but they do not add anything to the author's reputation as an essayist, unless it be to reveal his skill in controversy. They do, however, provide data relating to the history of the Irish Theatre worthy of preservation, as the original publications are difficult to obtain.

The priority of *Ideas of Good and Evil* would alone be sufficient to explain the precedence which it has taken in the works of W. B. Yeats. It was the first contribution of its kind made by him, and that, too, at a time when he had not yet obtained the degree of recognition which he now enjoys. The essays which appeared subsequently were not issued to catch the attention of the general public, so that it was not until nine years later that *The Cutting of an Agate* supplied a companion volume to that of 1903. During that interval Yeats had arrived; and his work was receiving the customary measure of conventional praise, instead of the no less traditionally suspicious criticism accorded to those not yet accepted. *Ideas of Good and Evil* met with the latter rather than the former reception, and, therefore, drew upon itself an amount of critical attention which his more recent essays have escaped. It was pronounced by some stilted and precious, by others, the clearest and most flexible prose Yeats had written. The accusation derives justification from a comparison between this book and *The Celtic Twilight*. The wistfulness and spontaneity of that early prose are gone, but gone also is the mood of which it was the expression. *Ideas of Good and Evil* is the work of the author of *The Secret Rose*, who is indeed a changed man from him who wrote *The Last Gleeman* and *A Visionary*. The Yeats who revealed in 1897 his preoccupation with magic and alchemy, whose mind had become filled with the dreams and images of mystic symbolism, could not but allow these things to colour his prose. The change which we saw creeping into his writing in *The Secret Rose*, and becoming more pronounced in *The Wind Among the Reeds*, had become a permanent condition when *Ideas of Good and Evil* appeared. Given, therefore, the complexion of Yeats's thought, it may be asked whether the last-mentioned work is really deserving of the censure passed upon it. If "the style is the man," then *Ideas of Good and Evil* is a perfect portrait of the author. Its defects are not literary but intellectual. Those who complain of preciosities and obscurities are simply engaged in denouncing the ideas of Yeats. Once it is recognised that the mysticism he teaches is merely an attempt to explain theoretically an artistic instinct, then the charge of artificiality and obscurity falls to the ground.

There are two motives which predominate in the essays of Yeats, the mystic and the literary. Where he speaks of literature he is clear and convincing, where he expounds his mysticism he is obscure and weak, and it is in the latter chapters precisely that he lays himself open to the accusations we have just noted. Compare the essays *What is "Popular Poetry"? Ireland and the Arts* and *The Celtic Element in Literature* with those entitled *Magic, The Symbolism of Poetry* and *The Philosophy of Shelley's Poetry*. Reading the three last mentioned the mind is soothed by the cadence of the author's phrases; he has the gift of enfolding generalities in a network of elusive images, and sentences which have all the impressive obscurity of a dream. But, when one has shaken off the suggestion, little remains except the familiar commonplaces which were the point of departure. On the contrary, the first three essays referred to are a concise statement of the postulates upon which the Literary Revival is based, and contain, incidentally, a definition of Yeats's own position in modern literature. "It was years before I could rid myself of Shelley's Italian light," he writes in *Ireland and the Arts*, "but now I think my style is myself. I might have found more of Ireland if I had written in Irish, but I have found a little, and I have found all myself."

This essay and *What is "Popular Poetry"?* are the most interesting pieces of self-criticism the poet has given us. In the latter he confesses his youthful error in believing that popular poetry—the poetry of

Longfellow or Mrs. Hemans, and of the generation of
Anglo-Irish writers preceding the Revival—had
special virtues which raised it above the verse of
"the coteries."   As he discovered, the people in Ireland do not separate "the idea of an art or a craft
from the idea of a cult with ancient technicalities
and mysteries."   Here, then, is a reason for the
return to folk-literature which has been so important
a feature of the Revival.   The unwritten tradition
may be found where "the counting house" has not
created "a new class and a new art without breeding
and without ancestry."   Irish folk-lore is, therefore,
not only valuable because of the Celtic breath that
lives in it, but because its literary traditions are unspoiled.   In *The Celtic Element in Literature* Yeats
shows how these traditions are of value to those who
would revitalise modern poetry. . . . "Literature
dwindles to a mere chronicle of circumstance, or
passionless phantasies and passionless meditations,
unless it is constantly flooded with the passions and
beliefs of ancient times."   The fountains of these
ancient passions and beliefs in Europe are the Sla-
vonic, the Finnish, the Scandinavian and the Celtic.
But as the Celtic has for centuries been closer to the
general stream of European literature, what could be
more natural, therefore, than to turn to it again
for the vivifying element contained within it?
"Irish legends move among known woods and seas,"
unlike those of Scandinavian and Slavic origin, and
have "so much of a new beauty that they may well
give the opening century its most memorable symbols."   These words were written in 1897, and
though the hope they reveal has been but partially
realised so far as English literature is concerned, the
realisation has been complete in Ireland.
It is possible, doubtless, to insist too much upon

"the Celtic note," so frequently pointed out in the work of certain English and American poets. Few, however, will deny that the return to national traditions on the part of the Irish poets has produced some of the best contemporary poetry in the English language. Yet Yeats himself does not claim this as a special virtue of the Celt, as such. In point of fact *The Celtic Element in Literature* may be recommended to all those Celtophobes who fear so greatly lest undue credit be given to Ireland and her literature. If Yeats accepts the too familiar judgments of Arnold and Renan on Celtic literature, he does so on condition of defining their now stereotyped terms. The "glamour" and "melancholy," the "magic" and "reaction against the despotism of fact" are obviously not the peculiar prerogatives of the Celt, but spring from causes common to all ancient peoples. It happens that, for various reasons partly suggested in the course of this work, Ireland has retained more of these primitive qualities, which have been preserved by the presence of a language uninfluenced by modern conceptions of life. Our "natural magic," writes Yeats, "is but the ancient religion of the world, the ancient worship of nature and that troubled ecstasy before her, that certainty of all beautiful places being haunted, which it brought into men's minds." No more effective and simpler statement of the case for the Irish literary renascence could be made than this essay. *Ideas of Good and Evil* is, in the main, a defence of Yeats's own ideas, and an exposition of the theories underlying the literature which he has helped by precept and example to create. There are few aspects of modern Anglo-Irish poetry which have not been treated in the course of this volume. *Speaking to the Psaltery*, for example, explains how the poet would have his

verses spoken, and forms a useful commentary on the
dramatic works of the author, especially when read
in connection with the later chapter, *The Theatre*.
When one has come to understand Yeats's feeling
for diction, his theory of spoken verse, an increased
measure of sympathy and attention is assured to the
performance of his plays.   The elaborate study of
elocution evidenced by his constant and serious preoccupation with this question confirms the well-
known suggestion of Lionel Johnson.   Johnson, it
will be remembered, held that Yeats's main interest
in the theatre came from his desire to hear his poetry
spoken.   At all events, that desire has been always
present, though it cannot have been the deciding
motive which led Yeats almost to forsake lyric
poetry in order to give his best energies to the stage.
    The affairs of the Irish National Theatre and the
Irish Players, the practical work incidental to the
Dramatic Movement, have so engaged the activities
of Yeats that he has not had the leisure to give
another volume like *Ideas of Good and Evil*.   In the
preface to *The Cutting of an Agate* he explains the
circumstances which prevented him from writing
any leisurely prose between 1902 and 1912.   "For
some ten years now I have written little verse and
no prose that did not arise out of some need of those
players or some thought suggested by their work.
. . . I have been busy with a single art, that of the
theatre, of a small, unpopular theatre."   With the
exception of *Discoveries*, reprinted from the little
book published semi-privately in 1907, the essays in
The Cutting of an Agate cannot be compared with
those of *Ideas of Good and Evil*, which remains the
most important work of its kind Yeats has yet
written.   As stated in the preface, this recent collection is the creature of circumstances, almost every

chapter having been written to meet the demand of the moment for propaganda or explanation. *J. M. Synge and the Ireland of his Time*, prefaces to works of Synge and Lady Gregory—these essays are typical of much of Yeats's prose-writing during the past decade. Three hundred pages of the Collected Edition are devoted to matters of this kind, rescued from the pages of *Beltaine, Samhain* and *The Arrow*, the first the organ of the Irish Literary Theatre, the others the "occasional periodical" of the Irish National Theatre. When considering the Dramatic Movement we shall have an opportunity of referring to this portion of Yeats's work, which is interesting in direct relation to the occasion of its production, rather than as a general contribution to literature.

Discoveries may be classed with *Ideas of Good and Evil*, to which, indeed, it might be considered an appendix, so brief and fragmentary are the majority of the essays. They belong to the same mood as the older book, though the lapse of years, with the exigencies of propagandist and practical work, has noticeably modified them. Yeats's concern for the Irish Theatre is constantly obtruding itself, his thoughts are haunted by the various problems and experiences which have come to him in the pursuit of this object. Characteristically, however, the old love of the remote and indefinite persists. *Prophet, Priest and King*, for all its grandeur of title, is simply a reminiscence of a visit to a country town with the Irish Players. Having described the unpromising material of which the audience was composed, and his dissatisfaction with the play as a means of awakening a loutish crowd to a sense of beauty and spirituality, Yeats concludes: "If we poets are to move the people, we must reintegrate the human spirit in our imagination . . . you cannot have health among a people if you have not prophet, priest and king." The title and concluding sentence are in the traditionally impressively vague manner, entirely incongruous with the subject of the poet's reflections. Abstract and symbolical embroidery upon some familiar theme, how difficult it is for him to resist it! Nevertheless, *Discoveries* is comparatively free from this peculiarity so marked in the earlier verse and prose of Yeats. Contact with practical questions has purged his mind of much that was mere decoration, and which gave to his writing an impersonal, almost inhuman touch. Cold, elaborate and visionary, he seemed often to be floating dreamily in a mist of half-divined ideas.

A most interesting passage, in this connection, occurs in the essay, *The Tree of Life*, where the artist is reproached with taking over-much to heart, "that old commandment about seeking after the Kingdom of Heaven." The poet had set out, he tells us, with the thought of putting his "very self" into poetry; which he understood to mean a representation of his own visions. Instead, however, of realising himself, he confesses he had come to care "for nothing but impersonal beauty," because, "as I imagined the visions outside myself, my imagination became full of decorative landscape and of still life." It would be difficult to find a phrase which summarises more aptly the impression carried away by many readers from Yeats's pages: "decorative landscape and still life." When the decoration has been beautiful in itself many are satisfied to enjoy the momentary pleasure of such contemplation. As was postulated in a previous chapter, this is sometimes the only method by which to derive satisfaction from the poet's utterances. Nobody will deny that still life has a charm of its own. But to those who seek in

184 IRELAND'S LITERARY RENAISSANCE

poetry something more than a sensuous appeal to the
eye and ear, Yeats's limitations are a very serious
defect. They find him, as he admits, "interested in
nothing but states of mind, lyrical moments, intellectual essences."

Such an attitude does not necessarily conflict with
the claims of poetry. Mallarmé and many of the
French Symbolists deliberately followed what Yeats
here considers a false light. Lovers of French verse
are, however, less exacting in this respect than those
whose admiration goes out whole-heartedly to the
poets of England. In fact, here we come upon an
explanation of the general inability of the average
English reader fully to appreciate French poetry.
Persons by no means swayed by patriotic feeling
have even denied that France has produced poets at
all comparable to those of England. Arnold, of
course, is responsible for the interesting fiction that
English is the language of poetry, and French the
language of prose. The truth is that the two countries have an almost entirely different conception of
poetry. In France the art of verse is almost wholly
a matter of rhythm and music, in England the poet
must have a philosophy; the one is addressed to the
senses, the other to the feelings. A Browning is as
inconceivable in French as a Mallarmé in English.
It will be found, in most cases, that the French poets
most popular in England are precisely those whose
attitude approximates to that of the English. In
many ways Yeats resembles his French rather than
his English contemporaries. The resemblance is
unintentional, it is true, it is even undesirable from
his own point of view, as his essays show. The element of mystic symbolism which he has put into his
work as an expression of his thought fails to satisfy
the reader in search of a "message." It will be

accepted, on the contrary, by those whose ear is attuned to the French tradition, for its musical and artistic value. The fact is not without significance that the first serious study of Yeats was by a French critic in *La Revue de Paris*. But whenever the artistry of his words and symbols is overcharged by the seriousness of his purpose, then he comes to the ground between two traditions.

The ultimate impression left by Yeats's prose, as by his verse, is one of beauty. Both are the creation of a mind skilled in the technique of words, the art which most completely absorbed the attention of the poet. Had Yeats brought the same concentration to the study of mysticism as to the creation of a style, his poetry might more worthily claim consideration on account of its content. But the philosophy which he has expressed in prose is no less vague, though less obscure, than certain poems, and resolves itself into a few commonplaces. Starting from a belief in the great mind and memory of nature, of which our minds and memories are a part, Yeats conceives the imagination as the link between the immortal memory and the memory of man, and symbolism as the instrument by which to awaken the correspondence between the two. The elaborate symbols he so frequently employs must be justified, therefore, because of the moods which they produce in him, enabling the poet to enter into communication with the world beyond. Unfortunately they do not always arouse the requisite emotion in the reader who is left, not in a state of mystic exaltation, but of mystification, by their abstruseness. Yeats has repeatedly described with precision the effect of these symbols upon himself, but the very wealth of detail casts a suspicion upon the authenticity of his visions. They are the fantastic dreams of a poet, rather than the glimpses of reality to which the true mystic attains. As we saw when discussing *The Secret Rose*, the author too often outrages one's transcendental common-sense. The doctrine of inertia, the shrinking from the problems of daily life, which is implicitly—indeed, explicitly—a part of Yeats's theory, does not fit into the mystic philosophy of which it is commonly supposed to be a part. The practical strength of mysticism, the heightened sense of power which it confers, is by no means compatible with the popular view fostered by writers like Yeats. Theirs is the aloofness, not of contemplation, but of the literary theorist, who professes to disdain the humble preoccupations of humanity. In short, examine it as we may, the mystic symbolism of Yeats leads inevitably to the conclusion that it is not mysticism but "mere literature."

Just as his verse has been drastically sifted and winnowed to free it from those romantic elements against which the poet now protests, so his later prose has reached the perfection of simplicity in *Reveries over Childhood and Youth* and *Four Years*, those charming fragments of an autobiography which will not be completely published until after his death. The former in its evocation of the child's life in his Western Irish home is indispensable to an understanding of the early stories and poems which he is too ready to disown. His memories of the years from 1887 to 1891 will explain, in his elusive and allusive fashion, that first period in London which turned his genius definitely in a new direction, and impressed upon the mould of his mind all those influences, occult, symbolic and æsthetic which have marked off his work from that of his contemporaries who remained in Ireland.

Although never inhuman in the sense which that

term implies in criticism of conventional biography, these chapters from the life of W. B. Yeats have a curious discarnate air, as though the mind of the writer had been emptied of all common preoccupations, and had retained only those memories that touched the mind and spirit. The result is to give a peculiar dignity and beauty to the prose in which they are written. The style is unencumbered by the preciosities, the pretentious obscurities which were once the besetting sin of the poet turned prosaist, when his theme was not polemical. In the prose as in the poetry of his maturity it is possible to discern an unexpected return to his origins, with the elimination of all the over-ornamentation of his middle period. The style of his autobiography is more akin to that of *The Celtic Twilight* than to that of *Ideas of Good and Evil*, but here the story over which he broods is not a folk-tale caught up by the vivid imagination of a young poet. It is his own story he has to tell, and into his narrative has come the sure, firm, skilled touch of the master of words, whose ripe mastery, however, does not suggest the mellow tang of old age.

CHAPTER IX

THE REVIVAL OF POETRY

LIONEL JOHNSON, NORA HOPPER, MOIRA O'NEILL,
ETHNA CARBERY AND OTHERS

THE ten years from 1890 to 1900, following upon the success of *The Wanderings of Oisin*, saw the rise of a great wave of poetry in Ireland. It was not that Yeats had obtained any decided material advantage from his work, but he had succeeded in imposing a new tradition. Even those who were most hostile admitted the presence in his verse of a new element, which was promptly labelled "the Celtic Renaissance." The phrase having been accepted, all the work of Irish poets was scrutinised in the hope of its revealing tendencies which might be covered by the label. As a consequence of the influences working in Ireland a number of poets ventured to express themselves in terms of the newly awakened tradition of their country. The result was that they found themselves greeted as "the Celtic School." It was impossible for them to write verse during the decade in question without incurring the pleasure or displeasure of critics armed with the word "Celtic." This is the chief factor common to the poets whose names are at the head of the present chapter. Arriving in the wake of Yeats, they were for some years wholly identified with the Revival, and were

the centre about which the storm of praise and con-
demnation, of argument and enthusiasm, raged.

LIONEL JOHNSON

With Todhunter, Rolleston and Yeats, Lionel
Johnson belonged to what may be termed the Irish
group in the Rhymers' Club. His first book of
verse, *Poems*, did not appear until 1895, when he had
already attracted attention by his contributions to
The Book of the Rhymers' Club (1892) and *The
Second Book of the Rhymers' Club* (1894). Although
of the same generation as Yeats, Johnson resembled,
in one essential, the older Irish poets who met at the
"Cheshire Cheese." The latter were described, it
will be remembered, as men whose chief work, and
whose style, were moulded by the English tradition,
which prevailed prior to the Revival. Consequently, the adherence of such poets as Todhunter
and Rolleston to the propaganda of Yeats, though it
awakened in them a new song, could not change fundamentally the general tone of their work. Similarly,
Lionel Johnson cannot be considered an Irish poet
in the sense that Yeats is. His English birth and
Oxford education left such an imprint upon him that
he was in the same position as his older Irish friends
of the Rhymers' Club; they could but partially re-
capture the tradition which had been reborn to displace in Irish literature the tradition in which they
had developed. Alone amongst his compatriots in
this group Yeats consistently preserved his nationality, as all his poems in the two books of the
Rhymers' Club testify. With the exception of
Johnson's beautiful *Celtic Speech*, none of the other
Irish contributions shows any decidedly national
characteristics.

His death at the age of thirty-five prevented Johnson from leaving more than a slender body of work to establish his fame: *The Art of Thomas Hardy* (1894), *Poems* (1895) and *Ireland and Other Poems* (1897). To these have now been added two posthumous volumes of essays, *Winchester Letters*, and a book of *Collected Poems* (1915), containing his complete work in verse. For reasons determined by the scope of the present study, only the two books of verse, and that but in part, need be considered. It is hardly necessary to say that this does not imply either that Johnson's prose work is negligible, or that his Irish poems are necessarily superior to those from which the spirit of the Revival is absent. That the greater part of his work concerns English rather than Irish literature has been already explained. Without insisting upon the question of relative merit, we may try to estimate that portion which belongs to the history of the Irish Literary Revival.

The best of the poems illustrating this side of Lionel Johnson's talent have been published in a selection made by W. B. Yeats, entitled *Twenty-one Poems*, which appeared in 1904. What differentiates these verses from those of the author's contemporaries is a certain classic hardness of outline, and a restraint not usually found in the loose reveries and wistful outpourings of the Irish muse. Johnson's Greek and Latin studies, his admiration for Pater, who was his tutor, could not but influence his own writing. Whether the theme be English or Celtic, there is always an aloofness in the passion of the poet; he does not abandon himself utterly to his mood. It was easier for Johnson to be reserved than it was for most of the Irish poets. Classical education, for instance, has rarely been their lot. They have approached the literatures of Greece and Rome, not as disciples of Pater, but as children seeking a

new field of romance and adventure. Nothing
would be more different, did we possess them, than
the impression of a man like Johnson and those of
Yeats or A. E., on reading Homer. But more
important, as enabling Johnson to exercise the classic
virtue of restraint, is the fact that he wrote of Ireland from the head more than from the heart. His
conversion to the political tradition of Ireland must
necessarily have been largely a matter of intellectual
conviction. The Irish strain in his blood was of the
slightest, and a generation or two of highly Anglicised
forbears, one of whom helped to crush the Rebellion
in 1798, did not tend to strengthen his sense of Irish
nationality. In view of these facts, Johnson's enthusiasm for Ireland may be described as that of a convert. His intellect was stirred before his heart,
otherwise it could be difficult to account for what
must have seemed an apostasy. Not by emotion,
but by argument, can the de-nationalised Irishman
be restored to his country, for the former would
appeal precisely to those instincts which he lacks.
It need not surprise us, therefore, if Johnson's poems,
arising out of a thought, possess qualities not commonly found in the verse of his contemporaries,
which are inspired by an emotion.

A further point of dissimilarity between Johnson
and the Irish poets with whom he was associated is
the strongly marked note of Catholicism which characterises so many of his poems. Whether he joined
the Catholic Church in the hope of thereby accentu-
ating his newly-found Irish nationality, or whether
he wished to be in the literary fashion of France, as
were so many of the English "decadents" of the
Eighteen Nineties, we cannot tell. It is possible he
may have been prompted by mixed motives, in which
literary, social, and even spiritual, considerations

played a part. Be that as it may, Johnson's Catholicism constitutes him the only poet of the Revival, apart from Katharine Tynan, whose religion has coloured his work. But here, again, his English education and training produced effects which distinguish him from the Irish Catholic. English Catholicism is, by comparison with that of Ireland, intellectual. If, by chance, an Irish poet gives expression to Catholicism, it is either in the instinctive, wild, half-Pagan fashion of the *Religious Songs of Connacht*, or after the simple, tenderly devout manner of Katharine Tynan. Compare the latter's charming poem, *St. Francis to the Birds*, with Johnson's *A Descant upon the Litany of Loretto* or *Our Lady of the May*. The lofty austerity of Johnson is very different from the humble reverence of the author of *Sheep and Lambs*. There is no introspection in her work, but just a natural movement of devotion before the creatures of God. Her verse is as typical of Irish as Johnson's is of English Catholicism. The intellectual fibre, the stern asceticism of the latter's religious poetry, is quite unknown to the few Irish poets of any importance who have written out of a like inspiration.

The statement that the Irish element in Johnson's work is the fruit of intellectual rather than emotional patriotism must not be taken to imply that it is weak and colourless. Putting the question on the lowest level we might say that the convert or proselyte frequently surpasses in zeal the older brethren in the faith. Perhaps, indeed, there was something of that enthusiasm in Johnson's adoption of Ireland. In his verse this ardour often resulted in impassioned lines of intense feeling and great beauty. *Celtic Speech, Ways of War* and *Ireland*, to name but three, are unsurpassed by none, and equalled by few, of his

contemporaries.   For perfection of form and depth
of emotion these poems are noteworthy.   As a master of words and technique Johnson ranks with
Yeats, but he had a more scrupulous regard for
classical tradition, as was natural, given the circumstances of his early life.   Indeed, so far as such a
slight contribution to Anglo-Irish poetry permits
the comparison, one might say that Johnson is Yeats
with an English classical education and the Oxford
manner.   For all the difference between their lives
and education, Yeats and Johnson are curiously
alike.   Both, each according to his literary tradition,
have a jealous care for the art of verse, both have
something aloof in their manner, as of men who live
remote from the passions of the common world.
Subsequent events have eliminated much of this in-
humanity from Yeats's work, but while Johnson was
living the two must have been very similar in this
respect, except that Yeats came more in contact with
humanity.   He had neither the instincts of a scholar
nor the habits of a recluse which heightened the
austere, ascetic traits in his friend's work.

In their literary theories they were at one, so far as
Ireland is concerned.   Johnson's *Poetry and Patriotism
in Ireland,* the only lecture of his to the Irish Literary Society that has been preserved, reads like a
pronouncement of Yeats's.   The arguments are the
same, only the voice and manner are different.   In
pleading for a wider conception of national literature
than that accepted from the poets of *The Nation,*
Johnson defines the aims of the Revival as Yeats has
done.   But, as one might expect from the delicate
critic of Thomas Hardy, there is a more catholic
understanding of literature in general, and above all,
a greater precision of thought and language than are
usual in Yeats's criticism.   We may note also an

accuracy of allusion and quotation whose absence has so constantly irritated or amused readers of Yeats's essays. As a worker in the early days of the Irish Literary Society, Johnson was a valuable second to Yeats, whose ideals and ideas he fully understood and supported. His broad culture and thorough literary education gave him an influence which must have been valuable to Yeats, who was almost alone in his concern for the general standards of literature. It must always be uncertain whether Johnson, if he had lived, would have continued to identify himself increasingly with the literature he was helping to foster. If one may judge by the somewhat analogous cases of his fellow Rhymers, Todhunter and Rolleston, he would not. The prior claims of literary interests and associations already formed would probably have drawn him. It is significant that the volume of critical essays, *Post Liminium*, contains but two dealing with Irish literature, one of them being the lecture just referred to, and the other a very journalistic sketch of Mangan. This fact does not suggest a deep interest in the work to which a part of him contributed. But with this part we may be satisfied, both because of the quality of the contribution, which compensates for the absence of quantity, and because of the act of contribution itself, which was a testimony to the strength of the cause. It is to the credit of the Revival that it should have attracted and influenced a writer who had every temptation to consecrate himself entirely to English literature, where his fame was well on the way to being established.

NORA HOPPER, MOIRA O'NEILL AND ETHNA CARBERY

In 1894 Nora Hopper's *Ballads in Prose* announced a newcomer to the group of young Irish poets in

London who were striving to add the evidence of their work to the theories for which Yeats had become sponsor. By this time the "Celtic Movement" had become an accepted fact in contemporary journalism, and Yeats, partly because of his incessant propaganda, and partly because of his own success, was the recognised leader of the so-called "school." If ever this word had any justification, it was in the case of Nora Hopper, who came forward manifestly as a disciple of Yeats. Although but a few verses were scattered through *Ballads in Prose*, the book bore unmistakable traces of being inspired by the poetry of Yeats. The prose stories had an air of fairy mystery, all were founded upon popular legends and Gaelic folk-lore and were, at that time, somewhat of a novelty. The retelling of folk-stories and the rewriting of Celtic myths had not then become so common as of late years. In a simple style the author had woven together a number of fanciful dreams, whose spirit and ornament were Irish. But the poems were flagrantly imitative, even to such a degree as:

> I will arise and go hence to the west,
> And dig me a grave where the hill-winds call. . . .

Yeats's *Innisfree* is here put under contribution as surely as are the verses, too numerous to quote, from which Nora Hopper borrowed her "long gray twilights," "sighing sedge" and "gray sea." There was, however, a promise in the very youthfulness of this volume. Not all the lyrics were weak imitations, and one, at least, *The King of Ireland's Son*, was to take its place amongst the most beautiful verses produced by the Revival. It appeared, in an expanded form, as the opening poem of Nora Hopper's first collection of poems, *Under Quicken Boughs*, published in 1896. Fiona MacLeod pronounced it one of the "three loveliest and most typical lyrics of our time," ranking it with *Innisfree,* and Moira O'Neill's *Corrymeela.* This statement belongs rather to what Yeats calls Fiona MacLeod's "too emphatic manner," but the poems are certainly "three of the loveliest and most typical lyrics" in Anglo-Irish literature. *The King of Ireland's Son* is best as originally conceived:

> All the way to Tir na n'Og are many roads that run,
> But the darkest road is trodden by the King of Ireland's son.
> The world wears down to sundown, and love is lost and won
> But he recks not of loss or gain, the King of Ireland's son.
> He follows on for ever, when all your chase is done,
> He follows after shadows—the King of Ireland's son.

The version in *Under Quicken Boughs* is nearly three times as long and has been weakened, in spite of one or two new lines of fine quality. The opening and closing stanzas will show the difference between the two poems:

> Now all away to Tir na n'Og are many roads that run,
> But he has ta'en the longest lane, the King of Ireland's son.
>
> .   .   .   .   .
>
> The star is yours to win or lose, and me the dusk has won.
> He follows after shadows, the King of Ireland's son.

The clumsiness of these lines, the triteness of thought and the stereotyped phrase which disfigure them, indicate the general quality of the volume in which they appear.

All the *clichés* which the parodists have found useful when exercising their talents upon Irish poetry are represented in these poems. "Silk of the kine," "dear black head," "beautiful dark rose"—none is missing. Worst of all, the conception is as stereotyped as the language; *The Passing of the Shee,* *Wild Geese,* *The Grey Fog* are but mechanical variations upon well-worn themes. Usually they are well done, for the author has decided skill and fluency, but they lack individual emotion. Yeats is probably right in suspecting that, though published later, *Under Quicken Boughs* was written, for the most part, prior to *Ballads in Prose*. Much as one feels the influence of Yeats in the latter, the verse has nevertheless a maturity lacking in the unequal poetry of Nora Hopper's second volume. Four years elapsed before she published *Songs of the Morning* (1900) which, with *Aquamarines* (1902), completes her work, so far as we are at present concerned. Her experiments in "circulationist" fiction belong neither to Ireland nor to literature. Both these later volumes are free from the excrescences of Celtic *cliché* to which reference has been made. Evidently the author has learned that, contrary to the general superstition, fairy raths, misty wraiths, and laments for the dead, do not necessarily constitute Irish poetry, not even when interspersed with Gaelic names and allusions to Celtic mythology. *A Pagan*, where the theme makes the mere "paraphernalia" of Celticism impossible, is more truly in its mood than the *Roisin Dubh* and *Ros Geal Dhu* of the earlier poems.

> Sad sobs the sea forsaken of Aphrodite,
>   Hellas and Helen are not, and the slow sands fall,
> Gods that were gracious and lovely, gods that were mighty,
>   Sky and sea and silence resume them all.

Yeats might have written this with more obviously Celtic allusion, but the attitude expressed could not, on that account, be more typical of the race.

Songs of the Morning has been pronounced the best volume of Nora Hopper's verse, although it contains fewer poems of outstanding merit than its predecessors. The level of workmanship is more even, but the freshness and fervour of some of the early poems is absent. In *Aquamarines*, particularly, there is a dead level of pretty, well-made verse, which would never have obtained for the poetess the degree of favour she enjoyed. A few poems such as that just quoted still have a little of the Celtic quality, but in *Songs of the Morning* and *Aquamarines* one feels how easily denationalised Nora Hopper's poetry became. One prefers the English poems of which the book is mainly composed to the desperate attempts at capturing the Irish spirit as *Kathleen Ny-Houlahan*. Nor is the book redeemed by the inclusion of the Irish play, *Muirgeis*, which we would willingly lose for the sake of the poem beginning:

> Beauty was born of the world's desire
> For the wandering water, the wandering fire. . . .

But *Beauty* belongs to the preceding volume and has not its equivalent in *Aquamarines*.

Nora Hopper's facile imagination surrendered itself too readily to passing influences. From the extravagant "Celticism" of her first books, and the conventional Anglicisation of the last, it is easy to estimate the instability of her talent. She had nothing of Lionel Johnson's almost fierce fanaticism in religion and politics, but she resembled him in that both were transplanted Irish, born in England and naturally absorbed by it to some extent. In the first enthusiasm of the emotions awakened by the call to patriotism in literature Nora Hopper was carried away by the charm and wonder of Irish legend. The personal and national prestige of Yeats doubtless appealed to her and she wrote in an exuberance of Celtic feeling. But, as time went on, the encroachment of her actual English life weakened the impulse towards Ireland, until finally her verse was undistinguishable from that of the multitude of minor English poets. The Revival held her just long enough to exhaust the slight vein of Irish poetry it discovered in her. What remained, outside her charming *Ballads in Prose*, was some half-dozen lovely lyrics which rightly entitle her to a place in the anthologies. It is doubtful if a strictly critical judgment would confirm the very personal choice which led to the publication of her selected works in five volumes.

The accusation of having written too much is not one that can be brought against either Moira O'Neill or Ethna Carbery. Moira O'Neill is known as the author of one book, *Songs of the Glens of Antrim*, just as Ethna Carbery's reputation rests solely upon the posthumous collection of her poems published in 1902 under the happy title, *The Four Winds of Erin*. Both, however, have written prose stories, whose substance derives from fairy and legendary lore, somewhat similar to those of Nora Hopper. Ethna Carbery's *In the Celtic Past* (1904) is probably more widely read in Ireland than *Ballads in Prose*, but the latter is better known than *The Elf Errant* (1895), in which Moira O'Neill, without detriment to her romance of fairyland, was able subtly to contrast and characterise her own and the English people.

Songs of the Glens of Antrim (1902) is the slenderest volume of verse to obtain general recognition which the Revival has produced. Twenty-five poems, each but a few stanzas, telling chiefly of the longing of an Irish peasant for his old home and the scenes associated with it—surely an unsubstantial bid for fame! Many poets have begun with equal modesty, but their first offerings have, as a rule, been followed by others more imposing. Moira O'Neill escaped the alternative usually presented to the young poet, who must either substantiate the promise of his first book, or see it pass out of memory. She made no attempt to exploit the vein which had brought her success, but rested at a point which would normally have been that of departure in search of further honours. The reason was doubtless that she fully recognised how insusceptible of expansion her little book was. At the same time we have to enquire why criticism was content to accept this new talent, without waiting for any riper development. The explanation is that *Songs of the Glens of Antrim* was so original, so novel and so perfect of its kind, that confirmation of the poet's power was not required.

Much had been said and written by Yeats and his colleagues of the force of the peasant element in the new Anglo-Irish literature, but many felt that precisely this element was far to seek in the work of the more prominent Irish writers. Moira O'Neill came, with a genuine peasant poetry, free from the intellectual subtleties held to be incompatible with the avowed folk-ideals of Yeats, and she convinced the sceptics. *Corrymeela* was as certainly good poetry as it was a natural utterance from the lips of an Irish peasant. When her verses were written the use of dialect was still rare amongst the poets—especially its serious use—and such of it as was employed had a certain anonymous character. Moira O'Neill localised her speech; she spoke the language of the Antrim Glens, and she demonstrated its application to literature. If her themes are not original, her manner of treating them was distinctly so. For the first time the voice of the Ulster countryside was heard, instead of the, even then, more familar tones of Munster and Connacht. Nowadays Anglo-Irish literature covers the whole field of characteristically Irish life, though Ulster is still less articulate than the provinces of the South and West. *Songs of the Glens of Antrim* was in this respect a pioneer volume, which realised completely the purpose of its author. For that reason we admire her discretion in not forcing the note she instinctively struck. Her reward was an immediate measure of esteem which lasted, despite the seeming inadequacy of its occasion. It was only after twenty years that the author added a sheaf of further songs to that little book, whose fame still disputes that of Moira O'Neill's more voluminous contemporaries.

Ethna Carbery's book, *The Four Winds of Eirinn*, owing to the great number of poems it contains, offers more variety than that of Moira O'Neill, though the two volumes are not, in essence, very dissimilar. Their common trait is the element of folk-poetry which distinguishes them from the more "literary" verse of the time. In Ethna Carbery this trait is more pronounced, because of the greater scope for its emphasis, and because the spirit of her work is intensely Gaelic. To use a stereotyped phrase, to say her poems smack of the soil, is to apply that now almost meaningless expression where its original force may be felt, so exactly do these words fit the case. For some years prior to their appearance in book form, Ethna Carbery's poems had been appearing in the newspapers read throughout the countryside, and they had become the possession of hundreds who had no care for the identity or standing of the author. They captured the popular heart because they breathed the authentic spirit of Gaelic Ireland. The successive editions into which they have passed in their collected form are evidence of the strength of the hold they obtained upon the people.

Examination of these poems will show some of the reasons for their success. They are never esoteric, they are written in the direct and simple language of the people, and they cover the whole field of Gaelic poetry. There are poems of love and of patriotism, poems which sing of Gaelic legend and of the idealism of the Celtic imagination. All are the utterances of a heart and mind passionately devoted to the land of the poet and her audience, for, characteristically, none is addressed to any but an Irish audience. It is doubtful if Ethna Carbery ever published her verse in an English journal; the acknowledged sources of the poems reprinted are either Irish or American. This selection on her part was probably intentional, but would, in most cases, have been involuntary, owing to the nature of her work. Such an admission naturally implies a narrowness of range incompatible either with great poetry or with the principles advocated by the leaders of the Revival. Irish literature can be national, without being isolated. The genius of Shakespere is none the less English because he has been almost "annexed" by Germany. Precisely this literary insularity, so marked in the literature of the early nineteenth century, was the substance of Yeats's complaint, when he urged his generation to make their work Irish without rendering it incapable of being appreciated abroad.

It may be frankly admitted that the adjective "great" is the last word one would apply to the poetry of Ethna Carbery, which does not even compare, from an artistic point of view, with that of her lesser contemporaries. Katharine Tynan and Nora Hopper, for example, have technical qualities which are not hers, though she is certainly their equal in force of poetic feeling. Although Nora Hopper's death was as premature as Ethna Carbery's—both having died at the age of thirty-five—the latter had not the opportunities for artistic development which came to the others. Writing solely in popular journals, for an uncritical audience, she escaped the discipline that must go towards the making of a great artist. In short, she paid the penalty which, as Yeats had pointed out, befell all who, like the poets of *The Nation*, put intense but narrow patriotism before art. They might write popular verse, and stirring verse, for association of patriotic ideas would often fill the place of technique. As Lionel Johnson pointed out in his lecture on *Poetry and Patriotism*, nobody would care to assert that *God Save the King* was even "decent verse," not to mention "poetry," but nobody would deny its appeal to Englishmen. This was the nature of the success of Irish poetry in pre-Revival times. Occasionally, as in the case of Mangan, ardently patriotic verse attained a high literary level, but, as a rule, the heart was stirred to the exclusion of the critical faculties. To a large extent Ethna Carbery's appeal was a reversion to the old type of poetry, and she met with an equally popular success. But this popularity is a significant confirmation of the great change brought about by the Revival in even the least esoteric circles. Whatever fault may be found with these poems, they remain essentially superior to their equivalents of the Fenian and *Nation* school. They are free from the political hates and lamentations of the older poetry, and, above all, they have substituted for these a love for the spiritual traditions of Celtic Ireland. The wider and deeper conception of nationality here implied is the great gift of the Revival to Anglo-Irish literature.

Almost as striking as the number of Irish poets who

became known during the Eighteen-Nineties, is the
large proportion of them who died young. In addition to Nora Hopper and Ethna Carbery we may
mention Rose Kavanagh and Frances Wynne, whose
work was well received, and would probably have
obtained more general recognition had they lived.
By far the more important of the two is Rose Kavanagh, although it was not until long after her death
that her poems were collected into a volume, *Rose
Kavanagh and her Verses* (1909). Frances Wynne's
Whisper! (1890) was a handful of pretty verse without
any of the personality and promise of Rose Kavanagh's. The latter's *Lough Bray* and *The Northern
Blackwater* are entitled to rank with the best of the
minor poetry produced by the Revival. There is a
deeper tone, a quality of thought, in her work which
one misses in that of her fellow-poets, where an at-
tenuated simplicity testifies to the prestige amongst
these young ladies of their older friend, Katharine
Tynan. Such is the case, for example, in Alice Furlong's *Roses and Rue* (1899), to cite from the living
an instance of this contagious *naïveté*, this attitude
of devotion, which is common to most of the women
poets of the time. It is highly probable that the
author of *St. Francis to the Birds* was, unconsciously,
responsible for an identity of attitude and manner
in the work of her friends which renders it unnecessary to examine at length what they have written.
With the exception of Rose Kavanagh, who began
to write about the same time as Katharine Tynan, all
took example by their successful predecessor in the
field of what we may term minor Catholicism.

Dora Sigerson Shorter was one of the group, including Rose Kavanagh, who contributed in 1889 to
Lays and Lyrics of the Pan-Celtic Society, a work to
which reference has been made in a previous chapter.

For this reason she does not belong to the category just mentioned. Having started out independently, as it were, she did not succumb to the influences of the personal circle in which she moved for some years. Moreover, as the author of more than a dozen books of verse, she differs measurably from the poets who have been the subject of this chapter. She rivals Katharine Tynan, as the most voluminous of the women poets, but the quantity of her work need not mislead us as to its quality or importance. In spite of George Meredith's championship, her poetry has been severely criticised for what has been politely described as its "incuriousness of form." The incredible offences against all known laws of metrics, style, and even grammar, which mar the verse of Dora Sigerson Shorter, have been so frequently pointed out that they need not detain us. It will be sufficient to note that these defects can be attributed only to ignorance or carelessness, and either must necessarily diminish her claim to be ranked with her contemporaries of the first class. Indeed, we might say that the former alternative would, within certain limits, be more acceptable than the latter. A native, uncultivated talent may well be found where circumstances exclude the accompaniment of commensurate technical power. While hoping, or waiting, for the development of an adequate technique criticism will recognise the presence of genius. In the case of Dora Sigerson Shorter, the accusation of ignorance is ludicrous, but the recurrence in successive volumes of similar flaws cannot but lead to the conclusion of carelessness.

In spite of disconcerting rhymes, and fault of style, the author of *The Fairy Changeling and Other Poems* (1898) is a poet of undeniable merit. In such forms as the ballad, where her peculiar weaknesses are less noticeable than in the lyrics, she has been specially successful. The absence of technique, the directness of her manner, save her here from the conventionality which usually prevents the modern ballad-writer from reproducing the effects of his models. Irish folk-lore provides her with plenty of material, and as might be expected, her best ballads are Irish. *The Fairy Changeling*, *The Fair Little Maiden* or *The Priest's Brother*, for example, are superior to *The Dean of Santiago*, which lacks emotion, as do many of the later poems. *Poems and Ballads* (1899) contains fewer ballads of the same order as those in *The Fairy Changeling*, which is probably the author's best volume. She does not always succeed, however, even with Irish themes, as witness *Uisneach and Deirdre*, where she essays, in turn, to treat the legend of the Irish Helen, but fails to challenge comparison with those of her contemporaries whom the subject has attracted. When making a selection for the volume published in 1907 as *The Collected Poems of Dora Sigerson Shorter*, she omitted this and many other of her less fortunate experiments, notably *The Me Within Thee Blind*. That "novelette in rhyming pentameters," as an English critic called it, was evidence of a desire to abuse the power of metrical narrative which George Meredith declared to be the chief gift of the author. In reviving the ballad, or, rather, in making this *genre* her principal concern, she has helped to restore to Irish literature one of its most characteristic forms. But one cannot help regretting that she did not check precisely that fatal fluency which enabled her to write so easily and so carelessly. In the many volumes she has published nothing essential will be found which is not in that single volume of collected poems for which George Meredith was sponsor. Even in the precarious position of a preface-writer he was obliged to admit the presence of that defective craftsmanship which has, from the beginning, detracted from the good work of Dora Sigerson Shorter.

Two writers of this period, Jane Barlow and Emily Lawless, deserve more than a passing reference to their poetical work. But as both have acquired and rested their reputations primarily upon their prose fiction, we must postpone the attempt to estimate adequately their contribution to Anglo-Irish literature. In the case of Emily Lawless this is all the more justifiable in that she had begun to establish herself as a novelist contemporaneously with the first manifestations of the poetic revival, with which she did not associate herself very prominently. Two volumes of her verse, *With the Wild Geese* (1902) and *The Point of View* (1909), were collected late in her literary life, and the third, *The Inalienable Heritage* (1914), appeared after her death. All three were privately printed, and only the first was afterwards published in the ordinary way. The circumstances, therefore, indicate that, as a poet, Emily Lawless did not wish to make any great claim to public attention. The reticent attitude she displayed towards her verse by no means implies that she had nothing to say to an audience larger than that of her personal friends and acquaintances. The historical ballads of seventeenth-century Ireland, which gave their title to her first collection of poems, are finer than most of modern experiments in this *genre*. The section entitled *Fontenoy*, in particular, has attained to the rank of a popular classic, disputed only by the equally beautiful *Dirge of the Munster Forest*, from the related group of poems, *The Desmond War*. For combined narrative strength, deep poetic and national colour, these ballads surpass most of the work by which Dora Sigerson Shorter has come to be recognised as a ballad-writer *par excellence*.

The Inalienable Heritage, though it contains the striking ballad of Penal days, *The Third Trumpet*, is most distinguished by its lyric qualities. These were present in *With the Wild Geese*, but were rather overshadowed by the prominence given to the title poems. The sense of nature which made so vivid the pictures in those earlier poems, comprehensively entitled *In the Aran Isles*, comes to fuller expression in the last book of Emily Lawless. *From the Burren* and *From a Western Shoreway* are two groups which illustrate at its best the author's gift of lyric poetry. Without any premeditated artifice she has the faculty of evoking the spectacle and the emotion of the splendidly wild, desolate landscape of the West, where the deep booming of the Atlantic affords the only adequate background. No Irish poet has more successfully imbued his verse with the tone and colour of Irish nature than the author of *A Bog-filled Valley*. Not that Emily Lawless is content to paint pictures only, or to write Nature poems for their own sake. Her enthusiasm as an entomologist did, it is true, inspire her to write of the "rare and deep-red burnet-moth only to be met with in the Burren." Excellent of its kind, this poem is an exception, for as a rule she never fails to voice the intimate relation of the human spirit to its natural surroundings. The roar of the great ocean, the mists veiling the brown stretches of bogland, the druid remains, the fairy mounds—as these pass before her eyes she identifies the mysterious spirit that broods over them with the spirit within herself. The Celtic imagination, which sees in the external world the evidence of the common identity of all life, as manifestations of the Great Spirit; which peoples the streams and

forests with supernatural presences serving to link
this world with the regions beyond Time and Space—
this imaginative element is not lacking in Emily
Lawless. She writes out of a detachment not usual
in Irish poetry, but this is probably due to the predominantly intellectual character of her emotion.
Of her strong feeling for Irish ideals and sufferings
many of her best poems are evidence, while all her
poetry is infused with an intense love for her native
soil. Exceptional, and most perfect, is her sensitiveness to the appeal of the mighty sea which breaks
upon the shores she knew and loved best.

At the outset of the Revival Jane Barlow, unlike
Emily Lawless, had made no advance in the direction
which ultimately brought her side by side with the
older writer. When T. W. Rolleston was editing
The Dublin University Review she was one of those
who, like Yeats, were rewarded by encouragement on
submitting their first poems for publication. These
Bogland Studies were collected some years later, and
appeared as her first book in 1892. It would be out
of place to judge this volume strictly upon its literary merits; its style and manner presuppose
metrical laxities, and lapses from most of the established rules of poetic literature. The author is not
concerned with such considerations, being interested
rather in the success of an experiment. *Bogland
Studies* is an attempt to give in verse form a series
of narratives of Irish peasant life. It was originally
written in a dialect perilously close to that caricature of Anglo-Irish speech with which Lever and
Lover endowed the "stage Irishman," and whose disappearance is due to the example of such masters of
the idiom as Douglas Hyde and J. M. Synge. In the
enlarged edition of 1894, Jane Barlow was wise
enough to modify or abolish some of the more out-

rageous distortions, such as rendering the pronunciation of the vowel sound "ie" by "a," a common mistake of superficial observers. At best, however, the
poems have an air of exaggeration and caricature
which makes them difficult to accept, now that a generation of dramatists and poets has familiarised us
with the true qualities of peasant speech.

Apart from this defect Jane Barlow's stories of
rural life are not without interest, and one can easily
imagine the novelty of her first volume could have
disarmed criticism to some extent. In spite of some
gross errors of transcription, due largely to the influence of a false literary convention, her poems reveal a
real knowledge of peasant turns of speech. The
later books, such as *Ghost-Bereft* (1901) and *The
Mockers* (1908) in which the themes of *Bogland
Studies* are largely repeated, show a greater restraint
in the employment of dialect, naturally to the advantage of the poems. But ingenious as the stories
are, they have little to support them but the narrative interest. Their psychology is primitive, most
of the happenings being of the novelette description,
and worst of all, it is conventional rather than real.
Jane Barlow's peasants are not human beings, but
stereotypes of the peasantry, as viewed by the upper
middle-class section of Anglicised Ireland. She is
not a hostile caricaturist, her desire is to be sympathetic, but she cannot see the country people except
through the conventions, literary and social, of her
class. In *Th'Ould Master*, for example, the first of
the *Bogland Studies*, and one that has been highly
praised, we find all the ingredients of the recipe for
Irish fiction bequeathed by the author of *Charles
O'Malley*. The impecunious landowner of ancient
family, adored by his starving tenants, the peasants
ragged, faithful, humorous and pathetic, whose

thoughts, and their expression, are a source of merriment to "the gentry"—these are too frequently the heroes of Jane Barlow's adventures. Occasionally she ventures to look at life from the point of view of the dispossessed, as in *The Souper's Widow*, or *Terence Macran*, to mention a later example, but one has the uncomfortable feeling that this is "mere literature," so fundamentally outside her characters does the author appear. Her fondness for the device by which inferiors appear to relate some event to their masters, or some otherwise sympathetic superior, is significant. Some have pointed to this as evidence of her inability to dissociate herself from the characters she studies. So completely does she identify herself with them that the narrator becomes inevitably the peasant himself. If this were so, we should not be so often reminded that the speaker is addressing one whom he considers above him socially. The truth is that Jane Barlow is too conscious of her social relation to the people described, and is, to that extent, debarred from glimpsing more of the peasant mind than can be revealed where such a relationship is emphasised.

CHAPTER X

THE DUBLIN MYSTICS

THE THEOSOPHICAL MOVEMENT. GEORGE W. RUS-
SELL (A. E.). JOHN EGLINTON

WHILE the poets mentioned in the last chapter were spreading the fame of the Literary Revival in England, where most of them lived or published their work, there had come together in Dublin a group of writers whose part in the building up of the new Anglo-Irish literature has been of far greater import-ance than is generally recognised. They created a literary life in Ireland just at a time when some fusion of intellectual activities was most essential to the future of the Revival, and, by living and working in and for their own country, strengthened the roots of Irish authorship. Their example made it possible to end the tradition which imposed upon every Irish author the necessity of going to London, or at least offering his work to English editors and publishers. Nowadays the greater part of Anglo-Irish literature is written and published in Ireland, following the precedent created in the period with which this chapter deals. Indeed, the work of publishing and editing was a considerable part of the activities which engaged the group of young men who now claim our attention. Towards the end of the Eighties there came into being what might certainly be termed a literary "movement" in Ireland, the presence in

Dublin of a number of writers working together, imbued with the same ideals, and in constant relation to one another. All were alive with the same enthusiasm for a national tradition in literature, and had found in O'Grady the necessary revelation. They concentrated and condensed, as it were, the hitherto scattered elements of revival, and gave a very desirable homogeneity to the rather isolated or unrelated efforts of individual writers in England and Ireland. Had they remained together longer we might still be able to speak of the "Irish literary movement," but they were obliged to separate, some without even leaving any contribution to our contemporary literature such as would mark their passage.

The study of mysticism was the common factor which brought together the younger writers, W. B. Yeats, Charles Johnston, John Eglinton, Charles Weekes and George W. Russell (A. E.), to mention only some of the names which have since come into prominence in Irish literature. By an irony of history, the late Professor Dowden seems to have given the impulse to the Theosophical Movement in Dublin. During the greater part of his life he was either hostile or indifferent to the literature which was being created about him, and not until recognition had come to it from abroad did Dowden permit himself to admire what his own literary eminence should have helped him to foster. Indirectly, however, he was responsible for the creation of a society of various talents whose importance in the history of the Revival cannot be exaggerated. It was at Dowden's house that W. B. Yeats heard the discussion of A. P. Sinnett's *Esoteric Buddhism* and *The Occult World* which induced him to read these two books, and to recommend them to his school-friend, Charles Johnston.   The latter, doubtless because of a more serious interest (we have already referred to the nature of Yeats's attraction to mysticism), was aroused sufficiently to wish to follow up his new study.   He talked of Sinnett to his friends, and interested a number to the point of forming in 1885 a "Hermetic Society," so named after Anna Kingsford's analogous society in London.   T. W. Rolleston, as editor of the *Dublin University Review*, proved his sympathy with the movement by publishing a long article by Charles Johnston on Esoteric Buddhism.   Thus the *Review* saw the beginnings, not only of the purely literary, but also of the philosophical side of the Irish Revival, as seen in W. B. Yeats and Charles Johnston, whose first contributions appeared almost simultaneously.

Johnston's interest did not stop at reading and commentary.   He went to London to meet Mr. Sinnett, through whom he became acquainted with various people of prominence in theosophical circles, and finally he returned to Dublin as a Fellow of the Theosophical Society.   It was not long before he obtained recruits, who in time became the Charter-members of the Dublin Lodge of the Theosophical Society.   This Lodge, whose charter was received in 1886, removed the *raison d'être* of the Hermetic Society, which ceased to exist until many years later, when the title was adopted by A. E., and those who formed the present Hermetic, to carry on the work of the Theosophical Society.   The corporate existence of the Dublin Lodge terminated in 1897, when a majority of the members were reorganised into the newly-formed "Universal Brotherhood."   These subsequent developments do not concern the present history, but the Dublin Lodge of the Theosophical Society was as vital a factor in the evolution of Anglo-Irish literature as the publication of Standish

O'Grady's *History of Ireland*, the two events being complementary to any complete understanding of the literature of the Revival. The Theosophical Movement provided a literary, artistic and intellectual centre from which radiated influences whose effect was felt even by those who did not belong to it. Further, it formed a rallying-ground for all the keenest of the older and younger intellects, from John O'Leary and George Sigerson, to W. B. Yeats and A. E. It brought into contact the most diverse personalities, and definitely widened the scope of the new literature, emphasising its marked advance on all previous national movements. For example, at a time when Russian literature was only beginning to penetrate to England, R. Ivanovitch Lipmann, who had just translated Lermontov, was bringing home directly to the writers of the Revival the literary traditions of his country. Lipmann is an instance indicating the remarkable fusion of personality and nationality effected by the Theosophical Movement in Dublin. It was an intellectual melting-pot from which the true and solid elements of nationality emerged strengthened, while the dross was lost. The essentials of a national spirit were assured by the very breadth of freedom of the ideals to which our writers aspired. Depth without narrowness was their reward for building upon a human, rather than upon a political, foundation.

Of the young writers who created the Theosophical Movement in Dublin, Yeats was the first to make his work known in book form, his *Mosada* having appeared the same year in which the Dublin Lodge received its charter, while *The Wanderings of Oisin* was published two years later. That mysticism was but a very small part of his inspiration seems confirmed by the fact that before his companions had become, as it were, articulate, he had produced five original works, had collaborated in two others, and was known as the editor of four collections of folk-tales. The only volume which bore distinctly the trace of those speculations with which the Dublin mystics were preoccupied was *The Celtic Twilight*, published in 1893, but written earlier. Its completion coincided, therefore, with the first coördinated effort of the mystics to make themselves known to the public, when *The Irish Theosophist* appeared in the autumn of 1892. This "monthly magazine devoted to Universal Brotherhood, the Study of Eastern literature and occult science," continued until 1897, when the title became *The Internationalist*, which was succeeded, in turn, by *The International Theosophist* in 1898. The former journals, without detriment to their breadth of aim, became veritable organs of the Literary Revival, whereas *The International Theosophist* had no very definite part in it, doubtless because of the termination of the Dublin Lodge's existence. When the Universal Brotherhood was constituted, the editorship of the magazine passed from Irish control. The life of the original journal, however, was most fruitful for contemporary Irish literature. With O'Grady's *All Ireland Review*, its successor, it was a comparatively successful attempt to give the Revival a worthy periodical literature.

There is no evidence of Yeats's collaboration in *The Irish Theosophist* or *The Internationalist*, the Irish contributors being mainly new men, unknown to even a restricted public. They constitute, therefore, an entirely different case from that of the writers who were attracted to the Theosophical Movement, but whose literary existence was independent of it. It would, of course, be rash to assert

that the newcomers would not have written but for
that Movement, but there can be no doubt of its
having helped many to find themselves, and of its
having given a definite mould and impulse to their
work.   George Russell (A. E.), John Eglinton,
Charles Weekes, and Charles Johnston were the
specific contribution of the Theosophic Movement
to the Revival.   As writers, editors and publishers
they are directly and indirectly responsible for a
considerable part of the best work in Anglo-Irish
literature.   Apart from his activity in initiating the
whole movement, Johnston translated *From the
Upanishads* in 1896, published by his companions as
part of that valuable enterprise to which we owe
A. E.'s *Homeward: Songs by the Way* and John Eglinton's *Two Essays on the Remnant*.   These little
books, for which Weekes was sponsor, were destined
to be the beginning of a new phase of Irish authorship.   The decent clothing of a volume of contemporary verse was no longer to be associated exclusively with the London imprint.

Circumstances   necessitated   the   departure   of
Charles Johnston to India, so that his share in the
ultimate success of the Movement he started was
not intimate.   It is likely that he would have contributed some more characteristic work to the literature of the Revival had he remained in Dublin.
His *Ireland: Historic and Picturesque*, which was
published in the United States in 1902, contains
passages which remind the reader of the eloquent
splendour of O'Grady, but it is the only book of the
kind he has written.   His essays in theosophical
literature do not bear the traces of nationality which
constitutes the Irish interest in the work of his
Dublin contemporaries.   He left Ireland so early
that it was impossible for him to blend the Eastern

and Celtic elements as A. E. has done. Similarly, Charles Weekes must be counted amongst those who did not leave behind them any enduring sign of their participation in this phase of the Revival. He published in 1893, and immediately suppressed, *Reflections and Refractions*, the first book to appear by one of the new school. A by no means discouraging reception was accorded to it, for, in spite of an inevitable unevenness, the majority of the poems were of a high level. The dominant note is intellectual rather than emotional, as witness those few verses which have been saved from destruction by the anthologists, *Titan, That* or *Think*. The transcendentalism of the mystic poet must be coloured with the vision of the artist if he would find acceptance. The themes of Weekes are often those which require but a little colour and emotion to lighten the burden of their thought. Probably it was this conviction which prompted him to withdraw the book, for it is remarkable how inferior those poems are in which the intellectual content is slight. Apparently he could not effect the necessary fusion of artistry and intellect, his verse being too frequently either colourless or superficial. Exception must be made, however, of *Louis Verger*, that powerful analysis which he calls "some sensations of an assassin." Here he succeeds in combining the emotional and intellectual qualities which are usually dissociated in his work. The appeal of this poem is more human than in those verses mentioned, where the mind only is stirred by the evocation of an idea. The almost perfect achievement of the purpose which Weekes renounced will be found in the work of the poet whom he introduced in the year following the withdrawal of his own book.

GEORGE W. RUSSELL (A. E.)

From the first number of *The Irish Theosophist*, in October, 1892, until the last issue of *The International*, in the spring of 1898, an almost uninterrupted outpouring of prose and verse attracted attention to a new writer, who sometimes wrote above his own name or initials, sometimes over the pseudonym "A. E." In 1894 he was persuaded by Charles Weekes to collect some of this verse, which appeared in Dublin under the title *Homeward: Songs by the Way*. This beautiful little book had a well-merited, and therefore unusual, success, both in England and the United States, where, after two Irish editions had been exhausted, new publishers were found. Henceforth the signature of A. E., above which it had appeared, was permanently identified and associated with the poetry of George W. Russell. A second collection of his contributions to the theosophical magazines was made, and a companion volume to the English edition of *Homeward* was published as *The Earth Breath and other Poems* in 1897. The repeated signs of favour which greeted this second book definitely established A. E. as the supreme poet of contemporary mysticism, and made him second only to Yeats in the poetic literature of the Revival. To many, indeed, he seems to have surpassed the latter, in spite of the modest place he has claimed for his work. For, amongst other remarkable qualities, A. E. possessed a sense of the value of letters which enabled him to resist the temptation to overwrite. Between 1897 and 1904 he published only ten new poems, and these were scattered through a semi-privately printed selection from his earlier works, *Nuts of Knowledge* (1903). The following year *The Divine Vision* appeared, his third, and in a

sense his last, volume of verse, almost as slender in
bulk as its predecessors. From that date until 1913
he was content to issue only another semi-private
edition of reprinted verse, *By Still Waters* (1906),
with the addition of half-a-dozen new poems.
Finally, in 1913, appeared his *Collected Poems*, one
volume which contains, as he says, "with such new
verses as I thought of equal mood, . . . what poetry
of mine I would wish my friends to read." The
book is, with slight modifications and omissions, a
complete reissue of his three volumes, the rejected
poems being only about twelve in number, the additions amounting to not quite twice as many. From
these details it will be evident that the work of A. E.
must possess some quality which is absent from the
more voluminous writers who have failed to over-
shadow him.

The basic element in A. E.'s work, both verse and
prose, is its absolute sincerity, and this is the quality
which has saved it from being lost in the multitu-
dinous over-production of printed matter. As is
possible for a writer to whom literature is not a
trade, he has written only out of a need for self-
expression, not out of the economic necessities of
journalism or book-making. In Ireland, as elsewhere, the degeneration of real talent, under the
pressure of newspaper popularity and the exigencies
of press work, is not infrequent, especially since
"Celticism" has become a commercial asset of incredible utility. To our credit it is true that the
greater part of the literature of the Revival has
been inspired by motives unconnected with commercialism, and the best is still free from the taint.
While it cannot be denied that a great deal of
worthless literature may be written by financially
disinterested idealists, the reverse seems to be the

case in Ireland. With one or two exceptions, our most valued writers have failed to make a pecuniary success even of a not too restricted popularity. On the contrary, the most popular authors, who succeeded where the others failed, have done so to their great detriment. Few Irish writers of any importance are financially successful, and they owe what is best in their work to the days when they wrote without a thought of material reward, it being explicitly understood, in fact, that none was forthcoming. Until recently an Irishman in need of money could not more certainly defeat his purpose than by submitting to the influences of the Revival. Success lay obviously in the direction of Anglicisation, or, at least, of "stage Irishness." Both are still more profitable, as witness the careers of our most distinguished expatriate, and of the Irish novelist who at present boasts the largest circulation.

It is the mark of the artistic and intellectual integrity of A. E. that he has not been spoiled by the very real success which has come to him. The form of the latter has been discriminate appreciation on the part of a public wide enough to escape the designation of a clique, yet sufficiently narrow to ensure the freedom of the artist, who is not exposed to the danger of commercial popularity. A. E. still writes as he wrote in *The Irish Theosophist*, with no care for the financial prospects of his work, concerned only for the truest expression of himself. He is no longer impelled to speak with the frequency of those early years, when the fullness of a new revelation, and the enthusiasm of youth, made silence arduous; when to have refrained from speech must, at times, have seemed almost an act of cowardice. Were he not restrained by the consciousness of the nature of his inspiration, he might with profit become a mystic-monger to suburban drawing-rooms. But A. E. deliberately chose to dissociate his material from his literary welfare, the latter being quite independent of the former. He could not see his way to continue spinning words, when he had been accustomed to weave a poetic fabric of ideas. In 1913 he collected such of his verse as seemed worthy to be preserved, and his intention to make no more verses was frustrated only by the stirring events which moved the world exactly one year after those *Collected Poems* were printed. To the emotions of the European war he responded in a fashion which enables us to enjoy some further characteristic songs by a voice whose threatened silence we should have regretted all the more because its latest utterances testify to an undiminished faculty of elevated poetry.

The mysticism of A. E. is entirely different from the symbolism which has given Yeats the reputation of being a mystic. That which is purely decorative in the poetry of the latter is, in A. E., the expression of fundamental truths. The author of *Homeward* chose to formulate his belief in verse, but, as the circumstances of his entry into literature show, he did so on behalf of a definite spiritual propaganda. Consequently, no desire for literary effect, no use of poetic licence, could sway him from his purpose, which was to illustrate from personal experience the mystic faith that was in him. Unlike Yeats, he did not seize merely upon the artistic opportunities of mysticism, though he does record his visions with the eyes and memory of an artist. The externals which attracted the instinct for beauty in Yeats were not lost upon A. E., but he was above all concerned for the inner meaning of the phenomena, whose plastic value alone captured the imagination of the former poet. We have already seen how Yeats allowed his æsthetic sense to outrage the transcendental common-sense of the true visionary. A. E. is not guilty of this, for the reality of his spiritual adventures imposes a restraint upon his artistic imagination, the latter being satisfied only in so far as is congruous with the former. This scrupulous obedience to the desire for veracity has, indeed, exposed the author to the reproach of repetition and monotony. If there be a certain resemblance between many of his pictures, we should rather admire the constancy of his vision than demand the introduction of effective novelties of phrase and image, probably as false as they are acceptable to a certain class of literary exquisite.

"I know I am a spirit, and that I went forth in old time from the Self-ancestral to labours yet unaccomplished; but, filled ever and again with homesickness, I made these homeward songs by the way." These words, with which A. E. introduced his first book of verse, should serve as a superscription to the *Collected Poems*, so completely do they summarise the whole message and tendency of his poetry. All his life he has sung of this conviction of man's identity with the Divine Power, the Ancestral Self of Eastern philosophy, from whom we are but temporarily divided. The occasion of his poems are those moments of rapture when the seer glimpses some vision reminding him of his immortal destiny, his absorption into Universal Being. The hours of twilight and dawn are those which most usually find the poet rapt in "divine vision," and to this circumstance must be attributed numerous landscapes whose beauty is undiminished by their being so frequently seen in the same light. A. E. never has recourse to mechanical repetition. For all their identity of setting, his pictures are endowed with a fresh beauty, by such varied impressions as the following:

> Its edges foamed with amethyst and rose,
> Withers once more the old blue flower of day;
> There where the ether like a diamond glows,
>   Its petals fade away.

and

> When the breath of Twilight blows to flame the misty skies,
> All its vaporous sapphire, violet glow and silver gleam,
> With their magic flood me through the gateway of the eyes;
>   I am one with twilight's dream.

or

> Twilight, a blossom grey in shadowy valleys dwells,
> Under the radiant dark the deep, blue-tinted bells
> In quietness reïmage heaven within their blooms. . . .

Both *Homeward* and *The Earth Breath*, from which these lines are quoted, contain frequent evocations of the same nature, and the later poems show no trace of *cliché*. For example,

> Dusk, a pearl-grey river, o'er
> Hill and vale puts out the day. . . .

or that charming line:

> Twilight, a timid fawn, went glimmering by.

Instead of reproaching the poet with the monotony of his descriptions, as some critics have done, one is tempted to admire the skill with which he contrives to render his impressions. The genuine feeling underlying them is doubtless the explanation. If sometimes the transcription suggests repetition, it is because words as fresh as the emotion prompting them are not always to be found. A. E. has not the verbal mastery of Yeats; the beauty of his verse is not so deliberate. His success, therefore, within the limits he has imposed upon himself, is all the more considerable.

Admitting that an essential part of a poet's function is to choose the words and images which render most fully and most beautifully his perception, one feels, nevertheless, that the beauty of A. E.'s verse is, so to speak, unconscious. That is not to suggest any lack of artistic discrimination in his use of language. At times he certainly exhibits an indifference to form of which Yeats is almost incapable, but, himself an artist, as well as a poet, he is keenly sensible of the poetic art. The unconsciousness referred to is of a different kind. It is the apparent absence of deliberate intention in the form and setting of the poems. The dusky valleys and twilight fields, the pictures which captivate the eye, are incidental, it might almost be said accidental. They occur merely as the accompaniment of an idea, the prelude to a statement which constitutes the real reason of the poem's existence. *Carrowmore, Oversoul, By the Margin of the Great Deep, Refuge*, to mention four well-known and typical poems, may be read for their wonderful descriptive quality. They are like the numerous others in their delicate colouring, and in their power of evoking starry landscapes, and the soft beauties of the Irish countryside. But neither they nor the others were written with that intention; whatever their value as word-pictures, to the poet they are essentially declarations of faith. Those acquainted with A. E.'s canvases will have no difficulty in recalling the peculiar effect of his introduction of superhuman phenomena into a material setting. Sometimes an angelic Being will hover above a plougher as he works, sometimes the body of a woman appears rising out of the ground. The abrupt juxtaposition of such figures in an otherwise ordinary landscape is characteristic. These supposedly supernatural phenomena are as much a part of the natural scene as the material objects the artist is painting. He simply describes what he sees. The poet and artist being closely related in A. E.—the themes and colouring of their work is identical—we find in his verse the same peculiarity as in his painting. A poem which reads at first as a simple picture of eveningtide, with no more than the usual undercurrent of reflection, gradually reveals the presence of the mystic seer. The "lonely road through bogland" leads to something more than the reïmaging in the reader's mind of a typical Irish landscape. Like the spirit Beings in his paintings, the mysticism of A. E. pierces through the word-pictures and remains the central *Motiv*.

It will be found that this *Motiv*, so far as it can be described in a phrase, is the relation of the soul to the eternal. With rare exceptions, and these of recent date, the poems of A. E. tell of the quest of his spirit for the Universal Spirit, they illustrate those moments of supreme ecstasy when the soul is rapt in communion with the Oversoul. The hours from nightfall until dawn are most propitious to these visions of Reality, for then the cares of daily life have ceased, and the seer can so concentrate his mind as to obtain communication with the spirit world. The frequency of the twilight setting in A. E.'s work has already been mentioned as due to this fact. It is also doubtless a part of that symbolism of which he says:

> Now when the giant in us wakes and broods,
> Filled with home yearnings, drowsily he flings
> From his deep heart high dreams and mystic moods,
> Mixed with the memory of the loved earth-things;
> Clothing the vast with a familiar face
> Reaching his right hand forth to greet the starry race.

"By the symbol charioted" the poet rises above earth, but "the loved earth-things" are coloured by his vision of the Beyond. The violet and amethyst, the pearl and silver shades of night are a happy reflection not only of actual nature but also of the celestial cities and starry regions of the soul. But this distinction between the natural and the supernatural is, after all, a mere convention which A. E. himself does not recognise. In using the term "supernatural" we must remember that it does not exist in the vocabulary of the true mystic.

The divinity of nature is an essential of A. E.'s faith. Earth is the Great Mother of whom we are born, and to whom we must return; deity is everywhere. Some of his finest songs have hymned the praise of earth, and it would be difficult to find anything surpassing them in pantheistic ecstasy, *The Joy of Earth*, *The Earth Breath*, *In the Womb*, *The Earth Spirit* and *The Virgin Mother*. Of the many poems upon this theme none is finer than the last mentioned:

> Who is that goddess to whom men should pray,
> But her from whom their hearts have turned away,
> Out of whose virgin being they were born,
> Whose mother nature they have named with scorn,
> Calling its holy substance common clay.

The recency of this poem makes comparison with earlier utterances interesting, as showing how steadfast is the belief expressed:

> Lover, your heart, the heart on which it lies,
> Your eyes that gaze and those alluring eyes,
> Your lips, the lips they kiss, alike had birth
> Within that dark divinity of earth,
> Within that mother being you despise.

The note of conviction is no less strong than in those youthful lines, *Dust:*

> I heard them in their sadness say,
> "The earth rebukes the thought of God;
> We are but embers wrapped in clay
> A little nobler than the sod."
>
> But I have touched the lips of clay,
> Mother, thy rudest sod to me
> Is thrilled with fire of hidden day,
> And haunted by all mystery.

One remembers that it was no legendary youth who preached to idle crowds the sacredness of the ground beneath their feet.   If A. E. no longer essays to convert the populace, as in those ardent early years of his crusade, we find *The Virgin Mother* closing on two lines expressing that original protest:

> I look with sudden awe beneath my feet
> As you with erring reverence overhead.

The soil of Ireland is sacred not only because of its common divinity as the source of all life, it has also the special appeal for us of being peopled by the gods and heroes of the Heroic Age.   In *A Call of the Sidhe*, *Dana*, *Connla's Well* and *Children of Lir*, for example, there is that fusion of the local and the universal which is peculiarly A. E.'s.   He has made the legendary lore of Ireland comprehensible in terms of Eastern mysticism, the result being verses which are at once specifically Irish and profoundly human in their world-wide appeal.   A. E. is intellectually a citizen of the universe, nay, of the cosmos, but he bears none the less the imprint of Irish incarnation.   The contrast between *A Call of the Sidhe* and Yeats's well-known *Hosting of the Sidhe* furnishes an interesting instance of the fundamental difference between the two poets. The charm of Yeats's lines is irresistible:

> The host is riding from Knocknarea,
> And over the grave of Clooth-na-bare
> Caolte tossing his burning hair,
> And Niamh calling: away, come away.

They capture the memory more easily than A. E.'s:

> Tarry thou yet, late lingerer in the twilight's glory:
> Gay are the hills with song: earth's faery children leave
> More dim abodes to roam the primrose-hearted eve
> Opening their glimmering lips to breathe some wondrous story.

But how empty they are of the profound undertone which finally becomes articulate:

> Come thou away with them, for Heaven to Earth is calling,
> These are Earth's voice—her answer—spirits thronging.
> Come to the Land of Youth: the trees grown heavy there
> Drop on the purple wave the starry fruit they bear.
> Drink: the immortal waters quench the spirit's longing.

It seems as if Yeats had contrived but an artistic, literary image of a popular superstition, whereas A. E. refers the folk legend back to its origins where he finds analogies with his own visions. For there is a certain incoherence of half-realised beauty, and personal emotion, in his attempt to transcribe what he has seen when "grown brother-hearted with the vast," his spirit soared "unto the Light of Lights in burning adoration."

The difference between the two poets is that Yeats is a symbolist, whereas A. E. is a mystic. They both make use of symbols, but the former does not succeed, as does the latter, in subordinating symbolism to the expression of truth. Yeats becomes enamoured, as it were, of the instrument and loses sight of its purpose. A. E. is so completely possessed by the reality of his vision that the end dominates the means. He cannot mistake "the perfect lifting of an arm" for the eternal moment, he looks beyond external appearances. In *The Symbol Seduces* he repudiates precisely that conception of Beauty which Yeats has, consciously or unconsciously, accepted:

> And while I sit and listen there,
> The robe of Beauty falls away
> From universal things to where
> Its image dazzles for a day.

Thus he describes the temptation to seek the Real in the Phenomenal, whereas his own attitude is defined as follows:

> Away! the great life calls; I leave
> For Beauty, Beauty's rarest flower;
> For Truth, the lips that ne'er deceive;
> For Love, I leave Love's haunted bower.

This is the renunciation of the true mystic, who cannot be seduced by the shadow of reality. A. E. rarely dwells with that insistence upon detail which so frequently characterises Yeats's dreams. Where the latter is prodigal of beautiful phrases and suggestive images, A. E. is content to give the merest hint of the wonders he has glimpsed in the hour of exaltation. He will even confess to a powerlessness which would be humiliating to the verbal mastery of Yeats:

> Our hearts were drunk with a beauty
> Our eyes could never see.

The author of *The Wind Among the Reeds* would prefer, in that case, to rely solely upon his imagination for the facts, however transcendental.

From the beginning A. E. has been conscious of the seriousness of his purpose, which is something other than the weaving of beautiful verses.   In the prelude to *Homeward* he cried:

> Oh, be not led away,
> Lured by the colour of the sun-rich day.
> The gay romance of song
> Unto the spirit life doth not belong.

His ears have been attentive to the lips through which "the Infinite murmurs her ancient story," and he has told only the messages thus heard.   Such later poems as *The Iron Age, The Heroes* and *On Behalf of some Irishmen not Followers of Tradition*, though in form a commentary upon current affairs, are all inspired by a deep conviction of man's divine potentialities.   They bear a closer relationship to the contemplative and visionary poems than do the similarly recent and topical verses of Yeats to their predecessors.   It is this fundamental unity of out-look, this steadfast hold upon a living idea, which constitute the special value of A. E.'s work.   His verse is not so much the utterance of a poet as the song of a prophet, and its importance is to be measured in other than purely literary terms.   He often falls below the standard of technical perfection which was set by Yeats, and is the latter's most valuable gift to Irish poetry.   But depth and sincerity, coupled with a general high level of workmanship, enable A. E. to take his place in the first rank.   If he has occasionally sacrificed the letter to the spirit we know with what intent.   We know that he has aspired to give us a revelation of Divine Beauty, and we are grateful that this should be his unique preoccupation.   In *The Veils of Maya* he voices the need for such concentration:

Mother, with whom our lives should be,
  Not hatred keeps our lives apart:
Charmed by some lesser glow in thee,
  Our hearts beat not within thy heart.

Beauty, the face, the touch, the eyes,
  Prophets of thee, allure our sight
From that unfathomed deep where lies
  Thine ancient loveliness and light.

More often perhaps than any other of his contemporaries A. E. has expressed his admiration for Standish O'Grady, upon whom he has written a short, but admirable essay, which was published in an American anthology of Irish literature. Like most of his prose work, critical and imaginative, this essay has lain for years uncollected, and it was not included in that long-desired volume, *Imaginations and Reveries*, which, in 1915, brought together a number of scattered writings. The files of various Irish reviews testify to the charm of A. E.'s prose, but only a small part has at last been issued in permanent form. With few exceptions, the contents of *Imaginations and Reveries* had already been reprinted since their first appearance in periodicals, but in such a manner as to render them inaccessible to a large public. The volume includes almost every one of the works which will here be enumerated in the order of their original publication, and may be considered representative, if not complete.

About 1897 A. E. republished two of his essays from *The Irish Theosophist*, under the titles, *The Future of Ireland and the Awakening of the Fires* and *Ideals in Ireland: Priest or Hero?* These brochures bear evidences of youthful composition, particularly the first mentioned, but the second is well written, and contains nothing the author would now disown. There is a fiery enthusiasm in this early profession of the lofty idealism with which the poet has since made us familiar. Viewing contemporary events in the light of spiritual Beauty, the author strikes a note which sings in the same key as that of O'Grady's passionate apostrophes. Thus he pictures the awakening of the people, called "to a temple not built with hands, sunlit, starlit, sweet with the odour and incense of earth . . . to the altars of the hills, soon to be lit up as of old, soon to be the blazing torches of God over the land." Since the epic historian of our Heroic Age had evoked the past by his brilliant gift of imagination and intuition, none had written such passages as:

"Ah, my darlings, you will have to fight and suffer: you must endure loneliness, the coldness of friends, the alienation of love; . . . laying in dark places the foundations of that high and holy Eri of prophecy, the isle of enchantment, burning with druidic splendours, bright with immortal presences, with the face of the everlasting Beauty looking in upon its ways, divine with terrestrial mingling till God and the world are one."

None of the other essays in the theosophical reviews were republished, however, until *The Hero in Man* and *The Renewal of Youth* appeared in 1909 and 1910. On the other hand, some of A. E.'s critical work formed part of that interesting collection *Literary Ideals in Ireland,* to which John Eglinton, Yeats and William Larminie contributed. This reprint of a series of articles discussing the claims of Anglo-Irish literature in general, and of the Irish drama in particular, is of special value to the student of the Revival. Here may be found literary history in the making, for the book furnishes one of those unique instances where the chief figures of the renascence publicly formulated their standards and discussed their differences. The original point at issue was O'Grady's statement that Heroic legends did not lend themselves to dramatic exploitation in the theatre. Yeats contended that they were susceptible of being staged, John Eglinton denied it. The discussion gradually covered all the conflicting theories held by various Irishmen as to the true function of Irish literature. A. E. aptly summarised the situation as a conflict between the nationalism advocated by Yeats and the individualism of John Eglinton, but, as he pointed out, "nationality and cosmopolitanism" were the true alternatives, and it appeared that at bottom all were agreed as to the desirability of the former. "To reveal Ireland in a clear and beautiful light, to create the Ireland in the heart, is the province of a national literature"; such was A. E.'s definition of the chief term used by the controversialists. With considerable critical acumen he succeeded in demonstrating how the conflicting ideals of John Eglinton and Yeats were reconciled in this conception of nationality, and how each contributed his share to its realisation.

The only other selection of similar studies by A. E. is the little booklet published in 1906 as *Some Irish Essays*, which contains that interesting examination of Yeats's poetry, *The Poet of the Shadows*. Having done generous homage to the beauty of the imagination which conceived *The Wanderings of Oisin*, A. E. complains of Yeats's attempt to make the "tropical tangle orthodox." "The glimmering waters and winds are no longer beautiful natural presences, but here become symbolic voices, and preach obscurely some doctrine." With a delicacy of phrase only equalled by the gentleness of the criticism, he censures the "esoteric hieroglyphs" which have made impossible the old delight in the poet of the Rose.

In a sentence he sums up the difference which separates *The Wind Among the Reeds* from *The Divine Vision:* "I am more interested in life than in the shadows of life." Surely, no more succinct differentiation between the mystic and the symbolist is possible? Of the three remaining essays, one is a reprint of *Nationality and Cosmopolitanism in Art* already mentioned, while another is a return to the controversy out of which that essay arose. In 1907, however, with the development of the Dramatic Movement nearing its apogee, A. E. was less confident of O'Grady's error. He expressly states that *The Dramatic Treatment of Heroic Literature* is to be considered as a tribute to "the finest personality in contemporary Irish literature," rather than as a refutation of O'Grady's argument against the dramatisation of the legends. Finally mention must be made of *On an Irish Hill*, that charming mystic reverie, which introduces two of A. E.'s best lyrics, and sets forth the reasons of that characteristic yearning for the hour and place when "twilight flutters the mountains o'er." It is hardly an essay in the sense that its companions are, and belongs to the order of those dream-stories which the author so frequently contributed to the theosophical reviews.

Several of these stories, as distinct from the essays, were published in book form in 1904, with the title *The Mask of Apollo*. Almost every chapter made its original appearance in *The Irish Theosophist* and *The Internationalist*, so that they attach themselves directly to the two brochures which were the earliest reprints of A. E.'s prose. The intervention of other interests, and the absence of any immediate attempt to continue those reprints, has produced an interval between *The Earth Breath* and *The Mask of Apollo*. In our account of them we have followed the chrono-

logical order, but the two books were written contemporaneously and belong to the same mood in
the author. The normal dissatisfaction at the dis-
persal and loss of most of A. E.'s prose-writing tends
to become acute in the present case, for it seems
unreasonable that out of a possible dozen sketches,
at least, only seven were selected to make up *The
Mask of Apollo*. Why were *The Meditation of Par-
vati*, *A Doomed City* and the more lengthy, *A Strange
Awakening*, rejected, when their neighbours, *The
Cave of Lilith*, *The Midnight Blossom* and *The Story
of a Star*, were chosen? Their omission deprived
us of what seemed almost destined to be the companion volume of prose which readers of A. E.'s
verse have demanded.

Having recorded the general objection to the material constitution of the book, we may unreservedly
express satisfaction with the intellectual substance
of its fifty-three pages. The author relates in a
preface how these stories "crept like living creatures"
into his mind, when he was but still a boy; they are
to be regarded, therefore, as his earliest literary conceptions. Although conceived so long ago they do
not appear, in execution, to differ materially from
the poetry A. E. was writing at the time these prose
fancies were first published. They are, in fact,
variations upon the theme which is the eternal subject of the mystic poet's meditations, and are an indication of the early date at which the mind of A. E.
had become possessed of the main tenets of his faith.
The characteristic correlation of Eastern and Celtic
legend is seen in *A Dream of Angus Oge*, but with this
exception, the inspiration is mainly Oriental. Doubtless the youth who first imagined *The Meditation of
Ananda* and *The Midnight Blossom* was fresh from his
initial contact with the Scriptures of the East, so

permeated are these stories with pure Oriental
mysticism.

In 1916 A. E. published *The National Being*, an
original and singularly beautiful contribution to the
otherwise hackneyed literature of contemporary Irish
politics. This eloquent plea for a co-operative com-
monwealth is at once a tract for the times and an
historical survey of Irish political ideals, in which
the splendid and generous faith of the author colours
and transcends the subject, until it becomes A. E.'s
own confession of faith and nationality. Without a
single concession to the tawdry claptrap of politicians, or the timid conventions of safe and sane
champions of society as it is, *The National Being*
achieved the fame and the popularity of a national
gospel. It was read alike by British statesmen, Sinn
Féin leaders, and the general public; it established
the author's fame as one of the few clear and absolutely disinterested minds engaged upon the Irish
problem, as part of the general problem of humanity's evolution towards a new social order.

Two years later there followed *The Candle of
Vision*, a unique spiritual autobiography, packed
with ideas and rich with beautiful reveries, an essential part of the work which A. E. had hitherto
given to the world in his verse. He describes these
meditations as "the efforts of an artist and poet to relate his own vision to the vision of the seers and
writers of the sacred books." He attempts to reveal the significance of a certain number of his spiritual adventures, and many wonderful pages are
given up to a narrative of dreams, visions and the
imaginations of the poet's boyhood, when the "mysterious life quickening within my life" began to reveal itself. His quest resolves itself into a search for
the element of truth that lies in imagination.

Assuming that our dreams are old memories re-fashioned, A. E. argues that it is "just as marvelous but not so credible" to assume that there is an artistic faculty in the subconscious memory, as to believe, with him, that dreams come "not by way of the physical senses transformed to memory," but "like the image thought transferred, or by obscure ways reflected from spheres above us, from the lives of others and the visions of others." Dreams are explicable in either of two ways; they are "self-created fantasy" or "the mirroring in the brain of an experience of soul in a real sphere of being."

Arising out of this interpretation of dreams, and governing the two-fold hypothesis of A. E., there is an interesting analysis of the difference between imagination and vision, although the two are often confounded. "If I look out of the windows of the soul," he writes, that is not an act of imagination, but a "vision of something which already exists, and which in itself must be unchanged by the act of seeing." On the other hand, "by imagination what exists in latency or essence is outrealised and is given a form in thought, and we can contemplate with full consciousness that which hitherto has been unrevealed, or only intuitionally surmised." Hence it follows that the images of imagination may be referred "definitely to an internal creator, with power to use or re-mould pre-existing forms and endow them with life, motion and voice."

An examination of the dream pictures and the visions recorded by the poet shows them to be coloured so definitely by his own artistic and metaphysical preoccupations, that the sceptical reader will be satisfied as to their being essentially refashioned memories. But *The Candle of Vision* is as free from dogmatism as from the cheap mystery-monger-ing of table-rappers and spook-hunters. It is the frank record of a mystic poet's own experiences and his speculations, inviting discussion rather than making oracular pronouncements. If, in the end, it brings us no nearer to the solution of the mystery of being, it does leave us with a more intimate conception of the poet of *Homeward*, and in possession of a beautiful piece of prose.

JOHN EGLINTON

The Theosophical Movement in Dublin not only gave us a great poet in A. E., but also our only essayist, and one of the most beautiful prose-writers in English at the present time. The subtle thinker who is known under the pseudonym of "John Eglinton" has rarely ventured outside the limits of the *genre* with which his reputation is wholly identified. He has written a few poems, but the essay has been the form most happily cultivated by him. None of his verse has been collected, and its almost anonymous publication in somewhat esoteric journals would indicate that the author does not wish to be credited with it. It would, however, be misleading to insist too strongly upon this supposition. Inaccessibility is a peculiar, but apparently essential, feature of all John Eglinton's work, and should not deter us from a reference to the deep, intellectual emotion of *The Omen*, *Acceptation*, and that tragic little poem, *Names*, rescued by Yeats for his *Book of Irish Verse*. There is a calm intensity of feeling in them, not unlike that which we have noticed in the poetry of Charles Weekes. One hears the cries and protests of the mind as it broods upon the mystery and tragedy of life. His utterances are reasoned rather than emotional or instinctive.

We must turn to the prose-writings of John Eglinton if we wish to find the thought coloured by emotion and imagination, particularly to his first book, *Two Essays on the Remnant*, published in 1895. Rarely has the passionate impatience of youth with the disillusion of first contact with the material realities of life been so finely expressed. The "heavy price the gods exact for citizenship" drives the young idealist from "the rude civic struggle" in which he has no part, and he proceeds to elaborate in harmonious prose the theory of society which will explain his own failure "to catch on as a citizen," and account for the evils of existence. It is his belief that the individual has outgrown the State, whose rate of progress is inevitably slower. The idealists are unemployed, for they must await the time when the community has come near enough to the point at which they find themselves to profit by their teaching and example. The "Remnant" must retire from society to the wilderness where, in communion with Nature, they may renew their inspiration, and preserve their faculties, until the day when the State has need of them. There would have been "no uneasy dreams for the Pharaoh of civilisation" had the Chosen People of each epoch withdrawn from a system in which they had no concern. By remaining, they become responsible for the social discontents which harass modern society. "The French Revolution was only the first of the great plagues," but many more will follow, so long as a Remnant is formed, out of sympathy with current ideals. The Unemployed Idealist, finding himself antagonised by the prevailing state of affairs, longs to escape, and "once man is glamoured with the thought of the wilderness he becomes indifferent. He is no longer a good citizen and he affects with his indifference those who should be so."

It is almost useless to summarise in dry outline
John Eglinton's thesis; the value and charm of the
book are in the writing or the quaint development
of the argument.   There is a remarkable characterisation of Wordsworth, "first and greatest of the
Unemployed," and of Goethe, who "by reason of his
prosperity became indirectly the cause of the captivity of his brethren." With great deftness of
phrase the author touches upon the various important events in the history of the Chosen People, the
"intellectuals," as he has more recently learned to
call them. He describes the Weimar of Goethe
and Schiller as "the very chief emporium of ideas in
Europe," and refers, with delightful irony, to the
"thought-raising districts of Germany" where one
may observe "how beautifully pedantry plays into
the hands of poetry." Striking is the picture of
Wordsworth in London. In spite of "the healthful
vacuity of a mind at ease," this "raw North-country
youth" is dangerous; "he exults no longer in citizenship and the flush of patriotism is withered within
him." He felt the glamour of Nature, "tremulous
with leaves," and the City became obnoxious to him,
and thus he unsettled the poets who came after him.
"No genuine child of light but is liable now to sudden
visitations from the wilderness," for "that Words-
worthian rapture, with all the mystic elements it
held in solution, has since permeated all idealism."
The revolt against city life and the artificialities of
our social organisation is, of course, an essential part
of John Eglinton's thesis and furnishes him with the
occasion for some remarkable fancies. He contrasts
the city "run to seed," when nature has deserted it,
with "a young barbaric town":

"From the engirdling walls to the threatening citadel every
hearth is kindled: there is noise of cutting and chopping and grind-

ing, a bee-like susurration of homogeneous employment; the sun-lit smoke is the city's breath, drawn freely from lungs nowhere decrepit. The young men exercise in the fields, the old men sit in council, and at sunset the daughters leap down the street to dance."

Two Essays on the Remnant is from beginning to end an appeal for such an ideal as this city symbolises. As the author so finely says, the test of the state of civilisation is "whether in assisting it the individual is astride of his proper instincts." So long as he must "crush his genius into his cleverness," so long as citizenship is possible only upon terms incompatible with the development of the best that is in him, so long will the "desire of the wilderness" disturb the peaceful coöperation of all classes. "Once the mind consents to labour for the body, that is slavery," but the Chosen People are doomed to be enslaved in this fashion, if they continue the pretence of being part of a community with which they have nothing in common. Book-making is substituted for the brick-making to which Pharaoh assigned the Chosen People of old, and the Remnant find themselves engaged to minister to "alien interests." They are set apart, because of their dexterity as "thought-artisans," and tolerated on condition that they "ply their trade" subserviently to the general need. There are valuable truths behind the fanciful form of John Eglinton's argument. His essay is a plea for the individual, in an age when the domination of the State is menacing; it is a criticism of society which carelessly allows the subjection of the creative mind to the exigencies of commercialism. The Words-worthian mysticism, or naturism rather, which has remained a constant element in the author's thought, forms an interesting corollary to the mystic panthe-

ism of A. E. The uncompromising individualism of
John Eglinton inevitably directed him to a more exclusive expression of the promptings of the mystic
faith. The ever-present nostalgia of the green fields
and rustic solitudes which runs through *Two Essays
on the Remnant* is the instinctive desire of the individualist to be literally alone with Nature. His attitude
towards life is dictated by the same feeling of revolt
against his fellowmen who have allowed life to "coag-
ulate into cities."

A. E. has always upheld the superior virtues of the
small community, he has sung of the freedom of life
in direct contact with the "Mighty Mother," yet
he never leaves the impression of fundamental antagonism to social conditions which one derives from
John Eglinton. This impression is, however, in part
erroneous, for he himself subsequently warned the
reader against the theory of the Chosen People, "in
which," as he says, "a metaphor is pressed to the
point of being recommended as a gospel." It would
be unfair to over-emphasise the exuberance of fancy
into which the young individualist was betrayed, as
it is unjust to essay a prosaic summary of his ideas.
His book is, after all, but a beautiful elaboration of
the individualistic commonplace that the majority
is always wrong. Against the excesses of an over-
strained metaphor we have to set innumerable
beauties of thought and language, which only frequent quotation could adequately convey. We
know what a magnificent structure of prose Rousseau
built upon the epigram *l'homme est bon, les hommes
sont mauvais*, and need not, therefore, resent too
sharply the almost identical, and equally paradoxical
generalisation from which *Two Essays on the Remnant* was written. This wonderful little book has
all the qualities and very few of the defects of the

writer's youth and his philosophy. It was written with uncommon skill, and balanced by the mind of an artist, at a time when the years had not yet transformed the *farouche* young idealist into the too diffident ironist of later essays. His own description of the Chosen People at work supplies the phrase which best characterises what he must then have been. In the first outpouring of divine discontent we see John Eglinton "as one who goes forth into the morning woods, in whose brain yet flaunt the pomps and processions of his dreams."

In 1902 John Eglinton collected some of the essays which he had contributed to the theosophical and other magazines. Published under the title *Pebbles from a Brook*, they are the best and most mature expression of the author. The untrammelled eagerness of *Two Essays* is gone; there are no experiments like "banausic murmur" or the "trikumia of its morning news-issue," to exasperate the misoneists. Instead we find an ironic detachment and a serene pleasure in the philosophic examination of modern ideals. A corresponding style has taken the place of the highly coloured tone of the first book. Occasionally the earlier exuberance breaks forth, as when he apostrophises the poets, taunting them with the poor subject they have in the man of these unheroic days:

". . . . a shell, his power gone from him, civilisation like a robe whirled down the stream out of his reach, in eddies of London and Paris, the truth . . . a cloudy, evaporated mass of problems over his head—this is he, homo sapiens, poor, naked, neurotic, undeceived, ribless wretch—make what you can of him, ye bards!"

But these passages are infrequent, having made way for a more subdued and more perfect dexterity of phrase. Daring similes which seemed previously to arise for the sole satisfaction of the literary sense are now employed with less disinterested intention, and have thereby acquired additional power. Noteworthy was the effect of the allusion "a palsied beldam with whiskey on thy breath and a crucifix in thy hand," in an address to Ireland, contained in the fine essay, *Regenerate Patriotism*.

It is, however, misleading to cite passages reminiscent of *Two Essays*. The pleasure which one derives from the later essays of John Eglinton is of a more intellectual and more substantial order than could be expected from the sustained *coloratura* of that admittedly extraordinary book. *Pebbles from a Brook*, particularly, is not a work to be estimated in terms of mere verbal affectiveness. Not that the graceful style, rich in subtle turns of speech, does not contribute greatly to its enjoyment. The form is a perfect clothing for the thought, so admirably adapted to it, in fact, that the idea of careless writing has become utterly dissociated from the name of the author. It seems as if John Eglinton can write only when manner and matter have blended into an exquisite harmony, making of each essay a well-embroidered tissue of ideas. But he no longer holds the attention by means of the bright designs which sparkle upon the literary fabric; for we are captured by the richness of the material itself. His fundamental attitude is still the same, he continues to measure all things from the standpoint of the individual. "Every man embodies in his own experience a fact which no omniscience can comprehend." "Man is still the measure of all things," "Give me myself; the best of yourself is for me the second best"—such are the recurring sentences, the thread upon which his reflections are strung. Every one of these essays is a pebble washed in the stream of his individualistic philosophy, an idea examined in the light of this faith in the potentialities of man. Identical as is the point of departure of this book and its predecessor, we shall find a notable modification of the initial petulance which demanded—even metaphorically, be it admitted—a withdrawal to the wilderness.

Pebbles from a Brook reveals John Eglinton as a transcendentalist of the same order as A. E., the master ideas of the poet and the essayist are identical. Man once carried within himself all the divine possibilities of human nature, he has fallen from that estate, but wisdom demands that he shall take cognisance of the fact. Now, of course, it is easy to understand the insistence upon the individual which has been noted as the chief characteristic of John Eglinton's work. He does not engage himself, like A. E., to illustrate from spiritual experience the truth of his postulate, but, assuming that it has been granted, he proceeds to a more impersonal investigation of the deductions to be drawn from it. In the first essay, *Knowledge*, his task is to demonstrate how utterly inadequate and unrelated to this fact of man's divinity is the greater part of the intellectual progress upon which modern civilisation prides itself. "The age of omniscience is the age of agnosticism," for we have failed largely to find an answer to the really vital interrogations of the human spirit: "the poet asks for truths and is given facts." We have relied in turn upon the scholar and upon the scientist, but they cannot help us; "we must begin to look to the original thinker and the poet." Unfortunately, literature aspires to live "for art's sake," an attitude which John Eglinton likens to "the declaration of a beauty past her prime, that she will have nothing more to do with men." Nor is this the only betrayal of the trust we have placed in literature, for our men of letters have allowed society to seduce them from high aims. "On occasion of each new heresy the world sends one of its representatives to be converted, and to hail the new prophet to dinner." The idealist lives on too friendly terms with popularity, he grows unmindful of the call to that mystical wilderness, whose necessity was affirmed in *Two Essays on the Remnant.* The world can be defeated only when man listens to the oracle within himself; then progress becomes, not actuality, but reality. "Unless knowledge issues in a personality our life is vain."

In *Heroic Literature* the essayist reminds us that the qualities in our Heroic Age which inspire the poet are precisely those whose absence, or neglect, are the basis of his criticism of existing conditions. Man was then "a great sombre fellow, shouting his pedigree at you when he spoke to you," for he bore latent in him the powers which have since gone out into the arts and inventions by which he is dwarfed to-day. Our endeavour, when we turn to heroic literature, must be "to get man once more into poetry." *Apostolic Succession* suggests how this vivifying conviction of human greatness may come to us. "Walking in the woods, or by the seashore, or among men, it often happens that a man experiences a rising of the tide of perception, life inundates consciousness, and as it recedes, casts up in his brain a melody, a gospel, an idea." It is after such moments of rapture as these that, as we have seen in the case of A. E., the poet renews his contact with Reality and gives us that "transcendental certainty" which John Eglinton defines as our greatest need. "We can take no delight in the infinite of nature, unless we feel that we too are infinite." In spite of the evolutionary hypothesis, so flattering to our present stage of development, the essayist asserts, with A. E., that we have suffered a declension of our powers. "Evolution knows nothing of exceptional temperaments. . . . It knows only of householders and shareholders who ride the central flood of evolutionary tendency, blown along by soft gales of natural selection." It fails to account for the appearance at the beginning of history of the conception of religion, but only from these exceptional temperaments can we get a religious certainty, "without which," as John Eglinton says, "poetry cannot be criticised, nor philosophical enquiry directed." The element wanting in modern experience will be found when our creative minds have realised that "it is not the function of genius to add new trophies to civilisation, but to disclose to men new depths within themselves."

The essays reprinted in 1906, under the title, *Bards and Saints,* differ from those just mentioned by a certain actuality previously noticeable only in *Regenerate Patriotism.* They were originally published in *Dana,* the brilliant little review edited by the author during the twelve months of its existence, from March, 1904, to April, 1905. The offence given by that analysis of popular patriotic sentiment was repeated in these later utterances, where John Eglinton comments upon similarly sacrosanct idols of the semi-political market-place, and drew upon him the hostility of the enthusiasts. An essay in *Pebbles from a Brook* entitled *The Three Qualities in Poetry* was the only republished literary criticism of his since the appearance of *Literary Ideals in Ireland* in 1899. A reprint, therefore, of some essays having literature for their subject was welcome, although a greater generosity in the number selected might have been permitted. Almost every issue of *Dana* con-

tained an article by John Eglinton as worthy of inclusion as those chosen for *Bards and Saints*.   Written with all the care and skill which the author has
devoted to the now rare art of the essayist, they
belong to the printed book rather than to the transitory pages of a review.   Those collected have been
termed literary, partly to distinguish them from the
more philosophical chapters of *Pebbles from a Brook*,
and partly because a reference to current literary discussion seems to have decided their selection.   It
would be more correct to describe them as essays
upon concrete topics of Irish life, as opposed to the
relatively abstract subjects of the former volume.

Needless to say, John Eglinton is incapable of
writing otherwise than out of a definite and ever-
present philosophy of life.   The use of the adjectives
"concrete" and "abstract" is purely relative, for
he has published essays, not journalistic articles.
The "Three Qualities" in Poetry, that most excellent
summary of the three stages in the history of poetic
literature, is typical of the best he can do when called
upon for literary criticism.   For all its abstractness
of title, it is as close to the actual as anything in
Bards and Saints.   Perhaps *The De-Davisisation of
Irish Literature* sounds less remote, but the train of
thought which runs through it is the same.   True,
the adverse criticism of Thomas Davis and his school
was calculated to displease the people who were
outraged by *Regenerate Patriotism*.   Both are the
expression of a conception of nationality, the one
relating to literature, the other to politics, somewhat
above the perception of vociferous patriots.   In the
former case John Eglinton merely anticipates a further extension of Yeats's criticism of *The Nation*
poets, in the latter, he declares his agreement with
A. E. that:

> We are less children of this clime
> Than of some nation yet unborn.

At the risk of being called an "alien" he affirms, with all the finest spirits of the Revival, that the aggressively patriotic literature associated with Davis and his followers, so far from being national, is merely political, and, at this time of day, morbid. "The expression of nationality, literature cannot fail to be," he concludes, "and the richer, more varied and unexpected that expression the better."

The Island of Saints and *A Neglected Monument of Irish Prose* are characteristic examples of the application of an ironical and detached curiosity to popular subjects, which has become so marked in the later John Eglinton. These two essays are related, in so far as both are an examination of certain religious phenomena in Ireland. In the first the author advances the theory that Irish Catholicism is an exotic, wholly out of sympathy with the natural aspirations of the Irish race. The hostility of bard and saint in Gaelic literature, the divorce of Catholicism and literature in subsequent times, and the peculiarly Protestant atmosphere of Catholic Ireland, with its Sabbatarianism and inartistic puritanism—these are the facts which, at all events, give the necessary background of reality to the slightly paradoxical contention. In the second essay, the ramifications of the problem are touched upon when the essayist explains the relation of cause and effect in the literary non-existence of the Irish Bible. Here are exhibited, in the light of a theory clearly postulated, some of the anomalies of our intellectual life, with its strange silence where certain fundamental ideas are concerned. John Eglinton has elsewhere enlarged upon the hopefulness of a recrudescence of religious bigotry. Until our system is cleared of the stifled

germs of seventeenth-century theological controversies, we shall never begin to discuss real problems
with becoming frankness. The history of the Irish
Bible becomes a symbol of the divorce between
things sacred and profane, which gives a certain
unreality to our public discussions.

Whether his subject is the Irish language (which
he rejects on æsthetic grounds) or the place of man
in society, John Eglinton is always the same master
of delicate prose. It is not necessary to agree with
him in order to feel the charm of his manner. In
Ireland we have so constantly heard unpleasant
truths unpleasantly stated that even the most *in-
transigeant* patriot should be grateful that one exception exists. Indeed, if some of our more vigorous
superstitions had more often encountered the wit of
John Eglinton their existence might be seriously
threatened, instead of being invigorated by the
blundering seriousness of "enlightened" bigots. The
controversial part of his work, however, is small, and
belongs mainly to the period of his editorial activities.
The brief existence of *Dana*, while demonstrating a
premature confidence in the capacity of our faction-
ised public to appreciate the interplay of ideas, was
far from being vain. Its sufficient justification is
found in the fact that the compatibility of literature
and journalism was proved in the person of its editor.
Apart from this, and beyond all matters of controversy, lies the fine collection of essays which have
established John Eglinton the first of our transcen-
dentalists. His is not the mysticism of A. E., but of
Wordsworth, for whom he has never ceased to express the profoundest admiration, since the day
when he greeted the name as "a far-fluttering, unat-
tainable carol to me in my prison." The contemplation of nature is not for him the occasion of those

visionary ecstasies we have found in the poet of *The Earth Breath*, but provokes the mood of philosophic revery associated with the author of *Lyrical Ballads*. John Eglinton is essentially a philosopher, not a seer or a man of action, like A. E.; he expresses the reflective, passive side of the faith of which the former is the intuitive and active exponent. The one is the complement of the other, and together they complete the record of the Theosophical Movement in Ireland. It is not in the nature of John Eglinton to become a leader, and he has regrettably allowed his most original and personal contribution to our literature, *Pebbles from a Brook*, to escape the wide publicity it deserves. In 1917, however, *Anglo-Irish Essays* appeared, and in this volume the author presents all that he wishes to preserve of what George Moore has so aptly termed his "odorous and bark-like prose." It is perhaps a too meagre sheaf of essays for those who have known and admired the earlier writings of John Eglinton, but it contains chapters which establish his right to rank with the finest English essayists.

CHAPTER XI

THE POETS OF THE YOUNGER GENERATION

IN spite of the absorption of literary talent by the Irish Theatre during the past ten years, the poetic impulse of the Eighteen Nineties was not allowed to expire. The dedication of A. E.'s *Divine Vision* indicated that a group of young poets, not yet known to the general public, was at hand to carry on the work of the generation represented by that volume—the last new book of verse to come from the original Theosophical Movement. Peculiarly fitted for intellectual leadership, A. E. became the link between his own and the rising generation when he selected the poems of this group for a collection entitled *New Songs*, which appeared shortly before *The Divine Vision*, in 1904. With this little volume he introduced the poets who had gathered about him, and were preparing, under his influence, to inaugurate the next phase of Anglo-Irish poetry. With the exception of Eva Gore-Booth, none of the contributors to *New Songs* had published verse in book form prior to its appearance. Padraic Colum, Thomas Keohler, Alice Milligan,

Susan Mitchell, Seumas O'Sullivan, George Roberts and Ella Young—these names were previously known only to readers of the more eclectic Irish periodicals. Many of the writers belonged to the Hermetic Society, where they learned from the mystic teaching of A. E. the truths which had fired his own youth. In a limited sense, therefore, *New Songs* may be described as the manifesto of a school, for its authors stood at least in that personal relation to A. E. which is called discipleship. He was their leader in a more intimate sense than was possible to any other prominent figure in the revival of our poetry.

The danger of concluding too easily that Anglo-Irish poetry has been the product of a school is illustrated, however, in this instance. Although all the facts pointed to the existence—for the first time—of such a school, the work of these young poets betrays less evidence of discipleship than did that of their predecessors, who lived in the shadow of Yeats. The latter, though rarely in personal contact with him, and too scattered to have any collective existence, were frequently imitative and constantly inspired by the author of *The Wind Among the Reeds*. The poetry of *New Songs* is the work of disciples, but A. E. is their intellectual, rather than their literary, master. His voice is not one that awakens mere echoes; it either reaches the understanding, or is unheard. Consequently, his presence must be traced in the thought, not in the literature, of his followers. It would be difficult to find grouped in one fellowship a more varied collection of verse than *New Songs*. Alice Milligan has no trace of mysticism, and sings, like Eva Gore-Booth, of legendary days. Even her pictures of the countryside are peopled with heroic figures. She cannot write of nature with the poignant simplicity of Eva Gore-Booth's *Waves of Breffny*, her inspiration is more tinged with politics. The volume of *Hero Lays*, which appeared in 1908, leaves a more characteristic impression of Alice Milligan, whose hero-worship confounds in an identical enthusiasm the heroes of legend and the leaders of modern Irish movements. She represents that modification of *The Nation* poetry, of which her friend Ethna Carbery was, as we saw, the chief voice. Her best verse is that in which the political is subordinated to the national emotion.

Ella Young and Susan Mitchell, on the other hand, could not have written as they do, had there been no Theosophical Movement. One slender volume each, *Poems* (1906) and *The Living Chalice* (1908), is all that they have offered, so far, for criticism,—a somewhat unsubstantial basis upon which to rest judgment. Both have evidently felt the touch of mysticism, and have essayed to express the profounder emotions awakened in them. If they are a little inarticulate, and profit too eagerly by the help afforded to their inexperience by more eloquent elders, we are content that this should be so, rather than that they should sacrifice obviously genuine feeling for the sake of greater independence or facility of rhyme. *The Star of Knowledge, Twilight* and *The Virgin Mother* vindicate the original quality of Ella Young's verse, and dispel the doubts which arise from *A Dream of Tir-nan-oge*—that prolonged echo. Susan Mitchell's *Living Chalice* and *Loneliness* are equally indicative of the power to give a personal inflection to the utterance of mystical verities. Her gift of parody and satire, as illustrated in her second book, *Aids to the Immortality of Certain Persons in Ireland* (1908), has been so evident as amply to justify the enlarged edition, which forms a companion volume to *The Living Chalice and other Poems*, as reissued, with additions, in 1913.

SEUMAS O'SULLIVAN

George Roberts and Thomas Keohler did not attempt to follow up the initial success which attended the publication of *New Songs*. The former preferred to give his attention to the publication of Anglo-Irish literature, while the latter abandoned authorship after the appearance of his *Songs of a Devotee* in 1906. There remain, however, the two most notable young poets of the group introduced by A. E., Seumas O'Sullivan and Padraic Colum, utterly dissimilar in every respect, except that of standing quite apart from their companions. By reason of the unmistakable originality of their work, its strong personal note evident from the beginning, Colum and O'Sullivan were very soon recognised as promising successors of Yeats and his contemporaries. It is, of course, impossible to confirm definitely such a statement. Their predecessors are fortunately still with us, and will no doubt continue to dominate the literary scene for many years. They themselves have not given more than a partial measure of their talent, and their success has been duplicated by one or two of their own generation who have since come into prominence. In the circumstances it will not be necessary to emphasise the obviously tentative nature of any contemporary estimate of their present achievement.

Seumas O'Sullivan was the first of the *débutants* in *New Songs* who ventured to publish an independent book of verse. Taking the most beautiful of his contributions to that volume as a title-piece, he issued *The Twilight People* in 1905. This was fol-

lowed three years later by *Verses Sacred and Profane*,
a smaller collection of like inspiration, the two being
representative of the earlier manner of O'Sullivan.
His very first poem gives the key in which this best
and most characteristic part of his book is set:

> It is a whisper among the hazel bushes;
> It is a long, low, whispering voice that fills
> With a sad music the bending and swaying rushes:
> It is a heart-beat deep in the quiet hills.

O'Sullivan's verse has been, for the most part, concerned with the gentle, pensive emotions of the
singer who celebrates the soft beauties of twilight.
The shadows of the poplars, the reeds and sedges of
lonely moorlands sway in a delicate rhythm which his
ears have caught. He would "seek out all frail,
immortal things," the white gleam of "foam-frail"
hands, the murmuring leaves, the gleam of "light
tresses, delicate, wind-blown" and of these he makes
his song in praise of beauty. He is unexcelled as a
painter of soft-toned pictures pervaded by the quiet
of evening solitude. *The Path, The Sheep* and *The
Herdsman* are striking examples of this faculty of
evocation, in which the interior harmony of the poet
with his surroundings is expressed:

> Slowly they pass
> In the grey of the evening
> Over the wet road
> A flock of sheep
>
> .   .
>
> Slowly they pass,
> And gleaming whitely
> Vanish away

and, as he watches, happy memories crowd in upon
him, but they pass away like the spectacle before
him:

> Whitely they gleam
> For a moment and vanish
> Away in the dimness
> Of sorrowful years;
> Gleam for a moment,
> All white, and go fading
> Away in the greyness
> Of sundering years.

Almost all O'Sullivan's poems are saturated with a wistfulness, springing from the consciousness that our moments of perfect happiness are gone before we can realise them, to return no more, except perhaps as the burden of some sad reverie. They are "delicate snatchings at a beauty which is ever fleeting," as A. E. describes them.

Seumas O'Sullivan has created a body of rare verse out of these impalpable dreams of "Shadowy Beauty," for his recent volume *An Epilogue and other Poems* (1914) shows a continuity of mood, with undiminished power of corresponding expression. In *Rain*, and that beautiful little lyric, *Lullaby*,

> Husheen the herons are crying,
> Away in the rain and sleet.

we assuredly hear the voice of the singer of *The Twilight People*. But he has learned to extend his sympathies for the capture of other themes. There seemed at one time to be a danger lest he should seek inspiration too persistently from the sources which first enchanted him. In spite, however, of the glamour of whispering shadows, and evanescent gleams of fairy-land, he began as early as 1909 to depart in a new direction from that indicated by *Verses Sacred and Profane*. In that year he published *The Earth Lover and other Verses*, a volume imbued with a less intangible spirit than its predecessors. The poems of city life are almost an innovation, so rarely have the poets of the Revival turned to the crowded street for their subjects. The more successful of O'Sullivan's efforts in this style were to come in 1912, when his collected edition *Poems* appeared. This is one of the finest books of contemporary Anglo-Irish verse, and enables the reader to form an idea of the scope and development of the poet's work. It contained almost every poem previously published by him in book form, and needs only to be supplemented by *An Epilogue* to form a complete statement of the author's position in the history of the Revival.

Although the traces of Yeats's influences are slight, he is the poet of whom one immediately thinks in studying the work of Seumas O'Sullivan. The latter is obviously of the same poetic lineage as the author of *The Wanderings of Oisin* and *The Countess Kathleen*, but his mood is very different from that of the later Yeats. He does not allow himself to be led away into symbolical elaborations of the kind that necessitate explanatory notes, whose bulk is no guarantee of increased understanding or poetical enjoyment. Such mysticism as O'Sullivan expresses belongs to the fairy order of Yeats's early work. He is thoroughly Celtic in his perception of the mystic voices and the spiritual suggestion of nature. As a rule this faith is latent and implied, rather than stated. Occasionally, as in his latest volume, he confesses his belief, which appears to be analogous with that of A. E. "I cannot pray, as Christians used to pray," he cries, "for I have seen Lord Angus in the trees." But these avowals are unusual in one whose introspection has been for the purpose of discovering within himself the emotional harmonies corresponding to certain much-loved phenomena. He is the typical disciple of A. E., revealing the influence of his master not so much in specific phrases as in the general attitude and colouring of his poetry.

With charming humility A. E. has referred to the technique of Seumas O'Sullivan: "he can get a subtle quality into his rhythms which I could not hope to acquire." This generous reference brings us to an important point of resemblance between Yeats and the younger poet. O'Sullivan is unique amongst his contemporaries by reason of his great technical skill. Even *The Twilight People* showed extreme diversity of metre, and considerable mastery of rhythmical effects and vowel combinations. He has all the love of verbal perfection which enabled Yeats to impose himself upon a generation careless of form. Seumas O'Sullivan writes slowly and with a constant care for the art of poetry, building up gradually a perfect fabric of verse, which shows a constant progression in technique. He is like Yeats, too, in so far as his work is free from a too obvious "Celticism," being profoundly national enough to take on the air of cosmopolitanism, in the best sense of the word. His verse reminds us at times of some of the modern French poets in its delight in the pure music of language. It is a pity he has not added to the three fine poems after Henri de Régnier which were republished in the collected *Poems*. There is a certain affinity of manner between the young Irish poet of the poplars and the exquisite artist of eighteenth-century French landscapes. They are both skilled in the evocation of the atmosphere attuned to the quiet melancholy of their reverie. It is as unreasonable to exact the formulation of a philosophy from Seumas O'Sullivan as to complain that he does not sing of the strenuous life of our own or the Heroic Age. He has written verses that are a delight to the ear and a joy to the spirit, in which he claims to give:

For that fierce olden ecstasy,
For that old singing, wild and brave,
Magic of wood and wind and wave,
For old high thoughts that clashed like swords,
A wisdom winnowed from light words.

It will be granted that he has succeeded in achieving that purpose. If all our poets fulfil so well their own promises we need not despair of the future.

PADRAIC COLUM

Padraic Colum's part in the constitution of *New Songs* was no less than that of O'Sullivan, either quantitatively or qualitatively. Radically different as was his verse, it incurred no risk of being overlooked in the favourable criticism bestowed upon the equally promising work of his fellow-contributor, and both were singled out for special praise. Colum, however, did not immediately attempt to confirm the encouraging judgment passed upon him. He waited three years before issuing *Wild Earth*, which appeared, with additional poems, in 1909. Although he has written a great deal of verse since then, that reissue of his first book is still the only volume of poetry he has so far published. The years following *New Songs* were claimed by the theatre, to which he contributed two of the most remarkable plays in our contemporary dramatic literature. We shall shortly have an opportunity to consider this side of the author's talent, when relating the history of the Irish Theatre, where his most complete successes were obtained. For the moment, this reference to the dramatist will suffice to explain why one small book is all that we have to represent a poet whose work is more significant than its volume would appear to warrant.

With a true instinct Padraic Colum found a title which not only fitted the particular collection of poems to which it was given, but was also a proclamation of the author himself. The fresh tang of "wild earth" comes into literature again with these songs of a peasant lad who still carries in his memory the simple, strong odour of the soil on which he was reared. He does not look at nature with the somewhat sophisticated eyes of the city-bred poet, who at best must bring to the contemplation of natural beauty a mentality coloured by the literary and philosophical theories of his *milieu*. We have already had occasion to notice how beautifully the charm and the secrets of nature may be revealed to one who seeks them, equipped with the necessary gift of vision and sympathy. We may rejoice at times, when highly cultivated art and intuitive simplicity combine to give us poetry which satisfies our sense of natural and artificial perfection. We cheerfully grant the necessary licence to the poetic artificer, so long as he shows himself conscious of the peculiar, innate quality of his material. The poet is measured by the skill and congruity of his selection and elaboration. Padraic Colum made but the slightest claim upon our artistic tolerance. With a minimum of artistic liberty he produced the maximum effect, giving us the stark poetry of life as it is felt by those living close to the soil:

Sunset and silence; a man; around him earth savage, earth broken:
Beside him two horses, a plough!

Such is the landscape in which his figures move. The poems are concerned only with these elementals, the plough, the land, the beasts of the field, and the human creatures who live for and by them. Colum excels in depicting the intimate relation of these

primordial factors of civilisation, and he knows how
to sum up existence, as it seems to men struggling
daily in contact with primitive forces. The peasant
speaks in such lines as:

> O! the smell of the beasts,
> The wet wind in the morn,
> And the proud and hard earth
> Never broken for corn.

If he allows himself to comment upon these pictures,
he does so in terms as simple as they are profound:

> Slowly the darkness falls, the broken lands blend with the savage;
> The brute-tamer stands by the brutes, a head's breadth only above
>   them.
> A head's breadth? Ay, but therein is hell's depth, and the height
>   up to heaven,
> And the thrones of the gods and their halls, their chariots, purples
>   and splendours.

There is a rugged strength in such poems of ploughers
and sowers and herdsmen, admirably reflected in the
hexameters just quoted. They are never marred
by the obtrusion of merely literary effects. In all
Wild Earth there is not an allusion which betrays
the background of a literature other than that which
one expects in the Irish countryside. The much-
admired *Poor Scholar of the Forties* supplies the only
legitimate atmosphere of learning, with its pathetic
reference to an essentially Irish tragedy. The author
had doubtless personal memories to assist him in
evoking that pitiable figure. There is a suggestion
of autobiography in the verse:

> And I must walk this road that winds
> 'Twixt bog and bog, while east there lies
> A city with its men and books,
>   With treasures open to the wise,
> Heart-words from equals, comrade-looks;
> Down here they have but tale and song,
> They talked Repeal the whole night long.

Another aspect of this absence of literary allusion is the freedom of Colum's poetry from any suggestion of imitation. It is possible for a more keen than friendly critic to ascribe a model to a large number of poems written in Dublin within the past decade. There is, of course, a trace of over-emphasis in such a proceeding, which makes no allowance for the unconscious influences of our literary atmosphere, tending inevitably to lend an air of homogeneity to the work of the younger poets. Many have, it is true, deliberately echoed their elders, especially in their first books, but this evidence of a weakness common to all beginners must not be insisted upon too harshly. So far as Padraic Colum is concerned, he appears to have escaped completely even the suspicion of being a borrower. *Wild Earth* presents no analogies with anything written by his immediate predecessors. The young poet had neither Yeats's passion for the music of verse, nor the mystic vision of A. E. Unlike his contemporaries he does not oscillate between the two, being as far removed from the one as the other. The impression conveyed by his work approximates rather to that Douglas Hyde's *Songs of Connacht*. Not that Colum's Catholicism ever becomes articulate, as in Hyde's *Religious Songs*, or that he displays any of the dialectic energy of the *Love Songs*. His thought is as devoid of specific religious colour as his language is devoid of that Gaelic exuberance which Synge caught from the same sources as Hyde. What then, it may be asked, is left of the suggested resemblance between *Wild Earth* and Hyde's translations? Very little, it must be confessed, that is tangible. There is, however, an undoubted kinship of spirit between the poet of the Midlands and the poets of the West in *The Songs of Connacht*. Probably it is their common origin which unites them. They all sing the same song of peasant life, the emotions they render, the scenes they describe, belong to an identical rural civilisation. Writing of the peasantry from the inside, while unspoiled by urban sophistications, Colum responded to the deeper race tradition which still survived from the days when the Connacht poets were similarly inspired. He has brought once more the peasant mind into Anglo-Irish poetry, which is thus renewed at the stream from which our national traditions have sprung, for it is the country people who still preserve the Gaelic element in Irish life, the beliefs, the legends and the usages which give us a national identity. So long as he continues to cherish those impressions of early life, so long as he retains his original imprint, Padraic Colum will contribute an essential part to the growth of the literature created by the Revival. Fortunately he has not lost that eagerness of mind peculiar to the imaginatively young. He still can view things with a certain fresh, all-consuming curiosity which lends a specially naïve charm to his work. He is at his best when he is simple.

JAMES STEPHENS

James Stephens was not one of the contributors to *New Songs*, but as he stands in the same relation to its editor as the young writers we have mentioned, it will be more convenient to overlook the chance which made his the latest name of distinction in literary Ireland. Had he come to A. E. with the others, we cannot doubt that he would have been included in their company, for it was largely because of identical encouragement that a new poet was formally introduced to us in 1909, as the dedication of *Insurrections* indicated. Shortly after the appearance of this volume the activities of Stephens were turned in another direction by the extraordinary success of two prose works, to which we shall return in a later chapter. His recognition as a prose writer at once dominated his reputation as a poet, having come to him in the short interval between 1909 and 1912, when *The Hill of Vision* was published as a successor to *Insurrections*. We notice, therefore, a point of resemblance between Colum and Stephens; both became widely known, immediately after they had been introduced as poets, in an entirely different branch of literature. However, Stephens did not allow this popularity to distract him from his original intention; the novelist did not absorb the poet so completely as did the dramatist in the case of Padraic Colum. He has found in himself the material for three books of verse, in addition to his prose work.

On its appearance in 1909, when the author was quite unknown, *Insurrections* did not receive very widespread attention. One or two critics, who were in touch with the literary undercurrents, used their influence to bring the book to the notice of the discerning, but influential comment was lacking, as a rule. It was not until James Stephens had become famous as the writer of *The Crock of Gold* that his first volume was favourably reconsidered. The conclusion to be drawn from this fact is too obvious to require emphasis. It is more interesting to note a probably contributory cause of neglect, as evidenced in some of the criticisms of a friendly nature. Even appreciative critics felt obliged to insist upon the absence of "the Celtic convention" in Stephens's verse. He evidently seemed unconvincingly Irish to that numerous class of readers, professional and otherwise, who have a formula for "Celtic" poetry, and are puzzled, disappointed or indignant, when an Irish poet departs from it. What this formula, this famous "convention" may be, only the English journalist can tell, since he has invented it. The poetry of Ireland has certainly national characteristics, like the poetry of France or England; all three have produced conventional poets, writing without originality or inspiration, but nobody has yet devised the terms English or French "convention," especially to denote the characteristic poetry of those countries. In Ireland, apparently, our poets are supposed to turn out rhyme according to some trade-marked pattern. When they do so, their admirers are charmed at the results of "the Celtic convention," while hostile critics dismiss contemptuously what they deem to be a mechanical product. The misunderstanding, whether it be friendly or otherwise, might be avoided if these critics would recollect that Irish verse is not more necessarily created by literary formulæ than that of any other country. Strange as it may seem, our poets do not manipulate *clichés* with a view to obtaining "Celtic effects." Many are weak and imitative, many are young and unformed, they deserve whatever censure befits that condition. But they are equally entitled to be considered as aiming at self-expression. In short, the benevolent use of the term "Celtic convention" is a denial of personal and national characteristics, its unfriendly use is an unwarranted extension of what might be legitimate criticism of unoriginal or immature poetry.

James Stephens is as truly Irish in *Insurrections* as if leprecauns, banshees and fairies, and all the other adjuncts of accepted Celticism, abounded on every page. So far as one can discover, these are the essen-

tial features of the convention to which Stephens
is alleged to be hostile. They are certainly as little
in evidence here as they are frequent in some of his
later work. Neither their presence nor their absence
has any relation to the poet's nationality, nor is a test
of his literary quality. Who would think of ignoring
Flaubert's *Salammbo* as a masterpiece of French
prose, in order to insist, with friendly or hostile
intent, upon its "Carthaginian Convention," as estimated by the frequency or infrequency of his references to specific aspects of the life of Carthage?
Preposterous as that would be, it is practically the
attitude of a great many critics of Anglo-Irish literature. Its admirers and detractors alike suffer from
the hallucination that our folk-lore, legends and customs are merely literary stereotypes applied mechan-
ically. The former appeal in desperation to "Celtic
convention," when confronted with an original talent, the latter entertain a superstitious enmity
against leprecauns and the like.

Insurrections does not offend the exclusive intoler-
ance of the second class of criticism referred to. It
was, however, a surprise for the worshippers of
formulæ, none of those in use being applicable.
Stephens can hardly have conceived an insurrection
against them as the reason of his title, which represented his attitude towards life rather than literature.
Rebelling against conventionality, he could not but
incidentally flout the laws of conventional Irish
poetry. For one thing, he wrote of the city more
than of the country, and his verse was uncoloured
by legendary lore or folk tradition. His imagination
is not haunted by any natural mysticism, the mysterious presences of hillside and valley do not whisper
to him, his fantasies are, as it were, intellectual, as
would be the dreams of a city child, as contrasted

with the child born in suggestive atmosphere of the country. *Seumas Beg*, for instance, in spite of its village scene, reveals the imaginative life of the boy who reads the adventure stories of urban childhood, and can invest with the same romance the old sailor who tells of stirring events in distant seas and who teaches him the use of tobacco. Similarly remote from the conventional "Celtic" imagination and peculiarly characteristic of Stephens is *What Tomas an Buile said in a Pub:*

> I saw God. Do you doubt it?
> Do you dare to doubt it?
> I saw the Almighty Man. His hand
> Was resting on a mountain, and
> He looked upon the world and all about it:
> I saw him plainer than you see me now,
> You mustn't doubt it.

The quintessence of James Stephens is in this combination of the grotesque and the profound, all part of that naïve irreverence with which the poet contemplates terrestrial and cosmic phenomena. The last verse of this poem expresses with perfect adequacy an idea which none but Stephens would have dared to treat so simply:

> He lifted up His hand—
> I say he heaved a dreadful hand
> Over the spinning earth, then I said, "Stay,
> You must not strike it, God; I'm in the way;
> And I will never move from where I stand."
> He said, "Dear child, I feared that you were dead,"
> And stayed His hand.

The insurgent note of *Insurrections* is not, however, limited to this almost colloquial treatment of profound themes, which is more characteristic of his later work, and is especially developed in his prose. His insurgency is shown rather in a general determination to see life stripped of conventionalised romance. *The Street Behind Yours* typifies Stephens's vision of the city:

> The night droops down upon the street
> Shade after shade. A solemn frown
>   Is pressing to
>   A deeper hue
> The houses drab and brown. . . .

O'Sullivan might have begun with such lines, but the harsh realism, and resignation in the face of ugliness, which mark the progress of the poem, are unlike anything written by Stephens's contemporaries. He sees the squalor of poverty with the dispassionate eyes of experience, without bitterness, perhaps, as one describing the familiar facts of daily existence. If the poet were not so buoyant and natural, he might be suspected of cynicism, but the term is quite inapplicable to these tragic little pictures. Candour and optimism are the springs of insurrection in Stephens. He is no more depressed by what he sees in the gutter than he is abashed by the magnificence of heaven. A strong sense of human fellowship enables him to retain his presence of mind, even in his relations with the superhuman.

The Hill of Vision, apart from one or two survivals from an earlier mood, brings us into a different world from that of *Insurrections*. Having ascended the eminence indicated by his title, Stephens is now more free to let his spirit wander in search of experience. Although no longer constrained to insist upon his right to view life from his own particular angle, he remains as insurrectionary as ever. He has left the city behind him, and adventures in realms more unconfined. Friends of the "Celtic convention" doubtless found *The Hill of Vision* more in harmony with their preconceptions, for here the poet has found his way into the country. He greets the fairies, however, in a tone of familiar friendship not quite in accordance with the prescribed rules. There is much of Stephens in that vagabond who says in *Mac Dhoul:*

> I saw them all,
> I could have laughed out loud
> To see them at their capers;
> That serious, solemn-footed, weighty crowd
> Of angels, or say resurrected drapers: . . .

It is with such whimsical fancies that Stephens recounts his visions of that super-terrestrial world of which the mystic poets have reverently written. By comparison he seems like the tramp Mac Dhoul, whose sense of humour is revolted by the staid company of angels:

> And suddenly,
> As silent as a ghost,
> I jumped out from the bush,
> Went scooting through the glaring, nerveless host
> All petrified, all gaping in a hush:
> Came to the throne and, nimble as a rat,
> Hopped up it, squatted close, and there I sat
> Squirming with laughter till I had to cry
> To see Him standing there. . . .

Mac Dhoul was hurled incontinently to earth for his irreverent intrusion, but announced himself impenitent by preparing to sing a song of less elevated beings. To some, no doubt, the poet's escapades appear of a similar character, and they have attempted to punish his irreverence accordingly. But we need have no fear that Stephens will violate the sanctities, where imagination allows him to play, with grotesque effect.

There has been, perhaps, too much emphasis of one side of James Stephens's talent, the side, moreover, which has been most adequately expressed in his prose. There, as we shall see, this exuberance of the fantastic spirit does not so easily incur the risk of being misunderstood. Not that *The Hill of Vision* really justifies any misunderstanding of the poet's sense of values. *The Fulness of Time* is an interesting example of the transition which prepares us for the more powerful verses of his riper manner. There is just the faintest suggestion of the early *Insurrections* in the matter-of-fact precision of:

> On a rusty iron throne
> Past the furthest star of space
> I saw Satan sit alone,
> Old and haggard was his face; . . .

but there is restraint and depth, announcing a capacity for philosophic emotion hardly suspected in his first book. *The Lonely God*, to which the poem quoted leads by natural progression, is a fine conception, whose fulfilment is accompanied by all the tokens of great poetic strength, descriptive, narrative and intellectual. Shorter, but equally significant, is *Eve*, which presents analogies with the poetry of A. E., being informed by an identity of thought. Evidence of A. E.'s influence upon Stephens can be found nowhere more beautifully revealed than in *The Breath of Life*, a poem unsurpassed by any of the younger Irish writers:

> The breath that is the very breath of life
> Throbbed close to me: I heard the pulses beat,
> That lift the universes into heat:
> The slow withdrawal, and the deeper strife
> Of His wide respiration, like a sea
> It ebbed and flooded through immensity.

The closing verses paint the coming of dawn in colours combined by an artist who can convey a new delight in that eternal wonder.

Published in 1915, *Songs from the Clay* is the book of a writer now known all over the English-speaking world. If the fame of the *Crock of Gold* tended to obscure the merits of *The Hill of Vision*, its influence has been the reverse in the present instance. Many readers of the poet's latest volume will have been procured by the charm of the prose-writer. *Songs from the Clay* does not need any reflected light to attract attention, but it cannot be said to mark any advance upon the poems which immediately preceded it. It has not the irregularities of *The Hill of Vision*, there is a firmness of technique indicating progress in the art of verse, but this even level of execution excludes the soaring as well as the falling of the earlier poetry. One is reminded more frequently of *Insurrections* than of the second volume, but now there is something a little too conscious in the grotesque which pleased when it seemed instinctive. *The Four Old Men*, for example, has a too deliberate air of unexpectedness to compare with *Hate*, that early poem in which, though entirely dissimilar, the same effect was secured in the last line. *The Satyr*, *The Snare* and some others, might be included in *The Hill of Vision;* they are an indication of a talent not fully exploited in the collection as a whole. It is a pity that the author did not wait until material for a book of verse was at hand ample enough to permit the exclusion of those attempts at recapturing the success of his first volume. The spontaneity of the original "insurrectionary" mood is not in them, and they merely detract from the quality of such poems as *The Road* or *The Liar*. Perhaps the destiny of Stephens was that he should find in prose the happiest exercise of his delightful imagination. His recognition has been so sudden and so rapid that positive assertion as to the significance of his separate achievements in prose and verse are of little assistance in estimating what may be the subsequent evolution of his work. He is happily at the outset of his career, which may ultimately be identified with the branch of literature to which he was first attracted. At the present time the contrary would seem to be indicated by the fact that *The Hill of Vision* remains his most noteworthy contribution to contemporary poetry.

JOSEPH CAMPBELL (SEOSAMH MACCATHMHAOIL)

Standing a little apart from the group of poets just mentioned is the writer who, until recently, signed his verse with the Gaelic form of his name, Joseph Campbell, the latter having been associated only with his later dramatic and prose work. Since he appears to have abandoned "Seosamh MacCathmhaoil," we may now use the English form, in spite of the fact that it was not identified with any of the verse we shall mention, prior to *Irishry* published in 1914.

In the same year as saw the publication of *New Songs*, the literary spirit of Ulster crystallised in the establishment of the Ulster Literary Theatre, and the creation of an interesting review, *Uladh*, whose first number appeared in November, 1904. The most important contributor to that issue was Joseph Campbell, one of the editors, whose synonymous Gaelic signature introduced him as the author of a prose fantasy of Northern legend, and a dramatic piece, *The Little Cowherd of Slainge*, also in prose, and dedicated to the Ulster Theatre. Shortly before this there had appeared a charming work of collaboration, *Songs of Uladh*, which contained the first publication of Campbell's verse in book form. This handsome work, illustrated by the poet's brother, is a collection of traditional Ulster melodies, in which Joseph Campbell's share was to provide English words for the songs, whose music had been gathered from the lips of the Donegal peasantry. The sympathy with the Ulster folk-tradition evidenced by these renderings of popular ballads, and the intimate interest of the explanatory notes, point to the subsequent development of the poet's talent. At the same time they explain why the author belongs to a different category from his contemporaries. He was moulded by other influences, and is, in spite of his later residence in Dublin, an Ulster poet, carrying with him the atmosphere of his early environment.

In the following year, 1905, Joseph Campbell's first collection of poems, *The Garden of the Bees*, was published in Belfast. It was a book of uncertain rhythms and faulty rhymes, containing more evidence of the young poet's reading than of himself. The inevitable memory of Yeats is present in certain characteristic phrases, although not so frequently as to stamp the author as a disciple. He is saved from this by the distinctly Northern Gaelic flavour of many of the more promising verses. *The Rushlight* followed in 1906, a more authentic herald of the poetry with which Campbell is now identified. It opens with that fine poem:

> I am the mountain singer—
> The voice of the peasant's dream,
> The cry of the wind on the wooded hill,
> The leap of the trout in the stream.

which is, so to speak, a declaration of the poet's intentions, so aptly does it summarise the scope of the volume:

Quiet and love I sing—
The cairn on the mountain crest,
That cailin in her shepherd's arms,
The child at its mother's breast.

Beauty and peace I sing—
The fire on the open hearth,
The cailleach spinning at her wheel,
The plough in the broken earth.

The Rushlight is a book of folk-poetry, written out of
the same inspiration as Colum's *Wild Earth*. The
author returns to the soil of Ulster with results which
make the reader forget the banalities of *The Garden
of the Bees*. The best poems of the latter are reprinted, *The Golden Hills of Baile-Eocain, I will go
with my Father a-Ploughing*, and even *Songs of
Uladh* is laid under contribution. In thus reverting
to his origins Campbell found his truest vein. When
he sings of the simple things of Irish life—the peasant
girls, the women at their doors, the tales of faery,
the tranquil, healthy joys and the natural tragedies
of the peasantry—he is unequalled. He attains the
same simplicity as Colum; he is free from literary
mannerism when he turns his attention to these
fundamental aspects of existence as seen and lived
in the face of nature. He has been rather naïvely
accused of treating the Christian mysteries as folk-
lore, as if he were not in harmony with an essential
feature of the still-living Gaelic tradition in so doing.
Preferable to the almost orthodox, if rather unex-
pectedly Whitmanesque, *O Beauty of the World*, is
The Gilly of Christ:

I am the gilly of Christ,
The mate of Mary's son;
I run the roads at seeding-time,
And when the harvest's done.

> I sleep among the hills,
> The heather is my bed;
> I dip the termon-well for drink,
> And pull the sloe for bread.

As indicating how much of the later Joseph Campbell—in a sense, the earlier and most original—was in *The Rushlight*, we may note that two of the poems most admired became the title-pieces of subsequent volumes, *The Gilly of Christ* (1907) and *The Mountainy Singer* (1909). These were preceded by a curious booklet, *The Man-Child*, also published in 1907. The latter is described by the author as "an attempt at the expression of the theory that Art, being a thing removed from Life, is unelemental, exaggerated, false." As for the title, it is to be understood as "a symbol of the virile and regenerate Ireland that is now springing into being." Formidable as all this sounds in the foreword to a mere handful of verse, the latter are not submerged by theories and intentions. Quotations, ranging from S. Chrysostom to Nietzsche, and including Carlyle, Whitman, and A. E., appear as mottoes to each poem, but, nevertheless, they do not obscure the natural beauties of such lines as:

> The silence of unlaboured fields
> Lies like a judgment on the air:
> A human voice is never heard:
> The sighing grass is everywhere—
> The sighing grass, the shadowed sky,
> The cattle crying wearily!

The Mountainy Singer, Campbell's first substantial volume of collected verse, contains the best of his work between 1905 and 1909, many additional poems being included with those previously published. The two manners which were indicated in *The Gilly of Christ* and the poem which gives its name to this collection, cover, broadly speaking, all that he has preserved in this book. On the one hand are the songs of country life and legend, on the other, the poems of Christian folk-lore. The latter, here revised and more numerous, are perhaps the most original part of Campbell's work. Others have sought and found close to the soil the material of poetry; in this respect Padraic Colum and he are very similar. But the author of *Wild Earth* has never cared to elaborate the Catholic mysteries into verse of a strange folk-charm. Joseph Campbell's handling of these themes owes nothing either to Yeats or to Lionel Johnson. Yeats found in the ritual of the Church a field of symbolism, Johnson's voice was that of the ascetic English Catholic. Campbell is unlike them, without, however, approximating to the simple, devotional spirit of Katharine Tynan. His simplicity is his own, and is best characterised by that criticism which reproached him with treating religion as folk-lore. *Every Shuiler is Christ, I met a Walking-Man,* and the like—what are they but skilful interpretations of Christian beliefs as they are coloured by the peasant mind? The poet has done in verse something analogous to the miracle plays of Douglas Hyde. We know how Hyde's profound knowledge of Gaelic, with its oral and written literature, has helped him in this work of reconstruction. In both Irish and English he has captured and preserved the fundamental traits of our native genius. We may therefore welcome this evidence that one of our younger poets has found a path which leads straight to the fountain-head of national tradition.

A certain similarity between the "mountainy singer" and the poet of *Wild Earth* has been suggested, but it would be erroneous to suppose that his religious poems constitute the sole originality of

Joseph Campbell. They are certainly unique, inasmuch as none of his contemporaries has followed or preceded him in this direction. To that extent, they are the most distinguishing feature of his poetry. As a delineator of peasant types and scenes, however, Campbell has a very distinctive manner. For proof it is only necessary to turn over the pages of *Irishry* (1914), his latest work. There is probably less in this volume than in *The Mountainy Singer*, which the more critical mood of later years will prompt him to excise. It is, to quote a phrase from the preface, "a pageant of types," drawn from every quarter of Ireland. A couple of years earlier, *Mearing Stones* (1911), a most unusual collection of prose sketches, recording a "tramp in Donegal," demonstrated the poet's capacity for impressionistic portraiture. Not only the verbal pictures, but the black and white designs with which the book was illustrated, showed that the eyes of an artist were the complementary gift of nature to a talent already well endowed. Much has been written of Synge's Wicklow and Kerry notebooks, but their interest is that which would naturally obtain concerning the raw material of the dramatist's art. In *Mearing Stones* there is certainly the material for the poems and plays of Campbell, but it is not raw material. The sketches are perfect of their kind, and were wisely published, not as an afterthought, but as the deliberate expression of a new phase of the author's development. Let us hope they are an earnest of future achievement in this *genre*.

Meanwhile *Irishry* has come to give us in verse something akin to those sketches of Donegal. Here it is not a county, but a country, which has been drawn upon by an impressionist in words. With the greater economy of line imposed by his medium

Joseph Campbell has drawn a series of pictures whose every stroke catches the eye of imagination. There is power in these outlines of typical figures: the horse-breaker, the fiddler, the turf-gatherer, the Orangeman, and the unfrocked priest. But he does more than indicate his figures, he endows them with the thoughts and language which constitute their class characteristics. When the poet's own voice is heard it is to remind us of the "royal dead" who peopled the land before those familiar characters of whom he writes. The decay of all things is recalled in *The Turf-Man*, who carries in his wicker-basket the last vestiges of the proud trees that flourished in the days of the Red Branch heroes. The representatives of humanity are changed, but, behind the humble ploughers, fiddlers and shepherds, Campbell sees the kings and warriors of old. As he views the Irish scene he is conscious of a continuity of tradition and spirit, which attaches the people to distant origins of which they know perhaps nothing but what is revealed by some remnant of the past, surviving in a legend or a phrase. With courage he approaches even the most conventionally unpoetic types, *The Gombeen* and *The Pig-Killer*, for example, or *The Labourer*, that remarkable vision of a most unpromising corner of Dublin life. He is quite modern, too, in his selection of studies, being free from the obsession of the Celtic, as well as many another convention. A finely conceived picture is that of *The Old-Age Pensioner:*

> He sits over the glimmering coal
> With ancient face and folded hands:
> His eye glasses his quiet soul,
> He blinks and nods and understands.
> In dew wetted, in tempest blown,
> A Lear at last come to his own.

In this little poem he conveys all the tragedy of existence for the poor in Ireland, with its now relatively happy ending. In no country can the sudden recognition of one of our social obligations have meant so much as to the many Irish recipients of the Old Age Pension.

Irishry observes the balance between excessive idealisation and the sanguinary, expletive realism recently so popular with the more widely read English poets. Campbell is realistic in that he is perfectly natural. Violent language is rarely necessary for his purpose, and he has done well to avoid superfluous occasions for it. To realise the superiority of this book one has only to compare it with the more or less kindred studies of humble life published within the past few years in England. All the beauty, dignity and pathos of Irish country life are preserved; the humour, the evil and the ugliness of certain conditions are faithfully reflected, but the whole is a well-balanced, encouraging achievement. Life drawn by the hand of an artist and coloured by the imagination of a true poet is very different from life chalked out by literary pavement artists, and melodramatised by "best-sellers." It is pleasant to notice that *Irishry*, with its predecessor, *Mearing Stones*, has secured a measure of attention and appreciation far beyond that enjoyed by any of the author's earlier works. For some reason Joseph Campbell has had to wait longer than others, not his superiors, for recognition. Perhaps this fact will ultimately be in his favour, as he is in no danger of failing to fulfil the promise of his first book. On the contrary, he has so greatly exceeded the hopes which might permissibly have been held of his youthful verse that he may be glad it escaped undue prominence. Technically his work has constantly improved. He has radically altered his style since *The Garden of the Bees,* and is now unquestionably amongst the first of the younger Irish poets. Fortunately for him, the usual process, where Irish literature is concerned, has been reversed. Instead of being hailed at first as a genius, in 1905, his merits are likely to be estimated by reference to his mature work, *The Mountainy Singer* and *Irishry.* The factor which has remained constant, in spite of changes of form and manner, is the content, which brings together his earliest and latest verse. When sympathy, instinct and knowledge sent him into Donegal to collect the *Songs of Uladh,* he was following the natural mould of his talent. The strength and charm of Joseph Campbell are in his intimate interpretation of the peasant, as he works and dreams, as a man and a symbol.

Enough has been said to indicate that the stream of Anglo-Irish verse has been renewed by fresh currents, whose force will guarantee a continuous flow of poetry for some years to come. The more individual talents have now been mentioned as representing the main tendencies of the present time, and because they illustrate most adequately the nature of the new generation's contribution to our poetic literature. It would be easy to extend enquiry to as many writers again as have been considered in this chapter, but the desire to be comprehensive would lead us far afield into the regions of very minor poetry. Some names call only for a passing reference because of their rapid disappearance from the active list, others, because they do not seem to stand for any important tendency not noticeable elsewhere. Of the former we have such instances as Paul Gregan, whose *Sunset Town* announced him as the first of A. E.'s disciples, some fifteen years ago. This book, bearing the imprint of the Hermetic Society, was an early indication of the impulse given to a second generation of poets by the Theosophical Movement, as it ultimately established itself in Dublin. Gregan, however, withdrew from public notice, and his verse remains isolated, like that of Thomas Boyd, a young writer who was instantly recognised as a poet of considerable charm, when his *Poems* appeared in 1906. It is a pity that he, too, depends solely upon the anthologists to save from oblivion some beautiful verses, the measure of a great loss.

James H. Cousins and Thomas MacDonagh belong to another category. Both have several volumes of verse to their credit, and are favourably known to the general public. Strictly speaking the former should not be counted amongst the poets of the younger generation, as his first book, *Ben Madighan and other Poems*, was contemporaneous with *Homeward: Songs by the Way*. But that volume and its immediate successors, in the purely imitative, eighteenth-century manner, did not bring the author the success he now enjoys, which dates approximately from the same period as saw the arrival of his younger contemporaries. He was engaged in the initial enterprise which led to the creation of the Irish National Theatre, and owes his reputation to the work he has written under the inspiration of Irish legend. It is noteworthy that the book which inaugurated his later and more successful phase, *The Quest*, was published in 1906, after the Dramatic Movement had fully expanded. The most interesting pages are those containing the poetic drama, *The Sleep of the King*, whose production in 1902 was the point of departure of the National Theatre Society. Since 1906 James H. Cousins has main-tained a good level of workmanship, without either serious retrogression or remarkable progress. He uses the sonnet form with skill, and in his latest work, *Straight and Crooked* (1915), he has preferred the short lyric to those lengthy narratives of legend like *The Marriage of Lir and Niav*, *The Going Forth of Dana* and *Etain the Beloved*, which constitute the bulk of his work. Whatever be his subject, he writes with a certain carefulness and absence of subtlety, which reveal him as following largely the pre-Revival tradition of Anglo-Irish poetry. Moore, Aubrey de Vere (and even Byron), are the names which friendly critics mention when instituting comparisons. It is curious that the interest in mysticism betrayed by his prose writing has not appreciably determined the character of his verse.

Thomas MacDonagh preceded the younger poets heretofore mentioned by one year, his *Through the Ivory Gate* having been published in 1903, but he is in every respect coeval with them. From the first, he showed himself strongly influenced by the Gaelic tradition, and his translations have been highly praised by competent critics. If one compares his renderings with those of the older writers, in cases where the theme is identical, the superiority of the newcomer is evident. His version of *The Fair-Haired Girl* may be cited as an example of his power, the more so, as Samuel Ferguson has also left us his interpretation of the same original. Reference has already been made to the weakness of Ferguson's adaptations from Gaelic. He is, as a rule, too conventional and "literary" to reproduce successfully the spirit of the Irish text. Mac-Donagh's verses are peculiarly fine in their Gaelic atmosphere:

> The stars stand up in the air,
>   The sun and the moon are gone,
> The strand of its waters is bare,
>   And her sway is swept from the swan.
>
> Three things through love I see,
>   Sorrow and sin and death—
> And my mind reminding me
>   That this doom I breathe with my breath

contrasted with Ferguson's:

> The sun has set, the stars are still,
> The red moon hides behind the hill;
> The tide has left the brown beach bare,
> The birds have left the upper air.
>
> I through love have learned three things;
> Sorrow, sin and death it brings;
> Yet day by day my heart within
> Dares shame and sorrow, death and sin.

But only detailed comparison can give an adequate idea of the relative merits of the two translations. Thomas MacDonagh is evidently at his best in such work, for in spite of occasional happy glimpses of the folk-mind in *Songs of Myself* (1911), the volume leaves the impression of not being very distinctive. The collected edition, *Lyrical Poems*, published in 1913, contains all that the author would wish remembered of his four books.

A species of premonition seems to have prompted the publication of this book, for it was destined to be the last work of MacDonagh's to be issued during his lifetime. He was executed in Dublin as one of the leaders of the Irish rebellion of April, 1916, closing his career in the midst of such a tragedy as inspired his play, *When the Dawn is Come* (1908), and many of his finest poems. In the verses entitled *Of a Poet Captain*, for example, he wrote his own epitaph.

As befits a teacher of literature, and the author of a treatise on metrics, MacDonagh's work shows him in complete control of his medium; he is rarely faulty or obscure. The best application of his talent was in the interpretation of Gaelic poetry, where his translations were marked by great metrical skill coupled with a passionate sense of nationality.

Another translator of distinction is Alfred Perceval Graves, whose *Irish Poems* (1908) collected into two volumes the verses of many years. He contributed in 1889 to *Lays and Lyrics of the Pan-Celtic Society*, but even before that time he had made a name as a writer of songs. A volume of mainly reprinted pieces, *Father O'Flynn and other Irish Lyrics*, was issued the same year, deriving its title from the song which has made the author universally famous. As a matter of fact, it is by his services to Irish music that A. P. Graves has established his reputation in a very special field of the Revival, rather than by his purely poetical labours. These, however, are not to be dismissed as negligible, and were it not that the song-writer has completely overshadowed the poet, we might have placed him beside his friends and contemporaries, George Sigerson and Douglas Hyde, with whom, as a translator, he presents many analogies. He resembles Samuel Ferguson perhaps more than any other writer, by reason of the variety of his interest in the renaissance of Irish culture. Music, folk-lore and country-songs have found in him a sympathetic student and interpreter, as his *Irish Literary and Musical Studies* (1913) recently testified. His editorial activities on behalf of Anglo-Irish literature have been numerous, from the time of his *Purcell Papers* and *Songs of Irish Wit and Humour*, in the Eighties, down to the recently inaugurated "Every Irishman's Library," to which he has also given a useful anthology of Irish poetry. He has played an important part in the building up of the Irish Literary Society, of which he was honorary secretary, and is now one of the vice-presidents. For all these evidences of active sympathy and participation, as well as for his more personal contributions to the poetic Revival, Alfred Perceval Graves is entitled to the serious attention of those interested in the Irish Literary Movement.

Of the most recent poets who have attracted attention it is difficult to speak or to prophesy, until they have given us more than the single volume of their début upon which to base our judgment. In the case of Joseph Plunkett, this hope has been dramatically extinguished by his death in the tragic company of Thomas MacDonagh and Padraic Pearse, another fine young talent of which Ireland is now intellectually the poorer. While Pearse's work was in Gaelic, and, therefore, outside the scope of the present history, Plunkett's was a part of the revival of Anglo-Irish literature. He had published only one book of verse, *The Circle and the Sword*, which appeared in 1911, and was favourably received by many who caught in it an echo of that Catholic mysticism associated with Francis Thompson and the English poets of Catholicism, rather than with their Irish contemporaries. Irish mysticism and Irish Catholicism, as we have already seen, are very differently manifested in the writers of Ireland's Renaissance. Plunkett died so young that we cannot do more than admit the undeniable promise of the brief record which has been left. A volume of his contributions to *The Irish Review* (1911–1914) would help to substantiate the claims of his first book.

The promise of a new talent was revealed by Lord

Dunsany in a lecture to the National Literary Society on Francis Ledwidge, whose *Songs from the Fields* in 1915 confirmed the lecturer's judgment, but the young poet's death during the war has left us with only the promise of the single posthumous volume in which all his work has been collected. More remarkable, however, was the discovery of a young poet, still in his 'teens when *The Vengeance of Fionn* revealed the name of Austin Clarke in 1911. The book was the occasion of some controversy between admirers and critics of the richly coloured style and florid romantic imagination which characterised this epic of Grania, the strangely neglected heroine of the old legends, whose glory has always been dimmed by that of Deirdre. But there is a note in this youthful poem which has not been heard so beautifully since the first appearance of *The Wanderings of Oisin*. Austin Clarke has also that prodigal wealth of colour and imagery, that enchanting magic of evocation, which gives a fire and a glamour to the adventures of both Oisin and Fionn. His second poem, *The Fires of Baal*, for all the difference of theme and inspiration, has substantiated the claim raised by A. E. amongst others on behalf of an accomplishment so rich and so young. The qualities and defects of his work may be seen in *The Vengeance of Fionn*.

If "Shelley's Italian light" troubled W. B. Yeats in his youth, as he has confessed, it is obvious that Austin Clarke, too, must rid himself of Yeatsian and similar influences, if he is ever to write the epic he has here undertaken so courageously. But it is the promise rather than the achievement of this young poet which justifies the hope he has aroused of more substantial work than the average volume of pretty lyrics.

CHAPTER XII

THE DRAMATIC MOVEMENT: FIRST PHASE

THE IRISH LITERARY THEATRE: EDWARD MARTYN
AND GEORGE MOORE

THE story of the Dramatic Movement in
Ireland has been so frequently told, its
protagonists and their works have been
the subject of so much commentary,
that a certain hesitation is natural in adding to the
criticism which has accumulated about the subject.
The creation of an Irish National Theatre is the
most familiar and most popular achievement of the
Revival. The dramatists have, consequently, obtained a degree of attention denied to the poets and
novelists. A critical bibliography of Anglo-Irish
literature will show dozens of books and articles
dealing with the drama, for one relative to poetry
or fiction. Yet, in all that has been written, there
has been a failure to bring out the important fact
that the Dramatic Movement falls into two distinct
phases, and that those now most conspicuously associated with its later developments were not the originators of the enterprise to which it owes its greatest
success. Reserving this latter point until we come
to discuss the Irish National Theatre, to whose
history it belongs, we shall consider the first phase
of the dramatic renascence. With the objects and
results of the Irish Literary Theatre before us, the

divergence between the original and the subsequent undertaking will be evident.

The production of W. B. Yeats's *Land of the Heart's Desire* at the Avenue Theatre, London, in 1894 doubtless awakened in him the definite ambition of giving Ireland a theatre where uncommercial drama might be fostered. He knew that for such plays as he could write there was no opening in London, except the Independent Theatre. Naturally it occurred to him that the intellectual awakening which was part of the Literary Revival in Ireland should render possible in Dublin a small theatrical enterprise modelled, like The Independent Theatre, upon the *Théâtre Libre* and the *Freie Bühne*. In this belief he was encouraged by his friend, Edward Martyn, who, as a devoted Ibsenite, was necessarily obliged to put his faith in such theatres, there being at that time not the slightest hope of seeing intelligent plays in the ordinary profiteering playhouses. Martyn and Yeats succeeded in interesting George Moore in their project, for he, too, was convinced that commercialism had made drama a literary impossibility in London. He was all the more disposed to support a theatre in Dublin as his confidence in the Independent Theatre had been lost. He felt that perhaps nowhere could the circumstances be more favourable to a repetition of Antoine's experiment than in Dublin, which had developed an artistic conscience, as a result of the propaganda of the Revival. In due course Lady Gregory, A. E., John Eglinton and other writers were secured as active supporters, a list of guarantors was published, and, under the auspices of the National Literary Society, the Irish Literary Theatre was established in the year 1899.

From the nature of the conditions which brought

Yeats, Martyn and Moore together for the execution of this purpose it is evident that folk-drama was not one of their preoccupations. They were united primarily in a revolt against theatrical conditions in London, which rendered impossible the production of plays whose character did not ensure immediate commercial success. As all their utterances showed, —the prefaces of Moore to his own and Martyn's plays, the articles in *Beltaine*, the organ of the Literary Theatre,—they were consciously inspired by the example of the *Théâtre Libre* and its German analogue. They thought of Ibsen as their master, and it was their avowed intention to do for Ireland what he had done for Norway. They certainly contemplated the creation of a national theatre, Yeats, particularly, showing himself anxious that this dramatic association in Ireland should distinguish itself from its kindred in London, by its use of national legend as the material of poetic drama. Martyn and Moore were more interested in social and psychological drama, as was natural, seeing that the one was an admirer of the Scandinavian dramatists, and the other was the author of *The Strike at Arlingford*, performed by The Independent Theatre in 1893. Although Moore and Yeats collaborated in *Diarmuid and Grania*, the last production of the Irish Literary Theatre, in 1901, we may notice in that difference of emphasis the fundamental cause of the ultimate scission in the Movement. It is significant that this play, which might have appeared to symbolise a reconciliation of literary ideals, marked, in reality, the disruption of the association.

Yeats's desire for poetic drama drawn from Irish sources did not necessarily conflict with the more cosmopolitan ideas of Moore and Martyn. At the first performance of the Irish Literary Theatre *The Countess Kathleen* wholly occupied the programme which it shared, at subsequent performances, with Martyn's *Heather Field*. Later on Alice Milligan's heroic play, *The Last Feast of the Fianna*, was produced with some success. But from legend to folklore was but a step with Yeats, and once that step was taken the peasant play became a mere question of time. Consequently there could be no continuity of ideas between the originators of the Movement. Their purpose was identical, but the bias of Martyn was away from folk-plays, while that of Yeats was inevitably in their direction. As the tone of the Irish Literary Theatre was that given by Edward Martyn and George Moore, they are the dramatists we must identify with it. Whatever be the merits of their work, it was, at least, consistent with the conception of national drama to which they professed at the beginning. Yeats, on the other hand, found elsewhere in embryo an enterprise more suitable for the realisation of the ideal he cherished, when he dreamed of the creation of an Irish National Theatre. If his efforts have resulted in a practical triumph denied to Edward Martyn, it must not be assumed that the latter has been less faithful to the original intention of their co-operation. We may find, indeed, that while Martyn's is a case of constancy unrewarded, Yeats has had to sacrifice much that is essential in the inevitable compromise whereby theory and practise are united in success.

EDWARD MARTYN

Although his name first became known in connection with the Irish Literary Theatre, which owed to him its designation and its material existence, Ed-

ward Martyn was not a novice in letters when he
was suddenly hailed as the chief dramatist of the
Revival.   Under the pseudonym of "Sirius" he had
published an extraordinary_ satire, *Morgante the
Lesser*, in 1890.   Written in a peculiarly unmodern,
eighteenth-century style, this book could hardly
count upon success with the average novel-reader,
but it deserves the attention of the curious who care
for the by-paths of contemporary literature.   Rabelais and Swift were obviously the masters whom
Martyn followed in an attempt to satirise the
growth of scientific materialism.   Morgante, the
symbolical giant of the narrative, is truly a Gar-
gantuan figure, the story of his birth and exploits
being as nearly akin to that of his great prototype
as nineteenth-century modesty permits the historian
to make it.   Needless to say, the author does not
approach any nearer to the Rabelaisian manner
than is implied in the statement that the plan of
Morgante's early years follows that of Gargantua's.
So far as the actual manner of the humour is concerned one is reminded rather of *Gulliver's Travels*.
The creation of Morgante and the invention of his
followers, the Enterists, provide opportunities for the
satirical illustration of various aspects of modern
society.   Religion, education, science, and even the
passing whims of the intellectually unemployed, all
contribute to the sum of absurdities composing the
narrative.

Edward Martyn shows a power of bitter, grotesque
imagination which is all the more remarkable because
it is sustained throughout a lengthy volume.   There
is a hint of his subsequent capacity for tenacious
fidelity to ideas, at the risk of isolation, in this first
book.   To the writing of such a work, remote from
anything in contemporary literature, and foredoomed

to inevitable comparison with the two mightiest satires outside antiquity, there went obviously unusual determination. We shall find this to be the most admirable quality in the author, his complete indifference to immediate popularity. He seems to consider literature, not as a bid for success, but simply as the expression of a personal impulse. He must have known that *Morgante the Lesser* would defy the casual reader, he must have felt how unique were its literary affiliations, yet, overshadowed by Rabelais and Swift, he wrote with a vigour and seriousness which has given us one of the strangest pieces of imaginative invective in recent times. The height of the only standards by which his book could be judged must be counted as the cause of its obscurity. But his dramas do not continue the mood which inspired *Morgante*, unless we count the trifle *Romulus and Remus* (1907), an extravaganza brutally ridiculing the composition of folk-drama, in a manner recalling faintly the author's first book. Satire is not his strong point, he lacks the concentration and lightness of touch which we demand nowadays from the satirist. The elaborate and leisurely conceptions of an earlier age, marvellously reproduced in *Morgante*, are not likely to find general appreciation, when related to our own time. In the theatre, expecially, where literary economy is essential, Edward Martyn was wise to strike out in another direction.

At the second performance of the Irish Literary Theatre, on the 9th of May, 1899, Edward Martyn's play, *The Heather Field*, was produced. Inadequate acting, and an unsuitable setting for poetic drama, had militated seriously against the success of *The Countess Kathleen*, with which the Theatre had opened the previous evening. *The Heather Field*, on the

contrary, was so successful as to cause a revision of
the unfavourable opinions expressed by the critics
on its appearance in book form, early in the year
1899. Recollecting the state of dramatic criticism,
which at that time had not yet recovered from the
shock of Ibsen, and was still in the distrustful, if
not hysterical, stage, we need not be surprised that
Edward Martyn found little favour. *The Heather
Field* belonged too obviously to the school of Ibsen
to be appreciated in London. Had it contained any
of those incidents which excited the hysteria of the
critics of *Ghosts*, it might have counted upon the
oppositional minority for support. The patrons of
"advanced drama" must, on principle, have championed any dramatist who defied the Censor. Martyn, unfortunately, did not adopt this easy road to
the limited fame of the literary martyr. His plays
were as surely devoid of offence, as they were unsus-
ceptible of commercial success. He had, with apparent perverseness, all the defects of the uncommercial playwright, without any of the corresponding advantages which delicate scenes, or daring
innovations, confer with certain select audiences.

In Dublin, where the sophistications of dramatic
reform controversies were ignored, *The Heather Field*
pleased every class of spectator. The initiated were
interested in this application of Ibsen's methods to
Irish conditions, the popular audiences were carried
away by the force of a conflict which was easily
understood. The symbolic value of Carden Tyrrell's
struggle to retain the heather field had no need of
explanation in a country where devotion to ideals,
at the cost of ruin and failure, has long been a familiar
phenomenon. There is fine drama in this story of
Carden Tyrrell, who is driven insane by the conflict
of reality, as personified in his wife and her matter-

of-fact friends, with the ideal, as symbolised by the wild field on his estate, to whose reclamation he would sacrifice everything. The heather field, in which he hears the voices that whisper of youth and happiness, was instantly recognised as part of that realm of dreams where man may satisfy the longings of the spirit. It is related that—characteristically —English playgoers sympathised with the doctors who pronounced Carden mad, whereas in Ireland the audience hissed the doctors and sided with the idealist against his wife. As George Moore has pointed out, the great triumph of Martyn's portrayal of Carden is that he makes him sympathetic, "although all right and good sense are on the wife's side."

Maeve, which was published in the same volume as the preceding play, met with an equally good reception, when performed during the second season of the Irish Literary Theatre, in 1901. If this "psychological drama in two acts" has not been played in England, Germany and the United States, like its predecessor, the reason must not be sought in any inferiority of workmanship. In a sense, *Maeve* corresponds more exactly to the type of play for which the author wished to found an Irish Literary Theatre, than *The Heather Field*. It is more peculiarly Irish in its atmosphere than the latter, and on that account precisely, its interest for the outside world may be slighter. Once again the motive is the clash of the real and the ideal, or as W. B. Yeats suggested, "Ireland's choice between English materialism and her own natural idealism." There is an entirely original use of fairy lore and legend in *Maeve*, found uniquely in the work of Edward Martyn. He shows how the old vagrant woman, Peg Inerny, who is transformed in the world of imagination into a queen of faery, fascinates the dreamy young girl, Maeve O'Heynes, by appealing to the latter's faith in the legendary traditions of the countryside. Maeve, who is about to marry a young Englishman of wealth, pays a last visit to the mountains where her visions have brought her into communion with the heroic figures of legend. Like Peg Inerny, who believes herself to be the great Queen Maeve of Red Branch history, Maeve is eager to enter the faery regions, where her super-human lover awaits her, and both may transcend the sordidness of their earthly existence. The girl longs to escape the poverty-stricken gentility of her father's home and the marriage which is to rehabilitate it; the old woman wants to leave beggary behind her. They go off in the cold night to their visions, and Maeve returning, sits at the open window in trance-like ecstasy, awaiting the arrival of the visitors from Beyond. They come to her, and as they fade out of sight, Maeve's spirit leaves her body to accompany them to the land of Tir-nan-Oge.

Thus, by the adaptation to local circumstances of the technique then associated with the great Scandinavian dramatist, Edward Martyn was able to give the Irish Literary Theatre two dramas of the kind which he desired to foster in Ireland. *The Heather Field* and *Maeve* could not have been written but for *The Wild Duck* and *The Lady from the Sea;* their ancestry is evident, but they are not imitations. They merely revealed at an early date that influence which has since profoundly modified the best modern drama.

George Moore has related, with his usual love of impressive detail, the fate of Edward Martyn's *Tale of a Town,* which the latter kindly allowed him to rewrite for production in 1900 as *The Bending of the Bough*. Two years later the original play, together with *An Enchanted Sea*, was published by Standish O'Grady. While the peculiar claims of *Morgante the Lesser* have been admitted, we have already suggested that satire is not the best exercise of the author's talent. In that elaborate romance, exaggeration and prolixity were part of the archaic convention of the form, but the effects secured by them are denied to Edward Martyn in the theatre. With all his efforts to prune his material, he fails to effect the necessary sharpening of the points he wishes to make. *The Tale of a Town* is actually a very legitimate satire on Irish municipal life, but the material has not been adapted to the stage. There is such exuberant caricature as to recall the symbolical figures of *Morgante*. The characters are drawn with strokes so broad that one cannot believe that they even believe in themselves. The subject is an excellent one, and in first approaching it, Edward Martyn pointed the way to a rich field, which has never been properly exploited by the Irish dramatists. *The Bending of the Bough* makes a convincing picture of that nameless, but familiar, municipality, whose leader, Jasper Dean, ultimately abandons the corporation whose private ambitions he had miraculously succeeded in subordinating to the general welfare. George Moore retains the first act of the original almost intact, but the remaining acts are radically different. The motives of Dean's sudden apostasy are more tangible, owing to the greater insight displayed by Moore in the characterisation of Millicent Fell, whose family, social and personal influence are the cause of the betrayal. The exaggerations of the first version have disappeared, and the dialogue is well written, making the

play one of the best in the repertory of the Irish
Dramatic Movement.

The Enchanted Sea is measurably superior to its
companion play, and justifies the publication of the
volume in 1902.   Here the author returns to his own
special subject, the expression of Irish drama in
terms as universal as those of Ibsen.   Mrs. Font
desires to get rid of her nephew Guy, so that the
estate which he has inherited from her late husband
may revert to her daughter, Agnes.   This *parvenu*
peasant woman imagines that the wealth of Agnes
would then be sufficient to tempt Guy's friend, Lord
Mask, to marry her.   Her purpose regarding her
nephew is facilitated by the general belief that Guy
is one of "the sea people."   The boy is strangely
drawn to the sea, and is under the suggestion of the
peasantry, who credit him with belonging there.
Mrs. Font lures the youth away to the cave on the
shore where he used to visit the sea fairies.   Her
return without him excites suspicion, but before she
can be arrested she learns the defeat of her plans.
Lord Mask is drowned while seeking, in a fit of
madness, to rejoin his friend, and all that is left for
her is suicide.   The play recalls *Maeve,* as both
recall, though very differently, *The Lady from the
Sea.*   In mere outline there is the typically melodramatic element which Ibsen did not disdain, but
the content of the drama is similarly suggestive of
something more than those "pure accidents," denounced by Bernard Shaw as merely "anecdotic,"
and not an essential part of "the quintessence of
Ibsenism."   The call of the sea is heard throughout
the play, and the general atmosphere of conflicting
aims and ideals, of superstition and poetry, raises it
above the level of melodrama.   If certain faults of
execution impair the conception, the latter is, never-

theless, powerful. In spite of defects, due largely
to the practical obstacles which have stood in the
way of the author's technical development, *The
Enchanted Sea* is a work of distinction.

The Place Hunters (1902) is a further attempt at
the species of satire we have seen in *The Tale of a
Town*. Compressed within the space of one act, and
treated in terms of farcical comedy, it is perhaps
a more successful tilt at the windmills of political
jobbery in Ireland. This comedy has more in common with the author's latest play, *The Dream Physician* (1914), than with its immediate successor,
Grangecolman (1912). The comic relief of the former,
in the person of George Augustus Moon, an old
journalist, was created in that spirit of broad caricature which always—though often unintentionally
—accompanies Edward Martyn's satire. The introduction of the element of comedy, in this case, was
an innovation, heretofore unknown in the dramatist's
work. His satire has usually been serious in intention whereas this caricatural portrait of a prominent
figure in the story of the Dramatic Revival was pure
farce. It was the first of his non-satirical plays to be
relieved by any evidence of the comic spirit. The
reproach of being gloomy and pessimistic had, in
consequence, been frequently made against the Irish
disciple of Ibsen. The accusation is neither more
nor less true in his case than in that of his master.

The years between 1902 and 1912, when Martyn's
last published play appeared, did not witness any
concession on his part to the demand for "cheerful"
plays. If anything, *Grangecolman* seems most nearly
to justify the criticism in question. There was a
breath of poetry and a strain of idealism animating
The Heather Field, Maeve and *The Enchanted Sea*
which disposed of the contention that Edward

Martyn's work was "morbid," to use the favourite term of those who criticise the school of drama to which he belongs. *Grangecolman*, however, is without any such quality to brighten its colourless realism. The plot centres about the effort of Katherine Devlin to free her father from his infatuation for the young amanuensis, Clare Farquhar, whom she herself introduced into the home, to escape the duties of secretaryship. Restless and disappointed, Katherine is jealous of the happiness which has come to her father in the companionship of a sympathetic woman. Having failed, with all her freedom, to find satisfaction in the emancipated ideas for which she abandoned her home, she is anxious to destroy what she has neither secured for herself nor given to others. When all means have proved fruitless, she decides to appeal to superstition by impersonating the ghost believed by her father to haunt Grangecolman. She does so with all the more readiness as she sees in the ruse a means of disturbing the quiet contentment of the household and obtaining for herself the only tranquillity possible—death. She counts on Clare Farquhar to expose the ghostly superstition in the most tragically effective manner. Nor is she mistaken, for Clare fires a revolver at the white figure which has no terrors for her, thereby ending her own dream of happiness, as well as Katherine's life.

Rosmersholm was immediately suggested to the critics by this play, but, it may fairly be asked, what but the slightest points of identity exist between the two? Katherine Devlin is rather the type of woman analysed by Ibsen in *Hedda Gabler*, the dissatisfied, vaguely ambitious product of the "emancipation" and "unrest" of modern feminism. Clare Farquhar, on the other hand, is in no way related to Rebecca West, who should be her prototype. Her power and influence are essentially those of the "womanly woman," abhorred by Ibsen, if we are to believe Bernard Shaw. She is certainly incapable of playing the part in Colman's life which Rebecca played in the career of Rosmer. The fact is, Edward Martyn has been too freely credited with Ibsenism. As has been admitted earlier in this chapter, the author of *The Heather Field* began frankly as an admirer of the Scandinavian dramatist, and, like his fellow-workers in the Irish Literary Theatre, he saw in the history of the Norwegian drama an example for Ireland. His own plays showed the influence of Ibsen more markedly than those of his colleagues, for the simple reason that the form of dramatic art in which he was chiefly interested has been largely created, and most certainly revolutionised, by the great Scandinavian master. It would be just as accurate to say that Edward Martyn is a disciple of Strindberg, with whose misogyny his work presents many parallels, and for whom he has expressed his admiration. He is an Ibsenite precisely in so far as he writes in accordance with the conventions which supplanted the old, well-made play of the pre-Ibsen era. In company with all the modern dramatists who were in revolt at that time against the conventional and commercial drama, he naturally turned to Russia and Northern Europe for his models. George Moore and he were agreed as to what direction the new movement in Ireland should take, Yeats was but partly in agreement with them. Consequently he did not write to foster the new drama as understood by Martyn, who soon found himself alone, owing to the dissolution of the original partnership. Had Moore written as extensively, he would have approximated to the ideal of Martyn rather than of Yeats.

It is easy to understand now why Edward Martyn's Ibsenism has been exaggerated. Circumstances were against him, and he was left the solitary exponent of the drama which he knew to be the next phase in the evolution of the English theatre. He wanted Ireland to start at once in the direction in which the future lay, he wanted Irish drama to be "modern," as the word was then understood. Not that he advocated the "talking" play, which Ibsen's most vociferous champion in England erroneously identified as the condition precedent of progress in the art of the theatre. His fundamental dissimilarity from Ibsen is most evident in his avoidance of those problems which give its *raison d'être* to the "drama of ideas." The mass of philosophic doctrine and social criticism extracted by Shaw in *The Quintessence of Ibsenism* is sufficient to show how slight is the relationship between *The Heather Field* and *The Wild Duck*. Edward Martyn does not discuss problems or launch theories, he is simply content to depict a *milieu*, give its atmosphere and allow the circumstances to suggest ideas to the intelligent spectator. He is the only Irish writer for the theatre who has sensed the dramatic possibilities of contemporary life in Ireland outside the peasantry. His material is more slender and more difficult of exploitation than that of his successors, the folk-dramatists, but who will say that he has been less fortunate in his own domain than many of the latter in theirs?

The history of the Irish Literary Theatre during the last portion of its early career calls for little comment. Alice Milligan's *The Last Feast of the Fianna* (1900) had that *succès d'estime* which is accorded at times to the innovator. It was the first of those Heroic dramas which were to become a feature of the Irish National Theatre. Douglas Hyde's *The*

Twisting of the Rope (1901) was an even greater innovation, being the first play to be performed in Irish in any theatre, and its success was commensurate with its actual fine qualities as well as with its sentimental value. The somewhat startling collaboration of George Moore and W. B. Yeats gave the Theatre its third drama of legend, *Diarmuid and Grania*, of which the only printed text made public is the fragment in French disclosed by George Moore in *Ave* (1911), that imaginative history of the first years of the Dramatic Movement. The strange story of that collaboration, and the inner workings of the creative machinery which produced the Irish Literary Theatre and its literature, have been exposed in a fashion which must debar more prosaic minds from reconstructing the narrative. The first volume of George Moore's trilogy contains all the facts (in addition to others) which concern us. Even had he repressed the desire for expansive reminiscence, a glance at the result of its three years activity would enlighten the student of the Irish Literary Theatre. The presence of conflicting aims and unrealised projects is revealed by the miscellaneous nature of the programmes. With the exception of Yeats's first play, which was not written specifically for production, the important contributions are those of Edward Martyn. If we credit him with the conception of *The Bending of the Bough*, it will be found that the three most successful plays produced, and those wholly congruous with the professed aims of the Theatre, were the work of the one man who has been constant to the first principles of the Movement.

The promise of *Diarmuid and Grania* was as negligible as the preposterous circumstances of its existence would lead one to expect. It was an obvious make-shift to give the programme an appearance of complying with Yeats's desire for legendary drama. *The Last Feast of the Fianna* was not calculated to enforce the claim to exploit the Heroic period, while *The Twisting of the Rope*, which followed *Diarmuid and Grania* the same night, was counted rather as a triumph for the Gaelic League. Inevitably there seemed but one conclusion to be drawn; the Irish Literary Theatre was best equipped for the production of dramas like *Maeve* and *The Heather Field*. Had Yeats written another play such as *The Countess Kathleen*, had Moore consecrated his great gifts of observation and satire to an original work of his own for the stage, there might have been further progress, with the greater success due to experience. But there came, instead, an abrupt halt. Almost all the elements of national drama were present in the achievement of the Irish Literary Theatre, the poetic play, the play of modern manners, the psychological, the historic drama. Some were only embryonic, but the possibilities of evolving a representative dramatic literature from these elements were clearly defined. But one thing was lacking, the folk-play, and this was enough to hasten a dissolution already threatened by the partial eclipse of the other form of dramatic art—the poetic—to which Yeats was most attached. As soon as he saw that neither Martyn nor Moore was sufficiently concerned for the comparative failure of the one to assert itself, and for the complete absence of the other, he was glad to start afresh. He had found a path which promised to lead to the goal he most ardently desired.

The Irish Literary Theatre did not die when its founders separated. Edward Martyn clung tenaciously to the plan which he had originally conceived. With the intermittent help of amateur organizations, notably The Players' Club and the Independent Theatre Company, he continued to devote himself to modern drama, encouraging the production of Scandinavian and Russian plays, as a means of keeping before us the ideal at which he aimed. All his later work, from 1902 on, was performed by these amateur companies, until he at last was able to secure a nucleus of players and playwrights with which to resuscitate the Irish Literary Theatre. There is now hope that the plans of fifteen years ago will materialise, and that Ireland will have a theatre open to the production of the best modern drama, national and foreign. After a preliminary season in 1914, to which only Irish dramatists contributed, a second year was begun with Tchekhov's *Uncle Vanya*. Should a public surfeited with peasant plays support the enterprise, Edward Martyn's many years of unappreciated effort will be rewarded. It must always be a regret that the fine talent revealed in *The Heather Field* and in *Maeve* should have been, in part, thwarted by the absence of favourable conditions for its development. The word "amateur" has not infrequently been applied in criticism of Martyn's work. There is, it is true, a certain stiffness of movement, in his later plays especially, and an absence of strong characterisation in the rather formal speech he employs. Everything that could help to broaden his work, that could make his style supple, has been lacking. The wider audience, the more experienced acting, and the more general criticism and appreciation, which have helped the Irish National Theatre, were denied to Edward Martyn. It seems, therefore, that he is all the more entitled to recognition for the good work he has done, both creative and other, on behalf of the literary drama in Ireland.

Nothing is easier, of course, than to be wise after the experience of others, and we have little difficulty in seeing the error of splitting up the Dramatic Movement, at the end of its experimental three years. The absence of folk-drama was, admittedly, a noticeable defect in an undertaking which was engaged in creating a dramatic literature representative of Ireland. But to the disinterested student there appears no reason why this need should not have been met, without involving the loss of what had already been established. The plays of Yeats and Martyn could just as well have been produced under the same auspices, they were not in any way mutually exclusive. In fact, as we shall see, in his second experiment, successful as it has been, Yeats was disappointed of his hope that the poetic drama would flourish. He is the only poet writing for the Irish National Theatre whose work has been in the least adapted for the stage. Peasant comedy and realism have been the chief title to fame of the theatre which succeeded his first experiment with Moore and Martyn. In consequence, we may say that Yeats's ideal has been hardly more fully realised than would have been possible had the Irish Literary Theatre been continued with his help. Had the literary energies of the time been concentrated, instead of scattered, that Theatre would have attracted all the talents, and doubtless folk-drama would, in due course, have asserted its claim to existence. As it was, the Movement continued its bifurcated career, and took on an unavoidable narrowness; too much of the folk element on one side, and none on the other. Justly celebrated as the Irish Players have become, it would be absurd to pretend that their repertoire mirrors more than a part of Irish life, yet they are absolutely debarred from the interpretation of that part which is missing. Their strength in folk-drama is their weakness outside it. To understand how this weakness has simultaneously made and unmade the success of our national drama, we must see why it was strong enough to shape the subsequent evolution of the Irish Dramatic Movement.

CHAPTER XIII

THE DRAMATIC MOVEMENT: SECOND PHASE

THE ORIGINS OF THE IRISH NATIONAL THEATRE:
W. G. FAY'S IRISH NATIONAL DRAMATIC COMPANY.
THE INITIATORS OF FOLK-DRAMA: J. M. SYNGE
AND PADRAIC COLUM

IT is rather generally believed that the present National Theatre Society developed out of the Irish Literary Theatre, although a strong effort of imagination is demanded to connect the two. How can a theatre justly famous for its school of folk-drama and peculiarly appropriate tradition of acting represent the further evolution of an institution which contained no trace of either, and ceased to exist because of its supposed inability to admit them? The truth is, it does not. The National Theatre Society traces its origins to an entirely different source, which existed prior to the separation of the founders of the Irish Literary Theatre. The brothers, W. G. and F. J. Fay, were responsible for bringing together the company of Irish actors which grew into what is now called the Irish Theatre. They had a native genius for acting which they imperfectly satisfied by giving amateur performances in different places throughout Dublin and its neighbourhood, but on coming into contact with A. E., through the intermediary of James H. Cousins, the Fays were encouraged to lay the foundations of the Irish National Theatre. A. E. had written that delicate prose poem, *Deirdre*, which was published five years later, in 1907, as his only contribution to our dramatic literature. This play at once appealed to Frank Fay and his brother, who recognised in it the sort of work which they had sought, and partially found, in Alice Milligan's *Deliverance of Red Hugh*, their performance of which had interested A. E. The desire of the Fays was all for purely national drama, acted by Irish players, and interpreted in the native tradition, far removed from that of the English stage, commercial or otherwise. Obviously, here were the collaborators required by Yeats, in his dissatisfaction with the English actors and the divergent aims of the Irish Literary Theatre. In a short time he, too, had made the acquaintance of this new company, which had independently been working along the lines he himself had wished the Literary Theatre to follow. Most conveniently he found an instrument ready to carry on the work which had not recommended itself to his original collaborators.

On the 2nd of April, 1902, A.E.'s *Deirdre*, for which he himself designed the costumes and scenery, was produced by the Fays and their group of actors, now styled the "Irish National Dramatic Company." On the same programme appeared *Kathleen ni Houlihan* by W. B. Yeats. The charm of the acting, into which the Fays infused that fine spirit whose service to the Theatre can never be overestimated, enhanced the success of these two beautiful little plays, and determined the fate of the Irish Theatre. There was now no doubt that native Irish drama could be developed with the assistance of this group of enthusiasts, whose energies were controlled by two actors of genius. Later on in the same year they moved to the Antient Concert Rooms, and on the scene of the Literary Theatre's *début*, repeated their initial triumph, in addition to producing four new plays: *The Sleep of the King* and *The Racing Lug*, by James H. Cousins; *A Pot of Broth*, by W. B. Yeats; and *The Laying of the Foundations*, by Frederick Ryan. With the exception of the last-mentioned, a satirical comedy of municipal life, recalling Edward Martyn's similar attempts, all these plays were definitely of the then new school, now so familiar. *The Sleep of the King* was a minor essay in the *genre* which Yeats's poetic dramas of ancient legend alone have illustrated successfully during the later years of the Irish Theatre. *The Racing Lug*, a peasant tragedy of the sea, foreshadowed Synge's little masterpiece, while *A Pot of Broth* was the legitimate ancestor of those comedies and farces which Lady Gregory has made specially her own, having been, in fact, largely written by her.

Thus, at the close of its second season the Irish National Dramatic Company, under the influence and direction of the brothers Fay, had traced, as it were, the boundaries of the domain in which the Irish Theatre was to become master. They had prepared the ground, collected the company and created the tradition of acting which was to give the fullest play to the peculiar quality of our national folk and poetic drama. Once they had the collaboration of playwrights whose work corresponded to their histrionic genius, the framework of a National Theatre was rapidly constructed. But this framework was essentially determined by the Fays, inasmuch as their limitations imposed the lines within which the drama was enclosed. We can now see why the second phase of the Dramatic Movement was dominated by that element which is at once its strength and its weakness. When W. B. Yeats and Lady Gregory turned to the Irish National Dramatic Company they had not the freedom enjoyed by the Literary Theatre. They had to accept, for the furtherance of their purpose, a medium already formed, and with certain pronounced characteristics. It so happened that these characteristics harmonised almost miraculously with their own conception of what the greater part of Irish drama should be. But a limit was necessarily imposed upon the development of the drama, outside of which failure was obvious. It became, therefore, the duty of Yeats to explain why the limitations of a theatre where only subjects drawn from legend and peasant life could be treated, were preferable to those of the theatre which Edward Martyn desired. To this question Yeats as editor of the Theatre's organ, *Samhain*, devoted many eloquent pages, to which we shall return.

In 1903 control passed out of the hands of W. G. and F. J. Fay, when the Irish National Theatre Society was formed, with W. B. Yeats as president. In a prospectus the Society claimed "to continue on a more permanent basis the work of the Irish Literary Theatre," whereas its real purpose was to carry on the work of the Fays, who remained in the Theatre until 1908, giving the best of themselves and helping it to distinction in a measure only surpassed by J. M. Synge. Indeed, the latter's stage success, as distinct from the recognition accorded to his published work, was due to them; to W. G. Fay for his wonderful interpretation of the title rôle in *The Playboy of the Western World*, and his creation of the chief male part in every other play of Synge's previously performed in Ireland; to Frank Fay for the training of a company, without which the Irish Theatre

would have been deprived of its most valuable asset.
It is noteworthy that its decline dates from their
departure, when the spirit which made the tradition
upon which the Theatre now lives began to fade.
But at this time there could be no question of decline, for the Dramatic Movement was surely approaching its apogee.   The year 1903 saw not only
the production of Yeats's admirable poetic plays, *The
King's Threshold* and *The Shadowy Waters*, but also
J. M. Synge's *In the Shadow of the Glen* and Padraic
Colum's *Broken Soil*, with which the two most notable of the new dramatists introduced themselves
as remarkable, but totally dissimilar, exponents of
peasant drama.   Then the Irish Literary Society
invited the players to London, where the appreciation of disinterested critics confirmed the wisdom of
the enterprise, the more so as it took, in one instance,
the form of a substantial deed.   Miss A. E. F. Horni-
man was so favourably impressed that she granted
the Irish National Theatre Society an annual subsidy,
provided the Abbey Theatre, and leased it to them
rent free for a term of six years.   From 1904 on we
have been possessed of a National Theatre, in the
material as well as the literary sense of the world.
The fact was signalised by the adoption in 1905 of
the title, The National Theatre Society, the ultimate metamorphosis of W. G. Fay's Irish National
Dramatic Company, and the final variation of its
nomenclature.

Perhaps the most succinct statement of the conception of national drama which separated W. B.
Yeats from Edward Martyn was that made by the
former in the 1902 issue of *Samhain:* "Our movement is a return to the people . . . and the drama
of society would but magnify a condition of life
which the countryman and the artisan could but

copy to their hurt. The play that is to give them a quite natural pleasure should either tell them of their own life, or of that life of poetry where every man can see his own image, because there alone does human nature escape from arbitrary conditions." Written at the beginning of the National Theatre's career, these words forecast definitely the nature of its work, and show precisely on what grounds Yeats preferred the limitations of the second to those of the first phase of the Dramatic Movement. The imaginative re-creation of history and legend, coupled with the study of life amongst those classes whose national characteristics are most marked, seemed to Yeats the best foundation upon which to build an Irish Theatre. Arguing before events had come to prove the truth of his assertions, he was obliged to refer to classical literature, English and foreign, for support of his contention. He knew, however, that the facts of Irish life would ultimately furnish contemporary evidence in his favour. The countryside still preserved that unwritten literature, poetic and legendary, whose exploitation in the theatre would at once create the bond of personal sympathy and interest which united the mind of the dramatist with that of the simple people in Elizabethan England. In another issue of *Samhain* he illustrates this advantage of the Irish writer, contrasting the absence of a common ground between the poet and the people in England, with the contrary condition in Ireland. "Milton set the story of Sampson into the form of a Greek play, because he knew that Sampson was, in the English imagination, what Herakles was in the imagination of Greece." But a censorship deprives the dramatist of such subjects nowadays, although the Bible stories occupy the same place in the popular mind of England as the tales of Finn and Ossian in Ireland.

If we add to this the closely related fact of Gaelic speech, we have all the circumstances that have helped to give substance to the theory from which Yeats started. The Anglo-Irish idiom, uncontaminated by cheap journalistic influences, full of vigorous archaisms, and coloured by the poetic energy of Gaelic, has done more than anything else to raise the peasant drama to the level of literature. This factor enters, of course, into the belief expressed by Yeats that a return to the people is necessary to the creation of national drama, but he was singularly fortunate in finding a dramatist who was to make of the popular idiom the most powerful vehicle of literary expression in modern times. It cannot be denied that he was, in any case, entirely justified in holding romantic, historical and peasant plays to be the true basis of our national dramatic art. The essence of nationality could be extracted from such material, and, although Yeats's plays have had no important successors, the folk-drama has flourished, with the help of a few original, and a host of imitative, dramatists. It is the latter, numerously present and to the exclusion of all others, who enable us to sympathise with Edward Martyn's plea for another class of play. Once the peasant convention had been reduced to a formula, it was natural to turn away impatiently in the hope of seeing some innovator prepared to renounce the assured success of repetition. In recent years there has been a noticeable decline in the quality of the plays produced in obedience to the principle, sound as it was, which Yeats invoked against Edward Martyn more than a decade ago. If the drama of peasant life had not transcended the limits of success which might, at the outset, have been assigned to it, the Irish Theatre would not find itself dominated by one particular *genre*. But the domination is largely the result of an unforeseen circumstance, the transfiguration of the peasant play by a writer of such genius that his work is already classic.

J. M. SYNGE

The great "event" in the history of the Irish Theatre has been the discovery and universal recognition of the genius of J. M. Synge, whose brief activity of six years (from 1903 to 1909) had a decisive influence upon contemporary drama in Ireland. There can be little doubt that the peasant play, now characteristic of the National Theatre, owes its success to this writer who at the outset revealed its dramatic and poetic possibilities. In a series of masterpieces Synge established his command of this form, whether adapted to tragedy or comedy, and proved his title to rank with the great dramatists of European literature. The circumstances of his *début* all combined to strengthen the prestige which he was to lend to the folk-drama. It has already been observed that the histrionic talent of the brothers Fay, and the tradition they imparted to their group of players, were peculiarly adapted to the development of the peasant play. Add to this the fact that Synge's very first piece, *In the Shadow of the Glen*, provoked that ignorant hostility which followed his later work with increased venom, and whose manifestation could not but awaken a sense of resistance. The natural determination of intelligent minds, in the face of unreasoning prejudice, is to persevere, in obedience to the faith that is engendered by the opposition of inferiors. The stand made by W. B.

Yeats for artistic freedom, when he championed Synge against mob-rule in literature, was as greatly to his credit as was his discernment in previously sensing that latent genius whose expression he had subsequently to defend so generously. Obviously such a struggle as was waged on behalf of its greatest exponent served only to enhance the claims of the folk-drama. The innumerable detractors of Synge contributed largely towards confirming his own reputation, as well as consolidating the hold of the peasant play upon a movement already predisposed in its favour.

J. M. Synge brought an equipment to his collaboration in the Irish Theatre very different from that of his fellow-workers. With the exception of Yeats, none of the new dramatists had come into direct contact with foreign peoples and culture, and Yeats's experiences of London and Paris were those of literature rather than of life. Synge, on the other hand, cared little for literature, and fled to the continent as soon as his university career was terminated, in order to satisfy that instinct of vagabondage which impels those who search for adventures, not among books, but among men. A sonnet in *Kottabos*, in 1893, the year of his departure from Trinity College, Dublin, was all that he left as evidence of his literary proclivities, before beginning those wander-years which culminated in his meeting with Yeats in Paris about 1898. When he returned, at the latter's suggestion, to the Aran Islands, he had already a sharpened sense of the realities of life as felt by those living in more direct contact with nature. Instinctively he had sought out the humbler companionships of the roadside, while his linguistic attainments permitted him to penetrate the exterior aspects of the foreign scenes through which he moved. His ears, trained by the sounds of several European languages in addition to English and Gaelic, were well fitted to catch the rhythms and music of that idiom which he brought into literature from the Western seashore and the Wicklow hills.

Whether he learned anything from the peasant plays of Hauptmann and Anzengruber is a matter of conjecture, but of his debt to French literature there is evidence in his desire to become known as its interpreter for English readers. The influence of Loti and Maeterlinck, of whom he had written in some of his rare essays in criticism, is occasionally visible in his dramatic work, but his obligations are general rather than particular. That he was attracted by the French ideal is evidenced by his love for Marot, Villon, Ronsard and Racine, especially Racine, upon whom he proposed to write a critical study. He abandoned this project at the instance of Yeats, whose object was less open to criticism, in this connection, than the argument employed to secure it. Fortunately the return of Synge to Ireland was not conditioned by a demand for proof of Yeats's monopolistic plea on behalf of an earlier English critic of French literature. Doubtless there was little reason to suppose that one so careless of ideas as Synge could adequately criticise literature. He certainly could not have challenged opinion as a critic with the extraordinary success which came to him as a dramatist. His reading of French, however, did not fail to leave its mark upon his work. He surely acquired thereby that highly cultivated sense of selection, that need of artistic order and method, which caused him to rewrite with meticulous conscientiousness, and helped him to fashion the Anglo-Gaelic idiom into a perfect instrument of poetic and dramatic speech. Perhaps, too, his contact with a literature which comprises a Voltaire and an Anatole France encouraged him to express his own sardonic humour and his ironic disillusionment in the presentation of human nature.

Most of the voluminous and repeated studies of Synge's indebtedness to France have been for the purpose of coupling his name with precisely those writers whom he expressly disliked, or with whom he had no point in common. This was the price he paid for coming into the Dramatic Movement with a wider and more varied experience than is usual in Irishmen of letters. Unfriendly critics gratified their nescient patriotism by attributing to "foreign devils" everything that displeased them in Synge. As they objected frequently to his most original and vital qualities, credit—or discredit—for these was given to "decadent" and alien influences. The same procedure was adopted to a lesser degree with Yeats, whose life lent colour to the awful suspicion that he was not wholly ignorant of French poetry. In both cases, as we have seen, whatever they may have owed to the influence of France was visible in their qualities rather than in their defects. It was just where Yeats and Synge expressed themselves most completely that they were accused of borrowing from contaminated sources. Industrious commentators have estimated and proved the relationship between Synge and Loti or Anatole France. Clear as are the facts, who will deny that the note is most original and personal precisely where something of an identity of attitude transpires? The author of *The Playboy of the Western World* shows the same irony as the creator of Monsieur Bergeret, but what depths of speculation separate the tempered intellectuality of the latter from the exalted simplicity of the former!

As if he had foreseen from the beginning what misapplied ingenuity would be brought to prove him an "alien" and a "decadent," Synge prepared to leave some tangible evidence of the sources whence his dramatic material was obtained. Although not published until 1907, *The Aran Islands* belongs to the period of his return to Ireland, and his repeated sojourns in that Western World which supplied him with the substance, and even the form, of his most notable contributions to the Irish Theatre. Read in conjunction with the notebooks compiled from his Wicklow experiences, this volume is a complete record of the dramatist and his work. These intensely interesting pictures of life in the Aran Islands have a charm independent of that which they derive from their relation to the plays. They reveal the personality of Synge almost as vividly as they evoke the colour, the tragedy and the comedy of a corner of the world unspoiled by industrial civilisation. The "drifting, silent man, full of hidden passion," as Yeats describes him, surrenders himself to the primitive yet highly sensitive race whose joys and sorrows we feel to be his own. There is a peculiar note of intimate understanding and sympathy in Synge's account of the Islanders which disposes at once of the accusation that he went there as a "literary" stranger bent upon securing "copy." His sensations are not those of an idle spectator; they are the response of the mind and soul of the race to the least corrupted manifestations of our national life and spirit. This response is all the more remarkable because of its sincerity. Synge is utterly unconscious of the extent to which the atmosphere and voice of Aran have penetrated his consciousness. A more self-conscious *amateur d'âmes* would never have confessed, like Synge, that he felt a stranger, so modestly did he estimate his capacity to assimilate those elements which fascinated his imagination.

By a strange irony, the geneses of the plays most obnoxious to Gaelic puritanism are so indicated in Synge's notebooks as to leave no doubt as to their native origin. *In the Shadow of the Glen*, the earliest of his offences in the eyes of the moral jingoists, was actually modified by the author. Pat Dirane's narrative in *The Aran Islands*, with its *dénouement* of adultery and murder, is a more disquieting reflection upon certain "patriotic" illusions than Synge's wonderful little play. Out of the familiar story of the husband who simulates death in order to test his wife's fidelity, known to Gaelic folk-lore no less than to Oriental legend, Synge made a characteristic tragedy in miniature. Faithful to the absence of didactic intention, which distinguished the author in a country whose breath is propaganda, he does not attempt to make Nora Burke the vehicle of any protest. He simply depicts her loveless life by the side of an old husband, in that lonely valley, drowned in mists from the mountains, where the only voice that speaks to her heart is the whispering wind, mysteriously eloquent. This is no "doll's house" whose door is banged by feminine revolt; Nora Burke is not an intellectual sister of her Scandinavian namesake. She is just a solitary woman, whose human instinct craves the adventure of freedom and youth. This impulse is satisfied, not by the youth, Michael, for whom she used to feel a sentimental attraction, but by the tramp, who takes her with him to share the wild joys of a roadside existence.

Synge's second one-act play, *Riders to the Sea*, graciously approved by his erstwhile, and subsequent, opponents, also had its roots in the Aran volume. It was written about the same time as *In the Shadow of the Glen,* and was produced shortly after the latter by the Irish National Theatre Society, in 1904. This almost perfect little tragedy, certainly the finest in our theatre, may be traced to certain definite incidents recorded in *The Aran Islands,* but it differs from the other plays thus traceable, in that it is the very quintessence of the spirit with which that book is informed. Into one act the dramatist has concentrated all the passionate horror of death, as it broods over the Aran fishermen, menacing them in their constant struggle with the sea. Old Maurya, whose husband and five sons have been taken from her by drowning, becomes a symbolic figure, as she personifies the grief of a people in the face of their common enemy. There is no suspense as to the fate of her sixth and last son, Bartley, who rides away to return no more. We know that he has gone to meet the same destiny as his father and brothers, and our interest is not in the particular event, tragic though it be. It is the great, universal tragedy of death which grips the attention already prepared and stimulated by a series of apparently unpremeditated incidents and accidents, which announce the approach of the dread protagonist. Maeterlinck's *Intruse* has an air of artificiality, perhaps because of its disembodied action, beside the spiritualised realism of *Riders to the Sea.* Maurya takes on the profound significance of an Æschylean figure, in her vain protest against Fate, and her ultimate resignation. She is widely human in her revolt and submission, as she is essentially a woman of the Islands. The *caoine* of the mourners is equally impressive, because of its local and general significance. Synge, with his marvellous sense of the theatre, an extension of his sense of life, was able to make this play at once a consummate technical achievement and a dramatic

summary of the Aran Islands.   The most powerful
effects are precisely those best illustrating the facts
of existence as realised by those who fight the waters
of the Atlantic for a difficult livelihood.   One of the
author's earliest impressions was the vital importance of this menace to the Islanders.   Describing
the keening he says:

> "In this cry of pain the inner consciousness of the people seems
> to lay itself bare for an instant, and to reveal the mood of beings
> who feel their isolation in the face of a universe that wars upon
> them with wind and seas.   They are usually silent, but in the
> presence of death all outward show of indifference or patience is
> forgotten, and they shriek with pitiable despair before the horror
> of the fate to which they all are doomed."

The poignancy of this cry is heard through every line
of *Riders to the Sea*.

Although not published until 1908, a year before
Synge's death, *The Tinker's Wedding* was written
contemporaneously with the one-act plays above
mentioned.   It may well have been the first play
conceived by him, as stated by Mr. John Masefield,
for it is the weakest.   W. B. Yeats has informed us
that the published version differs from the original
form in being more "unpopular."   If this change was
due—as the circumstances suggest—to any defiance
of popular prejudice by the author, who had just
passed through the *Playboy* "riot," one can only
regret that his courage did not equal his artistic
discrimination.   His experiences of Wicklow tramp
life should have provided Synge with something
more substantial than this farce, whose merits hardly
deserved two acts.   There is a fine energy of
grotesque humour in the anecdote of the two tinkers
whose belated desire to legalise their union results
in an utterly lawless outburst of contempt for religion and morality.   The complete freedom of mind

necessary to the appreciation of Synge's boisterous fun has not yet been forthcoming in Ireland, as might be expected, when one remembers the particular sanctities the author already stood accused of violating. If *In the Shadow of the Glen* and *The Playboy* seemed irreverent, *The Tinker's Wedding* is positively blasphemous, judged in the light of middle-class Irish propriety. Synge, of course, had no concern for such scruples, but he had an artistic conscience whose probity must eventually have condemned the play as inferior to the rest of his work.

The Well of the Saints was published in 1905 as the initial volume in the "Abbey Theatre Series" of plays, whose fifteen volumes now stand as a synthesis of the best work of the Dramatic Movement. The play was performed in the same year, and became one of the earliest international successes of the newly established Theatre, having been performed in German at Berlin in 1906. The experimental two acts of *The Tinker's Wedding* may be regarded as the point of transition to the full development of his power in the three acts of *The Well of the Saints* and its successors. Here Synge proclaims definitely that mastery of his art which subsequent achievement and criticism have confirmed. Relying upon the universally recognised dramatic potentialities of blindness as a theme, the author infuses his personality and his mood into a story whose origins are not traceable to any of his usual sources. Neither in Wicklow nor in West Kerry nor in the Aran Islands do his notebooks indicate the origins of this play, and much useless ingenuity has been wasted attributing it to Chaucer, Zola, Huysmans, Maeterlinck, Lord Lytton and Georges Clémenceau! The determination to unearth "sources" in the case of Synge has reached the point of an obsession with many critics, notably with those unfavourably disposed towards him.

The theme of *The Well of the Saints* is as universal as that of *Riders to the Sea*. The blind beggars who regain their sight by the operation of a miracle and lose it again, together with the desire to see, have an interest far exceeding that which could be diminished by the fact that they resemble the personages in Clémenceau's *Voile du Bonheur*. Whatever the analogies presented by "The Maid of Malines" in Lytton's *The Pilgrims of the Rhine*, Synge's Martin and Mary Dhoul are the specific creations of the author's genius. In their preference for the beauty of the imaginary world, as contrasted with the ugliness of reality revealed to them by the recovery of their sight, they are at once symbolic and personal. Surely we may see in their rejection of the commonplace facts of life a hint of that attitude which made Synge recoil from the horrors of industrial progress, and take refuge amongst a people whose imagination coloured reality? It is only necessary to observe in what beautiful terms Martin Dhoul and his wife interpret the world as transfigured by illusion, to conclude that they express the author himself. By a natural movement of the spirit he clothes his dream in the language whose rhythms had captured and held him far from the scene of modern civilisation. Preserving his characteristic interest in the picturesque realism of unspoiled life, Synge has given his peculiar imprint to the essentially Celtic drama of the conflict between the dream and the reality.

Until 1907 J. M. Synge was known, only to a limited public, as the author of three plays, two of which had procured him a reserve of enmity, whose fullest manifestation coincided with the extension of his fame to the English-speaking world of letters in that year. The incredible history of *The Playboy of the Western World* has been exhausted by numerous commentators, and may now be left for the notes of some future compiler of "Curiosities of Literature." The peculiarly hypercritical, over-strung nature of the criticism which followed Synge from the beginning has already been alluded to. It takes on the aspect of an uninterrupted pursuit of dubious literary ancestors, for the sole purpose of bringing some discredit upon the author, on moral, religious or political grounds. Most of these researches, though ostensibly directed towards estimating Synge's literary indebtedness, were undertaken with obvious intent to create prejudice, by associating the dramatist with names not honoured in Early Victorian circles. Where the appeal is not merely to preconceived moral verdicts, there is usually some suggestion of plagiarism. On the appearance of *The Playboy* all the antagonisms were aroused to a pitch of unusual violence, a veritable cult of hostility arose, and the anti-Synge campaign was launched. The noisy proceedings of Synge's opponents secured for the play a wide hearing, which might otherwise have been deferred. The obscure dramatist found himself famous in 1907, four years after the first public production of his work—such was the recognition he obtained when thrust, by unfriendly hands, upon the attention of competent critics.

The charm of *The Playboy* lies uniquely in its verbal and imaginative qualities. To enquire what are its moral intentions, to proclaim it libellous, to discuss its basis in reality, is to confess a complete understanding of the spirit in which such masterpieces are conceived. The fable of Christy Mahon's hour of triumph, when the belief that he has killed his father makes him at last conscious of his own identity, by reaction to the effect of his exploit upon the hearers of his narrative,—this is clearly no treatise on morals, to be refuted by reference to the well-known purity of Irish life.   Were all the evidence absent, which proves the Irish peasantry's very natural weakness for the fugitive from justice, the value of Synge's conception would be undiminished.   If Pegeen Mike were a grotesque exaggeration, instead of a wonderfully human personality, her admiration for the alleged parricide would still be one of those profound intuitions of which genius alone is capable. The play is a pure creation of the imagination, and its language responds to the intensity of the emotion in which it was conceived.   The singular beauty of the love-scenes between Christy and Pegeen Mike, the two characters in whom the exaltation of the dramatist's mood is most heightened, is the beauty of poetry in its essence.   It is poetry untrammelled by the mechanism of verse, as befits the natural simplicity of the speaker.   The rhythm and accent are there, coloured and emphasised by the Gaelic-English idiom, which has now become for the author a perfect instrument of poetic speech.   His knowledge of Gaelic, his work of selection on the Aran Islands, and the suggestions gleaned from Hyde's *Love Songs of Connacht*, have all formed in Synge's mind a well of literary strength, from which he derives the most diversely magnificent effects.   The amorous raptures of Christy, the angry interchanges of the women, the discourses of the publican—to every breath of passion there is a corresponding heightening of the key in which the language is pitched.   It is evident that Anglo-Irish is to Synge a medium in which he has obtained absolute freedom, he uses it with the same effect as the Elizabethans used

English. The savour and freshness of a language that is still unexploited, the wealth of imagery and the verbal magnificence of the Elizabethan tongue are felt and heard again in *The Playboy of the Western World.*

Nothing is more pathetic than to read Synge's attempted justification of this play in response to the demand for a statement of his purpose. His prefaces, and the testimony of his friends and biographers, show how averse he was to straining his art into the expression of "ideas," as the post-Shavian theory of drama demands. The stress of the riotous moment in which *The Playboy* appeared found the author unprepared. Critics and interviewers profited by his distress to drag from him some explanation of his play. He was first stampeded into describing it as an "extravaganza," then we find him writing to say that he was mistaken, and soon the point becomes obscured by his desire to produce evidence as to the probability or possibility of the incidents denounced in his play. The effect has been to confound this evidence, which replied only to specific accusations, with a general plea on behalf of the play itself. The controversies are dead, but there still remains the doubt they have sown as to the significance of *The Playboy.* The subject has been discussed in a manner which suggests nothing less absurd than an argument to determine whether Cervantes exaggerated, when describing the adventures of Don Quixote, or whether Tartarin de Tarascon was created by Daudet to illustrate the evils of mendacity. It is, of course, easier to recognise the creations of Daudet and Cervantes as belonging to pure fantasy; they are remote from us materially, but both writers gave offence to their immediate audiences.

We have seen in *The Well of the Saints* an example

of Synge's realistic treatment of a theme usually approached from the opposite direction. *The Playboy*, it may be said, is a further instance of the same kind. The scene of the play, the characterisation of the peasant types and the exteriorisation of the drama seem to indicate realism. Consequently, with the protests of the moralists and politicians in our ears, and the propagandist associations of dramatic realism to mislead us, we have attributed to Synge intentions which were never his, and to whose expression he vainly tried, at first, to adapt himself. Neither in *The Playboy* nor elsewhere did Synge attempt to contribute to the so-called theatre of ideas: "The drama," he says, "like the symphony, does not teach or prove anything." It is made serious "by the degree in which it gives the nourishment, not very easy to define, on which our imaginations live." This sentence defines exactly the serious purport of *The Playboy*, which is to nourish the imagination. The realism of the play is no more nor less than the realism of the language in which it is written. Both are the synthetic re-creation of very real elements in our life. Synge boasted that there was not a phrase of his dramatic speech but had its counterpart in the stories and conversations he heard in Gaelic Ireland, yet nobody pretends that Christy Mahon's talk is a literal transcription from life. The same is true of the play as a whole. It is a work of imaginative reconstruction, in which the moral and psychological elements are transfigured until they take on a universal significance. *The Playboy* stands in the same relation to the world of the Celtic imagination as Don Quixote did to the Spain of his day. In both cases the central figures have an existence which is at once personal, national and human.

The least important of Synge's two posthumous works is the volume, *Poems and Translations*, published in 1909, a few months after his death. These poems, written, for the most part, during his last period of illness, have the exaggerated strength, degenerating into brutality, which comes easily to a spirit strong enough to resent the restraint of a weak body. The latent pessimism, which always lurked behind Synge's most boisterous humour, stands out sharply in this handful of verses over which the shadow of his impending death crept, and finally closed in, before the book had passed through the press. Characteristically, he is at his best in the prose translations from Petrarch, Villon and others, where his command of Anglo-Irish idiom serves him well. Petrarch and Leopardi hardly lent themselves to this treatment, and his versions have rather the interest of an old song, re-sung in the accents of another age. Villon, however, remains admirably himself in the Gaelicised paraphrases which preserve much of the wild pathos of the original.

In 1910 the unfinished *Deirdre of the Sorrows* was given to the public, and brought home fully the great loss imposed upon Anglo-Irish letters by the death of Synge. That he could bring such originality and independence to the handling of a theme whose treatment a long line of poets had almost predetermined, indicated how far he was from having exhausted his talent. In the course of the Revival we have seen how the legend of Deirdre and Naisi attracted writers of the most diverse temperament, from the scholarly Ferguson to the mystic, A. E., and Yeats, the dramatic poet. A. E. and Yeats both failed, for very different reasons, to dramatise convincingly the story to which each of them gave his own personal, undramatic imprint. Synge projected himself perhaps more than they into his interpretation of the legend, but his instinctive feeling for drama, his sense of the theatre, saved him from their weakness. Unlike Yeats, who selected only the natural crisis as the moment of his tragedy, Synge followed A. E. and his predecessors, in taking the three episodes into which this part of the tragic history of the Red Branch falls. But it is not in technicalities of this kind that we must look for the originality of Synge, who made no innovations, beyond the introduction of that grotesque character, Owen. His success consisted in the skill with which he humanised the legendary figures, who were in danger of becoming stereotyped in a world of unreality, from which neither the delicate poetry of Yeats nor the mystic evocations of A. E. could save them. Synge did not approach the story as a poet or a visionary, but as a folk-dramatist, who could sense the relationship between the Ireland of the legend and that Gaelic Ireland in which the old spirit lingers. Still using the speech of his peasant plays he contrived to produce a tragedy, whose poetry surpasses that of Yeats's verse and A. E.'s prose, in dignity and beauty.

In Synge's version Deirdre is no longer a mere symbol or shadow, she steps out of legend and lives before us as an amorous woman, passionately devoted to beauty and happiness, which are her life. Her fear of old age, whose only meaning for her is death, has a poignancy enhanced by the author's power to communicate to her words something of his own despair in the presentiment that death was soon to rob him also of love and fame. The *Leitmotiv*, "death is a poor untidy thing at best, though it's a queen that dies," gives the play a tragic intensity, a human note absent from any other modern retelling of the

Deirdre saga. The heroic legend is translated into terms of universal tragedy, where the very real interest in the emotion of the protagonists by no means detracts from their value as legendary figures of symbolic significance. As Synge sees her, Deirdre is no less the passionate Queen of romance than the eternal victim of love, woman as she resigns herself to the inevitable passing away of what she holds dearest. There is an untamed fierceness in these people which marks them at once as belonging to that race of unspoiled children of nature whom Synge loved to study. In their primitiveness, and consequent resemblance to the peasant types of his other plays, they approximate more closely to the original personages of the legend. So we find, again, that his exterior realism does not involve any localism, but actually transcends the immediate occasion of it. Hence, for all its air of naturalistic peasant drama, *Deirdre of the Sorrows* most completely and dramatically satisfies the demand for a contemporary rehandling of heroic themes. In its freedom from the hampering effects of a too "literary" version, it achieves the swiftness and tension of high tragedy. With his sure instinct in these matters Synge clears his material of all beauties extraneous to the art of drama, he concentrates the action upon essentials, and by a wonderful employment of the means legitimately at his disposal, he causes the plays to move swiftly to the climax, whose inevitability broods over each scene. It is unnecessary to know the legend, every line and gesture involves the *dénouement* and prepares for it with consummate art.

It is easy to see what a future Synge might have enjoyed had he lived to extend to other aspects of our national life the methods he employed to such perfection. The material of legend revivified in the theatre after the manner of *Deirdre* might have given us a more varied dramatic literature than we possess. The absence of any followers of Yeats in his treatment of legendary lore, and the prestige of Synge, suggest that the latter could have led the way to the dramatisation of the Heroic cycles which he desired. As it is, his prestige has tended to effect quite contrary results. It was not his isolated essay in heroic drama that influenced his contemporaries, but his so-called "realistic" folk-plays. The ceaseless flow of peasant comedy and melodrama, in which the National Theatre has been almost submerged, is the penalty exacted by the success of Synge. But the query suggests itself: was Synge really a writer of realistic peasant plays? Is not the influence in question attributable to a misunderstanding of his work? Nobody has asserted that *Deirdre* belonged to that category. In fact regret has been expressed that Synge should, at the end, have forsaken his early manner. But, at bottom, *Deirdre* and *The Playboy* have more points of resemblance than of dissimilarity, so far as their peasant or legendary character is concerned. Reference has already been made to Synge's habit of treating realistically subjects which his compatriots invariably approach from a different angle, the conflict of imagination and reality, for example, in *The Well of the Saints*, and in *The Playboy* itself. The naturalness and actuality of the setting in the latter case are particularly misleading, but reflection would seem to confirm the belief that the adventures of Christy Mahon take place in the same world as did those of Peer Gynt.

In fine, Synge was a realist only in such a sense of the term as would embrace a Cervantes or the creator of Tartarin. But that is not the sense in which the peasant playwrights have understood him.

They have followed him only where he was most easily imitated, they have adopted his external procedure, ignoring the attitude of mind which brought him to the peasantry. His interest in the latter was of a purely spiritual and intellectual order. He saw in the Aran Islands what he termed "the last stronghold of the Gael" and his sole concern was for the spirit and tradition which he felt behind its inhabitants. A work of pure journalism—unique in his collected writings—are his articles on the Congested Districts, and there little of the genius of *The Playboy* is evident. But Synge was quite indifferent to the material aspects of peasant life, except in so far as they lent themselves to his artistic purpose. He regretted deeply any changes which seemed to threaten the richness of the literary vein which nourished his imagination. Of peasant realism, what, after all, has he given us but a few picturesque details which caught the eye of the dramatist? The language of his plays, the most tangible of his debts to the peasantry, has awakened no important echoes in the work of those who came after him. They use the speech of the people, but it is realistic speech, not the re-created dialect which Synge elaborated. As the folk-dramatists differ from him in this respect, so they differ from him in fundamentals. They have taken his realistic scenes, as they have taken the language of the people, and set up a framework of peasant drama, but they have not filled it with the subtle substance which transfigured the work of Synge. We should not expect them to do so. Genius is not added to every talent which the Dramatic Movement has encouraged. But in J. M. Synge the impulse of the Revival met with the response of genius. It did not create him, as it has done others, but it discovered in him that spark of originality which eventually burst into the flame of brilliant imagination. In that light he revealed Ireland to us, its beauty and its ugliness; but in so doing he enabled us to see beyond the limitations of place and time into the regions inhabited by the eternal spirit of mankind.

PADRAIC COLUM

The year which saw the production of *In the Shadow of the Glen* also marked the entrance upon the scene of the National Theatre of a young playwright whose originality entitles him to a place in its annals second only to that of Synge. Padraic Colum was the first of the peasant dramatists, in the strict sense of the word; he was, that is to say, the first to dramatise the realities of rural life in Ireland. Where Synge's fantastic intuition divined human prototypes, Colum's realistic insight revealed local peasant types, whose general significance is subordinate to the immediate purpose of the dramatist. Together they define the limits within .which our folk-drama has developed, for none of the later playwrights has added anything to the tradition initiated by Padraic Colum and J. M. Synge. With rare exceptions, which will be noticed, their successors have failed to give personality to their work, contenting themselves with certain general formulæ, whose elaboration leaves them as far from the restraint of Colum as from the flamboyancy of Synge. For, it is interesting to note, the former dramatist is the direct antithesis of the latter, nor has he been at all influenced by him, in spite of the disparity of their respective successes. Synge's fame and work made resistance difficult for all but the most original of his young contemporaries. But Colum has remained, at the cost of popular recognition, faithful to the spirit of *Broken Soil*, whose almost simultaneous appearance with Synge's first play precluded any possibility of imitation.

Broken Soil, however, was not the author's first dramatic work, although it introduced him to the public in 1903, under the auspices of the recently constituted Irish National Theatre Society. As early as 1901 Colum had come into contact with the brothers Fay, whose theatrical enterprise previously described had awakened in him the desire to write for the stage. He became an active member of the Fays' group, taking part in the production of A. E.'s *Deirdre* in 1902, the year of his first published plays, *The Kingdom of the Young* and *The Saxon Shillin'*, the latter being performed, with considerable propagandist success, in 1903. Once caught in the enthusiasm of the Fays and their company, Colum wrote a great deal of dramatic 'prentice work, which appeared, like the plays mentioned, in *The United Irishman*, that cradle of many contemporary Irish reputations. *The Foleys* and *Eoghan's Wife* were further essays of the same kind, all leading in the direction of those studies of peasant Ireland beginning with *Broken Soil*, which was followed by *The Land* in 1905, and by *Thomas Muskerry* in 1910. Unfortunately, for various reasons, attributable in part to the nature of his work, these three plays are all that we have upon which to form an estimate of his achievement. *The Miracle of the Corn* (1907) and *The Destruction of the Hostel* (1910) are trifles whose charm does not alter the fact that they are but slightly more characteristic of the author than *The Desert* (1912). It is true, he is but obeying his original impulse towards old legend in dramatising the incident of the destruction of the House of Da

Derga, for his most youthful effort was a play founded on the story of the *Children of Lir*, one of the tableaux produced by the brothers Fay. In his little miracle play he is still close to national tradition, but the oriental setting of *The Desert* breaks definitely the mould of his talent. It was followed, however, by *The Betrayal*, which is again in the direct line of the author's development, being a dramatisation of an incident arising out of the agrarian revolt in the closing years of the eighteenth century. Although successfully produced it has not yet been included among the dramatist's published works.

The Land, although his second play, was published in 1905 prior to *Broken Soil*, which did not appear in book form until its material had been recast as *The Fiddler's House*, two years later. It is at once more logical and more significant that Padraic Colum's published writings should begin with that "agrarian comedy," for there he handles the central and fundamental fact of peasant life, the call of the land. The struggle between town and country to hold the people, the problem of rural life, which is at last receiving serious attention, is the leading note of *The Land*. In Ireland it is against the attraction of the United States, no less than against the lure of urban civilisation, that resistance must be strengthened, and the dramatist shows us the drain upon the countryside resulting from the emigration of the young and vigorous. The conflict between Matt Cosgar and his father is not solved by the final submission of the old peasant to his son's threat that he will follow his kin to America. Ellen Douras, whose fancy is captivated by the wondertales of American life, infects Matt with her own restlessness, and they leave the land to

Cornelius and Sally and their parents. The inefficient and the old remain, while strength and enterprise are exported for the benefit of Transatlantic industrialism. The sadness and seriousness of the familar situation are heightened by the fact that the action takes place during the period when the hope of peasant ownership is at the point of realisation. The older men, who fought and suffered for the possession of the land, have arranged to purchase their holdings under the new Land Act. They are full of pride and joy at this final recognition of their savagely contested claims.

With the true sense of the peasant mind which characterises him, Colum seizes upon this tragedy, none the less poignant because the key is subdued. In various ways he succeeds in bringing out the revolt of the young people against the conventions and conditions of their elders. Matt Cosgar will not tolerate that implicit obedience to the father which is at the root of the family system, as practised in France and rural Ireland. He rebels against the law which prescribes that marriages must be arranged by the parents for financial considerations, without regard for the wishes of the young couples so united. The picture is one of peculiar power: the clash of wills between two generations of peasantry. Those who have won the soil find themselves abandoned by their children, who know only the hardships of the long struggle for possession, and are unable or unwilling to profit by the victory, which means so much to the men who fought for it. After all the crime and suffering of which the land was the occasion, the best energies of the countryside are not to be drawn upon for the work of reconstruction. The dearly-bought possession is left to the feeble, while the city and emigration absorb the strength of those to whom it should have been bequeathed. The rural exodus is being stemmed, but the subject of *The Land* has lost little of its interest for all who have a thought for the future of Ireland.

The Fiddler's House is a study of another aspect of peasant life. Having shown us the peasant face to face with the fundamental problem of his existence, in his relation to the land, the dramatist now portrays him in his spiritual and artistic manifestations. The ties of the soil are, of course, a part of the drama, for Conn Hourican is the peasant as artist, and the essential factor of that condition is not wanting. But while the land hunger finds its expression in his child Anne, the father is primarily a study in temperament. The old fiddler, for all his attachment to home, carries within him the yearning for change and freedom, the inability to remain settled, which we associate with the nature of genius. The trait which unites the artist and the vagabond brings Conn Hourican somewhat nearer to the symbolic types of Synge than is usual with the carefully realised figures of Colum's drama. Hourican hears and obeys the call of the road, and it is the same voice that draws him as called the tramps whom Synge reconstructed out of his Wicklow and West Kerry experiences. When the fiddler leaves his house the words which come to his lips show the same instinct for the poetry of natural beauty as was revealed by the blind beggar in *The Well of the Saints*, when they described their vision of nature. Not that the artistic faculty of Conn finds expression in the glowing phrases of Synge's fantasy. Nothing could more beautifully illustrate the complete independence of Colum than his treatment of this theme. The deep distrust entertained by respectable peasants towards the unattached man of the roads, the concern of Conn's daughters at his desire to resume his vagabondage, are the fitting background against which to set this fine old figure. The sympathy and realism which have gone to the portrayal of Conn Hourican make of him the personification of that element of our peasant life to which folk-art and folk-poetry owe their existence and preservation.

With the exception of the specifically agrarian problem, which was the point of departure of *The Land*, there is no question more vital than the patriarchal family system which obtains throughout rural Ireland. In selecting this theme for *Thomas Muskerry* Padraic Colum displayed his characteristic feeling for those situations and aspects of life which present themselves most readily to the mind of a people mainly composed of the peasant class. The sacrifice of the individual to the family unit is a tradition preserved most carefully in the agricultural communities of Western Europe. In France novelists have not been lacking to interpret this characteristic aspect of that country of small landholders. It is strange that no writer of Irish fiction has given us an equivalent to Henry Bordeaux's *Les Roquevillard*. But all through the work of Colum the sense of family life is evident. We have the problem suggested in *The Land*, where the revolt of the younger generation is, in part, accounted for by the exigencies of paternal authority. In *Thomas Muskerry* the full significance of the system is revealed.

Instead of illustrating his subject by the elaboration of those hints at revolt which are noticeable in the earlier plays, the dramatist has preferred to reverse the process. It is not the children who feel the restraints of family duty, but the old father, Thomas Muskerry, who dies a pauper in the workhouse of which he once was master, after being cruelly exploited by his relations. This middle-class family in a country town is aptly chosen for the development of such a theme. Being just one remove from the soil, they retain all the worst traits of their immediate peasant forerunners and serve best to emphasise the evils to which the exaggerated sense of domestic obligations may lead. The kindness and generosity of Muskerry have for years encouraged his children and their dependents to exercise their cupidity and unscrupulousness at his expense. When they find him no longer profitable, they cease to play upon the family relationship, and frankly abandon him, having robbed him of his good name, his dignity and his money. The tragic end of this victim of the claims of kinship is the culminating event in a grim story of petty meannesses and sordid motives, all arising out of the exploitation of kindness in the name of family solidarity. There are few writers who have disclosed with such insight the under-currents of existence in our provincial towns, where the virtues of the peasant are lost in the indirect contact with the ambitions and practises of urban civilisation. Living on the margin, as it were, between the city and the land the people develop only the inferior qualities of either life.

It would be misleading to leave the dramatic work of Padraic Colum without making clear his innocence of any avowedly didactic purpose. A brief analysis of his plays involves the use of phrases which are perhaps more convenient than accurate. *The Land* and *Thomas Muskerry* envisage certain phases of Irish life which constitute the "problems" of our sociologists, but the latter need not suspect him of any intention to anticipate their conclusions. The effort of the dramatist is not to propound or solve social questions, but is directed,

as he says, "towards the creation of situations."
"For character conceived as a psychological synthesis he has only a secondary concern." In thus
defining the attitude of the playwright, Colum
clearly demonstrates the character of his own work.
The three plays that have been mentioned are
primarily attempts to situate the Irish peasant
in such circumstances as to bring out the essential drama of rural life. Coming from the Midlands, and viewing the world from the standpoint
of the peasantry, he saw at once the naturally
dramatic situations in which they revealed themselves most characteristically. These restrained and
faithful pictures, from which every exaggerated or
adventitious element is eliminated, have a quality
which recalls Ibsen in their almost purely intellectual
action. Colum even avoids the melodramatic *dé-
nouements* which the author of *Hedda Gabler* did not
disdain.

In this last respect, but in that only, the later
peasant playwrights approach more closely to Ibsen.
The majority, indeed, show so marked an affection
for violent effects and purely external drama, that
the local setting of their work seems fortuitous. The
drama of Padraic Colum, on the other hand, is
peculiarly Irish, and has its very basis in peasant
conditions. One cannot imagine Conn Hourican,
Murtagh Cosgar or Thomas Muskerry transplanted
to another soil, their roots are too deep. Unlike so
many of their successors on the stage of the National
Theatre they could not develop just as well in London, Liverpool or New York. The greater part of
our pseudo "peasant" drama is merely melodrama
with an Irish accent. The situations are not inherent
in, or peculiar to, our national life, but are adapted.
They might serve equally as well to illustrate the

tragedy of an English slum or the dramatic possibilities of popular politics in the United States.   Even where the national and literary quality of the work done by his successors is beyond dispute, the achievement of Padraic Colum only gains by comparison. Without any predecessors of importance, he shares with Synge the right to be considered the most original of our folk-dramatists.   W. B. Yeats has said that Synge wrote of the peasant "as he is to all the ages; of the folk-imagination as it has been shaped by centuries of life among fields or on fishing grounds."   If it be admitted that, in this manner, Synge transcended the limits popularly ascribed to the peasant play, then, indeed, Padraic Colum is the first of our peasant playwrights.   By confining himself to the realistic interpretation of everyday country life he gives us the complement of Synge's transmutations.   Together their work completes, as it initiated, the dramatic realisation of peasant Ireland.

CHAPTER XIV

THE DRAMATIC MOVEMENT: THIRD PHASE

POPULARITY AND ITS RESULTS: "ABBEY" PLAYS AND
PLAYWRIGHTS. THE ULSTER LITERARY THEATRE:
RUTHERFORD MAYNE

A DEFINITE stage in the history of the
Irish Theatre was marked by the performance of *The Playboy of the Western World*
in 1907. The effect of the storm which
centred about Synge was to bring the Theatre notoriety, fame and, finally, popular success. As a
result of this sudden change of fortune, a host of
young dramatists came forward, some possessed by
real talent, others attracted by the popularity of the
Abbey Theatre. Almost all the names prominently
identified with that institution in recent years are
those of playwrights who came in on the wave of
success, after 1907. Those who helped to lay the
foundations of that success have either ceased to
figure on the programme of the Theatre, or their work
has been performed at such rare intervals as to con-
fine their public chiefly to the printed book, whenever
the plays were available in that form. It is true a
fairly constant effort has been made to keep the
work of Yeats and Synge before the public, but the
number of such performances is not commensurate
with the importance of these writers. Later dramatists of much inferior quality have come to domi-

344

nate the scene, at the expense of their more serious predecessors. Of the latter, only two have succeeded in holding popular attention to the same degree as the newcomers, probably because of their closer affinity. Lady Gregory and William Boyle may, for that reason, be classed with the later playwrights, rather than with the initiators of the Revival, although they have been associated with the National Theatre since an early date.

LADY GREGORY AND WILLIAM BOYLE

Lady Gregory's share in the Dramatic Movement has been adequately noticed by the various critics who have written the history of the Irish Theatre, and her own volume of reminiscences has served to complete the record. It is, therefore, only necessary to consider her work in so far as it concerns the literary history of the Revival. She has contributed more extensively to the repertoire of the Abbey Theatre than any other playwright, and since 1903, when her first play, *Twenty-Five*, was produced, up to the present time, her twenty, or more, comedies and dramas have been constantly performed, to the evident satisfaction of the general public. She has been the faithful coadjutor of W. B. Yeats from the time when she was appointed to control the policy of the National Theatre, and the practical value of her services has been widely recognised and acknowledged. Reference has already been made to the collaboration of Lady Gregory in certain of Yeats's plays, notably in *The Unicorn from the Stars*, which was published over their joint names. To this volume may be added the collection, *Seven Short Plays* (1908), *The Image* (1910), two volumes of *Irish Folk History Plays* (1912), and *New Comedies* (1913)—these represent the greater part of her original contributions to the Irish Theatre. She has published some of her translations from the Gaelic of Douglas Hyde in parallel editions of the latter's work, and *The Kiltartan Molière* (1910), peasant dialect versions of *Le Médecin Malgré lui*, *Les Fourberies de Scapin* and *L'Avare*. The latter have enjoyed a success which might not have been predicted of so daring an experiment, but these translations bear a remarkable affinity to the original. Lady Gregory has preserved much that must have evaporated had she employed the formal English of modern times. The nearest English to that of Molière's century is the idiom of peasant Ireland. The delight of her audiences was sufficient proof of Lady Gregory's superiority over the conventional translators of French classics. *The Kiltartan Molière* is an illustration of the real nature of her talent, which has been so happily exercised in translation.

Twenty-Five, the crude, amateurish, little drama with which Lady Gregory began her career as a dramatist, does not find a place amongst her collected plays, whereas its immediate successor, *Spreading the News*, was one of the first to be published. This farcical comedy in one act has lost none of its popularity since its production in 1904, and has been constantly seen at the Abbey Theatre and elsewhere. Having found favour so early and so permanently, it may fairly serve as the prototype of the long series of similar farces which are collected into the two volumes, *Seven Short Plays* and *New Comedies*. Starting with some utterly absurd incident,—the distortion of an innocent statement by village gossips in *Spreading the News*,—Lady Gregory infuses a wildly humorous spirit into the complications which ensue. The humour is always sharpened by the droll conversation and idiom in which it is clothed.

Frequently, indeed, the fun depends almost entirely upon the language and mimicry of the actors. Nothing she has written can vie with *The Workhouse Ward* as a source of laughter, and this is a comedy of words pure and simple. The exchange of flattery and abuse between the two old paupers as they lie in bed, their final and utterly unexpected refusal to be separated —of such characteristically simple elements are Lady Gregory's best comedies composed. Their weakness is, therefore, obvious. They are evidently written for the school of acting which performed them, they count in advance upon certain histrionic talents to create the comedy, and they are condemned to repeat themselves. Consequently, Lady Gregory's printed plays are of slight interest, except to those who have seen them acted, and, above all, they show no progress. *New Comedies* contains nothing that was not in *Spreading the News* or *Hyacinth Halvey*, the first two of their kind. In *The Image*, the longest comedy Lady Gregory has written, the attempt to strike out in a new direction is frustrated by the fact that the subject does not lend itself to three acts, being of the same tenuous, farcical material as the one-act comedies,—which she now describes as farces, it is interesting to note.

In addition to broad farce Lady Gregory has written six "Folk History Plays," where melodrama, as in *Kincora*, and comedy, as in *The White Cockade* and *The Canavans*, are the result of an innovation in the writing of historical drama. It is the author's purpose to make Irish history live in the popular imagination by interpreting legends and events in terms allied to those of the folk-play. From the beginning Lady Gregory made use of the Anglo-Irish idiom which she has termed "Kiltartan," after the district in which she heard it spoken, and its more obvious quaintness has given a special claim to her comedies. She did not secure the beautiful effects of Synge; his ear for the harmonies of language and his sense of poetic and dramatic style were part of his genius. But the Kiltartan dialect employed by Lady Gregory is a more faithful transcript of actual peasant speech, and, without being subjected to the selective and combinative process of a sensitive imagination, it has a natural savour which makes its use in comedy highly effective. Its application, however, to these "Folk History Plays" is far less successful, especially as comparison with Synge's *Deirdre* is at once suggested. *Deirdre* is a real folk-history play, with all the qualities of poetic tragedy bathed in the atmosphere and language of a folk-tale. In *Grania* Lady Gregory has caught something of Synge's rhythm and simple grandeur, and this tragedy stands out in contrast with the other plays of the group. But the *genre* is alien to her talent, and although credit must be given for her isolated treatment of the strangely neglected Grania story, her success lies elsewhere. The one-act form seems to be prescribed for her, whether in comedy or tragedy. *The Gaol Gate*, for example, is a poignant little play, in which the tragic note is clearer than in any of the more pretentious dramas. Lady Gregory has herself hinted at the exigencies of practical theatre management as the reason for her frequent contributions to the stage. She wrote to meet the need for one-act plays created by the conditions of the Irish theatre. Inevitably she has had to repeat the methods which had proved successful. But she has given us a sufficient number of well-written, diverting comedies to entitle her to a claim upon our remembrance, apart from her directorial assistance in the work of the Abbey Theatre.

Except that William Boyle's plays for the Irish
Theatre are in three or four acts they do not differ
essentially from those of Lady Gregory. But Kiltartan speech does not enter into their composition,
so they are deprived of one of Lady Gregory's
sources of humour and literary charm. This being
true of the rank and file of "Abbey" playwrights,
the author is more akin to them than to her, and the
fact explains their inferiority. William Boyle had
published a book of peasant sketches, *A Kish of
Brogues*, six years before *The Building Fund* announced his adherence to the Dramatic Movement
in 1905. He came forward, therefore, armed with
his experiences as a story-teller, and with a certain
preconception of the way in which the comedy of
rural Irish manners should be presented. His first
play was cast in the same setting as had provided
the material for *A Kish of Brogues*, and the peasantry
of County Louth are believable human beings, as
he portrays them. But very soon it became evident
that the author preferred to work from the machine-
made pattern rather than from life. Perhaps the
effort of attempting to express himself in a new
medium upon a familiar theme stimulated his imagination at the beginning, for *The Building Fund* has
remained unequalled by the plays which followed it.

The Eloquent Dempsey (1906) is merely grotesque
farce, and has no more bearing upon life than *The
Private Secretary* or *General John Regan*. The same
is true of *Family Failing*, the most recent comedy by
William Boyle, which suggests that no development
may be expected of such art as his. *The Mineral
Workers*, which was produced shortly after *The Eloquent Dempsey*, had more serious intentions, but the
multiplicity of persons and motives got beyond
the author's control, to the defeat of his purpose.

The clash of modern methods and ideas, personified by a returned Irish-American engineer, with the ignorance and conservatism of the peasantry, whose land he wishes to mine, would have made an excellent study, but the practical success of the plays has been as farcical comedy. Next to Lady Gregory, the most popular writer of farce has been William Boyle. Yet *The Building Fund* showed that the dramatist could evoke laughter by characterisation, instead of caricature. Unfortunately he has shown no tendency to make his success of 1905 a point of progressive departure. He has moved further and further in the opposite direction, obtaining applause as a purveyor of facile amusement.

The year 1908 was marked by the appearance of several new playwrights whose work expressed the changed condition in which the Abbey Theatre found itself. Its public had been widened by the notoriety and sympathy which were the immediate consequence of the Synge controversies, and this wider audience could not be reached without the sacrifice of many ideals and principles. It is impossible to reconcile the artistic programme which Yeats had defined in the early issues of *Samhain* with the evolution of the Irish Theatre from this point onwards, and, by a significant coincidence, that review ceased to exist in 1908. Of course, by this time the Theatre had become so well known that the necessity for a special propagandist organ like *Samhain* had lost its original justification. But those pages of doctrine and practice were never more precious than in recent years, when they seemed a bulwark against the rising tide of commercialism. It is regrettable that they should have disappeared just when all that they stood for was being undermined by concessions to "popular" audiences and "practical" advice. While W. B. Yeats adhered personally to the principles whose lofty idealism inspired the Dramatic Movement, the policy of the Theatre was governed by considerations which had again and again been repudiated by him in *Samhain* and elsewhere. It would appear as if the fight on behalf of *The Playboy* had exhausted the power of resistance which had kept the Theatre free from the pressure of financial and commercial wisdom.

Impressed by the reception accorded to Synge, and conscious of the ready hearing to be obtained by the playwright who could cater to the newly-found taste for peasant drama, numerous young writers awoke to find themselves dramatists. With neither the poetic genius of Synge, nor the psychological insight of Colum, they adopted a combination of the external features of both these dramatists' work. Naturally they could imitate only the more obvious and unessential elements. Synge's occasional violence of language, for example, becomes a regular part of the stereotyped peasant play, while Colum's quiet realism is transformed into sordid melodrama. Murder, drunkenness and crime are the favourite themes, and the playwrights combine the incidents with so careful a regard for the formulæ, that their work is almost indistinguishable. The language and setting are also prescribed by rule, and the reign of the fashionable folk-drama is inaugurated. In the course of time tours in England and the United States are found to be profitable undertakings, they become more and more frequent, the plays produced conform more and more to type, until finally the sole criterion of success is financial. The day-book and ledger replace *Beltaine* and *Samhain* as the organs of the National Theatre; the farces of William Boyle and the melodramas of W. F. Casey or T. C. Murray are substituted for the "unprofitable" plays of W. B. Yeats or Padraic Colum.

There is no reason why Ireland should not hear her voice speak in melodramatic tones, and the introduction of popular drama and comedy with the familiar accent of our own people is doubtless an improvement upon the imported article. The authors of *The Man who missed the Tide*, *The Cross Roads* and *The White Feather* have clearly demonstrated the possibility of successfully challenging the English monopoly of melodrama. It is no longer necessary to allow one's feelings to be harrowed simultaneously by the pronunciation and adventures of heroines and heroes from Camberwell or Fulham. Until the Abbey Theatre entered upon this latest phase, we were obliged to submit, when patriotic, to the tears and laughter of Boucicault, or when more emotionally inclined, to his English equivalents. Moreover, our Irish melodramatists are, in the main, less conventional than the imported variety, or perhaps it would be more correct to say, they are followers of newer conventions. The happy ending, the monologue, and the beautiful, yet virtuous, heroine are eliminated, in favour of more home-like virtues. Political feuds, family rivalries and the failure of idealists— these are the substitutes more in keeping with the external facts of Irish life. Mr. Walter Melville's wayward damsels might have referred to the "dreadful splendid life of the great city," as does the girl in S. L. Robinson's *Harvest*, but these are only occasional lapses. The same writer's first play, *The Clancy Name*, is more typical, while *Patriots* and *The Dreamers* prove that he is capable of rising above that level. In the former he has depicted the dramatic change which separates two political generations in Ireland, a change so profound as to render almost incredible *The Dreamers,* when this handling of Robert Emmet's story is compared with the conventional, Boucicaultian treatment of historic subjects.

The dramatist himself has more or less repudiated those crude first efforts, and in *The Whiteheaded Boy* and *The Lost Leader* he has completely vindicated himself. *The Whiteheaded Boy,* which had its first performance in Dublin in 1916, is one of the finest pieces of natural human comedy in the repertory of the Irish Theatre. It is free from the stale devices of Sardoodledom as from the rather stereotyped humours of the Kiltartan dialect farce. The element which gives its fine quality to this comedy is the complete naturalness of the dialogue and the intrinsic, unforced humour of the theme. The situations develop with the simplicity of life itself. There is not a "stagey" moment, nor a line that is theatrical, and the "curtains" are distressingly undramatic from the orthodox point of view. Yet, the whole play moves forward, irresistible in its cumulative effect, and with the constant motive of social satire always present, but never obtrusive. An interesting innovation in the printed text is the narrative form of the stage directions, which enable the reader to enjoy the illusion of listening to a spoken commentary on the actions of the characters. Lennox Robinson has avoided the technical jargon of the old stage direction, without imitating the garrulous confidences which Bernard Shaw likes to interpolate for the elucidation of his situations.

More daring and novel in theme is *The Lost Leader,* with its postulate of the popular Irish superstition that Parnell is not dead, but living in obscurity. Parnell is brought upon the stage and the dramatic interest develops out of the confrontation by modern Sinn Féin Ireland of its hero out of another phase of Irish revolt. It was too bold an experiment to be altogether successful, but it is an experiment which testifies to the increasing vitality and originality of Lennox Robinson's talent. A heightened dramatic sense and a surer craftsmanship are also revealed in the little volume of *Eight Short Stories*, his second essay in fiction. But neither this work nor its predecessor, *A Young Man from the South*, should lead the author away from his true vein, the theatre.

The little group of Munster dramatists to which Lennox Robinson belonged has more recently added several notable plays to the achievements of the Irish Theatre. T. C. Murray's *Birthright* was contemporaneous with Robinson's early plays, having been produced in 1910, but since the war the name of Daniel Corkery has emerged through the remarkable quality of *The Yellow Bittern* and *The Hermit and the King*. But it is as a novelist, rather than a playwright that, as we shall see, Daniel Corkery has established his fame in the forefront of contemporary Anglo-Irish literature. Nevertheless, the plays which he has collected under the title of *The Yellow Bittern and Other Plays* are a contribution to the poetic drama which recalls the early years of triumphant experiment in a *genre* now too frequently subordinated to peasant melodrama.

SEUMAS O'KELLY

The case of Seumas O'Kelly affords a not too unfavourable illustration of this tendency, inasmuch as he has not been definitely excluded from the National Theatre, but was admitted after he had proved the quality of his work elsewhere. *The Shuiler's*

Child was produced in 1909 by the company of amateurs known as the "Theatre of Ireland," which had previously performed the two less remarkable plays of his *début*. It was not until eighteen months later that the merit of *The Shuiler's Child*,—which had meanwhile been published,—was formally recognised by the directors of the National Theatre, where it is occasionally produced. Of recent peasant plays this is one of the most remarkable, by reason of its originality in the treatment of a subject apt to degenerate into *clichés* and melodrama. Avoiding high-strung violence, the dramatist has put a wild intensity into this story of the sacrifice made by a tramp woman who overcomes her desire to claim the child she once deserted. When she sees her little son thriving in the care of his adopted parents she recognises that his advantage lies in her renunciation. The portrayal of this struggle, and the characterisation of the vagabond, in whose heart the emotion of maternity is turned to something fierce and lawless as her own life, are admirable. Powerful also is the suggestion of two contrasted states of society, personified in the wild, instinctive woman of the roads and the peaceful affection of the foster parents in their prosperous farm home. A *dénouement* as effective as it is natural is the flight of the woman at the threat of the law to imprison her for deserting her child, when she had made the supreme sacrifice for her boy's welfare.

In spite of the need for one-act plays at the Abbey Theatre, explained by Lady Gregory by way of apology for her own efforts, *The Matchmakers, The Stranger* and *The Homecoming* have been performed only by amateurs, the two first mentioned having preceded *The Shuiler's Child*, the other having followed it. They appeared in a volume entitled *Three*

Plays, in 1912. Although not to be classed with the longer play, all three are free from any defect which would explain their exclusion as unfit to rank with the average comedy or one-act drama of the Abbey Theatre to-day. They may be cited, therefore, as instances of the increasing failure of the National Theatre to respond to the contemporary dramatic movement. The condition of proving oneself a good investment has resulted in a certain diversion of literary activity into channels undisturbed by the preoccupations of commerce. At the end of 1913, however, a second play by Seumas O'Kelly was produced on the scene of his former success. Significantly, it is here that he shows signs of conforming to the popular standard of "Abbey" melodrama. *The Bribe* is a belated, if not unworthy, successor to *The Shuiler's Child*, in the repertoire of the National Theatre. For his theme the author has chosen one of the most discreditable features of rural politics in Ireland, the corruption which characterises the making of public appointments. The tragic consequences of the election of an incompetent dispensary doctor is perhaps a little forced, and gives a melodramatic violence to the climax, but the exposition of motives and the picture of provincial manners are so skilful as to enable one to discount this fault.

GEORGE FITZMAURICE

A revival performance of *The Country Dressmaker* in 1912 drew attention to a young dramatist who had been almost forgotten during the five years which had elapsed since the first production of that play. George Fitzmaurice belongs to that neglected category of Irish playwrights whose work has been overshadowed by the popular successes of the newcomers to the Movement. *The Country Dressmaker* dates from the same year as *The Playboy*, having followed it in 1907, while the little "one-acter," *The Piedish*, was performed early in 1908, prior to the accession of the imitative school of peasant drama. George Fitzmaurice is, therefore, the legitimate successor of Synge and Colum amongst the serious exponents of folk-play, although he has had to wait long for recognition.   Rarely performed, his work was not published until 1914 when *The Country Dressmaker* appeared, to be followed shortly by *Five Plays*, a volume in which all that he cares to submit for criticism has been collected.   In addition to the two plays mentioned, he has added *The Moonlighter*, *The Magic Glasses* and *The Dandy Dolls*, making this book the most striking contribution to our dramatic literature since the death of Synge.

A noticeable feature of Fitzmaurice's work is the evident development of his talent between 1907 and 1914.   His first play does not, as is so often the case, represent the beginning and the end of the dramatist. Although he gave unmistakable indications of an original quality in his presentation of peasant comedy, *The Country Dressmaker* was marred by that gross exaggeration, amounting to caricature, which makes so many of our comedies degenerate into farce.   The influences doubtless responsible for this blemish have been referred to, but while they might betray the author at times, he could not write so as to be confounded with them.   The delineation of character in this story of match-making intrigue, with its central figure, the romantic novelette-reading dressmaker, places George Fitzmaurice apart from the average writer of farce.   The temptation to overemphasise the part of the dressmaker could not have been resisted by an author intent merely on raising a laugh by any species of buffoonery or horseplay. Avoiding the obvious, the dramatist depicts an effective study of a woman whose life has been largely moulded by the romance of cheap fiction, but who is extraordinarily natural and dignified in her sober translation of the fictitious into reality. With the exception of one caricatural effort, the characters are intensely true to human nature in general, and to rural Ireland in particular, and their language is a perfect expression of themselves. At this date it was already evident that George Fitzmaurice had a keen sense of the value of Anglo-Irish idiom as a literary medium.

The Piedish (1908), though a trifle, contained further evidence of promise, both in its use of peasant-speech and in its choice and treatment of a theme by no means sure of popular comprehension. The unintelligent laughter which greeted this fable of the dying old man, whose soul is concentrated upon his artistic purpose, cannot do the author an injustice, now that the printed text is available. But until recently he has had to suffer the penalty of hearing the play misrepresented by those who could see only the grotesque aspect of the old modeller's anxiety to complete the piedish before he dies. Accustomed to the farcical entertainment so frequently provided, audiences had gathered who were unable to appreciate this exposition in terms of folk-drama of the familiar struggle between the Paganism of the artist and the conventions of Christianity. Resting upon misapprehension, *The Piedish* could not, for several years, help in any way to extend the author's reputation, and became simply an obstacle to his success. In this way, the declining standard of taste encouraged by the Abbey Theatre has worked for the ruin of the Dramatic Movement, excluding some of the best short plays in the repertoire, and retarding the progress of original writers. At the lowest estimate both *The Piedish* and its predecessor deserved to be as well known as the works to which preference in recent years has been given.

The longest play which George Fitzmaurice has written is *The Moonlighter,* whose four acts approximate, more closely than usual with him, to the accepted notion of Irish peasant drama. The title itself indicates the nature of the play, which is set in the stormy period of the agrarian agitation. There are many characters and incidents of the type now familiar, the loud-mouthed violent heroes of rural melodrama, but again, the fine portrayal of the chief figures gives distinction to the play. The Fenian father whose blood has cooled, but whose son essays in theory to emulate him, only to abandon enthusiasm when physical danger is near; the hostility of the man of action to the young generation so full of words; and the final outburst of the old Fenian spirit, when these words become deeds with their inevitable sequence of brutality—these are the elements of which excellent drama is made. The presence of some stock figures of the "Abbey convention" is forgotten in the pleasure of observing the evolution of several wonderfully conceived types of Irish peasant.

The increasing mastery of Anglo-Irish idiom noticeable in the plays of George Fitzmaurice finds its consummation in *The Magic Glasses* and *The Dandy Dolls.* Both are in one act, and have neither the plot nor the substance which would justify detailed exposition. *The Magic Glasses* is situated professedly in some region subject to the laws of time and space, whereas *The Dandy Dolls* is a fantasmagoria pure and simple. But the two plays are essentially works of fantastic imagination, in which exuberant fancy is reflected in language of the same vigorous brilliance and superb colour as are found in Synge. Yet there is no *pastiche* of *The Playboy* in either. Except that both writers use the same instrument, the Gaelicised English of the West, they are dissimilar. The poetry of Synge hardly finds expression in these wildly humorous passages, where sentiment gives way to action. Fitzmaurice, however, shows the delight of the artist in the effects which may be obtained from the verbal wealth of the Anglo-Irish idiom, he has a sharp ear for those words and phrases which stimulate the intellectual palate by their savour and strength. There is something unreal in this dialectical imagery which accords perfectly with the strange, exotic world of which we get a glimpse. The dollmaker, who fears that "the Hag's son" will again steal the windpipe from the throat of his creations, is of the same race as the family who consult the doctor of magic that he may cure their son of his propensity for fairy music. These are all creatures of imagination, and we must greet them as we greeted the Trolds in *Peer Gynt*, of whose adventures, it may be said, *The Dandy Dolls* reminds us. With his extraordinary power of fantasy and grotesque vision, George Fitzmaurice may some day give us an Irish counterpart of the great Norwegian romance. He has proved, at least, that he possesses precisely that imaginative quality which, superadded to the genius of Synge, would have enabled the latter to conceive an Irish Peer Gynt. He has but to refine and cultivate a talent which possesses the somewhat uncouth vigour of undisciplined nature.

LORD DUNSANY

While the third phase of the Dramatic Revival is characterised, in the main, by the sacrifice of ideals and standards, there have, nevertheless, been occasions when the original spirit has re-asserted itself. The welter of undistinguished plays produced within the last five years should not blind us to the fact that the Abbey Theatre has periodically justified its fundamental purpose. Having referred to the revived interest shown in the work of some comparatively neglected dramatists, we may cite, in further extenuation, an instance of immediate recognition of unusual talent. Lord Dunsany is unique amongst recent Irish playwrights in every respect. He not only works in a different medium, but he has found favour with a directorate almost wholly absorbed in stereotyped folk-drama. His first play, *The Glittering Gate*, was performed in 1909, and, although utterly dissimilar from the work of any of his predecessors or contemporaries, it has not been suffered to lapse into oblivion. In 1911 *King Argimenes and the Unknown Warrior* followed, and both have been included in the volume of *Five Plays*, published in 1914. It is to the credit of the Abbey Theatre that Lord Dunsany should have been first recognised as a dramatist in his own country. Confirmation of this critical discernment is found in the fact that the three later plays in his book were successfully performed to wider audiences in England.

The Glittering Gate is a strange conception, best described as idealistic realism. An analysis of the state of mind of two dead burglars, who find themselves before the gate of heaven, constitutes the exposition of the piece. There is profound satire in this revelation of religious belief as moulded by earthly habits and practises. The constantly descending beer-bottles, eagerly seized by the burglar, but always empty, are the exteriorisation of a train of speculation whose symbolic summary forms the *dénouement*. Having forced in the door of heaven, the two protagonists are disgusted to find behind it "Stars. Blooming great stars." Disappointed in their personal illusions, they take refuge in the petulant agnosticism which conceals a conviction that deity is inspired by spite to thwart the faith of mankind. Rarely have such simple elements combined to make a play which appeals so powerfully both to the imagination and the intellect. The subject is one which Yeats might have treated with similar effect, but by what dissimilar means! He would probably have chosen the form of the miracle play, and given us a counterpiece to *The Hour Glass*. Yet, at bottom, Dunsany is more akin to Yeats than is any other dramatist of the Revival. *King Argimenes and the Unknown Warrior*, like *The Gods of the Mountain* and *The Golden Doom*, is a prose rendering of just such themes as belong to the Yeatsian drama. But, as becomes the original mythologist who created the *Gods of Pegana*, Dunsany has turned away from the field of national legend and history. The scenes of his plays are in that vague Orient whose fabulous cities witness the adventures of the Pegana deities. Such a story, however, as that of how Argimenes recovered his kingship, when the royal sword of some buried warrior comes into his hands, while he is working in the fields as a slave, is of the poetic lineage from which *The King's Threshold* sprang. The dramatic writings of both W. B. Yeats and Lord Dunsany are informed by a like sensitiveness to beauty, and their delicate charm is not always felt to advantage in the theatre. As in Yeats one returns always to the lyric poet, so in Dunsany we find, back of the dramatist, the genius for visionary narrative, whose expression will be noticed in a later chapter.

THE ULSTER LITERARY THEATRE

It would be a serious omission to close this account of the Irish National Theatre without a glance at the history of the Northern branch of the movement from which it derives. If the subject has been deferred it is because the earlier stages of the Ulster Literary Theatre were merely a repetition of what has already been recorded of the movement in Dublin. Further, the ultimate condition of the Ulster Theatre has been such as to constitute a practical demonstration of the result of those tendencies which have been described as marking the third phase of the Dramatic Revival. The over-production of conventionalised peasant plays, the neglect of dramatists whose commercial value is slight, and the necessity of meeting a new standard of financial success, have all played a part in radically altering the policy of the Abbey Theatre. Partly in order to satisfy the requirements of commercialism, and partly to escape the dilemma of constant repetition to audiences familiar with the limited popular repertoire, but unwilling to encourage revival of the good work of early years, the Irish Players have become largely a touring company. They are more frequently seen out of Ireland, either performing collectively, or competing in scattered groups with the "vaudeville artists" of English music halls. Their corporate existence has been weakened by the departure of the Fays and other talented members, and it has been of late more seriously threatened by the failure of the Abbey Theatre to keep open. In the circumstances, it will be instructive to see whether there is much hope to be placed in the belief of the directors that this policy of touring is temporary, and that the funds so collected will enable

the Theatre to reopen. The Ulster Literary Theatre furnishes a useful analogy, for it has passed more
rapidly through the stages leading to the position in
which the Irish National Theatre is now situated.

When W. G. Fay's Irish National Dramatic Company was formed in Dublin, affiliations were created
with the Belfast Protestant National Society, a
political organisation some of whose members, notably Bulmer Hobson and Lewis Purcell, were actively interested in literature. With the assistance
of the leading members of the Dublin company a
Belfast branch of the Dramatic Movement came into
existence in 1902, when two plays from the new
Dublin repertoire, *Kathleen ni Houlihan* and *The
Racing Lug*, by James Cousins, were produced at
St. Mary's Hall. Some months later A. E.'s *Deirdre*
was performed in Belfast, after its appearance in
Dublin, and in 1904 the Ulster Literary Theatre was
formally inaugurated. It was in that year the first
number of *Uladh* was issued, just on the eve of the
Ulster Theatre's opening season, and this journal of
Northern literature and drama served for a brief
period the same purpose as *Beltaine* and *Samhain*.
The inaugural performances in December, 1904, were
of unpublished plays by two Ulster playwrights,
Lewis Purcell's municipal satire, *The Reformers*,
and Bulmer Hobson's *Brian of Banba*, a poetic drama
of the heroic age. The following year saw the production of *The Little Cowherd of Slainge*, a dramatic
legend by Joseph Campbell, and *The Enthusiast*, in
which Lewis Purcell set forth the conflict between
Catholic and Protestant, and excited general interest
in his handling of this essentially Ulster problem.
The reputation of one of the most recent "Abbey"
playwrights, St. John G. Ervine, also an Ulsterman,
rests upon the great success of his *Mixed Marriage*

(1911), where the same problem is stated in similarly pessimistic terms.

In 1906 the Ulster Literary Theatre enjoyed its first real success, when *The Pagan*, by Lewis Purcell, and *The Turn of the Road*, by Rutherford Mayne, were produced—the former being the only play its author has published in book form, the latter introducing the most important of the Ulster dramatists. *The Pagan* is an amusing comedy of Ireland in the sixth century, where the humorous aspect of the struggle between Paganism and Christianity finds expression in the Pagan choice of a young Christian girl wooed by many suitors. It is the only play which attempts to visualise in comedic form the competition of two opposite moral tendencies in ancient Ireland. This gift of humour where the sacred conventions—political or literary—are concerned is a pleasant feature of the Ulster section of the Dramatic Movement. The farcical satire of Gerald MacNamara's *Thompson in Tir-na-n-'Og*, and *When the Mist does be on the Bog*, was appreciated by those who saw these plays at the Abbey Theatre, where the Ulster Players brought their literary irreverence into the very home of the traditions satirised. Like the greater part of the Ulster plays, these have never been printed, so it has been left to one dramatist to represent the share of Ulster in the literature of the Dramatic Movement.

Joseph Campbell has published his interesting play of Donegal peasant life, *Judgment* (1912), but it is not related to the Ulster Literary Theatre, and, in spite of an effective first act, it has failed to be dramatically convincing. The types of Northern peasantry are well drawn, and the faculty of observation and ear for language exhibited in the author's notebook, *Mearing Stones*, are put under valuable contribution. There is reason to hope for something from Joseph Campbell which will be a permanent addition to the Ulster drama, whose best exponent at present is Rutherford Mayne, the only one of his group to issue a representative volume. St. John Ervine's *Four Irish Plays* can hardly be so described, for they are about Ulster rather than of it, as must happen when the expatriate Irishman looks to his country for literary material. The success of *Mixed Marriage* has already been noticed, and the remaining plays call for no specific reference in a study of the Irish Theatre. They belong to the later type of "Abbey" melodrama, with the exception of *The Critics*, an unfortunate attempt at innovation. *The Orangeman*, the play next in interest to *Mixed Marriage*, was imported from the English to the Irish stage, a fact which indicates the unintimate relation between the author and the Irish Movement. He writes with equal facility for the theatres of his own and his adopted country, and seems to find Cockney London no less familiar than Belfast. His work can no more be identified with the literature of the Revival than can that of Bernard Shaw, to whom he has dedicated his latest play, of lower middle-class English life.

RUTHERFORD MAYNE

Even were he not the only Ulster dramatist to have published a considerable volume of work, Rutherford Mayne is peculiarly fitted to represent the Ulster Literary Theatre. His first play, *The Turn of the Road*, was also the first important production of the Ulster Theatre, and, with the exception of some minor, unpublished pieces, all his work has been associated with that organisation. In 1907 *The Turn of the Road* appeared in book form, in 1908 *The Drone* and *The Troth* were produced, and their success was confirmed by their publication the following year. Finally, in 1912, after *Red Turf* had stood the test of public performance, a collected edition of all four was published under the title, *The Drone and other Plays*. A farcical comedy in three acts, entitled *If!* (1914), has since been produced, but not published. If he estimates it as he estimated his only other departure from the folk-drama, we shall not find it printed. Although the author has shown himself more successful with this comedy than with the bourgeois tragedy, *Captain of the Hosts*, both essays in middle-class drama are outside the line of Rutherford Mayne's truest vision.

The Turn of the Road at once suggests comparison with Padraic Colum's *The Fiddler's House*, for the motive in both plays is similar. Here, however, it is a young man who renounces the land to follow the musical career which his love for his fiddle seems to promise him. Characteristic of the prudent North is the fact that, even where the conflict is one between artist and philistine, the former is not depicted as wholly careless of material considerations. Conn Hourican, in *The Fiddler's House*, is prepared to take to the roads in obedience to the artistic instinct that is in him. Robbie John Granahan makes the same choice, but the prize he has received at a recent *Feis*, and the favourable criticism of the judges, offer him more substantial hopes than were present to tempt the peasant of the Midlands in Colum's play. All the difference between Ulster and the rest of Ireland is felt in these two variations upon an almost identical theme. Rutherford Mayne's world is one in which imprudence has no place, his peasants are hardheaded and, in the main, comparatively well to do, their conversation turns incessantly upon money, and indifference where profit is concerned becomes a cardinal sin. Again, Protestant Puritanism, as distinct from the peculiarly Irish, Catholic variety, colours his work. In *The Turn of the Road*, the struggle of the artist is intensified by the puritan hostility which his gift encounters. He faces a world in which the love of art is not only an economic, but a moral, heresy. The dour Protestantism of the North throws a harsh light upon the scene of this play in curious contrast to the soft Catholic atmosphere in which *The Fiddler's House* is steeped.

The longest play of Rutherford Mayne is *The Drone*, whose original two acts have been lengthened to three, since it was first produced by the Ulster Literary Theatre in 1908. It is probably the purest and most natural comedy written in Ireland in recent years; it is certainly the best of all that the so-called realistic playwrights have given us. There are none of the extravagances of genius which would warrant comparison with the comedies of Synge, and for that reason we must turn to the "realists" for a parallel. Lady Gregory's joyous farces do not supply the necessary points of contact, but William Boyle has written out of a more analogous mood. There is an obvious identity of motive between several of his plays and *The Drone*, which tells of the manner in which a lazy old man imposes upon his relatives, by pretending that he is working at a great invention. All his life he has been suffering from the failing which forms the subject of William Boyle's popular comedy, but his laziness is not visible to those who believe they will one day share the fruits of his invention, as a reward for having kept him many years in idleness. The arrival of a Scotch engineer, who shows up the imposture, leads the pseudo-inventor to a display of unusual activity in a series of attempts to stave off the inevitable exposure, and it is a part of the dramatist's triumph that the defeated old man convinces us of his superiority to his victims.   The drone, Daniel Murray, is one of the most charming character studies in modern Irish drama, and the tragi-comedy of his humiliation has just that quality of good art which leaves the reader reflective.   The play goes far beyond the mere buffooneries of *Family Failing*, where laughter is not tempered by any intellectual emotion.   Rutherford Mayne succeeds in projecting genuine humour into situations which are at once the essence of comedy and the essence of life in rural Ulster.

Of the two one-act plays, *The Troth* and *Red Turf*, only the former calls for more than passing notice. They are both of the more conventional "Abbey" type, especially *Red Turf*, with its Galway setting and its purely external action.   The shooting of one farmer by another in a quarrel as to rights of turbary seems, perhaps, to differ very slightly from the shooting of a landlord by the prospective victims of an eviction.   The latter theme, however, assumes in *The Troth* an interest denied to the former.   Here the dramatist has the advantage of studying the people he knows best, and were it only for his portrayal of the Ulster peasant in tragic circumstances, the play would be interesting.   In Rutherford Mayne's series of Northern studies this is the only case in which he shows us the Ulsterman face to face with such a crisis as fell more commonly to the lot of his less fortunate countrymen in the South and West. As a rule he describes lives less sharply in conflict with the elemental realities of the struggle for existence.   Where the others talk of hunger and emigration and death, the characters of Rutherford Mayne's drama are preoccupied with cares of the prosperous, the driving of a good bargain, disputes as to dowries in terms of three figures, and the promptings of a Nonconformist conscience. *The Troth*, therefore, gives us a glimpse of the other side of the picture, and there is a peculiar significance in the natural way in which the fundamental problem in Irish affairs is solved. Without the slightest hesitation or apology the dramatist brings Catholic and Protestant together for the destruction of their common enemy. Ebenezer McKie and Francis Moore, in their joint action against the landlord, are Irish peasants first and religious opponents second. The oppression of intolerable wrong reveals the shallowness of the much emphasised difference between Orange and Green.

Rutherford Mayne has studied the speech and manners of the Ulster peasant with a care and insight too often absent from the attention lavished upon the West. His plays, both in form and content, are a faithful reflection of Irish conditions modified by prosperity and Protestantism. In the theatre a cottage scene in an Ulster play evokes circumstances absolutely different from those suggested by the same setting for a play by Synge or Colum. It is only necessary to see the Ulster Players to realise what an original and essential part is theirs in the presentation of Irish folk-drama. Peasant speech has come to be identified in the mind of the general public with the language of Synge, or the Kiltartan of Lady Gregory, and the anonymous dialect of her successors. But the Ulster Theatre has preserved an idiom which deserves to be known as well as these. If not so highly coloured as the Anglo-Irish of the West, it is full of striking terms and phrases, and has a faint Biblical rhythm which is not found elsewhere. Rutherford Mayne has made himself master of a speech whose force and quiet charm are visible in the printed text. He allowed himself to be betrayed into following the conventional line of least resistance when he turned to the West for his *Red Turf*. His isolation and originality are rewarded in the case of his other plays by the literary quality conferred upon them, but denied to the majority of recent imitative playwrights.

Unfortunately the absence of published Ulster plays has given an ephemeral air to the career of the Ulster Literary Theatre. A contributory factor has been the absence of an institution in Belfast corresponding to the Abbey Theatre in Dublin. A certain disintegration has been the consequence of this lack of a centre about which the activities of the Ulster playwrights might be grouped. *Uladh* ceased to exist after four quarterly numbers had been issued, and the plays, produced at first in small halls, found their way to the ordinary theatres of commerce, to whose conditions they had, of course, to submit. Naturally, commercialisation ensued. Moving about from theatre to music-hall, and touring in England and in the United States, the Ulster drama finally became submerged in the general stream of digestive amusements. It had not the visibly corporate existence which, in spite of increasing commercialisation, has kept the National Theatre Society a distinct entity, with aims and traditions of its own. But, as has been stated, the last two years have seen this distinction in the way of being effaced. The Irish Players, in popular plays, have found tours so necessary, or so profitable, that the Abbey Theatre has had to close its doors rather too frequently. The belief that the scattered elements of the Movement can be joined as before is not supported by the example of the Ulster Literary Theatre.

Now that Irish drama is thrown into competition with the ordinary playhouses and variety entertainments, the prospect of preserving the original spirit of the Revival is slight. A radical reconstruction of the vital factors of the movement must be effected under circumstances where the necessity for making profits will not arise. It was a mistake for the Ulster drama to be thrown back upon the commercial theatres when it found itself without a stage of its own. Instead of paying occasional visits to Dublin, the Ulster Society should have amalgamated with the National Theatre Society. Strange to say, none of the plays was first produced at the Abbey Theatre, even so recent a work as *Red Turf* (1911) had its *première* in Belfast. It would, of course, be preferable to have in Belfast a theatre standing in the same relation to the Dramatic Movement in Ulster as the Abbey Theatre has stood to the movement in the South. But the inability of the latter to escape commercialism indicates the necessity of an endowment, which was not forthcoming in Belfast, even to the limited extent enjoyed by the Abbey Theatre. It will probably be easier to obtain one endowed theatre than two, for which reason, amalgamation, with a subsidy, is essential to the welfare of the National Theatre.

To-day, as in the beginning, we find the division of forces to be the weakness of the Dramatic Revival. The various channels into which its activities flowed must be joined if a current is to be formed strong enough to resist the obstacles in the way of all artistic endeavour. These obstacles are so difficult that it is folly to increase them by emphasising points of difference which result in narrowness, sectionalism and monotony. Both the Irish Literary Theatre and its successor have given birth to writers who have enlarged the interest of Anglo-Irish literature. They have been promoted and fostered by men and women imbued with the single ambition of creative art, but each has paid, in its respective measure, the penalty of separatism.   No spirit of ingratitude has prompted this attempt to indicate the defects of the Dramatic Movement, which could not have developed at all but for the most patient and disinterested labours of many.   But its existence, now threatened, may be strengthened if the mistakes of the past are understood.   Too much indiscriminate enthusiasm has not only been largely responsible for the fatal popularity of the "Abbey" drama, but it has served to concentrate attention upon the successes, literary or otherwise, of the Movement, to the exclusion of all else.   But its failures are important, and never more so than now, when certain successes have conspired for its ruin.   National drama cannot live by such specialisation as has produced the stereotyped peasant play, it must embrace a wider field. The united forces of the two streams into which the Dramatic Revival originally diverged, with the consequent concentration of all minor activities, can alone assure the future of the Irish National Theatre.

CHAPTER XV

FICTION AND NARRATIVE PROSE

THE WEAK POINT OF THE REVIVAL. GEORGE MOORE.
DANIEL CORKERY. JAMES JOYCE. LORD DUN-
SANY. JAMES STEPHENS. LADY GREGORY. CON-
CLUSION

ANGLO-IRISH literature has been rich in poetry and drama, but the absence of good prose fiction is noticeable, when it is remembered that the romances of O'Grady were the starting point of the Revival. Indeed, were it not for the essays of John Eglinton, the occasional prose pieces of A. E., and Yeats's two volumes of stories, one might say that the art of prose has been comparatively neglected. For many years John Eglinton was the only writer of the Revival who wished to be known solely as a prosaist, but there is nowadays a perceptible tendency amongst the new writers to seek expression outside the limits of poetry and drama. They do not, however, seem interested in the novel as such, and prefer some even more amorphous form. Even those who write short stories, the most popular form of fiction in contemporary Anglo-Irish literature, rarely conform to the traditions of the *conte* or *nouvelle*. They either connect their narrative by some loose thread, or they reduce their stories to the dimensions of a sketch. Of novelists in the proper sense of the word we have very few, and they do not appear so intimately related to the literary movement in Ireland itself as the poets and dramatists. A vast quantity of purely "circulationist" fiction must be laid to the charge of Irish writers. Much of it is frankly potboiling; some of it is doubtless intended as a contribution to literature. For obvious reasons, only the more significant novelists call for such reference as is possible in dealing with a large field whose prevailing flatness is its most prominent characteristic.

EMILY LAWLESS AND JANE BARLOW

Emily Lawless was the first of the modern writers of fiction to obtain recognition, when *Hurrish* was published in 1886. This story of Land League times was an early manifestation of that interest in peasant conditions which has become the special feature of the Revival. It must, however, be said that at this point the connection ceases, for Emily Lawless wrote her book entirely as an unsympathetic observer. The agrarian movement is seen in the darkness of anti-national prejudice, not in the light of understanding, and the caricatural rendering of Irish dialect stamps the book as intended for foreign consumption. More fortunate was the choice of the Elizabethan wars in *With Essex in Ireland* (1890), followed in 1892 by *Grania*, an interesting picture of life in the Aran Islands, unspoiled by any misconception of Irish politics or Irish speech. *Maelcho* (1894) is a second attempt at historical fiction hardly to be compared with the earlier story of Essex's expedition, to which a certain charm is lent by the convention of a style contemporary with the events related. In her narrative of the Desmond rebellion there is something of that hostility to the "mere Irish" which was felt in *Hurrish*, and which contributed to the failure of Emily Lawless as an historical novelist. Compared with the glowing enthusiasm of O'Grady's Elizabethan stories her work appears colourless. She is most likely to be reread for the sake of *Traits and Confidences* (1898) and *The Book of Gilly* (1906), two delightful volumes of Western sketches and impressions. In these later works there is a modification of that attitude of aloof superiority, which seems to have sensibly weakened as a result of the changed conception of nationality effected by the Revival. In 1886 *Hurrish* expressed the only possible point of view in respectable circles. But, as time went on, Emily Lawless found that she could permeate her work with the spirit and colour of the West, without prejudice to her political and social convictions. Instead of uncouth, almost non-human beings, living in a savage land, she shows us the wild and simple beauty of life on the shores of the Atlantic, whose fascination haunted her verse, and finally found expression in her prose.

More properly to be counted among the prose writers of the Revival is the author whose poems, *Bogland Studies*, have already been mentioned as preliminary to that part of her work which now calls for attention. Jane Barlow had just only begun to write for *The Dublin University Review* when Emily Lawless was known as a novelist of some standing. Her career coincides, therefore, with that of the poets so exclusively identified with the renascence in Ireland. In 1892 *Irish Idylls* was published, the first of the long series of "bogland studies" which includes *Kerrigan's Quality*, *Maureen's Fairing*, *Strangers at Lisconnell* and many others. Sometimes, as in *Kerrigan's Quality* and *The Founding of Fortunes*, a slight plot gives an air of cohesion to these stories, but the author is always and essentially a short-story writer.   She depends entirely upon the natural charm of the scenes and incidents depicted, and reduces construction to a minimum.   She has a fine selective instinct which rarely betrays her into the trivial or absurd, and this, coupled with a remarkable knowledge of the simpler aspects of peasant life, enables the author to avoid the dangers with which the use of dialect is beset—dangers which threatened the success of *Bogland Studies*, as has been noted.

In most of Jane Barlow's work there is a suggestion of patronage, perhaps unavoidable in one who studies the peasant from outside, but the evident sympathy with which these idylls are written saves them from the reproach of offensiveness.   Frequent passages testify to a complete comprehension of the precarious position of the dependent landholder, and the familiar figures of the countryside are sketched with considerable skill.   There is, indeed, such intimacy with the life of the peasantry in its external aspects that one wonders how the necessary intercourse can have resulted in so scrupulous an absence of didacticism.   Nobody would wish to see these pictures spoiled by the crude colours of the propagandist, but the unconscious propaganda of deep feeling might have stimulated the reader to supply the data excluded by the artist.   It is precisely here that one feels that Jane Barlow lacks the requisite equipment for the study of rural Ireland. Everything she sees is softened in the glow of easy good humour or sentimental compassion, so that a rather superficial impression is all that remains when she has told her story.   She almost never shows herself conscious of the spiritual entity concealed in these people whom she depicts in all manner of circumstances.   Whether they are happy or sad, prosperous or ill-treated, they are portrayed solely as idyllic subjects whose problems are not stated in relation to any tangible reality. There is, in short, a decidedly unnatural detachment in Jane Barlow's conception of the Irish peasant. He is purely a creature of romance, whose existence is not to be measured by reference to unpleasant facts.

SEUMAS MACMANUS AND SHAN F. BULLOCK

Two Northern storytellers are Shan F. Bullock and Seumas MacManus, each of whom published his first book in 1893. The latter is known also as a poet and dramatist, but his popularity derives from the numerous tales of Donegal life and fairy lore which began in 1896 with *The Leadin' Road to Donegal*. This work came after *Shuilers from Heathy Hills* (1893), a collection of prose and verse, but it may be said to mark the beginning of the author's career. In spite of its flagrantly "stage Irishman" humour and exaggerated dialect, Seumas MacManus was not destined to follow in the tracks of Lover and Lever. *'Twas in Dhroll Donegal* (1897) and *The Humours of Donegal* (1898) were still in the rollicking Lover manner, but *Through the Turf Smoke* (1899) showed more restraint and closer observation of actual peasant life. Three volumes of folk-tales, *The Bewitched Fiddle*, *In Chimney Corners* and *Donegal Fairy Tales*, followed in immediate succession, and afforded evidence of the author's increasing literary skill, which soon attained its fullest expression. *A Lad of the O'Friels*, which appeared in 1903, is superior to anything else Seumas MacManus has published, and may be counted as one of the best idealistic novels of the Irish peasantry we possess. Like most of its kind, the book inevi-

tably tends to fall into a series of scenes, but the
thread is sufficiently substantial to constitute a
genuine story, instead of the more usual peg upon
which to hang detached sketches. The community
of Knocknagar is a living microcosm, studied with
eyes which have seen from the inside the people and
events described. Seumas MacManus succeeds in
shaking off the obsession of broad comedy which has
heretofore clung to him, and writes directly out of a
life he knows so well, that one regrets his concessions
to stereotype. The memorable picture of a Lough
Derg pilgrimage is a perfect example of the fine
material which lies at the disposal of the Irish
novelist.

Shan F. Bullock is a writer of a very different
calibre, and one who occupies an almost unique position in the literature produced under the influence
of the Revival. He is that rare phenomenon
amongst his contemporaries, a genuine novelist, who
has eschewed both poetry and drama, and whose
short stories are a very small part of his work.
Ring O' Rushes (1896) and *Irish Pastorals* (1901) are
the only volumes he has published in emulation of
Seumas MacManus or Jane Barlow. But to these
glimpses of rural manners in the County Fermanagh
he has imparted a seriousness not characteristic of
the more popular writers. *By Thrasna River*, his
first important novel, appeared in 1895, and to this
may be added *The Barrys* (1897), *The Squireen*
(1903) and *Dan the Dollar* (1905). From a list of
more than a dozen volumes these three will stand
as representative of the author who has most consistently worked to obtain for Irish fiction something of the prestige reserved for poetry and drama.
His novels deal almost exclusively with the people
of Ulster, although in *The Barrys* half the action

takes place in London, where the strange background throws into stronger relief the characteristics of the race from which the protagonists have sprung. Shan F. Bullock is not content to study Northern manners merely in their local manifestations. His two books of short sketches prove that he can write in the familiar, semi-idyllic manner as well as the chief exponents of the *genre*, but he is capable of more sustained effort. He alone has essayed to make the study of rural life simultaneously locally and universally human. He has analysed the Ulster temperament in conflict with fundamental problems, where deeper knowledge is demanded than is necessary to draw the picturesque outline of a peasant community. Consequently, one feels a gravity in his work utterly lacking in the romantic humour and pathos of Jane Barlow and Seumas MacManus. He does not see life as a sentimentalist, but as a realist, who cannot persuade himself that the smiles and tears of Hibernian romanticism are an adequate commentary upon the conditions he describes.

GEORGE MOORE

The three volumes of George Moore's *Hail and Farewell* might be included in the category of Irish fiction, were it not for their autobiographical form, coupled with the use of the names and attributes of living persons. Had the author chosen a more fictitious setting for this romance of literary Dublin, he would have spared us the pain of surrendering a remarkable work of imagination to the student of memoirs. Having previously drawn upon some of the people of his reminiscences for his novels, he might have continued the conventional disguise to the end. W. B. Yeats and A. E. were no less themselves when they figured successively as "Ulick Dean" in the early and later editions of *Evelyn Innes*. They would have lost nothing of their personality had they been similarly disguised in this narrative of a repatriated Irishman's adventures in the land of the Literary Revival. George Moore, however, crediting the subjects of his investigation, as well as the public, with his own capacity for artistic detachment, decided to elaborate the story of his return to Ireland, without troubling to conceal the identity of his material. With the perfect callousness of the realistic novelist, he took his "human documents" and arranged them with an eye only to their literary effectiveness. These were slices of life very much more personally alive than the anonymous *romans vécus* of his original French masters, but he exhibited them with the dispassionate enthusiasm of Zola reconstructing his picture of life during the Second Empire. *Ave*, *Salve* and *Vale*, in their strange juxtaposition of fact and fancy, form one of the most charming prose works associated with the Irish Literary Revival, of which they are the indispensable glossary and the sentimental history.

Fortunately, George Moore has left us a more enduring mark of his passage than his collaboration in the Irish Literary Theatre, and a less equivocal sign of his participation than *Hail and Farewell*. During his residence in Ireland he published one volume of short stories, *The Untilled Field* (1903), and one novel, *The Lake* (1905), which were, until recently, the only works of the first class in Irish fiction. In a preface to the Tauchnitz edition of the former book the author relates how, at the suggestion of John Eglinton, he began to write these stories, in order to preserve his impressions of Irish life, as it revealed itself to him after many years, absence.

They were ostensibly published, however, for the purpose of supplying Irish prose writers with models, both Gaelic and English, and several appeared in *The New Ireland Review* in parallel versions, after the manner of Douglas Hyde's Connacht songs. Whether the translated volume, *An T-U'r-Ghort*, which was published the same year as the English edition, was an equally remarkable contribution to contemporary Gaelic literature, is doubtful. The author himself has recounted with much humour his failure to command the same attention from his Irish-speaking as from his English-speaking readers. It is not improbable that moral rather than literary considerations guided the Gaels in this, as in many other instances, with the result that Anglo-Ireland is the richer of the modern Gaelic disdain for æsthetic truth. *The Untilled Field* is the most perfect book of short stories in contemporary Irish literature and need not fear comparison with *A Sportsman Sketches*, —the model proposed by John Eglinton. In the Tauchnitz preface Moore denies the hope of fulfilling the demands of his friend, but only with Turgenev's analogous volume can his own be compared, for its exquisite sense of natural beauty.

Not content with his achievement in this characteristically Irish *genre*, he proceeded to meet our greatest need, by giving the literature of the Revival its first and only novel of distinction, *The Lake*. The personal and national metamorphosis which separated the author and his country from the distant period of *Parnell and his Island* was dramatically revealed in *The Untilled Field*. The former volume of impressions, dated 1887, showed the Ireland of Land League days in the distorted view of an absentee landowner, even more thoroughly denationalised than usual by his literary apprenticeship

in Paris. Equally great is the distance separating
A Drama in Muslin (1886) and *The Lake* (1905),
both from a literary and chronological point of view,
but the difference between the two novels is of another quality. Whatever objections may have been
raised against *Muslin*,—to give the book its revised
title of 1915,—it is unjust to assume, as has been the
practise of Irish critics, that the author tried deliberately to calumny and misrepresent fashionable
society in Dublin. Although contemporaneous with
Parnell and his Island, the novel is a dispassionate
study, in the realistic manner, of social conditions,
not a personal criticism like the former work. After
the magnificent portrayal of English manners in
A Mummer's Wife, nothing could have been more
legitimately interesting than a similar analysis of
Irish society, and *Muslin* deserves no other criticism
than that which has been applied to all the earlier
works of George Moore prior to his return to Ireland. To make of it an occasion for patriotic indignation is merely to claim that preferential treatment
which no writer of genius has ever conceded to his
own people. The Irish setting is of no immediate
significance, for at that time the novelist was innocent of any suspicion of national bias, unless towards
France, his intellectual motherland.

It is precisely this fortuitous setting which constitutes the point of contrast between the earlier novel
and *The Lake*. The latter is Irish, the former is
about Ireland, and might, so far as its spirit is concerned, have been written by a foreigner. As befits
Irish fiction, *The Lake* is composed of the simplest
elements, and thereby stands in complete contrast
to all the author's other novels. Here one does not
find the amorous adventures, the rise and fall of fortunes, the amusing, discreditable and graphic inci-

dents of modern life,—the vast fabric of a complicated social organism unrolled with the patient,
unwearied gesture of the realistic novelist. On the
contrary, the vital action takes place within the
four walls of the parish-priest's house, in a remote
Western village, where he receives the letters which
are the occasion of an intensely interesting spiritual
drama. Father Oliver Gogarty is the only one of the
chief protagonists whom we meet face to face, after
the first glimpse of Rose Leicester, as she flees from
the parish under the shadow of sin. Her correspondence with her repentant accuser is all that we
have, for it is his evolution, under the subtle influence of the woman he unconsciously loves, which is
the interest of the story.

With delicate art Moore has outlined this drama of
revolt against celibacy and belief, so that the banal
theme is invested with a charm absent from the traditional rendering of the conflict. He avoids the
querulous didacticism of the familiar novel of prose-
lytism or agnosticism, just as he eliminates all suggestion of merely physical temptation. Oliver
Gogarty's relation towards Rose is a profound piece
of psychological analysis, in which the material
factor is diminished to such a point that the woman
becomes, as it were, a symbol. Having carefully
summarised the circumstances of Gogarty's priesthood, having postulated his spiritual and tempera-
mental disposition, he allows the interaction of ideas
and emotions to divest the priest of the accidental
and external accretions of his existence until, at last,
the man emerges. The latter has stripped off the
garments of convention, as well as the garb of his
calling, before he plunges into the lake, on whose
further shore the road to freedom lies open. The
bundle he leaves on the bank behind him is the mere

shell of a host of outworn ideals which have fallen away from him, and are abandoned on the threshold of his new life.

When one recalls the manner in which this subject has been treated by certain modern writers, and especially by George Moore's compatriots, it is not easy to be moderate in his praise. Add to this the tender beauty of the pictures forming the background of the story, the exquisite shading of light and colour, and the sensitive feeling for the landscape which seems, indeed, *un état d'âme*, so perfectly does it respond to the mood of the priest. Whether so intended, or not, like its companion volume of short stories, *The Lake* is a model for the prose-writers of the Revival. It was without an equal until the long-awaited Irish novelist appeared who has continued the work which George Moore so excellently began. Neither hypersensitive patriotism, nor a too strenuous desire for "literature at nurse," should obscure the fact that the author of that phrase has done most to restore the Anglo-Irish novel to literature. In the work of James Joyce we shall find that Moore's only successor has enriched Irish fiction with all that the older novelist might have given to it, had the portrayal of Irish life and character not been merely an incidental part of his great accomplishment.

FORREST REID AND SEUMAS O'KELLY

There has been a vast crop of entertaining fiction which has come to be regarded, especially outside Ireland itself, as "very Irish," as the characteristic Irish contribution to the modern novel. The greatest of these disciples of Charles Lever were Œ. Somerville and Martin Ross, whose partnership was terminated by the death of Miss Martin in 1915.

Their fox-hunting, rollicking tales of serio-comic peasants and devil-may-care Anglo-Irish gentry gave to *Some Experiences of an Irish R.M.* (1899), *Further Experiences of an Irish R.M.*, and *Dan Russell the Fox* the apparently irresistible charm of such literature for those who are satisfied with an effective convention. The popularity of the many volumes in this vein which these two collaborators published has somewhat overshadowed the real merit of the one novel of genuine power, originality and distinction which they wrote before they discovered the line of least resistance. *The Real Charlotte* (1894) is a Balzacian study of Irish provincial types, drawn with a seriousness and an impartial sense of reality, which serve to heighten regret for the subsequent squandering of the authors' great talent upon the trivialities of a superficial realism. The same attitude towards Irish life, but divorced from all semblance of reality, is found in the work of their successor, George Birmingham, whose *Seething Pot* (1905) and *Hyacinth* (1906) were the first of a long line of stories designed rather as aids to digestion than to the immortality of the author.

Here and there an isolated volume of more literary quality appears, William Buckley's powerful and well written study of the Irish Rebellion of 1798, *Croppies Lie Down* (1903), St. John Ervine's *Mrs. Martin's Man* (1914). For a moment it seemed as if the latter might be regarded as something more than a fortunate accident, but the pseudo-Dickensian *Alice and A Family* revealed an imitator of Pett Ridge, and the author's next Irish novel, *Changing Winds* (1917) indicated the arrival of another circulationist. It is obviously written in the manner of the later discursive, "sociological" novels of H. G. Wells, and its many pages are largely made up of

conversations in the now familiar manner of those
youths from the English universities whose post-
graduate philosophy has been recorded by a host of
younger English novelists. Well known London personalities and almost every prominent figure in Dublin are freely used by St. John Ervine, and no less
than three great catastrophes of recent history are
worked into the story, which nevertheless remains
lifeless. A curious economy is the introduction of
the same people once under their real names and
once in the feeblest of fictional disguise. The still
life pictures of England at the outbreak of the war
and Dublin during the insurrection in 1916 are the
measure of the novelist's failure to infuse the quality
of life into his book. His reflections on the Easter
Rising in Ireland, with their fantastic anti-Catholic
bias, and their complete blindness to the realities
of that desperate adventure, are more suitable to
the editorial columns of a Belfast newspaper than
to the work of a writer whom Bernard Shaw has described as "an Irishman of real genius." Both in
fiction and drama St. John Ervine seems unable to
fulfil the promise of his first work, *Mrs. Martin's
Man* and *Mixed Marriage*.

An Ulster novelist of a finer calibre is Forrest
Reid, who was a contributor to *Uladh*, the organ of
the Ulster Literary Theatre, in 1905, shortly after his
'prentice work, *The Kingdom of Twilight* was published. This was followed by another juvenile but
more promising book, *The Garden God*, after which
an interval of several years elapsed before the author
offered the first of his mature novels, *The Bracknels*
(1911). From the outset Forrest Reid showed his
preoccupation with occult naturism, and his first
books were rather naïve contributions to the cult of
Pan, after the manner of Arthur Machen and Al-

gernon Blackwood, but in *The Spring Song* (1916), this note of natural mystery is well sustained, and the vivid beauty of the author's visualisations of nature reveals a complete mastery over his style and his material. Out of the simplest elements an admirable work of art is contrived in this story of a group of children, whose adventures are described with so sure a sense of proportion that, while conscious of their intrinsic unimportance the reader is held by the intense interest which they assume in the sympathy and perspective of their creator.

A like simplicity of texture marks Forrest Reid's specifically Irish novels, *The Bracknels*, *Following Darkness* (1912), and *At the Door of the Gate* (1915). An ardent admirer of Henry James, he has been reproached for the tenuousness of the fabric on which he embroiders his delicate and usually elusive themes. The first of these three is an amazing dissection of the mean souls of a family whose head is a self-made Belfast merchant. The second, and most remarkable of the three, is a slow moving but arresting study of spiritual loneliness, whose scene is set in the Mourne Mountains and then in the shabby streets of Belfast, where a sensitive young artist is crushed by the crude religion and harsh people about him. To the same subject in another form the novelist returned in *At the Door of the Gate*, which shows the development of a young man in the typical environment of lower middle-class Protestantism as practised in North-East Ulster. Except in the plays of Rutherford Mayne no more faithful studies of Northern Irish conditions have been drawn. At the same time Forrest Reid has a Celtic feeling for the spiritual beauty of nature which, allied with subtle craftmanship and a capacity for writing excellent English, makes this aloof and isolated writer a figure of the utmost distinction amongst his contemporaries.

About the time when St. John Ervine was turning from the theatre to the novel, and had published a little volume of sketches and stories under the title of *Eight O'Clock*, there also appeared a collection of stories by Dermot O'Byrne, *Children of the Hills* (1913), to which the author has since added *Wrack and Other Stories* (1918), both showing unusual qualities. O'Byrne is steeped in Gaelic lore and the old language and history are an essential part of his art. His realism is the realism of Synge, with whom his work has many points in common, as may be seen in *Hunger*, *The Call of the Road* and the title story of the second volume. The rhythmic, highly coloured speech of the Gaelic-speaking peasant has been rendered by an ear no less sensitive than Synge's, and the atmosphere of Celtic Ireland is skilfully evoked in the weird and grim historical tales which are included in *Wrack*. At the same time, there is in Dermot O'Byrne a quality of mystic imagination which is nowhere perceptible in Synge, and which redeems him from the charge of mere imitation.

Prior to his death in 1918 Seumas O'Kelly was known chiefly as a dramatist, although his first book was a volume of short stories, *By the Stream of Kilmeen* (1902), but his fame is now certain to rest upon his posthumous masterpiece, *The Golden Barque and The Weaver's Grave*, which was published in Dublin in 1919. *The Weaver's Grave* is composed of the simplest elements, the quest of three old men for the site of a friend's grave, and the grotesque humours and quarrels arising out of that situation. Mortimer Hehir, the weaver, had died, and by traditional right he was entitled to be buried in the old cemetery of Cloon na Morav. His young widow enlists the services of Meehaul Lynskey and Cahir Bowes, whose antiquity qualified them to decide where the weaver had staked out his last claim. The superb comedy of this search in the graveyard, as full of memories for these old men as of graves, is the material out of which Seumas O'Kelly has made a story, vivid, humorous, haunting, bizarre. The setting is wonderful: the ancient country burial ground, still and forgotten beneath the tangle of shrubs and grasses, the mouldering tombstones, the relics of many centuries and generations. Into this place come the two aged figures, bent double over their sticks, but filled with the exciting sense of their belated recall to useful activity, wandering about "with the labour of age and the hearts of children."

Above the dispute of doddering age, youth, in the person of the widow and one of the gravediggers, has its immemorial struggle, in which the woman is vanquished by the soft eyes and lips of the young man. The process whereby one of the hitherto indistinguishable twin gravediggers suddenly begins to differentiate himself in the eyes of the woman from "the one who did not count" is described with charming subtlety, and there is real poetry and dignity in the closing scene, when at last the grave has been dug, and the man climbs out from his labour:

"Cloon na Morav was flooded with a deep, vague light. The widow scented the fresh wind about her, the cool fragrance of the earth, and yet a warmth that was strangely beautiful. The light of the man's dark eye was visible in the shadow which hid his face. The pile of earth beside him was like a vague shape of miniature bronze mountains. He stood with a stillness that was tense and dramatic. The widow thought that the world was strange, the sky extraordinary, the man's head against the red sky a wonder, a poem; above it the sparkle of a great young star. The widow knew that they would be left together like this for one minute, a minute which would be as a flash and as eternity."

In the same volume *The Golden Barque* is made up of a series of sketches concerned with a river barge of that name. The adventures of its crew and the chronicle of its voyages are composed of such incidents as must come into the existences described, but, as they pass through the imagination of Seumas O'Kelly, they become invested with a mysterious element of beauty. *Michael and Mary* is typical in its picture of a girl who stands on the bank of a canal and watches a barge slowly passing. A bent figure leads the horse along the towing-path, and a young man stands at the tiller. One day she goes from one lock to the next at his side, in the rain. Another day she hears that he has gone voyaging to an unknown destination, "for he had the blood in him for the wide ocean, the wild blood of the rover." The story is nothing, but in its sheer simplicity it has become the purest poetry, and is the loveliest thing in the book after *The Weaver's Grave*. The supreme achievement of that longer story tends to dwarf the slighter, but remarkable accomplishment of the briefer sketches, as it surpasses the author's other stories in *Waysiders* (1917) and *Hillsiders* (1920), although these rarely lack distinction. Seumas O'Kelly died while he was still at work upon *The Weaver's Grave* which, even without his final revision, remains a perfect story, and emphasises his loss to Irish literature.

A fine gift for narrative prose was revealed by Padraic Colum in his volume of impressions, *My Irish Year* (1912), where he evokes with sympathetic charm a series of pictures of peasant life in the Irish Midlands. The author's power of creating atmosphere, that intangible something which differentiates his plays from those of his contemporaries, is nowhere more remarkable than in this work.

Much of *My Irish Year* might be classified as fiction, so skilfully has Colum blended the material elements of his narrative with the imaginative qualities of intuition and instinct. No mere observer, on the outside of Irish life, could have reproduced so wonderfully the soul of rural Ireland. Similarly, in a later volume of prose, *A Boy in Eirinn* (1913), he contrives to invest a somewhat matter-of-fact presentation of Irish life and character with a delicate suggestion of the poetry and romance of childhood. Padraic Colum has since written several charming volumes of stories for children, such as *The King of Ireland's Son* (1916)—to mention the first, which is of specific Irish interest and confirms the hope that he may yet turn his genius for storytelling in the direction of the modern novel.

DANIEL CORKERY AND BRINSLEY MACNAMARA

Daniel Corkery was known chiefly as a playwright and an occasional contributor to Irish periodicals until 1916, when he published his first book, *A Munster Twilight*. This little volume at once proved to be something more than the inevitable collection of short stories which, as we have seen, has always tended to usurp the place of the novel proper in Irish fiction. In an essay on *The Peasant in Literature* the author has defined the bulk of our popular Irish peasant literature as "real in the non-essentials and very untrue in the essentials," and his own stories seem to be designed to fulfil the conditions which that criticism implies. *A Munster Twilight* is a work belonging to the same class as Padraic Colum's *Wild Earth* and Synge's *Riders to the Sea*, both of which were excepted from the judgment passed by Daniel Corkery on his predecessors. He knows his Cork and Kerry as Synge knew Wicklow and the Aran Islands, and Colum the Midlands, and he describes the people with the same harsh humour that gives its savor to the writing of the dramatist. *The Lady of the Glassy Palace* and *Vanity*, for example, treat of death in the manner which was denounced as "brutality" in Synge, but which is in reality a manifestation against the lachrymose, conventional pathos of the "pleasant" playwrights and storytellers. *The Wake* also may be commended to those who desire realities rather than the jocosities of Samuel Lover and the Dickensian variations upon deathbed themes, which are commonly accepted as the only possible alternatives. Corkery can evoke the grim humour, as well as the pathos, of this hackneyed situation by the simple process of telling the truth.

His most conventional story (though admittedly in the "new" Irish convention) is the first in the book, *The Ploughing of Leaca-na-Naomh*, although the press, as usual, singled it out for extravagant praise, doubtless because it is so "very Celtic." *The Return* is as grotesque and weird as anything in Poe but at the same time it is filled with a sense of Irish humanity. Not since *The Land* of Padraic Colum has the relation of the peasant to the soil been so finely expressed in prose as in that story of almost inarticulate emotion, *Joy*, which tells of the return to a rich farm of an old man who had been forced off the piece of poor land which he loved, and driven into the city. *The Spanceled* is another notable chapter, which reminds one of Synge in its challenging tragedy of a love which binds, or spancels, a man and a woman more irksomely because of the absence of legal bonds. In 1920 a second volume of short stories appeared under the title of *The Hounds of Banba*, vivid, imaginative studies of the Ireland of Sinn Féin, whose political interest naturally ensured their success. Political bias, though it may turn some readers away, is not by any means necessary to a proper appreciation of the artistic power of the book. Daniel Corkery has written the epic of resurgent and exalted nationalism, and his pictures of a whole people in revolt are admirable in the skill with which a single theme is developed without ever becoming forced or monotonous. The conditions portrayed are those which were outlined day by day in the newspaper reports of the Irish war, but here the outlines are filled in with the living matter of tradition, desperate devotion and heroic pride. Among a people aflame with the passion of nationality, harried yet undismayed, the author has found the stories of suffering and defeat, but never of despair. The rattle of machine guns and armoured cars, the tramp of men drilling in the darkness, the bitter memories of insurrection handed down from one generation to another, run through this book, giving it the value of an historical document which is, at the same time, literature. Here is the conflict of two races and two civilisations, not in terms of politics, but in terms of humanity.

The place of Daniel Corkery in Anglo-Irish literature is assured, however, not by his short stories, but by the novel which he published in 1917, *The Threshold of Quiet*. This work was written before *A Munster Twilight*, but the author was wise to offer the slighter book first, even at the risk of being expected to repeat himself in what was naturally regarded as his second book. There is not the slightest resemblance between them, for here he proceeds to unfold a leisured narrative in which the reader drifts along the quiet stream of provincial life. Connoisseurs of the picturesque phrase and those who cultivate literary plots will be rebuffed by Corkery's indifference to the dialectics of dialect and the requirements of "a good story." The substance of his novel is as tenuous as anything in the later works of Henry James; his manner is as garrulous and expansive as that of Dostoevsky. But his sentences have not the corresponding subtlety which makes or mars Henry James, according to one's fancy. "Swathed in relative clauses as an invalid in shawls," is not the description that can be aptly applied to them. Corkery writes a clear and forceful prose as devoid of mannerism as it is free from cliché; his style is as fresh and personal as his conception of character.

Reference has been made to the tendency of Irish fiction to resolve itself into a connected or unrelated series of episodes or incidents. The purveyors of humourous and sentimental novels for the libraries alone profess to tell a homogeneous story, and they are rewarded by a popularity denied either to the nouvelle, as such, or to the prose work of James Stephens. Although Corkery has shown in *A Munster Twilight* his ability to visualise the dramatic or humourous episode, his novel is innocent of all such effects. So completely has he emancipated himself from the common practice that one can easily imagine the impatient admirer of Katharine Tynan, Jane Barlow, George Birmingham, or Seumas MacManus turning aside from *The Threshold of Quiet*, with a complaint that it lacks incident, as it lacks a plot. It tells no story like *Spanish Gold*; it relates no scenes of country life, in the comic or sentimental manner of Jane Barlow and Seumas MacManus; it eschews the amiable idealisations of Katharine Tynan. If a parallel be sought it will be found, strange to say, in *A Portrait of the Artist as a Young Man*. Not that the morbid retrospection and analysis of

James Joyce have their counterpart in the work of
Daniel Corkery; but both writers have given their
books the inchoate form to which the Russian novelists have reconciled us. The former has written a
savage and, to some minds, a shocking indictment of
Dublin; the latter has gently drawn aside the cur-
tain, and softly illuminated the quiet and obscure
corners of Cork.

One thinks of Chekhov and Dostoevsky while reading *The Threshold of Quiet*, for only in Russian liter-
atuie does one find the portrayal of such secluded
and uneventful lives as drift through these pages,
as they drift through *The Cherry Orchard* or *Uncle
Vanya*. The mysterious death of Frank Bresnan
broods over the whole book; but it occurs at the beginning, and is the occasion of no greater suspense
in the reader than was Raskolnikov's crime in Dostoevsky's masterpiece, for all Corkery's skill in allowing the truth of suicide to crystallise slowly and
shyly in the minds of the circle whose existence is
described. As in the case of *Crime and Punishment*,
there is no attempt to exploit outward circumstance,
and the story is almost purely cerebral, so carefully
does the author restrict its movement to what is
passing in the minds of his characters. When the
book is closed all one has seen happening is the departure of Finnbarr Bresnan for America, after a
hesitation as to whether he had not a vocation for
the priesthood; the tragic ending to the story of
Stevie Galvin and his brother; the crossing of the
"threshold of quiet" by Lily Bresnan when she
finally feels free to enter Kilvirra Convent, renounc-
ing life and the love of Martin Cloyne. Even these
few dramatic moments are not developed, but just
cause a slight stir of the deep waters of consciousness
in which these lives are submerged.

Yet only the most hasty reader will fail to succumb to the appeal of the book, which captures the mind by its simplicity and sincerity, its absence of factitious interest. Corkery plunges us at once into the slow current of these lonely lives, whose struggle for peace and happiness is no less intense and moving because it takes place on a plane only discernible to the intimate comprehension of a writer whose eyes are fixed on the truth nearest to his own heart. The high lights of grand tragedy and the crude glare of melodrama do not light up these pages, steeped in tender and alluring half tones. As a *genre* picture of provincial society in Ireland, *The Threshold of Quiet* is unique in its serious realism, from which the ugliness of naturalism has been eliminated without detriment to its fidelity. With a skill that amounts to genius Daniel Corkery avoids the falsity and mawkishness of the popular idealisations, while preserving the purity at which they aim. A great deal of careful pruning has gone to the creation of the mood in which it is possible by the merest hints and suggestions to obtain effects which his contemporaries have laboured and spoiled. The religious note is particularly delicate and beautiful, spontaneous and reserved, eloquent but never didactic. It is not only a remarkable first novel, but it is the one work of modern Irish fiction which can be compared with that of James Joyce, not because of any identity of mood and matter, but because of the psychological depth and the originality of these two writers. Dissimilar as they are in every respect Daniel Corkery and James Joyce have brought the Irish novel back into literature.

A serious effort towards the same end is discernible in the work of several young novelists who came forward about the same time as Corkery. Darrell

Figgis with *Children of Earth* (1918), and *The House of Success* (1921), Eimar O'Duffy with *The Wasted Island* (1920), and Brinsley MacNamara, whose four novels, *The Valley of the Squinting Windows* (1918), *The Clanking of Chains* (1920), *In Clay and Bronze* (1921) and *The Mirror in the Dusk* (1921), deserve more than passing mention. The author is in evident revolt against the conventional Irish novel, and his work is a concerted attempt to break down the convention in fiction which the Abbey Theatre playwrights destroyed in Irish drama, to describe rural Ireland with realistic candour. Although the stories usually have their scene in the Midlands, Brinsley MacNamara closes his ears to the songs which the blackbird of Meath sang to Francis Ledwidge, nor does he bring the sympathy of Padraic Colum in describing the same countryside. Like the squinting windows of the valley of Tullanahogue as they peer malevolently at the doings of Garradrimna, the author's vision is not quite straight and clear. He is perhaps a little too complacently interested in the degrading existence of the "seven pubs" which absorb the time and money of the villagers, and his relish in the malicious gossip of the drunken men and back-biting women of the valley is not entirely unrelated to his own method of telling a story. He never loses an opportunity of emphasising the vileness of human nature in his portrayal of this agricultural slum. The theme is largely responsible for this one-sided characterisation. The story of the sin which wrecked the life of John Brennan's mother, defeated her ambitions for him, and brought him to the same ruin as his father, is developed through the gossip and feuds of Garradrimna, and the participants in these orgies of slander and hatred are the characters in Brinsley MacNamara's tragedy.

In *The Clanking of Chains* the subject is of more general significance, an exposure of the seamy side of Nationalist politics, as seen by an Irishman whose patriotism does not allow him to fall into the national habit of Narcissism. The malevolence of Tullanahogue was exercised under special conditions, and could have but a relative interest. The decadence of Ballycullen is the manifestation of a social disease which self-complacency has allowed the patrioteers to ignore. Michael Dempsey's struggle to stir his countrymen from their servile opportunism is, in a sense, the history of every Irish Nationalist leader. MacNamara allows no momentary gleam of hope or success to lighten these dark pages, and to that extent, it may be said, Michael Dempsey is not typical. He does not enjoy his hour of triumph even though it be merely the prelude to the ultimate disillusionment of rejected leaders, such as we have so often seen in this country. But the author has a vastly more important purpose than the creation of a tragic figure. Michael is never allowed to attain the dignity of tragedy—the brutal tragic-comedy of life is all powerful, and in the end he can do no more than retreat from the vindictive wrath of his inferiors. The Ballycullen community is composed of verbal patriots, who are content to belittle every heroic endeavour of Irish Nationalism until it succeeds. Then, when it is safe and profitable, they are the devoted admirers of each new political regime. In the course of the story these invertebrates evolve, with characteristic hesitations, from a soulless championship of constitutional Home Rule to an equally degrading conception of Sinn Féin. They touch nothing that they do not disfigure and destroy. The despairing idealist, Michael Dempsey, escapes, in order to avoid the fate of those tragic survivors of the Fenian and Agrarian movements, whom the author has described with the pitiless power of exasperated realism. Kevin Shanaghan and Connor Carberry, so different, yet alike in their misfortune of having outlived the day of their generation's glory, are remarkable studies.

The Clanking of Chains is an extremely effective study of the incurable loutishness of the undeveloped man. Brinsley MacNamara has chosen Ireland for the working out of his idea, but the *Leitmotiv* of the story is universal. Ibsen described it in *An Enemy of the People*, but, because we have not chosen to idealise the Scandinavians, nobody accuses Ibsen of having calumniated them. The romantic view of Nationalism will never lack exponents in Ireland and elsewhere. It is all the more necessary that a writer should come along who is not afraid to show us all the mean jealousies, the cowardice, and the corrupt servility, which shelter behind the deeds and words of great movements.

In his second novel the author shows a considerable advance upon his previous work. The characterisation is more distinct, and although the story in itself is not so "well-made," it is peopled by living types, Ambrose Donohoe, Gilbert McCormack, Marcus Flynn, and Mirandolina Conway. These are not just puppets serving the purpose of a thesis, but real men and women whose part in the shaping of Irish affairs is greater than that of the Michael Dempseys, because they are more numerous. It is they who have rivetted the chains whose heavy weight drags oppressively upon the community of which Ballycullen is a remarkable microcosm.

The autobiographical references of *In Clay and Bronze* date it as the second novel of Brinsley MacNamara, although circumstances deferred its publication, and eventually caused it to be published in London under the title of *The Irishman*, by "Oliver Blythe," although in New York the book appeared with its real title and over his own name. The story is that of Martin Duignan, a young farmer, who is drawn from the land to the city in pursuit of literary ambitions, has a disastrous spell of theatrical life in New York, and returns, disillusioned, to the clay from which he sprang. It is not until he has thus realised himself, and obeyed the traditional call of the soil to the peasant that is in him, that the artistically creative part of his being comes into play. At the close of the narrative his novel has been written and published, and he is back again in Dublin with high hopes in his breast. There the author leaves him with a slightly sardonic hint of the vanity of such hopes.

Brinsley MacNamara has an unrivalled faculty of seeing certain aspects of Irish life as they are. The peasantry, as he sees them, are neither the buffoons of Lover nor the visionaries of Yeats and Lady Gregory. They are the eternal peasant as Maupassant and others have described him, brutalised only too often by the intolerable conditions of existence in an agricultural slum. The types of Irish rural society which are elaborately and remorselessly exposed in *The Clanking of Chains* are sketched in here. MacNamara has a pitiless memory when he records the attitude of the mob mind towards Sinn Féin before it became patriotic to subscribe to that creed. In his pictures of Dublin he at once invites comparison with James Joyce's *A Portrait of the Artist as a Young Man* and *Ulysses*. Here, however, his effects are not so profound and his satire somewhat superficial. The "Tower Theatre" and its idiosyncrasies become the butt of many gibes, but they are neither good humoured enough to amuse nor serious enough to make a deep impression. But MacNamara has drawn an excellent picture of that curious pseudo-intellectual life of certain Dublin salons where an occasional fine talent may be found supporting a strange variety of parasites. Joyce has glanced at the fringe of that society, especially in *Ulysses*, but MacNamara's hero passes through it and returns to it.

It has been said of the Irish playwrights that they were too constantly preoccupied with the seamy side of Irish manners, with the ugly and sordid details of life. The riot over Synge's *Playboy* was a spectacular demonstration of the resentment felt by the romanticists. In his account of the "Tower Theatre" Mr. MacNamara hints satirically at the crude realism of peasant melodrama. His own novels, however, are the expression in fiction of precisely that mood of revolt and protest which enabled the dramatists of the Irish Theatre to drive out the old-fashioned stage Irishman of the Boucicault tradition. Brinsley MacNamara's work is a counterblast to the cheerful concoctions of George Birmingham, Dorothea Conyers, and even of Somerville and Ross, who never eliminated the Leveresque element from their novels. In the conventional form of the realistic school MacNamara's novels have widened the breach in the literary ramparts of romantic Ireland. But it is by the genius of James Joyce that the dilemma of the realists and the romanticists has been solved.

JAMES JOYCE

While the tranquil power and subtle qualities of *The Threshold of Quiet* have been recognised by discerning critics here and there, the book has had neither the popular suffrage of the general public nor the ardent championship of a coterie. The work of James Joyce, on the other hand, has enjoyed both in turn, and is now in danger of those antagonisms invariably aroused by extravagant enthusiasts and uncritical imitators. When he published his little booklet of Elizabethan songs, *Chamber Music*, in 1907, his name was unknown outside Ireland, and his first prose work, *Dubliners*, was actually accepted for publication about the same time by a Dublin publisher. Owing to a variety of peculiar circumstances, partly explained by the disadvantages under which the press always suffers when controlled by an alien administration, that first Irish edition of *Dubliners* was all destroyed except one copy delivered to the author, and the book did not appear until 1914, when it was published in London. Two years later a similar experience befell *A Portrait of the Artist as a Young Man*, which could not find a London publisher and was issued in New York. Finally neither London nor New York could meet the responsibility imposed by this daring and extraordinary genius, and his great experiment, *Ulysses* (1922), was issued in a limited edition for subscribers in Paris, but not until after *The Little Review* of New York had been rewarded with a fine for its praiseworthy attempt to publish portions of the work serially. With the exception of *Chamber Music* and his one play, *Exiles* (1918), the publication of Joyce's books has failed to answer to that definition of happiness which consists in having no history.

Charming as his little poems are they would no more have established James Joyce as one of the most original figures in the whole world of contemporary letters than would his remarkable psychological drama in three acts, which is undoubtedly the only Irish play to realise the first intentions of Edward

Martyn in helping to launch the Dramatic Movement. In its morbid and profound dissection of the soul, *Exiles* suggests the social analysis of Ibsen combined with the acute sexual perceptions of Strindberg. The originality of Joyce and the justification of the high esteem in which he is held must be sought in those three volumes of fiction, *Dubliners*, *A Portrait of the Artist as a Young Man* and *Ulysses*, which have rightly aroused the attention of the intelligent public in Europe and America, even though a French critic has rashly declared that with them "Ireland makes a sensational re-entry into European literature." Apart from its affecting and ingenuous belief in the myth of a "European" literature, this statement of M. Valery Larbaud's has the obvious defect of resting upon two false assumptions. It is natural, perhaps, that he should know nothing whatever about Irish literature, and prove it by comparing the living Irish language to Old French. But a Continental writer might, at least, have remembered the vogue of Thomas Moore, who shared with Byron the curious distinction of a peculiarly "European" reputation due apparently to the enchantment which distance lends to the view of a foreign literature. In other words, to the Irish mind no lack of appreciation of James Joyce is involved by some slight consideration for the facts of Ireland's literary and intellectual evolution, and the effort now being made to cut him off from the stream of which he is a tributary is singularly futile. The logical outcome of this doctrinaire zeal of the coterie is to leave this profoundly Irish genius in the possession of a prematurely cosmopolitan reputation, the unkind fate which has always overtaken writers isolated from the conditions of which they are a part, and presented to the world without any perspective.

Fortunately, the work of James Joyce stands to refute most of the theories for which it has furnished a pretext, notably the theory that it is an unanswerable challenge to the separate existence of Anglo-Irish literature. The fact is, no Irish writer is more Irish than Joyce; none shows more unmistakably the imprint of his race and traditions. Those who have with some difficulty weaned themselves from the notion that the harum-scarum sportsmen and serio-comic peasants of the Lever school represent Ireland, only to adopt the more recent superstition of a land filled with leprechauns, heroes out of Gaelic legend, and Celtic twilight, naturally find James Joyce disconcerting. Accordingly, they either repudiate him altogether, or attempt to explain him at the expense of all his Irish contemporaries. The syllogism seems to be: J. M. Synge and James Stephens and W. B. Yeats are Irish, therefore James Joyce is not. Whereas the simple truth is that *A Portrait of the Artist as a Young Man* is to the Irish novel what *The Wanderings of Oisin* was to Irish poetry and *The Playboy of the Western World* to Irish drama, the unique and significant work which lifts the *genre* out of the commonplace into the national literature. Like most of his fellow-craftsmen in Ireland, as we have seen, Joyce began characteristically with a volume of short stories. *Dubliners* differed from the others, not in technique, but in quality, and above all, in its affinity with the best work of the French Naturalists, from whom Joyce learned his craft as George Moore did before him. It is not mere coincidence that the greatest novels of contemporary Irish life should come from the only two writers who submitted to that French influence, until they had mastered it and created out of it something of their own. The genesis of all that the author has since published is in that superb collection of studies of middle-class Dublin life.

Dublin is the frescoe upon which James Joyce has woven all the amazing patterns designed by an imagination which is at once romantic and realistic, brilliant and petty, full of powerful fantasy, yet preserving an almost incredible faculty of detailed material observation. He is governed by a horror and detestation of the circumstances which moulded the life of his Stephen Dedalus, in that city which he has carried away with him during the long years of his expatriation, and whose record he has consigned to the pages of *A Portrait of the Artist* and *Ulysses*. With a frankness and veracity as impressive as they are appaling Joyce sets forth the relentless chronicle of a soul stifled by material and intellectual squalor. Stephen Dedalus, the son of a well-to-do Catholic family, passes through the various educational and social experiences of his class in Ireland. He is sent from school and college to the university, and these institutions, their pupils and staff are described with a candour which might have been considered more sensational had the victims moved in a more prominent world. The autobiographical and realistic character of the history of Stephen Dedalus is dismissed by certain critics as of no importance, but except for some disguises of name, the two volumes of his adventures are as effectively indiscreet as *Hail and Farewell*.

The gradual downfall of the Dedalus family provides the framework of the first book. A deep undertone of filth and sordid shiftlessness is the fitting accompaniment to the disintegration of Stephen's life. The atmosphere in which he is expected to respond to the stimulus of higher education is sardonically suggested in the chapter where he is shown preparing to attend his lectures:

"He drained his third cup of watery tea to the dregs and set to chewing the crusts of fried bread that were scattered near him, staring into the dark pool of the jar. The yellow dripping had been scooped out like a boghole, and the pool under it brought back to his memory the dark turf-coloured water of the bath in Clongowes. The box of pawn tickets at his elbow had just been rifled and he took up idly one after another in his greasy fingers the blue and white dockets, scrawled and sanded and creased, and bearing the name of the pledger as Daly or MacEvoy. . . .

"Then he put them aside and gazed thoughtfully at the lid of the box, speckled with louse marks, and asked vaguely:

"How much is the clock fast now?"

This hideous interior is typical of the material surroundings in which Stephen Dedalus lives. When he leaves the house we are told:

"The lane behind the terrace was waterlogged, and as he went down it slowly, choosing his steps amid heaps of wet rubbish, he heard a mad nun screeching in the nuns' madhouse beyond the wall:

"'Jesus! O Jesus! Jesus!'

"He shook the sound out of his ears by an angry toss of his head and hurried on, stumbling through the mouldering offal, his heart already bitten by an ache of loathing and bitterness. His father's whistle, his mother's mutterings, the screech of an unseen maniac were to him now so many voices offending and threatening to humble the pride of his youth."

It is not an escape, however, which the university provides, for he simply exchanges physical ugliness for intellectual ugliness, so far as Joyce reports his life there. The only ray of idealism which penetrates the gloom of his existence is the influence of religion, which comes upon him in college, when he recoils in terrified horror before the prospects of a hell, described with a wealth of dreadful detail which seems to be suggested by an elaboration of the filthiness of Stephen's moral and physical habits. It is apparently the author's purpose to empty Catholicism of all its spiritual content, in order to provide his hero with a congruous religious background. Similarly he is tempted to depart from the strictly horrible veracity of his pictures in order to romanticise the unclean initiation of Stephen into the adventure of love. It is, of course, possible, that the amourous and religious experiences of such a man should be on a level corresponding to the low quality of his own personality. But the redeeming feature of Stephen Dedalus is his sincerity, which enables him at all times to realise the significance of what he sees, and we find it hard to reconcile his realistic temperament with the preposterous idealisation of prostitution, in a city where it has not even a remote semblance of that disguise of joy, which is supposed to make it dangerous in more sophisticated places. So long as he describes the exterior of Dublin's underworld, Joyce is too good an observer to suggest anything more than its repulsiveness. It is the supreme irony of his portrait that the artist proceeds to Swinburnian romantics based upon material so unspeakably frowsy. The romance in Stephen's life is designedly of this degrading and degraded quality. For James Joyce shows himself throughout preoccupied with all that is mean and furtive in Dublin society, and so far as he permits his own views to emerge, he professes the greatest contempt for a social organisation which permits so much vileness to flourish squalidly, beneath a rigid formality of conduct. The pages of this book are redolent of the ooze of our shabby respectability, with its intolerable tolerance of most shameful social barbarism. Joyce shows how we breed and develop our Stephen Dedaluses, providing them with everything they crave, except the means of escape from the slime which envelops them. Culture for Dedalus is represented by the pedantries of medieval metaphysics, religion by the dread of hell. Left to drift abjectly between these extremes, the young artist disintegrates in a process whose analysis becomes a remarkable piece of personal and social dissection.

In *Ulysses* the analysis of Stephen Dedalus in particular, and of Dublin in general, is carried a step further, how much further may be imagined from the fact that this vast work, of more than seven hundred and twenty-five quarto pages, covers the events of less than twenty-four hours. It recounts a day in the life of Stephen Dedalus and Leopold Bloom, and shows in a marvellous microcosm the movement of the city's existence, in ever spreading circles and ripples of activity, correlated by a method which recalls that of Jules Romains and the *Unanimistes*. But its form is more akin to that of the German Expressionists. The technical innovations which began to show in *A Portrait of the Artist as a Young Man* are here advanced to the point of a deliberate stylistic method, whose cumulative effect is wonderful. The occasional use of monologue, the notation of random and unspoken thoughts as they pass through the mind of each character, the introduction without warning of snatches of conversation, of prolonged dialogues, now almost entirely takes the place of narrative. The final chapter, for instance, is a reverie of forty-two pages, without any kind of punctuation except the break of paragraphs, in which the whole sexual life of Leopold Bloom's wife rushes pell-mell into her consciousness. It is almost always in these passages of introspection that the author reveals the sex interests and experiences of his people, and in the emptying out of their minds naturally a great deal is uncovered to the discomfiture of convention. The charges of "immorality" which Joyce has had to face have been based as a rule upon such passages.

Yet, rarely in literature has eroticism appeared in such harsh and disillusioned guise as in the work of James Joyce, where it oscillates between contemptuous, Rabelaisian ribaldry, and the crude horror and fascination of the body as seen by the great Catholic ascetics. The glamour of love is absent, and there remains such an analysis of repressed and stunted instincts as only an Irishman could have made to explain the curious conditions of Irish puritanism. But the analysis is not put forward in any intention of criticism; didacticism is alien to all that Joyce has written. He has simply compiled the record, reconstructed a period in his life, and left us to draw conclusions. *Ulysses* is simultaneously a masterpiece of realism, of documentation, and a most original dissection of the Irish mind in certain of its phases usually hitherto ignored, except for the hints of George Moore. Dedalus and Bloom are two types of Dubliner such as were studied in Joyce's first book of stories, remarkable pieces of national and human portraiture. At the same time they serve as the medium between the reader and the *vie unanime* of a whole community, whose existence is unrolled before their eyes, through which we see, and reaches our consciousness as it filters into their souls. As an experiment in form *Ulysses* more effectively accomplishes its purpose than Jules Romains did in *La Mort de Quelqu'un*, for out of the innumerable fragments of which this mosaic is composed Joyce has created a living whole, the complete representation of life. The book might have been called *La Vie de Quelqu'un*, for it is not the personal existence of Dedalus and Bloom that matters so much as the social organism of which they are a part.

Hermann Bahr, in his *Expressionismus* (1916), describes the advent of Expressionism in terms which summarise appropriately the evolution of Joyce. "The eye of the body is passive to everything; it receives, and whatever is impressed upon it by outward charm is more powerful than the activity of the eye itself, more powerful than what it seizes of that outward charm. On the other hand, the eye of the mind is active and merely uses as the material of its own power the reflections of reality. . . . Now it seems that in the rising generation the mind is strongly asserting itself. It is turning away from exterior to interior life, and listening to the voices of its own secrets. . . . Such a generation will repudiate Impressionism and demand an art which sees with the eyes of the mind: Expressionism is the natural successor of Impressionism."

Much has been written about the symbolic intention of this work, of its relation to the Odyssey, to which the plan of the three first and last chapters, with the twelve cantos of the adventures of Ulysses in the middle, is supposed to correspond. Irish criticism can hardly be impressed by this aspect of a work which, in its meticulous detailed documentation of Dublin, rivals Zola in photographic realism. In its bewildering juxtaposition of the real and the imaginary, of the commonplace and the fantastic, Joyce's work obviously declares its kinship with the Expressionists, with Walter Hasenclever or Georg Kaiser.

With *Ulysses* James Joyce has made a daring and valuable experiment, breaking new ground in English for the future development of prose narrative. But the "European" interest of the work must of necessity be largely technical, for the matter is as local as the form is universal. In fact, so local is it that many pages remind the Irish reader of *Hail and Farewell*, except that the allusions are to matters and personalities more obscure. To claim for this book a European significance simultaneously denied to J. M. Synge and James Stephens is to confess complete ignorance of its genesis, and to invest its content with a mysterious import which the actuality of references would seem to deny. While James Joyce is endowed with the wonderful fantastic imagination which conceived the fantasmagoria of the fifteenth chapter of *Ulysses*, a vision of a Dublin Brocken, whose scene is the underworld, he also has the defects and qualities of Naturalism, which prompts him to catalogue the Dublin tramways, and to explain with the precision of a guide-book how the city obtains its water supply. In fine, Joyce is essentially a realist as Flaubert was, but, just as the author of *Madame Bovary* never was bound by the formula subsequently erected into the dogma of realism, the creator of Stephen Dedalus has escaped from the same bondage. Flaubert's escape was by way of the Romanticism from which he started, Joyce's is by way of Expressionism, to which he has advanced.

LORD DUNSANY AND JAMES STEPHENS

Until this revival of the art of fiction dealing with contemporary life, which has come about during the years of the war, the more original prose writers had shown no disposition to accept the novel proper as their medium. Prior to 1914 the two most important could not be classed as novelists except in the loosest sense of that term. Neither Lord Dunsany nor James Stephens had carried on the tradition of any previous writer of Irish fiction. They cannot be associated with the other storytellers. James Stephens began by making a slight concession to the accepted convention of the novel, but before *The Charwoman's Daughter* had reached many chapters that convention was abandoned. Lord Dunsany, on the other hand, has conceded only so much in his short stories as to suggest their ancestry in the fairy tale.

In 1905 *The Gods of Pegana* passed almost unperceived amidst the more avowedly Celtic literature of the moment. Indeed, it is unlikely that many readers who then saw the name of Lord Dunsany for the first time would have associated the book with the Irish movement in which its author was so generously interested. Coming forward as the creator of a new mythology, he could not readily be identified with a literary tradition whose strength was rooted in the soil of Gaelic legend and antiquity. Lord Dunsany invented his own antiquity, whose history was found in *The Gods of Pegana*. With a strange power of imagination he set forth the hierarchy of Pegana's gods, the greater and minor deities. Marvellous Beings, who play with worlds and suns, with life and death, their mere nomenclature is full of weird suggestion. There is not an event in the cosmic evolution known to us which Lord Dunsany has failed to elaborate into some beautiful legend. But, whereas the first volume was essentially the record of a new theogony, *Time and the Gods* (1908) is a collection of myths, which naturally attach themselves to the phenomena witnessed by the men whom the Pegana deities created for their amusement. In allowing his fancy to interpret the great elemental mysteries of nature, the rising of the winds or the coming of light, the author shows the same delicate poetic imagination as assisted him in the creation of the mighty figures who peopled his original cosmos. Yet, with a true sense of the mythus,

Lord Dunsany controls fantasy, so that he is never betrayed into any conflict with the natural laws, as understood by contemporary science. His fable of the *South Wind*, for example, is as accurate in its representation of the facts as it is charming in its tender poetry.

The *Leitmotiv* of his work, whether the narrative be of gods or men, is the mysterious warfare between the phenomenal world and the forces of Time and Change. Even the "gods of Pegana" live beneath the shadow of this conflict which must one day result in their overthrow. Lord Dunsany's later work, *The Sword of Welleran* (1908), *A Dreamer's Tales* (1910) and *The Book of Wonder* (1912), is concerned more specifically with this aspect of existence. Here we learn of those wonderful cities, Perdondaris and Babbulkund, whose fabulous beauties are obliterated in a moment of Time, when something swift and terrible swallows them up, leaving only the whispering sands above them. The most beautiful prose the author has written is in these stories, beginning with *In the Land of Time* from *Time and the Gods*, which tell of the passing away of human achievement at the assault of nature aided by her relentless accomplices. Yet he has demonstrated his mastery of the grotesque and horrible in tales which recall those of Poe or Ambrose Bierce. His later work lacks glamour and spontaneity, and does not give the measure of his power, which is best seen in *The Sword of Welleran* and *A Dreamer's Tales*. There Lord Dunsany showed a wealth of bizarre and terrible fantasy of the same high quality as characterised his previous essays in mythological narrative. The latter, however, are his enduring share in the reawakening of the Celtic imagination of which the Literary Revival is the manifestation.

While Lord Dunsany was for many years the most neglected of our prose-writers, James Stephens has enjoyed a very different fate, being probably the best known of all the younger generation. It has rarely been given to an Irish genius so national to become famous in the short space of three years, which separated his first little book of verse, *Insurrections*, from *The Crock of Gold*, published in 1912. The same year saw the publication of his first prose work, *The Charwoman's Daughter*, and his second volume of poems, *The Hill of Vision*, but these were of necessity somewhat obscured by the remarkable success of *The Crock of Gold*. As was suggested in reference to his verse, the poet was the beneficiary of the prosaist. It may be said that everything he published at that time, or previously, came into consideration as a consequent and subsequent part of that success.

The immediate popularity of James Stephens must be attributed to the fact that he revealed at once his power to use prose as attractively as others used verse. The Celtic spirit which breathes through the poetry of the Revival is at last felt in a work of prose fiction, which, by contrast with the novels and stories of previous years, seemed a wonderful innovation. Yet *The Crock of Gold* could not have been a surprise to those who read *The Charwoman's Daughter* as it appeared in the first volume of *The Irish Review*, during the year 1911. The realism of the latter story of the Dublin streets could not repress the irresistible grotesquerie and good-humour, the fanciful charm so characteristic of the better-known book. Mrs. Makebelieve and her daughter personified a side of their creator's mentality. Like them he has the faculty of rising above reality and transporting himself into a world of pure fantasy. The co-existence of the ugly material facts of life with the beauty of an imaginary state, as shown in the lives of Mary Makebelieve and her mother, is a symbol of Stephen's work. He is eternally hovering on the line which divides the sublime from the ridiculous. He crosses it with an insouciance which comes, not from a lack of perception, but from an innate sense of the relativeness of all values.

The title of his first book was the forecast of an attitude towards life which subsequent works have confirmed. The "insurrection" of James Stephens is the revolt of an unsophisticated mind against unnatural decorum. When the Philosopher in *The Crock of Gold* goes to interview Angus Óg, his frame of mind is not, perhaps, as reverential as might be expected from a man who desired the presence of such a Being. His familiar *bonhomie* springs from a conviction of the necessary humanity of one's relations with all creatures, heavenly and terrestrial. Thus Stephens will contrive the conversation of a fly, a cow, a god or a spider, upon the assumption of a common relationship between all phenomena. This is not a mere literary artifice, "sophisticated infantilism," as severe critics pronounce it. It is the reflection of the author's mind, which gambols in naïve irreverence about the gravest problems.

The Crock of Gold and *The Demi-Gods* (1914), his best works, are naturally most typical of his genius. At the same time, they are assertions of the claim of Irish prose to undertake some of the functions of poetry. Not that the author is prone to write "prose poems"; or to indulge in word-painting for its own sake. But his narratives are interwoven with the mysticism which we have heretofore found in A. E., and with the symbolism which has induced so many people to consider Yeats as a mystic. Irish mythology and fairy lore are skilfully blended, and the general impression left upon the reader is one entirely different from that of any other Irish story or fairy tale. The author's *gaminerie*, which enables him to contemplate the Cosmos with charming familiarity, has served him well, for he is not at all disconcerted when his fancy takes him from the domestic quarrels of the Philosopher and the farcical proceedings of the Policemen, to the realms of Pan and Angus Óg. The discourses of the gods are as much a part of his imaginative life as were of his actual life the charwomen, policemen and vagrants whose peculiarities he has not forgotten.

The dangers of this attitude were exemplified in *Here are Ladies* (1913) where the commonplace and the unusual jostle one another, this time to the discomfiture of the latter. In places one gets a glimpse of the author of *The Charwoman's Daughter* and *The Crock of Gold*, as in the grotesque fantasy of *The Threepenny Piece*, and in the delightful reverie of boyhood, *Three Happy Places*, where Stephens's peculiar power of visualising the outlook of a boy is exercised. Pessimists feared at one time that he was about to go the way of all Irish fiction writers, but *The Demi-Gods* has justified the optimists. Without breaking new ground the book marks an advance upon the earlier work to which it is closely akin. The author has firmer control of his material, and if there is a diminution of youthful exuberance, it is compensated by a note of deeper maturity. *The Demi-Gods* surpasses, where it does not equal, *The Crock of Gold*, which contains no character study to compare with Patsy MacCann.

When *The Demi-Gods* definitely placed James Stephens in the front rank of living prose-writers he was fortunately able to escape the compulsion to exploit the success which came to him so quickly after the appearance of *The Charwoman's Daughter*. He contented himself for six years by issuing an occasional little book of poems, none more beautiful than *Reincarnations*, a handful of exquisite variations upon themes from the later Gaelic poets. This slender work is a clue to the apparent inactivity of the author, who had plunged into the study of Irish, and was more absorbed in the Gaelic past than in the Irish present, although he had written that lively diary of an onlooker during the Rising of Easter 1916, *The Insurrection in Dublin*. He was at work upon a new version of the *Tain Bo-Cuailgne*, of which the two first volumes, as yet unpublished, promise his masterpiece. In prose, this time, he has achieved a "reincarnation" in which the great figures of legend, Deirdre and Naisi and Conchobar live and talk as they have never done since the days of the bards themselves. All the wit, the fantasy and the beauty which haunt the imagination and make the style of James Stephens have vivified those scenes and people, so often described since Standish O'Grady brought them back into literature, until they stand forth from his pages as the creations of the poet himself. Yet, with all this a scrupulous accuracy in details of chronology and local colour, carefully checked with reference to original documents and the findings of modern scholars and ancient bards.

Meanwhile a foretaste of this new quality in the work of Stephens, of this power of reincarnating from Gaelic material in a manner wholly original, may be found in the volume of *Irish Fairy Tales*, published in 1920, for which the author's major work was set aside temporarily. These are not the hackneyed fairy tales which usually serve, as this work has unfortunately done, as an excuse for a "gift-book" with illustrations by some artist in vogue. The author went to the fountain-head of Irish storytelling, the old legends and epics in which he was immersed, and the result is a volume as unmistakably of the soil of Ireland as it is the creation of the author's imagination. This fairyland is Irish, and were the characters of Grimm and Andersen to be substituted for Fionn, Tuan mac Cairill or Mongan, the tales would not lose their nationality in that universal land of fairy where no national frontiers hinder the wanderings of youthful adventurers. The descriptive passages are many and beautiful, but they are obviously meant for eyes and ears more sensitive than those of children. For example:

Even the wind had ceased, and there seemed to be nothing in the world but the darkness and himself. In that gigantic blackness, in that unseen quietude and vacancy, the mind could cease to be personal to itself. It could be overwhelmed and merged in space, so that consciousness would be transferred or dissipated, and one might sleep standing; for the mind fears loneliness more than all else, and will escape to the moon rather than be driven inwards on its own being.

or this:

A storm rose, and when I looked again from my tall cliff I saw that great fleet rolling as in a giant's hand. At times they were pitched against the sky and staggered aloft, spinning gustily there like wind-blown leaves. Then they were hurled from these dizzy tops to the flat, moaning gulf, to the glassy, inky horror that swirled and whirled between ten waves. At times a wave leaped howling under a ship, and with a buffet dashed it into the air, and chased it upward with thunder stroke on stroke, and followed again, close as a chasing wolf, trying with hammering on hammering to beat in the wide-wombed bottom and suck out the frightened lives through one black gape.

The author's power of grotesque fancy also adds to the effectiveness of his pictures of the strange and beautiful realm to which he acts as a guide. In *Mon-*

gan's Frenzy the spectacle of the warriors of Ulster perched in the trees to escape from a flock of savage sheep is irresistible. "They roosted among the branches like great birds, while the venomous sheep ranged below, bleating terribly and tearing up the ground." The incongruity of this idea resides largely in an association of ideas to a sophisticated reader, but it will hardly come within the appreciation of children. Then there is the description of Mannanan's dog, which rescued the warriors from their plight:

> Now if the sheep were venomous, this dog was more venomous still, for it was fearful to look at. In body it was not large, but its head was of great size, and the mouth that was shaped in that head was able to open like the lid of a pot. It was not teeth which were in that head, but hooks and fangs and prongs. Dreadful was that mouth to look at, terrible to look into, woeful to think about, and from it, or from the broad, loose nose that waggled above it, there came a sound which no word of man could describe, for it was not a snarl, nor was it a howl, although it was both of these. It was neither a growl nor a grunt, although it was both of these; it was not a yowl nor a groan, although it was both of these: for it was one sound made up of these sounds, and there was in it, too, a whine and a yelp, and a long-drawn snoring noise, and a deep purring noise, and a noise that was like the squeal of a rusty hinge, and there were other noises in it also.

The rhythm of this prose, this delight in words, the grotesque humour of each detail, are at once characteristic of the style of James Stephens and of the Gaelic storytellers. His study of Irish and prolonged absorption in the old literature have heightened the colour and strengthened the movement of his prose. His constructions have a delightful flavour of Gaelic; Irish forms are dexterously duplicated in English; cumulative epithets are effectively employed, yet the writing is as far removed from the manner of Synge as from the Kiltartan of Lady Gregory. The dignity and humour and easy, unaffected beauty of his style seem to find peculiarly happy expression in the re-clothing of these legendary tales, from which an episode, or even the hint of an episode, has enabled him to reconstruct a narrative of unsurpassed charm. These stories of the Fionn cycle are an indication of the direction in which James Stephens has been evolving, towards what already promises to be the greatest prose work in Anglo-Irish literature.

The retelling of the old stories of bardic literature has absorbed the energies of many Irish prose writers in recent years, apart from those who have been engaged in the work of translating and editing the classic texts of Gaelic literature. With the latter we are not concerned, except to note that this increasing knowledge of the Heroic Age has widened the field of tradition, and increased the resources of our poetry and drama. Those, however, who have contributed to the process of popularisation stand in a more direct relationship to Anglo-Irish literature. Their work has a literary rather than a scientific interest, although the intrinsic value of such work varies greatly, and interests the historian rather than the critic of literature.

Standish O'Grady had published his *History of Ireland: The Heroic Period* in 1878, but before the second volume was issued there appeared P. W. Joyce's *Old Celtic Romances* (1879), "the first collection of the old Gaelic prose romances that has ever been published in fair English translation," as the author described it in his preface. The book had none of the fire and poetic imagination of O'Grady's epic history; it did not, therefore, appeal in the same way to the young poets of the Eighties, but it was the forerunner of the popular literature of heroic Ireland. Its many editions prove that it can still survive the competition of numerous successors, some, fragmentary and fanciful, like Nora Hopper's *Ballads in Prose*, others, serious rivals, such as *The High Deeds of Finn* (1910) by T. W. Rolleston, where the value of a fine series of retellings is enhanced by the inclusion of material hitherto untranslated. Akin to O'Grady's *Finn and his Companions* is the recent volume, *Heroes of the Dawn* (1913), by Violet Russell, in which the wife of the poet essays, in turn, to bring the bardic heroes within the vision of boyhood. This work may be coupled with the *Celtic Wonder-Tales* (1910) of Ella Young as the two most charming collections of children's stories published in Ireland for many years.

Most of these versions have shown more regard for the literary and artistic quality of the stories than for the need of an ordered and accurate account of the bardic narratives. In this respect the best work is *The Cuchullin Saga in Irish Literature*, published by Eleanor Hull in 1898. A volume of fourteen stories embodying the history of Cuchulain, it was a valuable innovation in the manner of collating the Gaelic material. Its introduction and notes, and the careful selection of texts, made it at once a literary and scholarly contribution. But it was soon to make way for a similar volume outside the domain of scholarship, identical in content, but very different in form.

In 1902 Lady Gregory published her *Cuchulain of Muirthemne*, which was followed in 1904 by *Gods and Fighting Men*. The former is an ordered retelling of the Cuchulain legends, the latter treats of the gods and the Fianna, but, except in so far as it follows Eleanor Hull's choice of texts, Lady Gregory's work is very dissimilar. It is frankly a blend of scholarship and imaginative reconstruction. The author was no less desirous of clarifying the legendary material than was Eleanor Hull, but she did not allow considerations of fact to interfere with the success of her undertaking. Comparing all the translations of the scholars, she has co-ordinated and compressed them into a homogeneous narrative, by the simple expedient of making suppressions and additions of her own, whenever the textual versions threaten to disrupt her plan. Literary success came immediately to justify her experiments, but competent Gaelic criticism has severely condemned a procedure which has had the effect of conveying a very false idea of the classic age and literature of Ireland. Even so enthusiastic a commentator and apostle of Celticism as Fiona MacLeod felt constrained to admit the superiority of *The Cuchullin Saga in Irish Literature*.

Lady Gregory's "translations," however, are not to be judged for what that term implies. They are not so much translations as folk-versions of the old saga, adapted to literature. Their success has been mainly amongst readers already familiar with the correct text, or with those whose interest was of a less exacting nature. Both could submit to the undeniable charm of a style whose archaic flavour seemed peculiarly fitted to these evocations of ancient times. For Lady Gregory is the first and only writer of the Revival to employ the peasant idiom in narrative prose. That Kiltartan speech with which her comedies have made us familiar was consecrated to literary use by its effective elaboration in *Cuchulain of Muirthemne*. With the previous example of *The Love Songs of Connacht* before her, Lady Gregory was encouraged to extend the scope of Gaelicised English by adopting peasant speech in

her most serious contribution to Anglo-Irish literature. It was a fine literary instinct that guided her
in making this innovation, for, stripped of their language, her stories of Cuchulain and the Fianna would
have been lost in the almost anonymous mass of
similar popularisation. As it is, she has been saluted
by many as an Irish Malory, and her work has
shared in the general admiration for the beauties of
an idiom illustrated shortly afterwards by the genius
of J. M. Synge. The young writers of a generation
unfamiliar with the emotion aroused by O'Grady, in
the distant days when his rehandling of the bardic
material was a revelation, may derive from Lady
Gregory's pages that enthusiasm for heroic beauty
which inspired the first movement of the Revival.

The literature of the Celtic Renaissance has been
predominantly the creation of poets and dramatists,
and in retrospect it presents a somewhat unequal
appearance, owing to the absence of prose writers.
The novel has fared badly, but criticism has fared
worse, being unrepresented, except for the intermittent essays of John Eglinton, and that interesting, if
isolated, work of collaboration, *Literary Ideals in
Ireland*, of which some account has been given. The
æsthetic reveries of W. B. Yeats, like the scattered
articles of A. E. and others, do not bear witness to
any deliberate critical effort on their part. Impartial criticism is a more than usually delicate task
where a small country like Ireland is concerned.
When the intellectual centre is confined within a restricted area, personal relations are unavoidable, and
the critic finds discretion imperative, if he is to continue to dwell peaceably in the midst of his friends.
Nevertheless, the Irish reviews have not shrunk
from publishing the most candid criticism, and if
little of this material has been collected, it is the

fault of the critics. An interesting and hopeful innovation was the publication of Thomas MacDonagh's *Literature in Ireland*. This thoughtful volume of "studies in Irish and Anglo-Irish" was published shortly after the author's execution, and promised to be an introduction to further works of a similar character. MacDonagh was well equipped for the task he had set himself, and this book is an important contribution to the study of Anglo-Irish poetry.

The effect upon the literature of the smaller countries of this absence of critical judgment, publicly expressed, has been that honest criticism prefers to be silent where it cannot praise. Consequently, there is lack of intellectual discipline which allows the good and the mediocre to struggle on equal terms for recognition. In Ireland we have become accustomed to hearing Irish writers either enthusiastically advertised by the English press, or denounced as charlatans, usurping the fame reserved for the genuine heirs of England's literary glory. The phenomenon rarely calls for more than casual attention, so fortuitous does it seem. Yet, so far as it has any reasonable basis, it may be traced to our habit of allowing every writer who so desires to submit his work to outside criticism on the same terms as our most distinguished literary representatives. We cannot expect others to show more discrimination than ourselves, and when the storm of facile applause has broken over the head of the confiding poet or dramatist, we need not be surprised if some spirit more enquiring than the others leads an abusive reaction. So long as we continue to have our criticism written for us by journalists in England, these disconcerting alternations of idolatry and contempt will follow Irish literature abroad.

However flattering the cult of Celticism may seem

to us, it is unwise to attach any significance to it. Anglo-Irish literature, as a whole, has not grown up to meet the desires of the devotees of this cult, but to meet the need of Ireland for self-expression. Should it incidentally produce a writer of such proportions as to entitle him to a place in comparative literary history, let us, by all means, encourage him to challenge the attention of the outside world. The main purpose, however, of the Literary Revival has not been to contribute to English literature, but to create a national literature for Ireland, in the language which has been imposed upon her—a circumstance which effectively disposes of the theory that Ireland is merely an intellectual province of England. The provincial Irishman is he who prefers to identify himself with the literary movement of another country but his own, and those writers who have addressed themselves to the English, rather than to the Irish, public are obviously in that category. They are always expatriates to their adopted countrymen.

The only question, therefore, which must be answered by such a survey as the present is: has the Literary Renaissance accomplished its purpose? Has it given us a body of work which may fairly be described as the nucleus of a national literature? In spite of various weaknesses, it seems as if Anglo-Irish literature had proved its title to be considered as an independent entity. It has not altogether escaped the literary traditions of the language in which it is written, but it has shown a more marked degree of originality, in respect of form and content, than Belgian or any other literature similarly dominated by a powerful neighbour. Possessing the advantage, denied to Switzerland and Belgium, of a great native literature, with all the traditions thereby implied,

Ireland has been able to mould her second language according to the literary genius of the race.

It does not matter in the least whether the poetry of the Revival deserves, or does not deserve, the honours which enthusiasts have claimed for it. We must, first of all, determine whether the literature of the Revival is really national, and then attempt to estimate the relative importance of those who created it. If this history has helped in any way to attain that object, it will have corresponded to the intention with which it was conceived. Comparative criticism will in due course decide that question which obsesses certain minds, namely: is W. B. Yeats a greater poet than Shelley? France did not assign his status to her supreme poetic genius, Racine, by reference to Dante and Shakespeare. National (or local) values invariably take precedence of international, however disappointing that fact may seem to lovers of the absolute.

BIBLIOGRAPHY

The following bibliography is intended primarily as a summary of the achievement of the Literary Renaissance in Ireland. In the case of the more important writers a complete list of their works has been given. Many of these do not fall within the scope of this book but are of interest to bibliophiles. Works of fiction having no relation either to literature in general, or to the history of the Revival in particular, have been omitted.

As detailed statements of the plays produced by the Irish Players are available elsewhere, only the more significant dramatists have been included.

In every instance the dates given are those of first publication in book form.

A few works announced for publication have been included.

A. E. (GEORGE W. RUSSELL)

Homeward: Songs by the Way, 1894. The Future of Ireland and the Awakening of the Fires, 1897. Ideals in Ireland: Priest or Hero?, 1897. The Earth Breath, 1897. Literary Ideals in Ireland, 1899 (in collaboration). Ideals in Ireland, 1901 (in collaboration). The Nuts of Knowledge, 1903. Controversy in Ireland, 1904. The Divine Vision, 1904. The Mask of Apollo, 1904. New Poems, 1904 (edited). By Still Waters, 1906. Some Irish Essays, 1906. Deirdre, 1907. The Hero in Man, 1909. The Building up of a Rural Civilisation, 1910. The Renewal of Youth, 1911. The United Irishwomen, 1912 (in collaboration). Co-operation and Nationality, 1912. The Dublin Strike, 1912. The Rural Community, 1913. Collected Poems, 1913. Gods of War and other Poems, 1915. Imaginations and Reveries, 1915. Templecrone, 1916. The National Being, 1916. Thoughts for a Convention, 1917. Salutation, 1917. The Candle of Vision, 1918. Conscription for

Ireland, 1918. Michael, 1919. The Economics of Ireland, 1920. A Plea for Justice, 1920. The Inner and the Outer Ireland, 1921. Ireland and the Empire at the Court of Conscience, 1921.

WILLIAM ALLINGHAM (1824–1889)

Poems, 1850. Peace and War, 1854. Day and Night Songs, 1854. The Music Master, 1855. Nightingale Valley, 1862. Laurence Bloomfield in Ireland, 1864. Fifty Modern Poems, 1865. Songs, Ballads and Stories, 1877. Ashby Manor, 1882. Evil May Day, 1883. The Fairies, 1883. Irish Songs and Poems, 1887. Rhymes for the Young Folk, 1887. Flower Pieces and other Poems, 1888. Life and Phantasy, 1889. Thought and Word, 1890. Varieties in Prose, 3 vols., 1893. Blackberries, 1896. Sixteen Poems, 1905 (edited by W. B. Yeats).

JANE BARLOW (1857–1917)

Bogland Studies, 1892. Irish Idylls, 1892. Kerrigan's Quality, 1893. The Battle of the Frogs and Mice, 1894. The End of Elfintown, 1894. Maureen's Fairing, 1895. Strangers at Lisconnell, 1895. Mrs. Martin's Company, 1896. A Creel of Irish Stories, 1897. From the East unto the West, 1898. From the Land of the Shamrock, 1900. The Ghost-Bereft, 1901. The Founding of Fortunes, 1902. By Beach and Bog Land, 1905. Irish Neighbours, 1907. The Mockers and other Verses, 1908. Irish Ways, 1909. Flaws, 1911. Mac's Adventures, 1911. Doings and Dealings, 1913. Between Doubting and Daring, 1916. In Mio's Youth, 1917.

WILLIAM BOYLE

A Kish of Brogues, 1899. The Building Fund, 1905. The Eloquent Dempsey, 1907. The Mineral Workers, 1907. Family Failing, 1912.

SHAN F. BULLOCK

The Awkward Squads, 1893. By Thrasna River, 1895. Ring o' Rushes, 1896. The Charmer, 1897. The Barrys, 1899. Irish Pastorals, 1901. The Squireen, 1903. The Red Leaguers, 1904. Dan the Dollar, 1905. The Cubs, 1906. Robert Thorne, 1907. Master John, 1909. Hetty, 1911. Thomas Andrews, 1912. The Race of Castlebar, 1913 (in collaboration). Mr. Ruby Jumps the Traces, 1917.

ETHNA CARBERY (ANNA MACMANUS)
(1866–1902)

The Four Winds of Eirinn, 1902. The Passionate Hearts, 1903. In the Celtic Past, 1904.

AUSTIN CLARKE

The Vengeance of Fionn, 1918. The Fires of Baal, 1921. The Sword of the West, 1921.

PADRAIC COLUM

New Songs, 1904 (in collaboration). The Land, 1905. The Fiddler's House, 1907. Studies, 1907. Whitman, 1907 (edited). Wild Earth, 1907. Thomas Muskerry, 1910. Eyes of Youth, 1910 (in collaboration). The Desert, 1912. My Irish Year, 1912. Oliver Goldsmith, 1913 (edited). A Boy in Eirinn, 1913. Broad Sheet Ballads, 1913 (edited). Gerald Griffin, 1918 (edited). Poems of the Irish Revolutionary Brotherhood, 1916 (edited). The King of Ireland's Son, 1916. The Irish Rebellion of 1916, 1916 (in collaboration). Wild Earth and other Poems, 1916. Mogu the Wanderer, 1916. The Adventures of Odysseus, 1918. The Boy Who Knew What the Birds Said, 1918. The Girl Who Sat by the Ashes, 1919. The Boy Apprenticed to an Enchanter, 1920. The Children of Odin, 1920. The Golden Fleece, 1921. Anthology of Irish Verse, 1922 (edited).

DANIEL CORKERY

A Munster Twilight, 1916. The Threshold of Quiet, 1917. The Labour Leader, 1920. The Yellow Bittern and other Plays, 1920. The Hounds of Banba, 1920. I Bhreasail: A Book of Lyrics, 1921.

LORD DUNSANY

The Gods of Pegana, 1905. Time and the Gods, 1906. The Sword of Welleran, 1908. A Dreamer's Tales, 1910. The Book of Wonder, 1912. Five Plays, 1914. Fifty-One Tales, 1915. Tales of Wonder, 1916. A Night at an Inn, 1916. Plays of Gods and Men, 1917. Nowadays, 1918. Tales of War, 1918. Unhappy Far-Off Things, 1919. Tales of Three Hemispheres, 1920. If, 1921. The Chronicles of Rodriguez, 1922.

JOHN EGLINTON (W. K. MAGEE)

Two Essays on the Remnant, 1895. Literary Ideals in Ireland, 1899 (in collaboration). Pebbles from a Brook, 1901. Some Essays and Passages, 1905 (edited by W. B. Yeats). Bards and Saints, 1906. Anglo-Irish Essays, 1917.

ST. JOHN G. ERVINE

Mixed Marriage, 1911. The Magnanimous Lover, 1912. Eight O'Clock and other Studies, 1912. Four Plays, 1914. Mrs. Martin's Man, 1914. Jane Clegg, 1914. Alice and a Family, 1915. John Ferguson, 1915. Sir Edward Carson, 1915. Changing Winds, 1917. The Foolish Lovers, 1920. The Ship, 1922.

SIR SAMUEL FERGUSON (1810–1886)

Inheritor and Economist, 1849. Dublin, 1849. The Cromlech on Howth, 1864. Lays of the Western Gael, 1865. Congal, 1872. Deirdre, 1880. Poems, 1880. The Forging of the Anchor, 1883. The Hibernian Nights' Entertainments, 3 vols., 1887. The Remains of St. Patrick, 1888. Lays of the Red Branch, 1897.

DARRELL FIGGIS

A Vision of Life, 1909. The Crucibles of Time, 1911. Shakespeare: A Study, 1911. Broken Arcs, 1911. Studies and Appreciations, 1912. Queen Tara, 1913. Jacob Elthorne, 1914. The Mount of Transfiguration, 1915. A. E.: A Study of a Man and a Nation, 1916. A Chronicle of Jails, 1917. The Gaelic State, 1917. Children of Earth, 1918. The Historic Case for Irish Independence, 1918. Bye-Ways of Study, 1918. Carleton's Stories of Irish Life, 1918 (edited). A Second Chronicle of Jails, 1919. The Economic Case for Irish Independence, 1920. The House of Success, 1921.

GEORGE FITZMAURICE

The Country Dressmaker, 1914. Five Plays, 1914.

EVA GORE-BOOTH

Poems, 1898. Unseen Kings, 1904. The One and the Many, 1904. The Three Resurrections and the Triumph of Maeve, 1905. The Egyptian Pillar, 1907. The Perilous Light, 1915. The Death of Fionavar, 1916. The Sword of Justice, 1918. Broken Glory, 1918.

ALFRED PERCEVAL GRAVES

Songs of Killarney, 1873. Irish Songs and Ballads, 1880. Joseph Sheridan Lefanu's Purcell Papers, 1879–1880 (edited). Lays and Lyrics of the Pan-Celtic Society, 1889(in collaboration). Father O'Flynn and other Irish Lyrics, 1889. Songs of Irish Wit and Humour, 1894. The Irish Song Book, 1894. Sheridan Lefanu's Poems, 1896 (edited). Songs of Erin, 1900. The Irish Poems of A. P. Graves, 2 vols., 1908. The Irish Fairy Book, 1909. Welsh Poetry Old and New, 1912. Irish Literary and Musical Studies, 1913. Harpstrings of the Irish Gael, 1914 (edited). The Book of Irish Poetry, 1915 (edited). Sir Samuel Ferguson's Poems, 1918 (edited). A Celtic Psaltery, 1917 (edited).

LADY GREGORY

Ideals in Ireland, 1901 (in collaboration). Cuchulain of Muirthemne, 1902. Poets and Dreamers, 1903. Spreading the News, 1904. Gods and Fighting Men, 1904. Kincora, 1905. The White Cockade, 1905. A Book of Saints and Wonders, 1906. Spreading the News and other Comedies, 1906. The Unicorn from the Stars, 1908 (in collaboration). Seven Short Plays, 1909. The Kiltartan History Book, 1909. The Kiltartan Wonder Book, 1910. The Kiltartan Molière, 1910. The Image, 1910. The Full Moon, 1911. Irish Folk History Plays, 2 vols., 1912. New Comedies, 1913. Our Irish Theatre, 1913. The Golden Apple, 1916. The Kiltartan Poetry Book, 1918. The Dragon, 1920. Visions and Beliefs in the West of Ireland, 2 vols., 1920. Hugh Lane, 1921. The Image and other Plays, 1922. Three Wonder Plays, 1922.

NORA HOPPER (1871–1906)

Ballads in Prose, 1894. Under Quicken Boughs, 1896. Songs of the Morning, 1900. Aquamarines, 1902. Selected Poems, 5 cols., 1906.

*DOUGLAS HYDE

Poems and Ballads of Young Ireland, 1888 (in collaboration). Lays and Lyrics of the Pan-Celtic Society, 1889 (in collaboration). Beside the Fire, 1890. The Love Songs of Connacht, 1893. The Revival of Irish Literature, 1894 (in collaboration). The Three Sorrows of Storytelling, 1895. The Story of Early Gaelic Literature, 1897. A Literary History of Ireland, 1899. Ideals in Ireland, 1901 (in collaboration). Irish Poetry, 1903. Songs ascribed to Raftery, 1903. The Religious Songs of Connacht, 1906. Legends of Saints and Sinners, 1915 (edited).

JAMES JOYCE

The Day of the Rabblement: An Essay, 1901. Chamber Music, 1907. Dubliners, 1914. A Portrait of the Artist, 1916. Exiles, 1918. Ulysses, 1922.

LIONEL JOHNSON (1867–1902)

Sir Walter Raleigh in the Tower, 1885. The Book of the Rhymers' Club, 1892 (in collaboration). The Second Book of the Rhymers' Club, 1894 (in collaboration). Poems, 1895. The Art of Thomas Hardy, 1896. Ireland and other Poems, 1897. Twenty-one Poems, 1904 (edited by W. B. Yeats). Selections from the Poems of Lionel Johnson, 1908. Poetry and Ireland, 1908 (in collaboration). Post Liminium, 1911. Collected Poems, 1915. Some Winchester Letters, 1919. Reviews and Critical Papers, 1921.

THOMAS KEOHLER

New Songs, 1904 (in collaboration). Songs of a Devotee, 1906.

WILLIAM LARMINIE (1850–1899)

Glanlua, 1889. Fand, 1892. West Irish Folk Tales, 1893. Literary Ideals in Ireland, 1899 (in collaboration).

EMILY LAWLESS (1845–1913)

A Millionaire's Cousin, 1885. Hurrish, 2 vols., 1886. Major Lawrence, F. L. S., 3 vols., 1887. The Story of Ireland, 1887.

---

* Works in Gaelic are not included.

Plain Frances Mowbray, 1889. With Essex in Ireland, 1890. Grania, 1892. Maelcho, 1894. Traits and Confidences, 1898. A Garden Diary, 1901. With the Wild Geese, 1902. Maria Edgeworth, 1904. The Book of Gilly, 1906. The Point of View, 1909. The Race of Castlebar, 1913 (in collaboration). The Inalienable Heritage and other Poems, 1914.

SEOSAMH MACCATHMHAOIL (JOSEPH CAMBPELL)

The Songs of Uladh, 1904. The Garden of the Bees, 1905. The Rushlight, 1906. The Man Child, 1907. The Gilly of Christ, 1907. The Mountainy Singer, 1909. Mearing Stones, 1911. Judgment, 1912. Irishry, 1914. Earth of Cualann, 1917.

THOMAS MACDONAGH (1884–1916)

Through the Ivory Gate, 1903. April and May, 1904. The Golden Joy, 1906. When the Dawn is come, 1908. Songs of Myself, 1910. Thomas Campion and the Art of English Poetry, 1913. Lyrical Poems, 1913. Literature in Ireland, 1916. Collected Poems, 1916. Pagans, 1920.

SEUMAS MACMANUS

Shuilers from Heathy Hills, 1893. The Leading Road to Donegal, 1896. 'Twas in Dhroll Donegal, 1897. The Bend of the Road, 1897. The Humours of Donegal, 1898. Through the Turf Smoke, 1899. In Chimney Corners, 1899. The Bewitched Fiddle, 1900. Donegal Fairy Stories, 1902. The Red Poocher, 1903. A Lad of the O'Friels, 1903. The Hard-Hearted Man, 1904. Ballads of a Country Boy, 1905. The Woman of Seven Sorrows, 1905. Plays, 1906. Dr. Kilgannon, 1907. Yourself and the Neighbours, 1914. Lo and Behold Ye, 1919. The Story of the Irish Race, 1922.

JAMES CLARENCE MANGAN (1803–1849)

Anthologia Germanica, 1845. Poets and Poetry of Munster (First Series), 1850. The Tribes of Ireland, 1852. Poems, 1859 (edited by John Mitchel). Essays in Prose and Verse, 1884. Selected Poems, 1897 (edited by Louise J. Guiney). Life and Writings, 1897 (by D. J. O'Donoghue). Prose Writings, 1903. Poems, 1904.

EDWARD MARTYN

Morgante the Lesser, 1890 (pseudonym "Sirius"). Maeve and the Heather Field, 1899. The Tale of a Town and an Enchanted Sea, 1902. Grangecolman, 1912. The Dream Physician, 1918.

BRINSLEY MACNAMARA

The Valley of the Squinting Windows, 1918. The Clanking of Chains, 1919. In Clay and Bronze, 1921. The Mirror in the Dusk, 1921. The Irishman, 1921 (over pseudonym of Oliver Blyth).

RUTHERFORD MAYNE (S. WADDELL)

The Turn of the Road, 1907. The Drone, 1909. The Troth, 1909. Collected Plays, 1912.

ALICE MILLIGAN

The Last Feast of the Fianna, 1900. New Songs, 1904 (in collaboration). Hero Lays, 1908. The Daughter of Donagh: A Cromwellian Play, 1920.

SUSAN MITCHELL

New Songs, 1904 (in collaboration). The Living Chalice, 1908. Aids to the Immortality of Certain Persons in Ireland, 1908. Collected Poems, 2 vols., 1913. George Moore, 1916.

GEORGE MOORE

Flowers of Passion, 1878. Martin Luther, 1879 (in collaboration). Pagan Poems, 1881. A Modern Lover, 3 vols., 1883. A Mummer's Wife, 1885. Literature at Nurse, 1885. A Drama in Muslin, 1886. A Mere Accident, 1887. Parnell and His Island, 1887. Confessions of a Young Man, 1888. Spring Days, 1888. Mike Fletcher, 1889. Impressions and Opinions, 1891. Vain Fortune, 1891. Modern Painting, 1893. The Strike at Arlingford, 1893. Esther Waters, 1894. Celibates, 1895. The Royal Academy, 1895. Evelyn Innes, 1898. The Bending of the Bough, 1900. A Loan Collection of Pictures: Modern Landscape Painters, 1901. Ideals in Ireland, 1901 (in collaboration). Sister Teresa, 1901. The Untilled Field, 1903.

The Lake, 1905. Memoirs of My Dead Life, 1906. Reminiscences of the Impressionist Painters, 1906. The Apostle, 1911. Ave, 1911. Salve, 1912. Esther Waters. A Play, 1913. Elizabeth Cooper, 1913. Vale, 1914. The Untilled Field, 1914 (enlarged edition). Muslin, 1915 (revised edition of A Drama in Muslin). The Brook Kerith, 1916. Lewis Seymour and Some Women, 1917 (revised edition of A Modern Lover). The Story-Teller's Holiday, 1918. Avowals, 1919. The Coming of Gabrielle, 1920. Abélard and Héloïse, 1921. Fragments from Héloïse and Abélard, 1921. In Single Strictness, 1922.

T. C. MURRAY

Birthright, 1911. Maurice Harte, 1912. Spring and other Plays, 1917.

DERMOT O'BYRNE (ARNOLD BAX)

Seafoam and Firelight, 1910. The Sisters and Green Magic, 1911. Children of the Hills, 1913. A Dublin Ballad, 1918. Wrack and other Stories, 1918. Red Owen, 1919.

STANDISH O'GRADY

History of Ireland: The Heroic Period, Vol. I, 1878. Early Bardic Literature, 1879. History of Ireland: Cuculain and his Contemporaries, Vol. II, 1880. History of Ireland: Critical and Philosophical, Vol. I, 1881. The Crisis in Ireland, 1882. Cuculain: An Epic, 1882. Toryism and the Tory Democracy, 1886. Red Hugh's Captivity, 1889. Finn and his Companions, 1892. The Bog of Stars, 1893. The Story of Ireland, 1894. The Coming of Cuculain, 1894. Lost on Du Corrig, 1894. The Chain of Gold, 1895. In the Wake of King James, 1896. Pacata Hibernia, 1896 (edited). Ulrick the Ready, 1896. The Flight of the Eagle, 1897. All Ireland, 1898. Queen of the World, 1900 (pseudonym Luke Netterville). In the Gates of the North, 1901. Ideals in Ireland, 1901 (in collaboration). Hugh Roe O'Donnell, 1902. The Masque of Finn, 1907. The Departure of Dermot, 1917.

SEUMAS O'KELLY (1881-1918)

By the Stream of Killmeen, 1902. The Matchmakers, 1908. The Shuiler's Child, 1909. Three Plays, 1912. The Bribe,

1914. The Lady of Deerpark, 1917. Waysiders, 1917. Ranns and Ballads, 1918. The Leprechaun of Killmeen, 1918. The Golden Barque and the Weaver's Grave, 1919. Hillsiders, 1921. Wet Clay, 1922.

MOIRA O'NEILL (MRS. M. SKRINE)

An Easter Vacation, 1893. The Elf Errant, 1895. Songs of the Glens of Antrim, 1900. More Songs of the Glens of Antrim, 1921.

SEUMAS O'SULLIVAN (JAMES STARKEY)

New Songs, 1904 (in collaboration). The Twilight People, 1905. Verse Sacred and Profane, 1908. The Earth Lover, 1909. Selected Lyrics, 1910 (with a Preface by A. E.). Impressions, being a Selection from the Note-books of the late J. H. Orwell, with a Foreword by the Editor, 1911. Poems, 1912 (collected edition). An Epilogue to the Praise of Angus, 1914. Requiem, 1917. Mud and Purple, 1917. The Rosses, 1918.

FORREST REID

The Kingdom of Twilight, 1904. The Garden God, 1905. The Bracknels, 1911. Following Darkness, 1912. The Gentle Lover, 1913. At the Door of the Gate, 1915. W. B. Yeats: A Critical Study, 1915. The Spring Song, 1916. A Garden by the Sea, 1918. Pirates of the Spring, 1919.

LENNOX ROBINSON

The Cross Roads, 1911. Two Plays, 1911. Patriots, 1912. The Dreamers, 1915. A Young Man from the South, 1917. Dark Days, 1918. Eight Short Stories, 1918. The Lost Leader, 1919. The White-Headed Boy, 1920.

T. W. ROLLESTON (1857–1920)

The Encheiridon of Epictetus, 1881. Uber Wordsworth und Walt Whitman, 1883. The Teaching of Epictetus, 1886. Poems and Ballads of Young Ireland, 1888 (in collaboration). Grashalme (Leaves of Grass), 1889 (German translation in collaboration). The Prose Writings of Thomas Davis, 1889 (edited). The Book of the Rhymers' Club, 1892 (in collaboration). The Second Book of the Rhymers' Club, 1894 (in collaboration). A

Treasury of Irish Poetry, 1900 (in collaboration). Imagination
and Art in Gaelic Literature, 1900. Parallel Paths, 1908. Sea
Spray: Verses and Translations, 1909. The High Deeds of
Finn, 1910. Myths and Legends of the Celtic Race, 1911.
Tannhauser, 1911. The Story of Parsifal, 1912. Lohengrin,
1913. Sacred and Profane Love: A Trilogy after Richard
Wagner, 1915. Thomas Davis: Selections from his Prose and
Poetry, 1915 (edited). Ireland's Vanishing Opportunity, 1919.

DORA SIGERSON SHORTER (1818–1918)

Lays and Lyrics of the Pan-Celtic Society, 1889 (in collabo-
ration). Verses, 1894. The Fairy Changeling, 1898. My
Lady's Slipper, 1898. Ballads and Poems, 1899. The Woman
who went to Hell, 1902. As the Sparks Fly Upward, 1903.
The Song and Story of Earl Roderick, 1905. Collected Poems,
1907. The Troubadour, 1910. New Poems, 1912. Madge
Linsey and other Poems, 1913. Love of Ireland: Poems and
Ballads, 1914. The Sad Years, 1918. A Legend of Glenda-
lough, 1919. Sixteen Dead Men and other Poems of Easter
Week, 1919.

GEORGE SIGERSON

The Poets and Poetry of Munster, 1860. Poems and Ballads of Young Ireland, 1888 (in collaboration). The Revival
of Irish Literature, 1894 (in collaboration). Bards of the Gael
and Gall, 1897. The Saga of King Lir, 1913.

Œ. SOMERVILLE AND MARTIN ROSS

An Irish Cousin, 1889. Naboth's Vineyard, 1891. In the
Vine Country, 1893. The Real Charlotte, 3 vols., 1894. Beg-
gars on Horseback, 1895. The Silver Fox, 1898. Some Ex-
periences of an Irish R.M., 1899. Further Experiences of an
Irish R.M., 1900. All on the Irish Shore, 1903. Some Irish
Yesterdays, 1908. Dan Russell, The Fox, 1911. In Mr. Knox's
Country, 1915. Irish Memories, 1918. Mount Music, 1919.
Strayaways, 1920.

JAMES STEPHENS

Insurrections, 1909. The Charwoman's Daughter, 1912.
The Hill of Vision, 1912. The Crock of Gold, 1912. Here are
Ladies, 1913. Five New Poems, 1913. The Demi-Gods, 1914.

Songs from the Clay, 1915. The Adventures of Seumas Beg, 1915. The Insurrection in Dublin, 1916. Green Branches, 1916. Hunger, 1918. Reincarnations, 1918. Irish Fairy Tales, 1920.

J. M. SYNGE (1871–1909)

Riders to the Sea. In the Shadow of the Glen, 1905. The Well of the Saints, 1905. The Playboy of the Western World, 1907. The Aran Islands, 1907. The Tinker's Wedding, 1908. Poems and Translations, 1909. Deirdre, 1910. Collected Works, 4 vols., 1910.

JOHN TODHUNTER (1839–1916)

The Theory of the Beautiful, 1872. Laurella and other Poems, 1876. Alkestis, 1879. A Study of Shelley, 1880. Forest Songs, 1881. The True Tragedy of Rienzi, 1881. Helen in Troas, 1886. Poems and Ballads of Young Ireland, 1888 (in collaboration). The Banshee and other Poems, 1888. How Dreams Come True, 1890. A Sicilian Idyll, 1890. The Poison Flower, 1891. The Book of the Rhymers' Club, 1892 (in collaboration). The Second Book of the Rhymers' Club, 1894 (in collaboration). Life of Sarsfield, 1895. Three Bardic Tales, 1896. Sounds and Sweet Airs, 1905. Heine's Book of Songs, 1907 (translation). From the Land of Dreams, 1918. Essays, 1920.

KATHARINE TYNAN (MRS. K. HINKSON)

Louise de la Vallière, 1885. Shamrocks, 1887. Poems and Ballads of Young Ireland, 1888 (in collaboration). Lays and Lyrics of the Pan-Celtic Society, 1889 (in collaboration). Ballads and Lyrics, 1891. Irish Love Songs, 1892 (edited). Cuckoo Songs, 1894. Our Lord's Coming and Childhood: Six Miracle Plays, 1895. A Lover's Breastknot, 1896. The Wind in the Trees, 1898. Poems, 1901. Innocencies, 1905. Twenty-one Poems, 1907 (edited by W. B. Yeats). Rhymed Life of St. Patrick, 1907. Experiences, 1908. Ireland, 1909. Lauds, 1909. New Poems, 1911. Twenty-five Years: Reminiscences, 1913. The Wild Harp, 1913 (edited). Irish Poems, 1913. The Flower of Peace, 1914. Flower of Youth, 1915. Late Songs, 1917. The Middle Years, 1916. Herb o' Grace, 1918. The Years of the Shadow, 1919.

CHARLES WEEKES

Reflections and Refractions, 1893. About Women, 1907.

W. B. YEATS

Mosada, 1886. Poems and Ballads of Young Ireland, 1888 (in collaboration). Fairy and Folk Tales of the Irish Peasantry, 1888 (edited). The Wanderings of Oisin, 1889. Stories from Carleton, 1889 (edited). Representative Irish Tales, 2 vols., 1890 (edited). John Sherman and Dhoya, 1891 (pseudonym Ganconagh). Irish Fairy Tales, 1892 (edited). The Countess Kathleen, 1892. The Book of the Rhymers' Club, 1892 (in collaboration). The Works of William Blake, 1893 (edited). The Poems of William Blake, 1893. The Land of Heart's Desire, 1894. The Second Book of the Rhymers' Club, 1894 (in collaboration). Poems, 1895. A Book of Irish Verse, 1895 (edited). The Secret Rose, 1897. The Tables of the Law, 1897. Literary Ideals in Ireland, 1899 (in collaboration). The Winds Among the Reeds, 1899. The Shadowy Waters, 1900. Ideals in Ireland, 1901 (in collaboration). Cathleen ni Hoolihan, 1902. Where There is Nothing, 1903. Ideas of Good and Evil, 1903. In the Seven Woods, 1903. The Hour Glass, Cathleen ni Hoolihan, The Pot of Broth, 1904. The King's Threshold and on Baile's Strand, 1904. Stories of Red Hanrahan, 1904. Poems (1899–1905), 1906. Poems of Spenser, 1906 (edited). Deirdre, 1907. Discoveries, 1907. Collected Works, 8 vols., 1908. The Golden Helmet, 1908. Poetry and Ireland, 1908 (in collaboration). Poems: Second Series, 1909. The Green Helmet and other Poems, 1910. Plays for an Irish Theatre, 1911. J. M. Synge and the Ireland of his Time, 1911. Poems, 1912 (new edition, revised). The Cutting of an Agate, 1912. Stories of Red Hanrahan, The Secret Rose and Rosa Alchemica, 1913. A Selection from the Love Poetry of W. B. Yeats, 1913. Poems Written in Discouragement, 1913. Selection from the Poetry of W. B. Yeats, 1913 (Tauchnitz edition). Responsibilities, 1914. Reveries over Childhood and Youth, 1916. Eight Poems, 1916. Easter Nineteen Sixteen, 1917. The Wild Swans at Coole, 1917. Per Amica Silentia Lunae, 1918. Two Plays for Dancers, 1919. Michael Robartes and the Dancer, 1920. Four Years, 1921. Four Plays for Dancers, 1921. The Trembling of the Veil, 1922. Seven Poems and a Fragment, 1922.

ELLA YOUNG

New Poems, 1904 (in collaboration). Poems, 1906. The Coming of Lugh, 1909. Celtic Wonder Tales, 1910.

WORKS OF REFERENCE

The following list includes works announced for publication:

Andrews (Charlton)   The Drama To-day. Philadelphia, 1913.

Archer (William)   Poets of the Younger Generation. London, 1902.

Bennett (E. A.)   Fame and Fiction. London, 1902.

Bickley (Francis)   J. M. Synge and the Irish Dramatic Movement. London and Boston, 1912.

Bithell (Jethro)   W. B. Yeats. Paris, 1913.

Borsa (Mario)   Il Teatro Inglese Contemporaneo. Milan, 1906; London and New York, 1908.

Bourgeois (Maurice)   J. M. Synge and the Irish Theatre. London and New York, 1913.

Boyd (Ernest A.)   The Contemporary Drama of Ireland. Boston, 1917; Dublin, 1918.
Appreciations and Depreciations. Dublin, 1917; New York, 1918.

Brown (Stephen J.)   A Guide to Books on Ireland. Dublin, 1912.
Ireland in Fiction. Dublin, 1919.

Chandler (F. W.)   Aspects of Modern Drama. New York, 1914.

Chevalley (Abel)   Le Roman Anglais de notre temps, London and Paris, 1921.

Clark (Barrett H.)   British and American Drama of To-day. New York, 1915.

Cunliffe (John W.)   English Literature During the Last Half Century. New York, 1919.

Elton (Oliver)   Modern Studies. London, 1907.

Engel (E.)   Geschichte der Englischen Literatur. Leipsig, 1907.

Figgis (Darrell) — Studies and Appreciations. London and New York, 1912.
A. E. (George W. Russell). Dublin and New York, 1916.

Freeman (John) — A Portrait of George Moore in a Study of his Work. London, 1922.

Graves (Alfred P.) — Irish Literary and Musical Studies. London, 1913.

Gregory (Lady Augusta) — Our Irish Theatre. New York, 1913; London, 1914.

Gwynn (Stephen) — To-day and To-morrow in Ireland. Dublin, 1903.
Irish Books and Irish People. Dublin, 1919.

Hamilton (Clayton) — Studies in Stagecraft. New York, 1915.

Herts (B. Russell) — Depreciations. New York, 1915.

Hone (J. M.) — W. B. Yeats. Dublin, 1915; New York, 1916.

Howe (P. P.) — The Repertory Theatre. London, 1912.
J. M. Synge: A Critical Study. London and New York, 1912.

Huneker (James) — Overtones. New York and London, 1904.
The Pathos of Distance. New York and London, 1913.
Unicorns. New York, 1917.

Jackson (Holbrook) — All Manner of Folk. London and New York, 1912.
The Eighteen Nineties. London and New York, 1913.

Joyce (James) — The Day of the Rabblement. Dublin, 1901.

Kellner (Leon) — Die Englische Literatur im Zeitalter der Koenigin Viktoria. Leipsig, 1909.

Kennedy (J. M.) — English Literature: 1880–1905. London and Boston, 1912.

Krans (Horatio S.)	W. B. Yeats and the Irish Literary Revival. New York, 1904; London, 1905.
Le Gallienne (Richard)	Retrospective Reviews. 2 vols. London and New York, 1896.
Lewisohn (Ludwig)	The Modern Drama. New York, 1915.
MacDonagh (Thomas)	Literature in Ireland. Dublin, 1916.
Mair (G. H.)	Modern English Literature. London and New York, 1914.
Malye (Jean)	La Littérature Irlandaise Contemporaine. Paris, 1913.
Masefield (John)	John M. Synge. London and New York, 1915.
Mason (Eugene)	A Book of Preferences in Literature. London and New York, 1915.
Maury (Lucien)	Figures Littéraires. Paris, 1911.
Mitchell (S. L.)	George Moore. Dublin, 1916.
Monahan (Michael)	Nova Hibernia. New York, 1914.
Montague (C. E.)	Dramatic Values. London and New York, 1911.
Moore (George)	Hail and Farewell. 3 vols. London and New York, 1911–1914.
More (Paul E.)	Shelburne Essays. Vol. I. New York, 1904.
Nevinson (H. W.)	Books and Personalities. London and New York, 1905.
O'Donoghue (D. J.)	The Poets of Ireland: A Biographical and Bibliographical Dictionary. Dublin, 1912.
Oliver (D. E.)	The English Stage: Origins and Modern Development. London, 1912.
Olivero (F.)	Studi sul Romanticismo Inglese. Bari, 1914.
Orage (A. R.)	Readers and Writers. London and New York, 1922.
Paul-Dubois (L.)	L'Irlande Contemporaine. Paris, 1907; Dublin, 1911.

Peck (H. T.)   The Personal Equation. New York,
                             1898.
Reid (Forrest)   W. B. Yeats: A Critical Study. Lon-
                             don and New York, 1915.
Ryan (W. P.)   The Irish Literary Revival. London,
                             1894.
Sturgeon (Mary C.)   Studies of Contemporary Poets.
                             London, 1920.
Walbrook (H. M.)   Nights at the Play. London, 1911.
Walkley (A. B.)   The Drama and Life. London, 1907;
                             New York, 1911.
Weygandt (C.)   Irish Plays and Playwrights. Boston
                             and London, 1913.
Yeats (W. B.)   The Cutting of an Agate. New York,
                             1912; London, 1919.
Williams (Harold)   Modern English Writers. London,
                             1918; New York, 1919.

INDEX